Advanced Elasticsearch 7.0

A practical guide to designing, indexing, and querying
advanced distributed search engines

Wai Tak Wong

BIRMINGHAM - MUMBAI

Advanced Elasticsearch 7.0

Commissioning Editor: Pravin Dhandre
Acquisition Editor: Nelson Morris
Content Development Editor: Roshan Kumar
Senior Editor: Jack Cummings
Technical Editor: Dinesh Chaudhary
Copy Editor: Safis Editing
Project Coordinator: Namrata Swetta
Proofreader: Safis Editing
Indexer: Rekha Nair
Production Designer: Nilesh Mohite

First published: August 2019

Production reference: 1220819

Published by Packt Publishing Ltd.
Livery Place
35 Livery Street
Birmingham
B3 2PB, UK.

ISBN 978-1-78995-775-4

www.packtpub.com

I would like to thank the Almighty One for His encouragement and this opportunity, and my wife's constant support and patience throughout the long process of writing this book. Thanks also to those companies and teams, such as Elastics, Investor Exchange (ETF APIs), TD Ameritrade (commission-free ETF), Pivotal Software (Spring Tool Suite), Google (Postman), and Docker, that support open source software so that I can use their technologies as part of the book and make it a success.

– Wai Tak Wong

`Packt.com`

Subscribe to our online digital library for full access to over 7,000 books and videos, as well as industry leading tools to help you plan your personal development and advance your career. For more information, please visit our website.

Why subscribe?

- Spend less time learning and more time coding with practical eBooks and Videos from over 4,000 industry professionals

- Improve your learning with Skill Plans built especially for you

- Get a free eBook or video every month

- Fully searchable for easy access to vital information

- Copy and paste, print, and bookmark content

Did you know that Packt offers eBook versions of every book published, with PDF and ePub files available? You can upgrade to the eBook version at `www.packt.com` and as a print book customer, you are entitled to a discount on the eBook copy. Get in touch with us at `customercare@packtpub.com` for more details.

At `www.packt.com`, you can also read a collection of free technical articles, sign up for a range of free newsletters, and receive exclusive discounts and offers on Packt books and eBooks.

Contributors

About the author

Wai Tak Wong is a faculty member in the Department of Computer Science at Kean University, NJ, USA. He has more than 15 years professional experience in cloud software design and development. His PhD in computer science was obtained at NJIT, NJ, USA. Wai Tak has served as an associate professor in the Information Management Department of Chung Hua University, Taiwan. A co-founder of Shanghai Shellshellfish Information Technology, Wai Tak acted as the Chief Scientist of the R&D team, and he has published more than a dozen algorithms in prestigious journals and conferences. Wai Tak began his search and analytics technology career with Elasticsearch in the real estate market and later applied this to data management and FinTech data services.

About the reviewers

Marcelo Ochoa works for Dirección TICs of Facultad de Ciencias Exactas at Universidad Nacional del Centro de la Prov. de Buenos Aires and is the CTO at Scotas, a company that specializes in near real-time search solutions using Apache Solr and Oracle. He divides his time between university jobs and external projects related to Oracle, open source, and big data technologies. Since 2006, he has been part of an Oracle ACE program and was recently incorporated into a Docker Mentor program.

He has co-authored *Oracle Database Programming Using Java* and *Web Services and Professional XML Databases*, and as a technical reviewer for several books and videos such as *Mastering Apache Solr 7*, *Mastering Elastic Stack*, *Learning Elasticsearch 6*, and others.

Saurabh Chhajed is a machine learning and big data engineer with 9 years of professional experience in the enterprise application development life cycle, using the latest frameworks, tools, and design patterns. He has experience of designing and implementing some of the most widely used and scalable customer-facing recommendation systems with extensive usage of the big data ecosystem – in the batch and real-time and machine learning pipelines. He has also worked for some of the largest investment banks, credit card companies, and manufacturing companies around the world, implementing a range of robust and scalable product suites.
He has written *Learning ELK Stack* and reviewed *Mastering Kibana* and *Python Machine Learning* with Packt Publishing.

Craig Brown is an independent consultant, offering services for Elasticsearch and other big data software. He is a core Java developer with 25+ years of experience and more than 10 years of Elasticsearch experience. He is also experienced with machine learning, Hadoop, Apache Spark; is a co-founder of the Big Mountain Data user group in Utah; and is a speaker on Elasticsearch and other big data topics. Craig founded NosqlRevolution LLC, focused on Elasticsearch and big data services, and PicoCluster LLC, a desktop data center designed for learning and prototyping cluster computing and big data frameworks.

Packt is searching for authors like you

If you're interested in becoming an author for Packt, please visit `authors.packtpub.com` and apply today. We have worked with thousands of developers and tech professionals, just like you, to help them share their insight with the global tech community. You can make a general application, apply for a specific hot topic that we are recruiting an author for, or submit your own idea.

Table of Contents

Section 3: Programming with the Elasticsearch Client

Preface

Building enterprise-grade distributed applications and executing systematic search operations calls for a strong understanding of Elasticsearch and expertise in using its core APIs and latest features. This book will help you master the advanced functionalities of Elasticsearch and learn how to develop a sophisticated real-time search engine confidently. In addition to this, you'll also learn how to run machine learning jobs in Elasticsearch to speed up routine tasks.

You'll get started by learning how to use Elasticsearch features on Hadoop and Spark and make search results faster, thereby improving the speed of queries and enhancing customer experience. You'll then get up to speed with analytics by building a metrics pipeline, defining queries, and using Kibana for intuitive visualizations that help provide decision makers with better insights. The book will later guide you through using Logstash to collect, parse, and enrich logs before indexing them into Elasticsearch.

By the end of this book, you will have comprehensive knowledge of advanced topics such as Apache Spark support, machine learning using Elasticsearch and scikit-learn, and real-time analytics, along with the expertise you need to increase business productivity, perform analytics, and get the very best out of Elasticsearch.

You will do the following:

- Pre-process documents before indexing in ingest pipelines
- Learn how to model your data in the real world
- Get to grips with using Elasticsearch for exploratory data analysis
- Understand how to build analytics and RESTful services
- Use Kibana, Logstash, and Beats for dashboard applications
- Get up to speed with Spark and Elasticsearch for real-time analytics
- Explore the Java high/low-level REST client and learn how to index, search, and query in a Spring application

Who this book is for

The book is aimed at beginners with no prior experience with Elasticsearch, and gradually introduces intermediate and advanced topics. The chapters walk through the most important aspects to help audiences to build and master the powerful search engine. Search engine data engineers, software engineers, and database engineers who want to take their basic knowledge of Elasticsearch to the next level can use it to its optimum level in their daily core tasks.

What this book covers

Chapter 1, *Overview of Elasticsearch 7*, takes beginners through some basic features in minutes. We just take a few steps to launch the new version of the Elasticsearch server. An architectural overview and a core concept introduction will make it easy to understand the workflow in Elasticsearch.

Chapter 2, *Index APIs*, discusses how to use index APIs to manage individual indices, index settings, aliases, and templates. It also involves monitoring statistics for operations that occur on an index. Index management operations including refreshing, flushing, and clearing the cache are also discussed.

Chapter 3, *Document APIs*, begins with the basic information about a document and its life cycle. Then we learn how to access it. After that, we look at accessing multiple documents with the bulk API. Finally, we discuss migrating indices from the old version to version 7.0.

Chapter 4, *Mapping APIs*, introduces the schema in Elasticsearch. The mapping rules for both dynamic mappings and explicit static mappings will be discussed. It also provides the idea and details of creating static mapping for an index. We also step into the details of the meta fields and field data types in index mapping.

Chapter 5, *Anatomy of an Analyzer*, drills down in to the anatomy of the analyzer and in-depth practice different analyzers. We will discuss different character filters, tokenizers, and token filters in order to understand the building blocks of the analyzer. We also practice how to create a custom analyzer and use it in the analyze API.

Chapter 6, *Search APIs*, covers different types of searches, from terms-based to full-text, from exact search to fuzzy search, from single-field search to multi-search, and then to compound search. Additional information about Query DSL and search-related APIs such as tuning, validating, and troubleshooting will be discussed.

Chapter 7, *Modeling Your Data in the Real World*, discusses data modeling with Elasticsearch. It focuses on some common issues users may encounter when working with different techniques. It helps you understand some of the conventions and contains insights from real-world examples involving denormalizing complex objects and using nested objects to handle relationships.

Chapter 8, *Aggregation Framework*, discusses data analytics using the aggregation framework. We learn how to perform aggregations with examples and delve into most of the types of aggregations. We also use IEX ETF historical data to plot a graph for different types of moving averages, including forecasted data supported by the model.

Chapter 9, *Preprocessing Documents in Ingest Pipelines*, discusses the preprocessing of a document through predefined pipeline processors before the actual indexing operation begins. We also learn about data accessing to documents through the pipeline processor. Finally, we cover exception handling when an error occurs during pipeline processing.

Chapter 10, *Using Elasticsearch for Exploratory Data Analysis*, uses the aggregation framework to perform data analysis. We first discuss a comprehensive analysis of exploratory data and simple financial analysis of business strategies. In addition, we provide step-by-step instructions for calculating Bollinger Bands using daily operational data. Finally, we will conduct a brief survey of sentiment analysis using Elasticsearch.

Chapter 11, *Elasticsearch from Java Programming*, focuses on the basics of two supported Java REST clients. We explore the main features and operations of each approach. A sample project is provided to demonstrate the high-level and low-level REST clients integrated with Spring Boot programming.

Chapter 12, *Elasticsearch from Python Programming*, introduces the Python Elasticsearch client. We learn about two Elasticsearch client packages, elasticsearch-py and elasticsearch-dsl-py. We learn how the clients work and incorporate them into a Python application. We implement Bollinger Bands by using elasticsearch-dsl-py.

Chapter 13, *Using Kibana, Logstash, and Beats*, outlines the components of the Elastic Stack, including Kibana, Logstash, and Beats. We learn how to use Logstash to collect and parse log data from system log files. In addition, we use Filebeat to extend the use of Logstash to a central log processing center. All work will be run on official supported Elastic Stack Docker images.

Chapter 14, *Working with Elasticsearch SQL*, introduces Elasticsearch SQL. With Elasticsearch SQL, we can access full-text search using familiar SQL syntax. We can even obtain results in tabular view format. We perform search and aggregation using different approaches, such as using the SQL REST API interface, the command-line interface, and JDBC.

Chapter 15, *Working with Elasticsearch Analysis Plugins*, introduces built-in Analysis plugins. We practice using the ICU Analysis plugin, the Smart Chinese Analysis plugin, and the IK Analysis plugin to analyze Chinese texts. We also add a new custom dictionary to improve word segmentation to make it generate better results.

Chapter 16, *Machine Learning with Elasticsearch*, discusses the machine learning feature supported by Elasticsearch. This feature automatically analyzes time series data by running a metric job. This type of job contains one or more detectors (the analyzed fields). We also introduce the Python scikit-learn library and the unsupervised learning algorithm K-means clustering and use it for comparison.

Chapter 17, *Spark and Elasticsearch for Real-Time Analytics*, focuses on ES-Hadoop's Apache Spark support. We practice reading data from the Elasticsearch index, performing some computations using Spark, and then writing the results back to Elasticsearch through ES-Hadoop. We build a real-time anomaly detection routine based on the K-means model created from past data by using the Spark ML library.

Chapter 18, *Building Analytics RESTful Services*, explains how to construct a project providing a search analytics REST service powered by Elasticsearch. We combine lots of material and source code from different chapters to build a real-world end-to-end project and present the result on a Kibana Visualize page.

To get the most out of this book

Readers should have a basic knowledge of Linux, Java, Python, Virtualenv, SQL, Spark, and Docker.

All installation steps are described in detail in each relevant chapter.

Download the example code files

You can download the example code files for this book from your account at www.packt.com. If you purchased this book elsewhere, you can visit www.packt.com/support and register to have the files emailed directly to you.

You can download the code files by following these steps:

1. Log in or register at www.packt.com.
2. Select the **SUPPORT** tab.
3. Click on **Code Downloads & Errata**.
4. Enter the name of the book in the **Search** box and follow the onscreen instructions.

Once the file is downloaded, please make sure that you unzip or extract the folder using the latest version of:

- WinRAR/7-Zip for Windows
- Zipeg/iZip/UnRarX for Mac
- 7-Zip/PeaZip for Linux

The code bundle for the book is also hosted on GitHub at https://github.com/PacktPublishing/Advanced-Elasticsearch-7.0. In case there's an update to the code, it will be updated on the existing GitHub repository.

We also have other code bundles from our rich catalog of books and videos available at https://github.com/PacktPublishing/. Check them out!

Download the color images

We also provide a PDF file that has color images of the screenshots/diagrams used in this book. You can download it here: https://static.packt-cdn.com/downloads/9781789957754_ColorImages.pdf.

Conventions used

There are a number of text conventions used throughout this book.

CodeInText: Indicates code words in text, database table names, folder names, filenames, file extensions, pathnames, dummy URLs, user input, and Twitter handles. Here is an example: "Mount the downloaded WebStorm-10*.dmg disk image file as another disk in your system."

A block of code is set as follows:

```
html, body, #map {
  height: 100%;
  margin: 0;
  padding: 0
}
```

When we wish to draw your attention to a particular part of a code block, the relevant lines or items are set in bold:

```
[default]
exten => s,1,Dial(Zap/1|30)
exten => s,2,Voicemail(u100)
exten => s,102,Voicemail(b100)
exten => i,1,Voicemail(s0)
```

Any command-line input or output is written as follows:

```
$ mkdir css
$ cd css
```

Bold: Indicates a new term, an important word, or words that you see onscreen. For example, words in menus or dialog boxes appear in the text like this. Here is an example: "Select **System info** from the **Administration** panel."

Warnings or important notes appear like this.

Tips and tricks appear like this.

Get in touch

Feedback from our readers is always welcome.

General feedback: If you have questions about any aspect of this book, mention the book title in the subject of your message and email us at customercare@packtpub.com.

Errata: Although we have taken every care to ensure the accuracy of our content, mistakes do happen. If you have found a mistake in this book, we would be grateful if you would report this to us. Please visit www.packt.com/submit-errata, selecting your book, clicking on the Errata Submission Form link, and entering the details.

Piracy: If you come across any illegal copies of our works in any form on the Internet, we would be grateful if you would provide us with the location address or website name. Please contact us at copyright@packt.com with a link to the material.

If you are interested in becoming an author: If there is a topic that you have expertise in and you are interested in either writing or contributing to a book, please visit authors.packtpub.com.

Reviews

Please leave a review. Once you have read and used this book, why not leave a review on the site that you purchased it from? Potential readers can then see and use your unbiased opinion to make purchase decisions, we at Packt can understand what you think about our products, and our authors can see your feedback on their book. Thank you!

For more information about Packt, please visit packt.com.

Section 1: Fundamentals and Core APIs

In this section, you will get an overview of Elasticsearch 7 by looking into various concepts and examining Elasticsearch services and core APIs. You will also look at the new distributed, scalable, real-time search and analytics engine.

This section is comprised the following chapters:

- Chapter 1, *Overview of Elasticsearch 7*
- Chapter 2, *Index APIs*
- Chapter 3, *Document APIs*
- Chapter 4, *Mapping APIs*
- Chapter 5, *Anatomy of an Analyzer*
- Chapter 6, *Search APIs*

Overview of Elasticsearch 7

Welcome to *Advanced Elasticsearch 7.0*. Elasticsearch quickly evolved from version 1.0.0, released in February 2014, to version 6.0.0 GA, released in November 2017. Nonetheless, we will use 7.0.0 release as the base of this book. Without making any assumptions about your knowledge of Elasticsearch, this opening chapter provides setup instructions with the Elasticsearch development environment. To help beginners complete some basic features within a few minutes, several steps are given to launch the new version of an Elasticsearch server. An architectural overview and some core concepts will help you to understand the workflow within Elasticsearch. It will help you straighten your learning path.

Keep in mind that you can learn the potential benefits by reading the *API conventions* section and becoming familiar with it. The section *New features* following this one is a list of new features you can explore in the new release. Because major changes are often introduced between major versions, you must check to see whether it breaks the compatibility and affects your application. Go through the *Migration between versions* section to find out how to minimize the impact on your upgrade project.

In this chapter, you'll learn about the following topics:

- Preparing your environment
- Running Elasticsearch
- Talking to Elasticsearch
- Elasticsearch architectural overview
- Key concepts
- API conventions
- New features
- Breaking changes
- Migration between versions

Preparing your environment

The first step of the novice is to set up the Elasticsearch server, while an experienced user may just need to upgrade the server to the new version. If you are going to upgrade your server software, read through the *Breaking changes* section and the *Migration between versions* section to discover the changes that require your attention.

Elasticsearch is developed in Java. As of writing this book, it is recommended that you use a specific Oracle JDK, version 1.8.0_131. By default, Elasticsearch will use the Java version defined by the JAVA_HOME environment variable. Before installing Elasticsearch, please check the installed Java version.

Elasticsearch is supported on many popular operating systems such as RHEL, Ubuntu, Windows, and Solaris. For information on supported operating systems and product compatibility, see the Elastic Support Matrix at https://www.elastic.co/support/matrix. The installation instructions for all the supported platforms can be found in the *Installing Elasticsearch* documentation (https://www.elastic.co/guide/en/elasticsearch/reference/7.0/install-elasticsearch.html). Although there are many ways to properly install Elasticsearch on different operating systems, it'll be simple and easy to run Elasticsearch from the command line for novices. Please follow the instructions on the official download site (https://www.elastic.co/downloads/past-releases/elasticsearch-7-0-0). In this book, we'll use the Ubuntu 16.04 operating system to host Elasticsearch Service. For example, use the following command line to check the Java version on Ubuntu 16.04:

```
java -version
java version "1.8.0_181"
java(TM) SE Runtime Environment(build 1.8.0_181-b13)
Java HotSpot(TM) 64-Bit Server VM (build 25.181-b13, mixed mode)
```

The following is a step-by-step guide for installing the preview version from the official download site:

1. Select the correct package for your operating system (**WINDOWS, MACOS, LINUX, DEB, RPM,** or **MSI (BETA)**) and download the 7.0.0 release. For Linux, the filename is elasticsearch-7.0.0-linux-x86_64.tar.gz.
2. Extract the GNU zipped file into the target directory, which will generate a folder called elasticsearch-7.0.0 using the following command:

```
tar -zxvf elasticsearch-7.0.0-linux-86_64.tar.gz
```

3. Go to the folder and run Elasticsearch with the −p parameter to create a `pid` file at the specified path:

```
cd elasticsearch-7.0.0
./bin/elasticsearch -p pid
```

Elasticsearch runs in the foreground when it runs with the command line above. If you want to shut it down, you can stop it by pressing *Ctrl + C*, or you can use the process ID from the `pid` file in the working directory to terminate the process:

```
kill -15 `cat pid`
```

Check the log file to make sure the process is closed. You will see the text `Native controller process has stopped, stopped, closing, closed` near the end of file:

```
tail logs/elasticsearch.log
```

To run Elasticsearch as a daemon in background mode, specify −d on the command line:

```
./bin/elasticsearch -d -p pid
```

In the next section, we will show you how to run an Elasticsearch instance.

Running Elasticsearch

Elasticsearch does not start automatically after installation. On Windows, to start it automatically at boot time, you can install Elasticsearch as a service. On Ubuntu, it's best to use the Debian package, which installs everything you need to configure Elasticsearch as a service. If you're interested, please refer to the official website (`https://www.elastic.co/guide/en/elasticsearch/reference/master/deb.html`).

Basic Elasticsearch configuration

Elasticsearch 7.0 has several configuration files located in the `config` directory, shown as follows. Basically, it provides good defaults, and it requires very little configuration from developers:

```
ls config
```

The output will be similar to the following:

```
elasticsearch.keystore  elasticsearch.yml  jvm.options  log4j2.properties
role_mapping.yml  roles.yml  users  users_roles
```

Let's take a quick look at the `elasticsearch.yml`, `jvm.options`, and `log4j2.properties` files:

- `elasticsearch.yml`: The main configuration file. This configuration file contains settings for the clusters, nodes, and paths. If you specify an item, comment out the line. We'll explain the terminology in the *Elasticsearch architectural overview* section:

```
# --------------------------- Cluster ---------------------------
# Use a descriptive name for your cluster:
#cluster.name: my-application
# --------------------------- Node ---------------------------
# Use a descriptive name for the node:
#node.name: node-1
# --------------------------- Network ---------------------------
# Set the bind address to a specific IP (IPv4 or IPv6):
#network.host: 192.168.0.1
# Set a custom port for HTTP:
#http.port: 9200
# --------------------------- Paths ---------------------------
# Path to directory where to store the data (separate multiple
# locations by comma):
#path.data: /path/to/data
# Path to log files:
#path.logs: /path/to/logs
```

- `jvm.options`: Recalling that Elasticsearch is developed in Java, this file is the preferred place to set the JVM options, as shown in the following code block:

```
IMPORTANT: JVM heap size
# Xms represents the initial size of total heap space
# Xmx represents the maximum size of total heap space
-Xms1g
-Xmx1g
```

You rarely need to change the **Java Virtual Machine (JVM)** options unless the Elasticsearch server is moved to production. These settings can be used to improve performance. When configuring heap memory, please keep in mind that the Xmx setting is 32 GB at most, and no more than 50% of the available RAM.

- `log4j2.properties`: Elasticsearch uses Log4j 2 for logging. The log file location is made from three given properties, `${sys:es.logs.base_path}`, `${sys:es.logs.cluster_name}`, and `${sys:es.logs.node_name}` in the `log4j2.properties` file, as shown in the code block:

```
appender.rolling.fileName =
${sys:es.logs.base_path}${sys:file.separator}${sys:es.logs.cluster_
name}.log
```

For example, our installed directory is `~/elasticsearch-7.0.0`. Since no base path is specified, the default value of `~/elasticsearch-7.0.0/logs` is used. Since no cluster name is specified, the default value of `elasticsearch` is used. The log file location setting `appender.rolling.filename` will generate a log file named `~/elasticsearch-7.0.0/logs/elasticsearch.log`.

Important system configuration

Elasticsearch has two working modes, development mode and production mode. You'll work in development mode with a fresh installation. If you reconfigure a setting such as `network.host`, it will switch to production mode. In production mode, some settings must be taken care and you can check with the Elasticsearch Reference at `https://www.elastic.co/guide/en/elasticsearch/reference/master/system-config.html`. We will discuss the file descriptors and virtual memory settings as follows:

- **File descriptors**: Elasticsearch uses a large number of file descriptors. Running out of file descriptors can result in data loss. Use the `ulimit` command to set the maximum number of open files for the current session or in a runtime script file:

```
ulimit -n 65536
```

If you want to set the value permanently, add the following line to the `/etc/security/limits.conf` file:

```
elasticsearch - nofile 65536
```

Ubuntu ignores the `limits.conf` file for processes started by `init.d`. You can comment out the following line to enable the `ulimit` feature as follow:

```
# Sets up user limits according to /etc/security/limits.conf
# (Replaces the use of /etc/limits in old login)
#session required pam_limits.so
```

- **Virtual memory**: By default, Elasticsearch uses the `mmapfs` directory to store its indices, however, the default operating system limits setting on `mmap` counts is low. If the setting is below the standard, increase the limit to `262144` or higher:

```
sudo sysctl -w vm.max_map_count=262144
sudo sysctl -p
cat /proc/sys/vm/max_map_count
262144
```

By default, the Elasticsearch security features are disabled for open source downloads or basic licensing. Since Elasticsearch binds to localhost only by default, it is safe to run the installed server as a local development server. The changed setting only takes effect after the Elasticsearch server instance has been restarted. In the next section, we will discuss several ways to communicate with Elasticsearch.

Talking to Elasticsearch

Many programming languages (including Java, Python, and .NET) have official clients written and supported by Elasticsearch (`https://www.elastic.co/guide/en/elasticsearch/client/index.html`). However, by default, only two protocols are really supported, HTTP (via a RESTful API) and native. You can talk to Elasticsearch via one of the following ways:

- **Transport client**: One of the native ways to connect to Elasticsearch.
- **Node client**: Similar to the transport client. In most cases, if you're using Java, you should choose the transport client instead of the node client.
- **HTTP client**: For most programming languages, HTTP is the most common way to connect to Elasticsearch.
- **Other protocols**: It's possible to create a new client interface to Elasticsearch simply by writing a plugin.

Transport clients (that is, the Java API) are scheduled to be deprecated in Elasticsearch 7.0 and completely removed in 8.0. Java users should use a Java High Level REST Client.

You can communicate with Elasticsearch via the default 9200 port using the RESTful API. An example of using the curl command to communicate with Elasticsearch from the command line is shown in the following code block. You should see the instance details and the cluster information in the response. Before running the following command, make sure the installed Elasticsearch server is running. In the response, the machine's hostname is wai. The default Elasticsearch cluster name is elasticsearch. The version of Elasticsearch that is running is 7.0.0. The downloaded Elasticsearch software is in TAR format. The version of Lucene used is 8.0.0:

```
curl -XGET 'http://localhost:9200'
{
  "name" : "wai",
  "cluster_name" : "elasticsearch",
  "cluster_uuid" : "7-fjLIFkQrednHgFhOUfxw",
  "version" : {
  "number" : "7.0.0",
  "build_flavor" : "default",
  "build_type" : "tar",
  "build_hash" : "a30e8c2",
  "build_date" : "2018-12-17T12:33:32.311168Z",
  "build_snapshot" : false,
  "lucene_version" : "8.0.0",
  "minimum_wire_compatibility_version" : "6.6.0",
  "minimum_index_compatibility_version" : "6.0.0-beta1"
  },
  "tagline" : "You Know, for Search"
}
```

Using Postman to work with the Elasticsearch REST API

The Postman app is a handy tool for testing the REST API. In this book, we'll use Postman to illustrate the examples. The following are step-by-step instructions for installing Postman from the official download site (https://www.getpostman.com/apps):

1. Select Package Management (Windows, macOS, or Linux) and download the appropriate 32-/64-bit version for your operating system. For 64-bit Linux package management, the filename is Postman-linux-x64-6.6.1.tar.gz.

2. Extract the GNU zipped file into your target directory, which will generate a folder called Postman:

```
tar -zxvf Postman-linux-x64-6.6.1.tar.gz
```

3. Go to the folder and run `Postman` and you'll see a pop-up window:

```
cd Postman
./Postman
```

4. In the pop-up window, use the same URL as in the previous `curl` command and press the **Send** button. You will get the same output shown as follows:

In the next section, let's dive into the architectural overview of Elasticsearch.

Elasticsearch architectural overview

The story of how the ELK Stack becomes Elasticsearch, Logstash, and Kibana, is a pretty long story (https://www.elastic.co/about/history-of-elasticsearch). At Elastic{ON} 2015 in San Francisco, Elasticsearch Inc. was renamed Elastic and announced the next evolution of Elastic Stack. Elasticsearch will still play an important role, no matter what happens.

Elastic Stack architecture

Elastic Stack is an end-to-end software stack for search and analysis solutions. It is designed to help users get data from any type of source in any format to allow for searching, analyzing, and visualizing data in real time. The full stack consists of the following:

- **Beats master**: A lightweight data conveyor that can send data directly to Elasticsearch or via Logstash
- **APM server master**: Used for measuring and monitoring the performance of applications
- **Elasticsearch master**: A highly scalable full-text search and analytics engine
- **Elasticsearch Hadoop master**: A two-way fast data mover between Apache Hadoop and Elasticsearch
- **Kibana master**: A primer on data exploration, visualization, and dashboarding
- **Logstash master**: A data-collection engine with real-time pipelining capabilities

Each individual product has its own purpose and features, as shown in the following diagram:

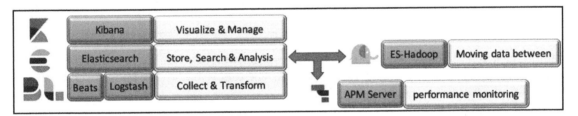

Elasticsearch architecture

Elasticsearch is a real-time distributed search and analytics engine with high availability. It is used for full-text search, structured search, analytics, or all three in combination. It is built on top of the Apache Lucene library. It is a schema-free, document-oriented data store. However, unless you fully understand your use case, the general recommendation is not to use it as the primary data store. One of the advantages is that the RESTful API uses JSON over HTTP, which allows you to integrate, manage, and query index data in a variety of ways.

An **Elasticsearch cluster** is a group of one or more Elasticsearch nodes that are connected together. Let's first outline how it is laid out, as shown in the following diagram:

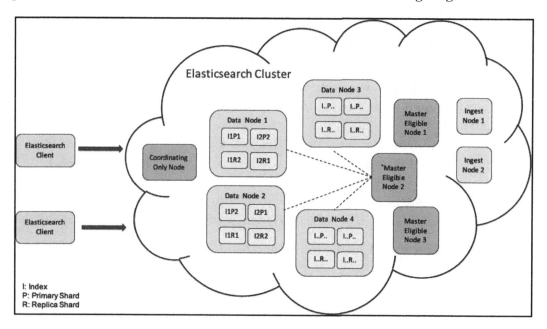

Although each node has its own purpose and responsibility, each node can forward client requests (coordination) to the appropriate nodes. The following are the nodes used in an Elasticsearch cluster:

- **Master-eligible node**: The master node's tasks are primarily used for lightweight cluster-wide operations, including creating or deleting an index, tracking the cluster nodes, and determining the location of the allocated shards. By default, the master-eligible role is enabled. A master-eligible node can be elected to become the master node (the node with the asterisk) by the master-election process. You can disable this type of role for a node by setting `node.master` to `false` in the `elasticsearch.yml` file.

- **Data node**: A data node contains data that contains indexed documents. It handles related operations such as CRUD, search, and aggregation. By default, the data node role is enabled, and you can disable such a role for a node by setting the `node.data` to `false` in the `elasticsearch.yml` file.

- **Ingest node**: Using an ingest nodes is a way to process a document in pipeline mode before indexing the document. By default, the ingest node role is enabled—you can disable such a role for a node by setting `node.ingest` to `false` in the `elasticsearch.yml` file.

- **Coordinating-only node**: If all three roles (master eligible, data, and ingest) are disabled, the node will only act as a coordination node that performs routing requests, handling the search reduction phase, and distributing works via bulk indexing.

When you launch an instance of Elasticsearch, you actually launch the Elasticsearch node. In our installation, we are running a single node of Elasticsearch, so we have a cluster with one node. Let's retrieve the information for all nodes from our installed server using the Elasticsearch cluster nodes info API, as shown in the following screenshot:

The cluster name is `elasticsearch`. The total number of nodes is 1. The node ID is `V1P0a-tVR8afUqJW86Hnrw`. The node name is `wai`. The `wai` node has three roles, which are `master`, `data`, and `ingest`. The Elasticsearch version running on the node is `7.0.0`.

Between the Elasticsearch index and the Lucene index

The data in Elasticsearch is organized into indices. Each index is a logical namespace for organizing data. The document is a basic unit of data in Elasticsearch. An inverted index is created by tokenizing the terms in the document, creating a sorted list of all unique terms, and associating the document list with the location where the terms can be found. An index consists of one or more shards. A shard is a Lucene index that uses a data structure (inverted index) to store data. Each shard can have zero or more replicas. Elasticsearch ensures that the primary and the replica of the same shard will not collocate in the same node, as shown in the following screenshot, where **Data Node 1** contains primary shard 1 of **Index 1 (I1P1)**, primary shard 2 of **Index 2 (I2P2)**, replica shard 2 of **Index 1 (I1R2)**, and replica shard 1 of **Index 2 (I2R1)**.

A Lucene index consists of one or more immutable index segments, and a segment is a functional inverted index. Segments are immutable, allowing Lucene to incrementally add new documents to the index without rebuilding efforts. To maintain the manageability of the number of segments, Elasticsearch merges the small segments together into one larger segment, commits the new merge segment to disk and eliminates the old smaller segments at the appropriate time. For each search request, all Lucene segments of a given shard of an Elasticsearch index will be searched. Let's examine the query process in a cluster, as shown in the following diagram:

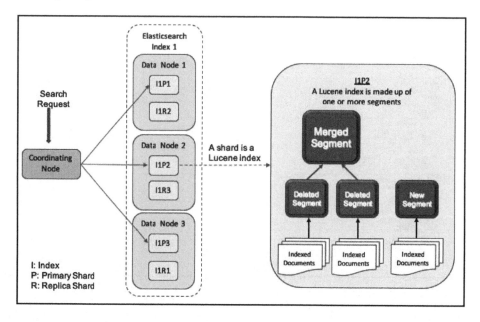

In the next section, let's drilled down to the key concepts.

Key concepts

In the previous section, we learned some core concepts such as clusters, nodes, shards, replicas, and so on. We will briefly introduce the other key concepts in this section. Then, we'll drill down into the details in subsequent chapters.

Mapping concepts across SQL and Elasticsearch

In the early stages of Elasticsearch, mapping types were a way to divide the documents into different logical groups in the same index. This meant that the index could have any number of types. In the past, talking about index in Elasticsearch is similar to talking about database in SQL. In addition, the discussion of viewing index type in Elasticsearch is equivalent to a table in SQL is also very popular. According to the official Elastic website (`https://www.elastic.co/guide/en/elasticsearch/reference/5.6/removal-of-types.html`), the removal of mapping types was published in the documentation of version 5.6. Later, in Elasticsearch 6.0.0, indices needed to contain only one mapping type. Mapping types of the same index were completely removed in Elasticsearch 7.0.0. The main reason was that tables are independent of each other in an SQL database. However, fields with the same name in different mapping types of the same index are the same. In an Elasticsearch index, fields with the same name in different mapping types are internally supported by the same Lucene field.

Let's take a look at the terminology in SQL and Elasticsearch in the following table(`https://www.elastic.co/guide/en/elasticsearch/reference/master/_mapping_concepts_across_sql_and_elasticsearch.html`), showing how the data is organized:

SQL	Elasticsearch	Description
Column	Field	A column is a set of data values in the same data type, with one value for each row of the database, while Elasticsearch refers to as a field. A field is the smallest unit of data in Elasticsearch. It can contain a list of multiple values of the same type.
Row	Document	A row represents a structured data item, which contains a series of data values from each column of the table. A document is like a row to group fields (columns in SQL). A document is a JSON object in Elasticsearch.
Table	Index	A table consists of columns and rows. An index is the largest unit of data in Elasticsearch. Comparing to a database in SQL, an index is a logical partition of the indexed documents and the target against which the search queries get executed.

Schema	Implicit	In a **relational database management system** (**RDBMS**), a schema contains schema objects, which can be tables, columns, data types, views, and so on. A schema is typically owned by a database user. Elasticsearch does not provide an equivalent concept for it.
Catalog/database	Cluster	In SQL, a catalog or database represents a set of schemas. In Elasticsearch, a cluster contains a set of indices.

Mapping

A schema could mean an outline, diagram, or model, which is often used to describe the structure of different types of data. Elasticsearch is reputed to be schema-less, in contrast to traditional relational databases. In traditional relational databases, you must explicitly specify tables, fields, and field types. In Elasticsearch, schema-less simply means that the document can be indexed without specifying the schema in advance. Under the hood though, Elasticsearch dynamically derives a schema from the first document's index structure and decides how to index them when no explicit static mapping is specified. Elasticsearch enforces the term schema called **mapping**, which is a process of defining how Lucene stores the indexed document and those fields it contains. When you add a new field to your document, the mapping will also be automatically updated.

Starting from Elasticsearch 6.0.0, only one mapping type is allowed for each index. The mapping type has fields defined by data types and meta fields. Elasticsearch supports many different data types for fields in a document. Each document has meta-fields associated with it. We can customize the behavior of the meta-fields when creating a mapping type. We'll cover this in Chapter 4, *Mapping APIs*.

Analyzer

Elasticsearch comes with a variety of built-in analyzers that can be used in any index without further configuration. If the built-in analyzers are not suitable for your use case, you can create a custom analyzer. Whether it is a built-in analyzer or a customized analyzer, it is just a package of the three following lower-level building blocks:

- **Character filter**: Receives the raw text as a stream of characters and can transform the stream by adding, removing, or changing its characters
- **Tokenizers**: Splits the given streams of characters into a token stream
- **Token filters**: Receives the token stream and may add, remove, or change tokens

The same analyzer should normally be used both at index time and at search time, but you can set `search_analyzer` in the field mapping to perform different analyses while searching.

Standard analyzer

The standard analyzer is the default analyzer, which is used if none is specified. A standard analyzer consists of the following:

- **Character filter**: None
- **Tokenizer**: Standard tokenizer
- **Token filters**: Lowercase token filter and stop token filter (disabled by default)

A standard tokenizer provides a grammar-based tokenization. A lowercase token filter normalizes the token text to lowercase, where a stop token filter removes the stop words from token streams. For a list of English stop words, you can refer to `https://www.ranks.nl/stopwords`. Let's test the standard analyzer with the input text `You'll love Elasticsearch 7.0`.

Since it is a `POST` request, you need to set the `Content-Type` to `application/json`:

The URL is `http://localhost:9200/_analyze` and the request **Body** has a **raw** JSON string, `{"text": "You will love Elasticsearch 7.0."}`. You can see that the response has four tokens: `you'll`, `love`, `elasticsearch`, and `7.0`, all in lowercase, which is due to the lowercase token filter:

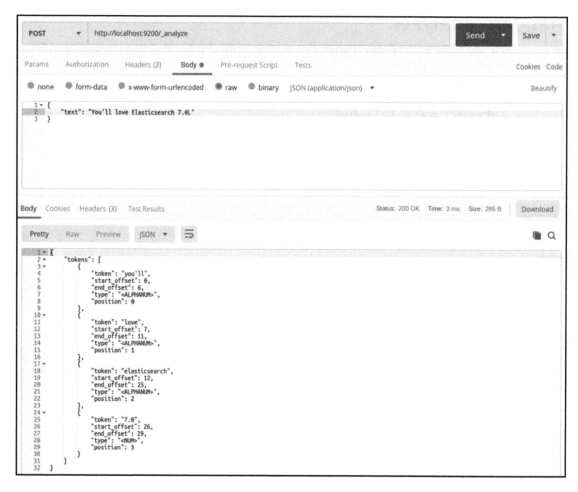

In the next section, let's get familiar with the API conventions.

API conventions

We will only discuss some of the major conventions. For others, please refer to the Elasticsearch reference (`https://www.elastic.co/guide/en/elasticsearch/reference/master/api-conventions.html`). The following list can be applied throughout the REST API:

- **Access across multiple indices**: This convention cannot be used in single document APIs:
    - `_all`: For all indices
    - `comma`: A separator between two indices
    - `wildcard (*,-)`: The asterisk character, `*`, is used to match any sequence of characters in the index name, excluding the index afterwards

- **Common options**:
    - **Boolean values**: `false` means the mentioned value is false; `true` means the value is true.
    - **Number values**: A number is as a string on top of the native JSON number type.
    - **Time unit for duration**: The supported time units are `d` for days, `h` for hours, `m` for minutes, `s` for seconds, `ms` for milliseconds, `micros` for microseconds, and `nanos` for nanoseconds.
    - **Byte size unit**: The supported data units are `b` for bytes, `kb` for kilobytes, `mb` for megabytes, `gb` for gigabytes, `tb` for terabytes, and `pb` for petabytes.
    - **Distance unit**: The supported distance units are `mi` for miles, `yd` for yards, `ft` for feet, `in` for inches, `km` for kilometers, `m` for meters, `cm` for centimeters, `mm` for millimeters, and `nmi` or `NM` for nautical miles.
    - **Unit-less quantities**: If the value specified is large enough, we can use a quantity as a multiplier. The supported quantities are `k` for kilo, `m` for mega, `g` for giga, `t` for tera, and `p` for peta. For instance, `10m` represents the value 10,000,000.
    - **Human-readable output**: Values can be converted to human-readable values, such as `1h` for 1 hour and `1kb` for 1,024 kilobytes. This option can be turned on by adding `?human=true` to the query string. The default value is `false`.

- **Pretty result**: If you append `?pretty=true` to the request URL, the JSON string in the response will be in pretty format.
- **REST parameters**: Follow the convention of using underscore delimiting.
- **Content type**: The type of content in the request body must be specified in the request header using the `Content-Type` key name. Check the reference as to whether the content type you use is supported. In all our `POST/UPDATE/PATCH` request examples, `application/json` is used.
- **Request body in query string**: If the client library does not accept a request body for non-POST requests, you can use the `source` query string parameter to pass the request body and specify the `source_content_type` parameter with a supported media type.
- **Stack traces**: If the `error_trace=true` request URL parameter is set, the error stack trace will be included in the response when an exception is raised.

- **Date math in a formatted date value**: In range queries or in date range aggregations, you can format date fields using date math:
    - The date math expressions start with an anchor date (`now`, or a date string ending with a double vertical bar: `||`), followed by one or more sub-expressions such as `+1h`, `-1d`, or `/d`.
    - The supported time units are different from the time units for duration in the previously mentioned *Common options* bullet list. Where `y` is for years, `M` is for months, `w` is for weeks, `d` is for days, `h`, or `H` is for hours, `m` is for minutes, `s` is for seconds, `+` is for addition, `-` is for subtraction, and `/` is for rounding down to the nearest time unit. For example, this means that `/d` means rounding down to the nearest day.

For the following discussion of these data parameters, assume that the current system time `now` is `2019.01.03 01:20:00`, `now+1h` is `2019.01.03 02:20:00`, `now-1d` is `2019.01.02 01:20:00`, `now/d` is `2019.01.03 00:00:00`, `now/M` is `2019.01.01 00:00:00`, `2019.01.03 01:20:00||+1h` is `2019.01.03 02:20:00`, and so forth.

- **Date math in index name**: If you want to index time series data, such as logs, you can use a pattern with different date fields as the index names to manage daily logging information. Date math then gives you a way to search through a series of time series indices. The date math syntax for the index name is as follows:

  ```
  <static_name{date_math_expr{date_format|time_zone}}>
  ```

  The following are the terms used in the preceding syntax:

  - `static_name`: The unchanged text portion of the index name.
  - `date_math_expr`: The changing text portion of the index name according to the date math to vary.
  - `date_format`: The default value is `YYYY.MM.dd`, where `YYYY` stands for the year, `MM` for the month, and `dd` for the day.
  - `time_zone`: The time zone offset and the default time zone is UTC. For instance, the UTC time offset is `-08:00` for PST. Given that the current system time is 1:00 PM, January 3, 2019, the index name interpreted from the date math is expressed by `<logstash-{now/d{YYYY.MM.dd|+12:00}}>` and is `logstash-2019.1.4`, where `now/d` means the current system time rounded down to the nearest day.

- **URL-based access control**: There are many APIs in Elasticsearch that allow you to specify the index in the request body, such as multi-search, multi-get, and a `Bulk` request. By default, the index specified in the request body will override the `index` parameter specified in the URL. If you use a proxy with URL-based access control to protect access to Elasticsearch indices, you can add the following setting to the `elasticsearch.yml` configuration file to disable the default action:

  ```
  rest.action.multi.allow_explicit_index: false
  ```

For other concerns or detailed usage, check out the official Elasticsearch reference (https://www.elastic.co/guide/en/elasticsearch/reference/master/api-conventions.html). In the next section, we will review the new features in version 7.0.0.

New features

New features are introduced and documented in the 7.0.0 release notes (`https://www.elastic.co/guide/en/elasticsearch/reference/current/release-notes-7.0.0.html`). There are many new features involved in the new release, however, some of them are not our interests and some of which are beyond the scope of this book. Therefore, we show them with two sub-sections. The first sub-section lists those new features to be discussed in the later chapters. The second sub-section lists those new features with description and their issue number.

New features to be discussed

The new features to be discussed include the following:

- Analysis (see the examples in `Chapter 15`, *Working with Elasticsearch Analysis Plugin*):
    - Added support for inlined user dictionary in Nori's tokenizer
    - Added a prebuilt ICU analyzer
- Geo (see the examples at `https://www.elastic.co/guide/en/elasticsearch/reference/master/geo-shape.html`):
    - Integrated Lucene's LatLonShape (BKD-backed geoshapes) as the default `geo_shape` indexing approach
- Java High Level REST Client (see the examples in `Chapter 11`, *Elasticsearch from Java Programming*):
    - Added `rollup` search
- Java Low Level REST Client (see the examples in `Chapter 11`, *Elasticsearch from Java Programming*):
    - Made warning behavior pluggable for each request
    - Added `PreferHasAttributeNodeSelector`
- Machine learning (see the examples in `Chapter 16`, *Machine Learning with Elasticsearch*):
    - Added a delayed `datacheck` to the `datafeed` job runner

- Mapping (see the examples in `Chapter 4`, *Mapping APIs*):
    - Made typeless APIs usable with indices whose type name is different from `_doc`
    - Added nanosecond field mapper `date_nanos` for the `Date` datatype
    - Added `rank_feature` and `rank_features` datatype to expose `Lucene`'s FeatureField
- Search (see the examples in `Chapter 6`, *Search APIs*):
    - Added `intervals` query
    - Added soft limit to open scroll contexts
    - Added `took` timing info to response for the `_msearch/template` request
    - Added `allow_partial_search_results` flag to search requests with default setting
    - Introduced ability to minimize round-trips parameter `ccs_minimize_roundtrips` in cross-cluster search requests
    - Added `script` filter query to `intervals` query
    - Added `track_total_hits` parameter to enable the setting of the number of hits to track accurately
- SQL (see the examples in `Chapter 14`, *Working with Elasticsearch SQL*):
    - Introduced the `HISTOGRAM` grouping function
    - Introduced `DATABASE()` and `USER()` system functions
    - Introduced `INTERVAL` query
    - Introduced SQL `DATE` data type
    - Introduced `FIRST` and `LAST` aggregate function

New features with description and issue number

These new features include:

- Allocation:
    - Introduce the elasticsearch-node repurpose tool to clean up the problematic data for repurposed nodes, Elasticsearch GitHub issue `https://github.com/elastic/elasticsearch/pull/39403`

- Analysis:
  - Add support for field types other than `text` field type to work with TermVectors API, Elasticsearch GitHub issue `https://github.com/elastic/elasticsearch/pull/31915`

- Authentication:
  - Add support for API keys to access Elasticsearch, Elasticsearch GitHub issue `https://github.com/elastic/elasticsearch/pull/38291`
  - Add support for for authentication in the `OpenID Connect` realm, Elasticsearch GitHub issue `https://github.com/elastic/elasticsearch/pull/37787`
  - Add support for `OpenID Connect` realm JWT+JWS related functionality, Elasticsearch GitHub issue `https://github.com/elastic/elasticsearch/pull/37272`
  - Add support for `OpenID Connect` realm base functionality, Elasticsearch GitHub issue `https://github.com/elastic/elasticsearch/pull/37009`

- Authorization:
  - Allow custom authorization with an authorization engine, Elasticsearch GitHub issue `https://github.com/elastic/elasticsearch/pull/38358`
  - Wildcard IndicesPermissions don't cover security, Elasticsearch GitHub issue `https://github.com/elastic/elasticsearch/pull/36765`

- CCR:
  - Generalize `search.remote` settings to `cluster.remote` (See the cross-cluster search setting from the Setting changes sub-section of the Breaking Changes section in this chapter)
  - Add support for cross cluster replication follow info api, Elasticsearch GitHub issue `https://github.com/elastic/elasticsearch/pull/37408`

- Distributed:
  - Add support for log messages from `allocation` commands, Elasticsearch GitHub issue `https://github.com/elastic/elasticsearch/pull/25955`

- Features/Index life cycle management:
  - Add support for the `unfollow` action for CCR follower indices, Elasticsearch GitHub issue `https://github.com/elastic/elasticsearch/pull/36970`

- Features/Ingest:
    - Remove support for the Hashing processor, Elasticsearch GitHub issue `https://github.com/elastic/elasticsearch/pull/32178`
    - Add support for the `indexed_chars_field` parameter in ingest attachment processor plugin to specify the size of indexed characters on a per document basis, Elasticsearch GitHub issue `https://github.com/elastic/elasticsearch/pull/28977`

- Features/Java high-level REST client:
    - Add support for the GraphClient for the high level REST client, Elasticsearch GitHub issue `https://github.com/elastic/elasticsearch/pull/32366`

- Features/Monitoring:
    - Add support to collect only the `display_name` cluster metadata setting, Elasticsearch GitHub issue `https://github.com/elastic/elasticsearch/pull/35265`

- Geo:
    - Add support for the `geotile_grid` aggregation, Elasticsearch GitHub issue `https://github.com/elastic/elasticsearch/pull/37842`

- Infrastructure/Core:
    - Skip shard refreshes if a search request happens on a search idle shard, Elasticsearch GitHub issue `https://github.com/elastic/elasticsearch/pull/27500`

- Infrastructure/Logging:
    - Unify log rotation for index/search slowlog, Elasticsearch GitHub issue `https://github.com/elastic/elasticsearch/pull/27298`

- Infrastructure/Plugins:
    - Reload secure settings for plugins, Elasticsearch GitHub issue `https://github.com/elastic/elasticsearch/pull/31383`

- REST API:
    - Adds support for `include_type_name` option to the `indices.create`, `indices.get_mapping` and `indices.put_mapping` APIs, which defaults to true, Elasticsearch GitHub issue `https://github.com/elastic/elasticsearch/pull/29453`

- Machine Learning:
  - Filter undefined job groups from update job calendar actions, Elasticsearch GitHub issue `https://github.com/elastic/elasticsearch/pull/30757`

- Mapping:
  - Add a `feature_vector` field to index sparse feature vectors, Elasticsearch GitHub issue `https://github.com/elastic/elasticsearch/pull/31102`
  - Give precedence to index creation when mixing typed templates with typeless index creation and vice-versa, Elasticsearch GitHub issue `https://github.com/elastic/elasticsearch/pull/37871`

- Ranking:
  - Add support for ranking evaluation API to evaluate the search results over a set of given search queries, Elasticsearch GitHub issue `https://github.com/elastic/elasticsearch/pull/27478`

- Recovery:
  - Ass support to allow to trim all ops above a certain sequence number with a term lower than X, Elasticsearch GitHub issue `https://github.com/elastic/elasticsearch/pull/31211`

- SQL:
  - Add support for Adds basic support for `ST_AsWKT` function, Elasticsearch GitHub issue `https://github.com/elastic/elasticsearch/pull/34205`
  - Add support for `SYS GEOMETRY_COLUMN` system command, Elasticsearch GitHub issue `https://github.com/elastic/elasticsearch/pull/30496`
  - Add support to allow sorting of groups by aggregates, Elasticsearch GitHub issue `https://github.com/elastic/elasticsearch/pull/38042`

- Search:
  - Add `took` timing info to response for `_msearch/template` API, Elasticsearch GitHub issue `https://github.com/elastic/elasticsearch/pull/30961`
  - Add support to expose the `Lucene Matches` API to search query, Elasticsearch GitHub issue `https://github.com/elastic/elasticsearch/pull/29631`

- Enable adaptive replica selection by default, Elasticsearch GitHub issue `https://github.com/elastic/elasticsearch/pull/26522`
- Add setting `http.search.max_content_length` for the search, msearch and template search APIs to set the maximum search request size, Elasticsearch GitHub issue `https://github.com/elastic/elasticsearch/pull/26423`

- Security:

    - Switch internal security index to security-7 to match the version, Elasticsearch GitHub issue `https://github.com/elastic/elasticsearch/pull/39337`

- Suggesters:

    - Serialize suggestion responses as writeable instead of streamable which makes custom suggestion response types possible, Elasticsearch GitHub issue `https://github.com/elastic/elasticsearch/pull/30284`

In the next section, let's pay attention to the breaking changes in version 7.0.0.

Breaking changes

You need to be aware of the breaking changes when migrating your application to Elasticsearch 7.0. The following document that describes the breaking changes will be listed in the subsequent sub-sections:

- Breaking changes in 7.0 (`https://www.elastic.co/guide/en/elasticsearch/reference/current/breaking-changes-7.0.html`)

If you are a novice, just jump to `Chapter 2`, *Index APIs*, and come back later. We will only point out important changes from the 7.0 documentation here.

Aggregations changes

The changes related to aggregation are as follows:

- The execution hints (`global_ordinals_hash` and `global_ordinals_low_cardinality`) for the term aggregations are eliminated.

- The max limit of buckets allowed in a single response for bucket aggregations is controlled by the `search.max_buckets` cluster setting, with the default value of `10,000`. An attempt to return a request that exceeds the limit will fail with an exception.
- You should use the `missing_bucket` option instead of the `missing` of the parameter `sources` in the composite aggregation to include documents that have no value in the response. The deprecated `missing` option is eliminated.
- The `params._agg` script parameter, or `params._aggs` in the scripted metric aggregation, should be replaced by the new `ScriptContext state` and `states` variables.
- In previous versions, the `map_script` parameter was the only parameter required in the `Script Metric Aggregation`. Now, the `combine_script` and `reduce_script` parameters are also required.
- The response of `percentiles` and `percentile_ranks` aggregation will return `null` instead of `NaN` if its input is empty.
- The response of `stats` and `extended_stats` aggregation will return 0 instead null if its input is empty.

Analysis changes

The changes related to analysis are as follows:

- The max limit for tokens that can be obtained in the `_analyze` API is `10000`.
- The max limit for input characters analyzed during highlighting is `1000000`.
- Use the `delimited_payload` parameter for the delimited payload token filter, instead of the deprecated `delimited_payload_filter`. For existing pre-7.0 indices, a deprecation warning is logged. The new index will fail with an exception.
- The standard filter is eliminated.
- The `standard_html_strip` analyzer is deprecated.
- Using the deprecated `nGram` and `edgeNGram` token filter will throw an error. Use the name `ngram` and `edge_ngram` respectively instead.

API changes

The changes related to APIs are as follows:

- The internal versioning support for optimistic concurrency control is eliminated.
- In the document `bulk` API, use the `retry_on_conflict` parameter instead of `_retry_on_conflict`; use `routing` instead of `_routing`; use `version` instead of `_version`; and use `version_type` instead of `_version_type`. Use the `join` meta-field instead of the `_parent` in mapping. All previous underscore parameters are eliminated. The camel-case parameters such as `opType`, `versionType`, and `_versionType` have been eliminated.
- The cat thread pool API has renamed some field names from 6.x to 7.0 to align the meaning in the fixed thread pools and scaling thread pools. Use `pool_size` instead of the original `size` and `core` instead of the original `min`. For the corresponding alias, use `psz` instead of `s`, and `cr` instead of `mi`. In addition, the alias for max has changed from `ma` to `mx`. A new `size` field that represents the configured fixed number of active threads allowed in the current thread pool is introduced.
- For the `bulk` request and `update` request, if a request contains an unknown parameter, a **Bad Request (400)** response will be returned.
- The feature for the `Suggest` statistics obtained during the `Search` statistics operation on the indices stats `_stats` API is eliminated.
- The `copy_setting` parameter in the split index operation will be removed in 8.0.0. These settings are copied by default during the operation.
- Instead of using the stored search template `_search` API, you must use the stored script `_scripts` API to register search templates. The search template name must be provided.
- Previously, the response status of the index alias API depended on whether the security feature was turned on or off. Now, an empty response with a status of **OK (200)** is always returned.
- The feature for the response object to create a user using the `/_xpack/security/user` API with an additional field created outside the `user` field is eliminated.
- Use the corrected URL `_source_excludes` and `_source_includes` parameters instead of the original `_source_exclude` and `_source_include` parameters in the query.

- Unknown keys in the multi search `_msearch` API were ignored before, but will fail with an exception now.
- The graph `/_graph/_explore` API is eliminated.
- Term vector can be used to return information and statistics in specific document fields in the document API. Use the corrected plural-form `_termvectors` method instead of the singular form, `_termvector`.
- The `Index Monitoring` APIs are not authorized implicitly anymore. The privileges must be granted explicitly.
- The deprecated parameter fields of the `bulk` request is eliminated.
- If the document is missing when the `PUT Document` API is used with version number `X`, the error message is different from previous version. The new message is shown in the code block below:

```
document does not exist (expected version [X]).
```

- The `compressed_size` and `compressed_size_in_bytes` fields are removed from the Cluster State API response.
- The `Migration Assistance` API is removed.
- When the cluster is configured as read-only, 200 status will be returned for a GET request.
- The `Clear Cache` API support POST or GET request previously. Using GET request for such API is eliminated.

Cluster changes

The changes related to cluster are as follows:

- The colon (`:`) is not a valid character for the cluster name anymore due to cross-cluster search support.
- The number of allocated shards (`wait_for_active_shards`) that must be ready before the open index API can be proceeded has been incremented from 0 to 1.
- The shard preferences in the search APIs, including `_primary`, `_primary_first`, `_replica`, and `_replica_first`, are eliminated.
- The cluster-wide shard limit used to prevent user error now depends on the value of `max_shards_per_node * number_of_nodes`.

Discovery changes

The changes related to Discovery are as follows:

- The `cluster.initial_master_nodes` setting must be set before cluster bootstrapping is performed.
- If half or more of the master-eligible nodes are going to remove from a cluster, those affected nodes must be excluded from the voting configuration using the `_cluster/voting_config_exclusions` API.
- At least one of the following settings must be specified in the `elastiscearch.yml` configuration file.
    - discovery.seed_hosts
    - discovery.seed_providers
    - cluster.initial_master_nodes
    - discovery.zen.ping.unicast.hosts
    - discovery.zen.hosts_provider
- Use the setting name `cluster.no_master_block` instead of `discovery.zen.no_master_block`, which is deprecated.
- The default timeout for heartbeat fault detection ping operation between cluster nodes is 10 seconds instead of 30 seconds.

High-level REST client changes

The changes related to the high-level REST client are as follows:

- Methods that accept headers as the header `varargs` argument have been eliminated from the `RestHighLevelClient` class.
- Previously, the cluster health API was a shard-level base, but now it is a cluster-level base.

Low-level REST client changes

The changes related to low-level REST client are as follows:

- The `maxRetryTimeout` setting of the `RestClient` and `RestClientBuilder` class is eliminated.
- Methods that do not take `Request` objects, such as `performRequest` and `performRequestAsync`, have been eliminated from the `RestClient` class.

- The `setHosts` method is removed from the `RestClient` class.
- The minimum compiler version is bumped to JDK 8.

Indices changes

The changes related to indices are as follows:

- By default, each index in Elasticsearch is allocated 1 primary shard and 1 replica.
- The colon (`:`) is no longer a valid character in the index name anymore due to the cross-cluster search support.
- Negative values for `index.unassigned.node_left.delayed_timeout` settings are treated as zero.
- The undocumented side effects from a `_flush` or a `_force_merge` operation have been fixed.
- The difference between `max_ngram` and `min_ngram` in `NGramTokenFilter` and `NGramTokenizer` is limited to 1 before. This default limit can be changed with the `index.max_ngram_diff` index setting. If the limit is exceeded, it will fail with an exception.
- The difference between `max_shingle_size` and `min_shingle_size` in `ShingleTokenFilter` was limited to 3 before. This default limit can be changed with the `index.max_shingle_diff` index setting. If the difference exceeds the limit, it will fail with an exception.
- New indices created in version 7.0.0 will have a default value for the `number_of_routing_shards` parameter. The requirement of the split index API for the source index must be associated with this setting . In order to maintain the exact same distribution as a pre-7.0.0 index, you must make sure the values in the split index API and the value at the index creation time are the same.
- Background refreshing is disabled. If you don't set the value of `index.refresh_interval`, no refresh operation will be acted on for the search idle shards.
- The Clear Cache API allows you to clear all caches, or just specific caches. The original usage of the specific cache name is eliminated. Use `query` instead of `query_cache` or `filter_cache`. Use `request` instead of `request_cache`. Use `fielddata` instead of `field_data`.

- The `network.breaker.inflight_requests.overhead` setting has changed from 1 to 2. The estimated memory usage limit of all currently active incoming requests at transport or HTTP level on a node has been increased.
- The parent circuit breaker defines a new setting `indices.breaker.total.use_real_memory`. The starting limit for the overall parent breaker `indices.breaker.total.limit` is 95% of the JVM heap if it is true (`default`), otherwise it is 70%.
- The field data limit for the circuit breaker of index `indices.breaker.fielddata.limit` has been reduced from 60% to 40% of the maximum JVM heap by default.
- The `fix` option of the index setting `index.shard.check_on_startup`, which checks the corruption of shard, has been eliminated.
- The `elasticsearch-translog` tool has been eliminated. Use the `elasticsearch-shard` tool instead.

Java API changes

The changes related to the Java API are as follows:

- Use the `isShardsAcknowledged()` method instead of the `isShardsAcked()` method in the `CreateIndexResponse`, `RolloverResponse`, and `CreateIndexClusterStateUpdateResponse` classes. The `isShardsAcked()` method is eliminated.
- The aggregation framework has had some classes moved upward. The new location of the classes in `org.elasticsearch.search.aggregations.metrics.*` packages is under the `org.elasticsearch.search.aggregations.metrics` package. The new location of the classes in `org.elasticsearch.search.aggregations.pipeline.*` packages is under the `org.elasticsearch.search.aggregations.pipeline` package. The new location of the `org.elasticsearch.search.aggregations.pipeline.PipelineAggregationBuilders` class is under the `org.elasticsearch.search.aggregations` package.
- Regarding the `org.elasticsearch.action.bulk.Retry` class, the `withBackoff()` method usage with the `Settings` field is eliminated.
- Regarding the Java client class, use the method name of the plural form, `termVectors()`, instead of the singular form, `termVector()`.

- The `prepareExecute()` method has also been eliminated.
- The deprecated constructor `AbstractLifeCycleComponent(Settings settings)` is eliminated.

Mapping changes

The changes related to mapping are as follows:

- The original indexing meta field, `_all`, which indexed the values of all fields, has been eliminated.
- The original indexing meta field, `_uid`, which combined `_type` and `_id`, has been eliminated.
- The original default mapping meta field, `_default_`, which was used as the base mapping for any new mapping type, has been eliminated.
- For search and highlighting purposes, the `index_options` parameter controls which information has been added to the inverted index. However, it no longer supports numeric fields.
- The max limit of nested JSON objects within a single document across all nested fields is `10000`.
- In the past, specifying that the `update_all_types` parameter update the mappings would update all fields with the same name of all `_type` in the same index. It has been eliminated.
- The classic similarity feature, which is based on the TF/IDF to define how matching documents are scored, has been eliminated since it is no longer supported by Lucene.
- The error for providing unknown `similarity` parameters in the request will fail with exception.
- The `geo_shape` datatypes in the indexing strategy now defaults to using a vector-indexing approach based on Lucene's new `LatLonShape` field type.
- Most options of the `geo_shape` mapping will be eliminated in a future version. They are `tree`, `precision`, `tree_levels`, `strategy`, `distance_error_pct`, and `points_only`.
- The max limit of `completion` context is 10. A deprecation warning will be logged if the setting exceeds.
- The default value of `include_type_name` has changed from `true` to `false`.

If you use tree as a mapping option for geo_shape mapping and also use a timed index created from a template, you must set geohash or quadtree as the option to ensure compatibility with your previously created indices.

ML changes

The change related to machine learning is as follow:

- `Types` parameter is eliminated from the `datafeed` configuration

Packaging changes

The changes related to packaging are as follows:

- If using `rpm` of `deb` package, to override the settings of the `systemd` elasticsearch service, it should be made in `/etc/systemd/system/elasticsearch.service.d/override.conf`
- The `tar` package will not include the files in bin directory for Window platform
- Stop supporting `Ubuntu` 14.04 version
- Stop supporting secrets input from command line input

Search changes

The changes related to search are as follows:

- By default, the adaptive replica selection, `cluster.routing.use_adaptive_replica_selection`, is enabled to send copies of data to replicas. You may disable it to use the old round-robin method as in 6.x.
- In the following error situations, a `bad request (400)` will be returned instead of an `internal server error (500)`:
  - The resulting window is too large, from + size must be less than or equal to: `[x]` but was `[y]`.
  - Cannot use the `[sort]` option in conjunction with [rescore].
  - The rescore window, `[x]`, is too large.
  - The number of slices, `[x]`, is too large.

- Keep alive for scroll, `[x]`, is too large.
- In adjacency matrix aggregation, the number of filters exceeds the max limit.
- An `org.elasticsearch.script.ScriptException` compile error.

- The `request_cache` setting in the scroll search is eliminated. A bad request (400) will be returned if you still use it.
- The method of including a `rescore` clause on a query to create a scroll search is eliminated. A bad request (400) will be returned if you still use it.
- Use the corrected name, `levenshtein`, instead of `levenstein`, and `jaro_winkler` instead of `jarowinkler`, for the `string_distance` term `suggest` options in the term **suggester**.
- The meaning of `suggest_mode=popular` in the suggesters (term and phrase) is now the doc frequency from the input terms to compute the frequency threshold for candidate suggestions.
- Search requests that contain extra tokens after the main object will fail with a parsing exception.
- The completion suggester provides an auto-complete/search-as-you-type feature. When indexing and querying a context-enabled `completion` field, you must provide a context.
- The semantics of `max_concurrent_shard_requests` has changed from cluster level to node level. The default number of concurrent shard requests per node is `5`.
- The format of the total number of documents that matches the search criteria in the response has changed from a value type to an object of a value and a relation.
- When `track_total_hits` is set to `false` in the search request, the total number of matching documents (`hits.total`) in the response will return `null` instead of `-1`. You may set the option as `rest_total_hits_as_int=true` in the request to return to the old format.
- The `track_total_hits` defaults to 10,000 documents in the search response.
- The default format for `doc-value` field is switched back to 6.x style. The `Date` field can take any `date` format and the `Numeric` fields can take a `DecimalFormat` pattern.
- For `geo` context completion `suggester`, the context is only accepted if the `path` parameter points to a field with `geo_point` type.

Query DSL changes

The changes related to query DSL are as follows:

- The default value of the `transposition` parameter in a fuzzy query is changed from `false` to `true`.
- The query string query options of `use_dis_max`, `split_on_whitespace`, `all_fields`, `locale`, `auto_generate_phrase_queries`, and `lowercase_expanded_terms` have all been eliminated.
- If a bool query has the `must_not` clause, a score of `0` for all documents is returned instead of `1` because the scoring is ignored.
- Treats geohashes as grid cells, instead of just points, when the geohashes are used to specify the edges in the `geo_bounding_box` query.
- A multi-term query (a wildcard, fuzzy, prefix, range, or regex query) against non-text fields with a custom analyzer will now throw an exception.
- If the resulting polygon crosses the dateline, the GeoJSON standard will be applied to the `geo_shape` query to disambiguate the misleading results.
- Boost settings are not allowed on complex inner span queries.
- The number of terms in the terms query (`index.max_terms_count`) is limited to `65536`.
- The maximum length of a regex string (`index.max_regex_length`) allowed in a regex query is limited to `1000`.
- No more than 1,024 fields can be queried at a time. It also limits the auto explanation of fields in the *query_string* query, the `simple_query_string` query, and the `multi_match` query.
- When a score cannot be tracked, the return value of `max_score` will return `null` instead of `0`.
- Boosting is a process that enhances the document relevance. The matching document placed at the top of the result can be given a negative boost value to move it to the last position. Negative boosting support is eliminated.
- The score generated by the `script_score_function` or `field_value_factor` must be non-negative, otherwise it will fail with an exception.
- The difference between the `query` and `filter` context in `QueryBuilders` is eliminated. Therefore, bool queries with `should` clauses that don't require access to scores do not need to set the `minimum_should_match` to `1` .
- More constraints on the `scores` value. It must not be negative, must not decrease when `term freq` increases, and must not increase when `norm` increases.

- Negative support for the `weight` parameters for the `function_score` query is eliminated.

Settings changes

The changes related to settings are as follows:

- The default `node.name` is the `hostname` instead of the first eight characters of the `node _id`.
- Use the `index.percolator.map_unmapped_fields_as_text` setting instead of the deprecated `index.percolator.map_unmapped_fields_as_string` setting to force unmapped fields to be handled as strings in a percolate query.
- Since the indexing thread pool no longer exists, the `thread_pool.index.size` and `thread_pool.index.queue_size` settings have been removed.
- The `thread_pool.bulk.size, thread_pool.bulk.queue_size,` and `es.thread_pool.write.use_bulk_as_display_name` settings, which were supported as the fallback settings have been removed.
- Use `node.store.allow_mmap` instead of `node.store.allow_mmapfs` to restrict the use of the `mmapfs` or the `hybridfs` store type of indices.
- The HTTP on/off switch setting `http.enabled` has been eliminated.
- The HTTP pipeline support has been eliminated. However, the `http.pipelining.max_events` setting is still the same as in the previous version.
- The setting name `search.remote.*` used to configure cross-cluster search was renamed to `cluster.remote.*`. The previous setting names fall back in version 7.0.0 and will be removed in version 8.0.0.
- To audit local node information security settings, you must use `xpack.security.audit.logfile.emit_node_host_address` instead of the deprecated `xpack.security.audit.logfile.prefix.emit_node_host_address;` use `xpack.security.audit.logfile.prefix.emit_node_host_name` instead of the deprecated `xpack.security.audit.logfile.emit_node_host_names;` and use `xpack.security.audit.logfile.prefix.emit_node_name` instead of the deprecated `xpack.security.audit.logfile.emit_node_name`. In addition, the default value of `xpack.security.audit.logfile.emit_node_name` has changed from `true` to `false`.

- For all security realm settings, instead of using the explicit `type` setting, the realm type must be part of the setting name. Consider the following for instance:

```
xpack.security.authc.realms:
    realm1:
        type: ldap
        order: 0
        ...
    realm2:
        type: native
        ...
```

  This must be updated as follows:

```
xpack.security.authc.realms:
    ldap.realm1:
        order: 0
        ...
    native.realm2:
        ...
```

- The default TLS/SSL settings are removed.
- The TLS v1.0 is disabled by default.
- The security is only enabled if xpack.security.enabled is true, or xpack.security.enabled is not set, and a gold or platinum license is installed.
- Some of the security settings' names are changed, you must use `xpack.notification.email.account.<id>.smtp.password` instead of `xpack.notification.email.account.<id>.smtp.secure_password`, `xpack.notification.hipchat.account.<id>.auth_token` instead of `xpack.notification.hipchat.account.<id>.secure_auth_token`, `xpack.notification.jira.account.<id>.url` instead of `xpack.notification.jira.account.<id>.secure_url`, `xpack.notification.jira.account.<id>.user` instead of `xpack.notification.jira.account.<id>.secure_user`, `xpack.notification.jira.account.<id>.password` instead of `xpack.notification.jira.account.<id>.secure_password`, `xpack.notification.pagerduty.account.<id>.service_api_key` instead of `xpack.notification.pagerduty.account.<id>.secure_service_api_key`, `xpack.notification.slack.account.<id>.url` instead of `xpack.notification.slack.account.<id>.secure_url`.
- The settings under the `xpack.security.audit.index` and `xpack.security.audit.outputs` namespace and have been removed.

- The `ecs` setting for the user agent ingest processor now defaults to true.
- The `action.master.force_local` setting is removed.
- The limit of cluster-wide shard number is now enforced, not optional.
- If `http.max_content_length` is set to Integer.MAX, it will not be reset to 100mb.

Scripting changes

The changes related to scripting are as follows:

- The getter methods for the date class have been eliminated. Use `.value` instead of `.date` on the date fields. For instance, use `doc['start_time'].value.minuteOfHour` instead of `doc['start_time'].date.minuteOfHour`.
- Accessing the missing field of the document will fail with an exception. To check if a document is missing values, you can use `doc['field_name'].size() == 0`.
- A `bad request (400)` instead of an `internal error (500)` is returned for malformed scripts in search templates, ingest pipelines, and search requests.
- The deprecated `getValues()` method of the `ScriptDocValues` class has been eliminated. Use `doc["field_name"]` instead of `doc["field_name"].values`.

If an upgrade is needed, follow the advices for the migration between versions in the next section.

Migration between versions

The rules of thumb when migrating your application between Elasticsearch versions are as follows:

- When migrating between minor versions (for example, 7.x to 7.y), we can upgrade one node at a time.
- Migrating between two subsequent major versions (for example, 6.x to 7.x) requires a full cluster restart.
- Migrating between two non-subsequent major versions (for example, 5.x to 7.x) requires reindexing documents from Elasticsearch 5.x to Elasticsearch 6.x. Then, you follow the procedures for migrating between two subsequent major versions.

A reindexing API can be used to convert multi-type indices to single-type indices during migration. See the example in Chapter 3, *Document APIs*.

 Elasticsearch 7.0 will not start on a node with documents indexed prior to 6.0.

Summary

So far, we have run the Elasticsearch server and performed some simple tests. We also familiarized ourselves with some basic concepts from an architectural point of view to reduce the trauma of our learning curve. We have listed and briefly discussed the new features and major changes in the new release. We also covered the best way to handle the migration between major versions.

In the next chapter, we'll delve into index APIs. An index is a logical namespace for organizing data in Elasticsearch. Becoming familiar with the index infrastructure is the first step in solving Elasticsearch performance issues. We'll first understand the APIs for index management, index settings, and index templates. After we practice some advanced examples of index status management operations, we will also discuss monitoring indices statistics.

2
Index APIs

In the previous chapter, we gained basic knowledge of Elasticsearch. We also covered the latest features and breaking changes that were introduced in version 7.0. In this chapter, we will discuss the index APIs. Documents are indexed, stored, and made searchable by using the index API. The main purpose of an index is to logically group documents that have certain similar characteristics. An index is identified by a name (all in lowercase), and this name is referenced in index, search, update, and delete operations for the documents belonging to it.

In subsequent sections, you'll learn how to use index APIs to manage individual indices, index settings, aliases, and templates. Monitoring statistics for operations that occur on an index will also be covered. We will also look at index management operations, including refreshing, flushing, and clearing the cache.

By the end of this chapter, you'll have learned about the following topics:

- Index management APIs
- Index settings
- Index aliases
- Monitoring indices
- Index persistence
- Advanced index management APIs

Index management APIs

Index management operations allow you to manage the entire life cycle process via its settings, mappings, creation, opening, closing, deletion, and updating indices in an Elasticsearch cluster. Let's explore the basic CRUD APIs for working with indices first.

Basic CRUD APIs

Some of the basic APIs for working with indices are as follows:

- **Index creation**: The name of the index must follow these requirements:

    - Lowercase only
    - Cannot include \, /, *, ?, ", <, >, |, spaces, commas, or #
    - The colon (:) character can't be used
    - Cannot start with -, _, or +
    - Cannot be . or ..
    - The maximum bytes for the index name is 255

Let's practice index creation by using a **PUT** request with a valid index name and then use an invalid index name in the Postman app. For example, the valid index name we will use is cf_etf. The request URL is http://localhost:9200/cf_etf. The successful response to the valid case is **200 OK**, as shown in the following screenshot:

The invalid index name that we will use for the illustration is `cf:etf`, where the index name has a colon symbol. As we can see in the following screenshot, the response is **400 Bad Request**, with an `invalid_index_name_exception` error:

- **Check whether the index exists**: Use a **HEAD** request to check whether the index exists. The response should be **200 OK**; otherwise, you will get an **INVALID REQUEST 404** response. This API also applies to index alias operations. We'll introduce index alias operations in the following section:

- **Get the index**: This API allows you to retrieve information about one or more indices (for multiple indices, see the *API convention* section in Chapter 1, *Overview of Elasticsearch 7*). We use a **GET** request to get the cf_etf index that we have just created. The response is **200 OK**, and the response body contains three parts of the index, which are aliases, mappings, and settings, as shown in the following screenshot:

The mappings part will be described in Chapter 4, *Mapping APIs*. The settings part will be explained in the next section, *Index settings*. The aliases will be illustrated in a later section, *Index aliases*.

If the index is not found, you will get a **404 Not Found** response, and the root clause in the response body will throw an index_not_found_exception error. For example, let's issue a **GET** request with the non-existent index, cf:etf, which has got failure in the index creation request, as shown in the following screenshot:

- **Delete index**: This API allows you to delete one or more existing indices. As shown in the following screenshot, the response of a successful deletion is **200 OK**:

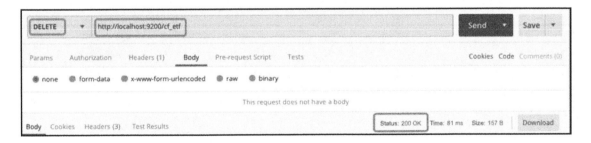

When getting the same response as in the **GET** index request with a non-existent index, you will get a **404 Not Found** response. The root clause in the response body will be an `index_not_found_exception` error. It is worth mentioning here that using an alias name instead of the index name in the **DELETE** operation will not delete the corresponding index.

- **Update index**: There is no such operation to directly update the contents of the index (that is, `PUT/index`). Instead, you update the mapping of the index, such as `PUT/index/_mapping`, or update the settings of the index, such as `PUT/index/_settings`.

- **Open/close index**: Elasticsearch supports online/offline mode for indices. When using offline mode, the data is maintained with almost no overhead on the cluster. Read/write operations will be blocked after the index is closed. When you want the index to come back online, just open it. However, closing the index can take up a lot of disk space. You can disable the close index feature by changing the default value of `cluster.indices.close.enable` from `true` to `false` to avoid accidents.

The following is an example of a `_close` index API. This operation uses a **POST** request. If the operation is successful, the response is **200 OK**:

The following is an example of an open index API. This operation uses a **POST** request. If the operation is successful, the response is **200 OK**:

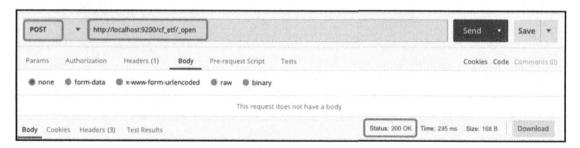

When an index is closed and a read/write document request uses that index, the operation will fail with a **400 Bad Request** response.

Now that you know about the basic CRUD APIs and know how to create a new index, you may need to adjust the characteristics of the index. In the next section, we will discuss the index settings that we can customize as needed.

Index settings

The index settings are divided into per-index level and global level. Basically, the purpose of global-level settings is to manage the settings for all indices rather than configuring them one by one. Global-level index settings include circuit breakers, field data caches, node query caches, indexing buffers, shard request caches, and recovery. They are controlled by the so-called indices module. Go to the reference (`https://www.elastic.co/guide/en/elasticsearch/reference/master/modules-indices.html`) for more details.

On the other hand, per-index level settings are controlled by index modules. Per-index level settings are also distinguished as static and dynamic. Static settings can only be set when the index is created or on a closed index, while dynamic settings can be changed on the live index. The following is a brief description of the per-index level settings:

Per-index level settings		
Static	`index.number_of_shards`	This is the number of primary shards that an index should have: default (5) and limit (1024).
	`index.shard.check_on_startup`	These are the options to check for corruption before opening: `true`, `false` (default), and `checksum`.
	`index.codec`	This is the compression method that's used: the options are `LZ4` (default) and `best_compression`.
	`index.routing_partition_size`	This is the number of shards that are allowed for a document to fan out for a search request. The options are 1 (default) ≤ x < `index.number_of_shards`.

Dynamic	`index.number_of_replicas`	This is the number of replicas for each primary shard. The default is 1.
	`index.auto_expand_replicas`	The number of replicas is automatically increased to accommodate spikes in read-heavy environments; the options are `false` (default), `x-y`, and `x-all`, where `x` is the lower bound and `y` is the upper bound.
	`index.search.idle.after`	This is the inactive time period for a shard to become a search idle shard. The default is 30s.
	`index.refresh_interval`	This is how often to perform a refresh operation. The default is 1s.
	`index.max_result_window`	This is the maximum amount of hits allowed to be returned from the search requests to this index. The default is 10000.
	`index.max_inner_result_window`	This is the maximum amount of hits allows to return from a query for inner nested objects or top hits aggregations to this index. The default is 100.
	`index.max_rescore_window`	This is the maximum amount of hits allows to be returned from rescore requests to this index; it's the same as `index.max_result_window`.
	`index.max_docvalue_fields_search`	This is the maximum number of `doc_values` fields allowed to be returned from each hit. The default is 100.
	`index.max_script_fields`	This is the maximum number of `script_fields` allowed in a query. The default is 32.
	`index.max_ngram_diff`	Max difference between `max_ngram` and `min_ngram` allows for `NgramTokenizer` and `NGramTokenFilter`. Default is (1).
	`index.max_shingle_diff`	Max difference between `max_shingle_size` and `min_shingle_size` allows for `ShingleTokenFilter`. Default (3).
	`index.blocks.read_only`	Enables read-only operations. The default is `false`.
	`index.blocks.read_only_allow_delete`	This is similar to `index.block.read_only` but allows deletion operations when it is `true`.
	`index.blocks.read`	Disables read operations. The default is `false`.
	`index.blocks.write`	Disables write operations. The default is `false`.
	`index.blocks.metadata`	Disables access to metadata. The default is `false`.
	`index.max_refresh_listeners`	This is the maximum number of refresh listeners available on each shard of the index.
	`index.analyze.max_token_count`	This is the maximum number of tokens allowed to be produced in the `_analyze` API. The default is 10000.
Dynamic	`index.highlight.max_analyzed_offset`	This is the maximum number of characters allowed to be analyzed in a highlight request. The default is 1000000.
	`index.max_terms_count`	This is the maximum number of terms allowed in a terms query. The default is 65536.
	`index.max_regex_length`	This is the maximum length of regex allowed in a `regexp` query. The default is 1000.
	`index.routing.allocation.enable`	This specifies on which node/nodes to control shard allocation for this index. The options are `all` (default), `primaries`, `replicas`, and `none`.
	`index.routing.rebalance.enable`	This specifies on which node/nodes to enables shard rebalancing for this index. The options are `all` (default), `primaries`, `replicas`, and `none`.
	`index.gc_deletes`	This is the garbage collection deletion period. The default is 60s.
	`index.default_pipeline`	This is the default ingest node pipeline name for this index. `_none` means no pipeline.

For other index settings in *Index Modules,* refer to `https://www.elastic.`
`co/guide/en/elasticsearch/reference/master/index-modules.html`.

Now, let's work on the index settings API, `_settings`:

- **Get settings**: This API allows you to retrieve index/indices settings. The default
  settings includes index creation date, `creation_date`; the number of
  shards, `number_of_shards`; the number of replicas `number_of_replicas`;
  `uuid`, the Elasticsearch version ID; and the given index name, `provided_name`.
  We use a **GET** request to get the settings of the `cf_etf` index. As we can see in
  the response body, all of the settings of the `cf_etf` index are in default values:

- **Update dynamic per-index settings**: Let's use the **PUT** request and the request body on the `ct_etf` index to update the `number_of_replicas` setting from 1 to 2. You can issue the get settings API to verify `num_of_replicas` has been updated from 1 to 2. Let me remind you that the `Content-Type` header has been set to `application/json`:

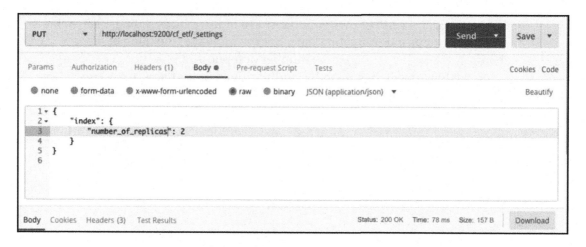

- **Update static per-index settings**: If you update the static settings on an open index, you'll get a **400 Bad Request** response with `illegal_argument_exception`. We must first close the `ct_etf` index and then the update request to set `index.codec` to `best_compression`:

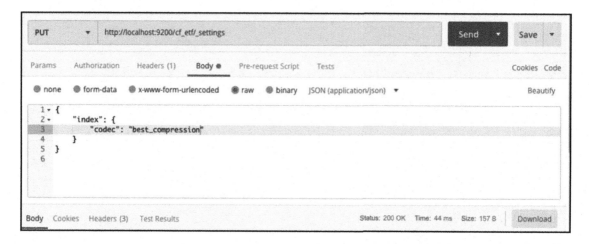

- **Delete index settings**: The deletion of index settings is not supported.
- **Reset an index settings**: Specifying the `null` value to the index setting in the update API will reset it back to its default value.

Index templates

Index settings can be defined in index templates and applied when the index is created so that the settings can be reused. However, changing the template has no effect on any existing indices. The settings in the template will also be overridden by the settings in the create index API. In this section, we will introduce the basic index template CRUD APIs and practice each one:

- **Create the index template**: Let's create an index template, `cf_etf_template`, using the two options that are available. We'll set `number_of_replicas` to 2 and `codec` to `best_compression`. In the template, there is a field called `index_pattern` that can be specified a glob style pattern. Any index being created that matches the index pattern will apply the settings of the template. In the following screenshot, we are using `["cf_etf*"]` as the index pattern:

- **Get index template**: This API allows you to retrieve the settings of an index template. Let's issue a **GET** request to retrieve the information from `cf_etf_template`, as shown in the following screenshot:

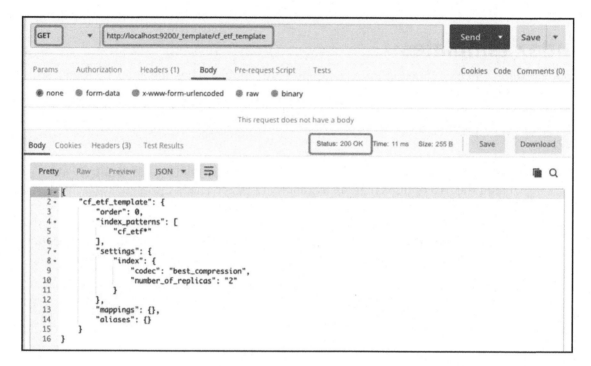

There is a field name, `order`, in the response body that shows the order ranking in which multiple matching templates are merged. The lower order applies first and the higher order overrides them.

- **Delete index settings**: Use DELETE/_template/cf_etf_template to delete the index template.
- **Check whether the index exists**: Use HEAD/_template/cf_etf_template to check whether the index template exists.
- **Create index with index template**: Let's create a new index, `cf_etf_large`, and check whether the settings of `cf_etf_template` have been applied to it.

The following screenshot is an example of creating the `cf_etf_large` index, where its name matches the index template, `cf_etf*`:

When you use the get index API with the `cf_etf_large` index, you can see that the index settings, `number_of_replicas` to `2` and `codec` to `best_compression`, are applied, as shown in the following screenshot:

An index template is a way to reuse settings so that you can create different indexes. In the next section, we will discuss how to use different names of an index in alternative or varied ways.

Index aliases

The index aliases API allows you to create another name for an index or multiple indices and then use it as an alternative name in an index operation. The alias APIs give us flexibility in the following aspects:

- Re-indexing with zero downtime
- Grouping multiple indices
- Views on a subset of documents

For a simple case, use _alias. For complex operations, _aliases. In this section, we will introduce the basic index alias CRUD APIs and practice each one:

- **Create Index Alias API**: Create an alternative name for an index or multiple indices. The following screenshot shows the creation of the index alias, cf_etf_1, for the index, cf_etf:

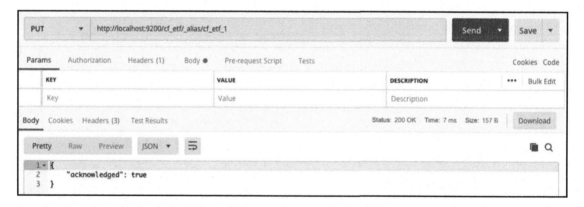

The syntax of the index (that is, cf_etf) can be * | _all | glob pattern | name1, name2, and so on. This means that a single alias can reference multiple indices.

- **Get Index Alias API**: This API allows you to retrieve information from the alternative name of the index. The following screenshot shows the **GET** request of the `cf_etf_1` index alias:

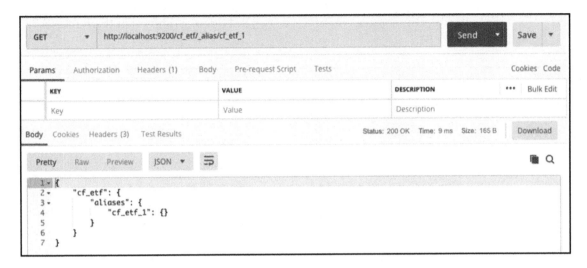

- **Delete Index Alias API**: Use `DELETE/cf_etf/_alias/cf_etf_1` to eliminate the index alias.
- **Check whether the index alias exists**: Use `HEAD/cf_etf/_alias/cf_etf_1` to check whether the index alias, `cf_etf_1`, exists.

> The syntax of the term (`cf_etf`) and the term (`cf_etf_1`) can be any of `*` | `_all` | `glob pattern` | `name1`, `name2`, and so on, which means you can eliminate one or more aliases from one or more indexes.

- **Aliases action API**: `_aliases` can perform multiple operations on an index/indices as an atomic operation. Supported actions include `add`, `remove`, and `remove_index`. Let's create a dummy index, `cf_etf_to_be_deleted`, by using the Index Create API, as shown in the following screenshot:

Then, we can issue an aliases API with three actions:

1. Add a new `alias` named `cf_etf_2` to the `index` named `cf_etf`.
2. Delete the `alias` named `cf_etf_1`.
3. Delete the dummy `index`, `cf_etf_to_be_deleted`, as shown in the request body:

Reindexing with zero downtime

It is recommended to use aliases instead of indices in production. Since your current index design may not be perfect, you'll need to reindex later. For example, some fields of the documents have changed. By using an alias, you can transparently switch your application from using the old index to the new index without downtime. Suppose you use the index alias `cf_etf_production`, instead of the `cf_etf` index in your application. You successfully re-index the data from `cf_etf` to the new index, `cf_etf_new`. Then, you delete the alias from the old index and create the same alias for the new index. The index that's used in the application is switched. The operations of the whole process are shown in the following screenshot:

Grouping multiple indices

Too many documents under the index may degrade search performance. If most queries are based on the same field of the index, such as category, class, and type, then you can logically group data by that field. Let's assume that there is a category field in the documents. There are four categories, which are large, mid, small, and others. If the documents can be evenly divided into each category, we can create four indices based on the category to index the documents. Then, we can create an alias called cf_etf_alias to contain all four indices. If you want to search for records from all categories, just use the index alias, cf_etf_alias. The following steps are used to create the index alias for all four indices.

1. Recall that we have created the cf_etf_large index in the previous section. Here, we are creating the cf_etf_mid index:

2. Here, we are creating the cf_etf_small index:

3. Here, we are creating the `cf_etf_others` index:

4. Finally, we are creating the index alias, `cf_etf_alias`:

5. Retrieve information from the alias that is, `cf_etf_alias`. It includes indices large, mid, small, and so on:

Alias APIs are point-in-time-based, which means they only point to the current index. It will not be automatically updated when indices that match the alias' pattern are added or removed later.

Views on a subset of documents

In a SQL database, a view is a SQL statement that is stored in the database using a name. In Elasticsearch, a filtered alias provides a similar capability to access a subset of documents from the underlying indices. A filtered alias can be applied to search APIs, count APIs, delete by query APIs, and so on. To create a filtered alias, you need to ensure that the x field already exists in the index mapping, and then you can create an alias that uses the filter on the x field. Although we haven't yet presented the document and mappings yet we will still have a quick look through an end-to-end example. The step-by-step instructions are as follows:

1. Create a new index, cf_view, with a mapping to tell Elasticsearch that the symbol and category fields are using the keyword datatype:

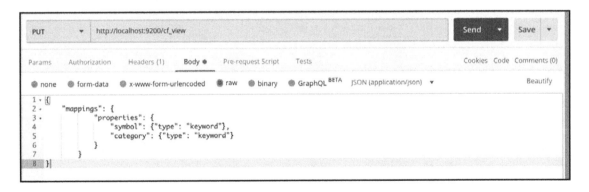

2. Index two documents to the `cf_view` index (one for `Equity` and one for `International`). The following is the first document:

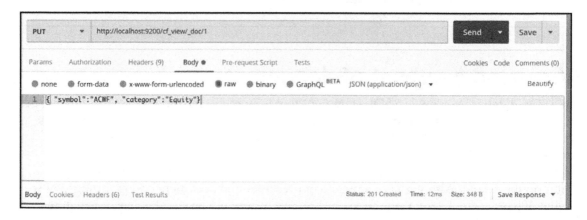

3. The following is the second document:

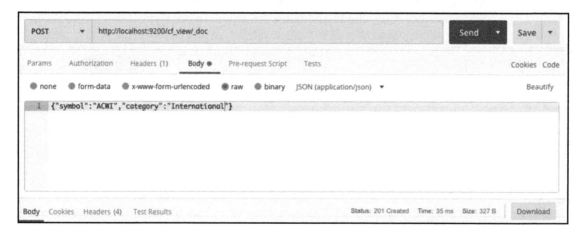

4. Create an index filtered alias, `cf_view_international`, which is a view of the documents with the `category` field equal to `International`:

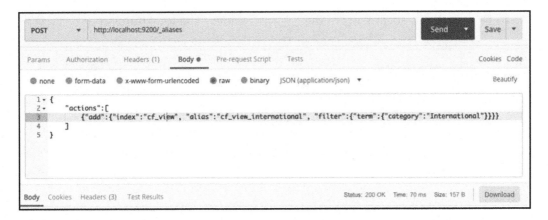

5. Search all the documents in the `cf_view_international` alias. The total number of `hits` is 1:

6. Search all the documents in the `cf_view` index. The total number of `hits` is 2:

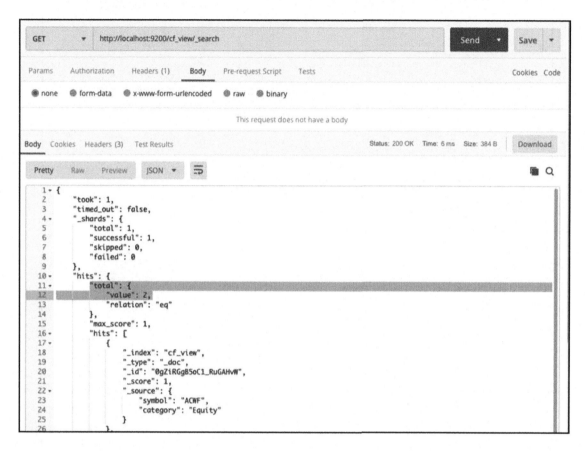

We have practiced a round-trip example to demonstrate how to benefit from using index aliasing, which is created as a subset of `cf_view`. By using `cf_view_international`, we can retrieve the ETFs from the `International` category.

Miscellaneous

The following are two other settings related to performance, which are also commonly used in the _aliases API:

- **Routing**: A document is routed to a particular shard to store or search. Elasticsearch has a simple formula to calculate the route. However, users can customize their routing method. This feature can be used together with filtering aliases in order to avoid unnecessary shard operations. You can specify the parameter `routing` value according to your design when the index alias is created.
- **Write index flag**: If an alias points to multiple indices, a question will arise. Which index will take the write operations, such as indexing or updating? To resolve this issue, the `is_write_index` flag must be associated with one of the aliasing indices. Only one index per alias can be assigned. If none are specified among the aliasing indices, then no write operation is allowed. You can just specify the `is_write_index` parameter of the target index as true according to your design.

Let me remind you that filtered aliases for document-level security fields are not recommended. For more information, please refer to `https://www.elastic.co/guide/en/x-pack/current/security-limitations.html`.

Advanced users may want to gather information to solve performance issue. In the next section, we will discuss how to monitor indices.

Monitoring indices

Basically, index-centric statistics report aggregated data from different physical machines that are running in different environments. Monitoring such statistics seems less helpful when compared to node statistics or cluster statistics. Let's take a quick look at four different APIs.

Indices stats

It is useful to see statistics from the indices stats API, _stats. You can get an answer such as the number of search requests in terms of the specific index received, the total time to fetch documents in that index, or identify the hot indices inside your cluster. Let's take a look at cf_view. As shown in the response body of the following screenshot, the result reports two aggregations, which are primaries and total:

The `primaries` field reports aggregation in the scope of the primary shards, while the `total` field is the cumulative values in both shard types. Since we have only indexed two documents in `cf_view`, `primaries.docs.count` is equal to 2. It takes 14 **milliseconds** to fetch a document from `cf_view` (`primaries.search.fetch_time_in_millis`). The `cf_view` index has received 7 search requests (`primaries.search.query_total`) in total.

There are many metrics that you can dig from the result of indices stats, but we won't go into them any further because it is beyond the scope of this book. You can refer to the following link for more information:

`https://www.elastic.co/guide/en/elasticsearch/reference/master/indices-stats.html.`

Indices segments, recovery, and share stores

Other important indices statistics-related APIs are as follows:

- **Get indices segments information**: This provides low-level segment information for the Lucene index (shard level) that builds indices in the cluster:

- **Get indices recovery information**: This provides detailed information about the recovery status for the shards that builds indices in the cluster:

- **Get indices shard stores information**: This provides insight information about the stores for the shards that builds indices in the cluster:

Now, we know how to monitor an index. In the next section, we will talk about the internals of index persistence and maintenance APIs.

Index persistence

Elasticsearch solves the persistence in different ways. The transaction log, `translog`, and the temporary storage in-memory buffer are used during index operations. Later, the data in the in-memory buffer will move to a new segment. Finally, segments will be flushed to the disk storage. A few APIs that manage the persistent stage of the indexed data are as follows:

- **Clear Cache**: When Elasticsearch determines that a bitset is likely to be reused in the future, it will be cached directly in memory and reuse it as needed. This API allows you to clear all caches or specific caches such as query, request, and field data for one or more indices.

  The following is an example of clearing the `query` cache of the `cf_view` index:

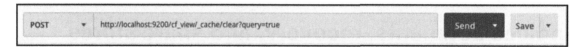

  The following is an example of clearing the shard request cache of the `cf_view` index:

  The following is an example of clearing the field data cache of the `cf_view` index:

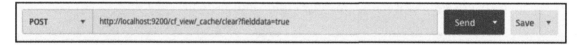

- **Refresh and flush**: In a refresh operation, the in-memory buffer flushes the contents to a newly created segment and makes the new documents visible for searching. In a flush operation, the in-memory buffer is written to a new segment. Then, all of the existing in-memory segments are merged into the merged segment, and then written to disk. Finally, the translog is cleared (for more step-by-step details, see the resources at `https://qbox.io/blog/refresh-flush-operations-elasticsearch-guide`). The following diagram depicts the state changes of the translog, memory buffers, and segments in the index, refresh, and flush operations:

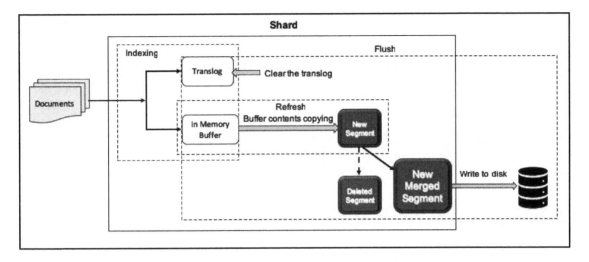

The following is an example of refreshing the `cf_view` index:

The following is an example of flushing the `cf_view` index:

- **Synced flush**: Perform a normal flush operation and add `sync_id` to all the shards to avoid waiting for the default 5 minutes inactivity period to mark the index as idle:

- **Force merge**: The `_forcemerge` API allows you to reduce the number of segments by merging them together. This optimization can make the search operations faster:

In the next section, we'll discuss the advanced index management APIs that can help to improve performance.

Advanced index management APIs

Some index APIs can reduce overhead in specific use cases and improve overall query performance. In this section, we'll discuss how to split the index into more than one primary shard by using the Split API or vice versa by using the `_shrink` API. Moreover, you can roll over from an old index to a new index on purpose.

Split index

This API allows you to transform an existing index into a new one while the original primary shard is split into two or more primary shards. The primary shards of the new index must be a factor of the original primary shard. The steps are as follows:

1. Use a **PUT** request to set the source index in read-only mode by updating the setting of the index, and it must have a green health status:

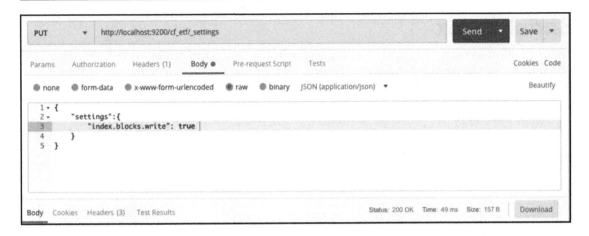

2. Use the **POST** request with the _split API to split the cf_etf index into a new index called cf_etf_split:

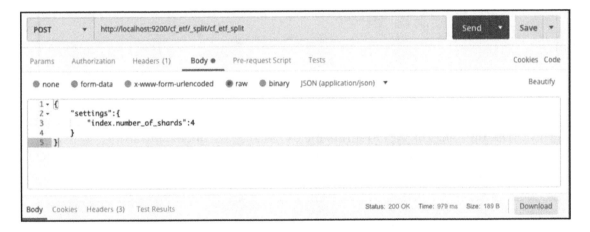

The requirement of the split index operation for the source index regarding the existence of the number_of_routing_shards parameter in previous version is removed in Elasticsearch 7.0.

Shrink index

This API allows you to shrink an existing index into a new one with fewer primary shards. The number of the primary shards of the new index must be a factor of the original primary shards. The steps are as follows:

1. The source index is marked as read-only using the `index.blocks.write:true` setting. Its states must be in green health. The relocation of a copy of each shard must be the same node, `shrink_node_name` (https://www.elastic.co/guide/en/elasticsearch/reference/master/shard-allocation-filtering.html):

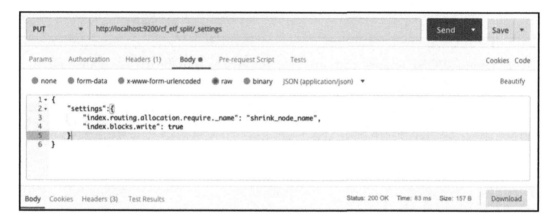

2. Use the `_shrink` API to shrink the `cf_etf_split` index into a new `cf_etf_shrink` index. The original setting of the `cf_etf_split` index will be copied to the new index:

Rollover index

This API request accepts a list of conditions and a single alias name that must be associated with only one index. If the existing index satisfies the specified conditions such as aging or capacity issues, then a new index will be created and the alias is switched to point to the new index:

1. For example, let's use a **PUT** request to create the `rollover-000001` index with its alias, `rollover_alias`, in the request body, as shown in the following screenshot:

The alias will be created at the same time. The successful response will be **200 OK**.

2. Then, we rollover the index using a **POST** request with the `_rollover` API and the `rollover_alias` alias in the URL with an empty request body. The new `rollover-000002` index is created and pointed by the alias, as shown in the following screenshot:

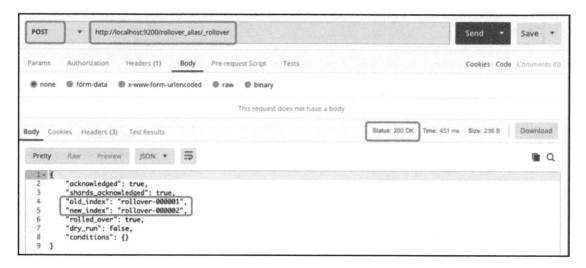

There is a little trick on the index naming. If the name ends with a dash — and a number with a leading zero, then the new index will follow the same pattern with an increment.

Summary

Wow! We have completed Chapter 2, *Index APIs*. In this chapter, we learned the basic APIs for managing indices, important settings, and index templates. We also went through a few practices of index aliases APIs. After some indices statistics were introduced to monitor, we experienced several advanced index management operations to improve performance issues.

In the next chapter, we'll delve into document APIs. Basically, Elasticsearch can be viewed as a document-oriented database designed to store, retrieve, and manage document-oriented data. First, we'll learn about single-document APIs, then multi-document APIs. Finally, we will look at a reindex example so that we can migrate indices from the old version of Elasticsearch to 7.0.

Document APIs 3

In the previous chapter, we learned how to use the index API to manage indices and perform indexing and search operations on simple documents. We also looked at a number of APIs related to index persistence maintenance work. In this chapter, we will extend our understanding from the viewpoint of documents.

Elasticsearch is a document-oriented database, which means it stores the entire object or document. **JavaScript Object Notation (JSON)** is the document format used in the API. Not only is the document stored, but its content is also indexed to make it searchable. We will start by learning about the basics of a document and its life cycle and then we will learn how to access it. Then we continue with how to access multiple documents with the bulk API and migrating indices from the old version to the version 7.0. API.

By the end of this chapter, you'll learn the following topics:

- The Elasticsearch document life cycle
- Basic CRUD for single document management APIs
- Multi-document management APIs
- Migration from a multiple mapping types index

The Elasticsearch document life cycle

The Elasticsearch document life cycle can be defined as a series of phases in forms and functional activities, through indexing operations until deletion. Let's first start with the major components of a document and then go through the cycle.

What is a document?

Documents in Elasticsearch are represented in JSON format. JSON objects are written in key/value pairs. A key must be a string and must always be enclosed in quotation marks. The value must be a valid JSON datatype. Keys and values are separated by colons and with the key/value pair separated by commas. A document will be associated with metadata elements during indexing operations including the given index name, the mapping type, and the document identifier.

The document identifier can be given or autogenerated. Recall that Elasticsearch has a simple hashing formula to calculate the route that routes a document to a particular shard for storage or search. The simple formula is as follows, and the default `routing` value is the document identifier:

```
shard = hash(routing) % number_of_primary_shards
```

The document life cycle

You may have a few questions about the changes in forms and functional activities of the document. For example, what happens when indexing? How is the document replicated? Does the document deletion operation actually remove the document from the disk? The following diagram illustrates the indexing operation and document retrieval:

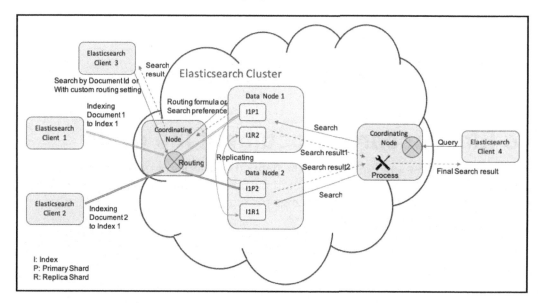

In the indexing operation, we can describe the whole procedure in the following steps:

1. The Elasticsearch client sends the document to the **Elasticsearch Cluster**; the first stop is the coordination node.
2. The document is then forwarded to the target primary shard determined by the routing formula. For example, the document sent from **Client 1** will be forwarded by the **Coordinating Node** to **Data Node 1**, and the document sent by **Client 2** will be forwarded to **Data Node 2**.
3. The analyzer generates terms from the document and creates the inverted index and stores it in the Lucene segment. For the storing process of the Lucene segment, please refer to the *Between Elasticsearch Index and Lucene Index* section of `Chapter 1`, Overview of Elasticsearch 7.
4. The Primary Shard is responsible for forwarding the document to another replica for replication at the appropriate time.
5. Once the indexing operation is done, the document identifier, `_id`, will be returned in the response body. If we retrieve the document by `_id` or set the custom routing setting, as in the example of **Client 3**, the search request will be routed to the specific shard/shards. Otherwise, as in the example of **Client 4**, all shards associated with the index/indices of the query will receive the search request, and partial search results will be gathered together in the coordinating node.
6. After the merge and sort process from the partial search results, the final search results will be sent back to **Client 4**.

As mentioned earlier, the index segment is immutable. When a document deletion request is operating in a shard, it is not actually removed immediately. Instead, it is only marked as deleted and not physically removed from the segment. The principle is the same when updating a document: the original document is actually marked as deleted and replaced by a new document with the corresponding field changes. Physical removal of the mark deleted documents occurs during the merge process because they are not written to new segments. We have made clear the life cycle of the document. Now, let us look at the single document APIs in the next section.

If you are interested in understanding more about the performance degradation in the search performance caused by the deleted documents, you can refer to a document about Lucene's handling of deleted documents: `https://www.elastic.co/blog/lucenes-handling-of-deleted-documents`.

Single document management APIs

The basic document CRUD APIs are targeted at a single document. Before we jump into those APIs, let's get familiar with our sample document first.

Sample documents

The contents of the sample documents describe the commission-free ETF. The list contains 314 ETFs provided by TD Ameritrade (`https://research.tdameritrade.com/grid/public/etfs/commissionfree/commissionfree.asp`). Each ETF has seven fixed fields and two optional fields. They are described in the following table:

Field name	Fixed/optional	Description
symbol	Fixed	The ticker symbol of the ETF.
fund_name	Fixed	The name of the ETF.
rating	Optional	The given risk rating to the ETF by Morningstar, with one star being the worst ranking and five stars being the best. Not all ETFs are rated.
morningstar_category	Fixed	The given category to the ETF in the Morningstar classification system. The system is based on the similarity of investment.
category	Fixed	The category given by TD Ameritrade.
family	Fixed	The brand name of the investment company that manages the fund family to which the ETF belongs.
market_cap	Optional	The size of the companies in which the ETF invests. Not all ETFs can be classified.
description	Fixed	The detailed description of the ETF.
exchange	Fixed	The facility where the trading of the ETF occurs.

The following is one of the sample documents:

```
{
    "symbol":"ACWF",
    "fund_name":"iShares Edge MSCI Multifactor Global ETF",
    "rating":3,
    "morningstar_category":"World Large Stock",
    "category":"Equity",
    "family":"iShares",
    "market_cap":"large",
    "description":"The investment seeks to track the investment results of
the MSCI ACWI Diversified Multiple-Factor Index.\\n The fund generally will
invest at least 90% of its assets in the component securities of the
underlying index and in investments that have economic characteristics that
are substantially identical to the component securities of the underlying
index. The underlying index is designed to contain equity securities from
the MSCI ACWI Index (the \\\"parent index\\\") that have high exposure to
four investment style factors: value, quality, momentum and low size, while
maintaining a level of risk similar to that of the parent index.",
    "exchange":"NYSE Arca"}
```

In our GitHub repository (`https://github.com/PacktPublishing/Mastering-Elasticsearch-7.0/tree/master/Chapter06`), you can find two sample files, `acwf.json` and `acwi.json`. The contents in the sample files are used as the request body in Postman for indexing operations.

Indexing a document

You can index a document with an `_id` or without it. Elasticsearch will automatically generate one for you if the `_id` field is not filled:

- **Indexing with _id**: The following code block describes the syntax of indexing a document with an identifier:

```
PUT /{index}/_doc/{_id}
```

Let's specify `_id` as 1 to create an `ACWF` ETF document in the `cf_etf` index, as shown in the following screenshot:

In the response body, the aforementioned metadata is index name (`_index: cf_etf`), mapping type (`_type: _doc`), and the document identifier (`_id: 1`). Besides, there is a bit more metadata, such as the version number (`_version`), the sequence number (`_seq_no`), and the primary term (`_primary_term`). The default version number is 1, and it will be incremented when the document is modified. The sequence number is a global checkpoint that tracks the order of documents between the primary and the replica shards after the indexing operation. The primary term is to address the race conditions of operations due to the old primary shard failure, and a shard is promoted to a new primary shard concurrently.

The starting value of the primary term is 1, and it will be incremented by one when the primary shard is restarted or a shard is promoted to be a primary.

- **Indexing without _id**: The following code block describes the syntax of indexing a document without an identifier:

```
POST /{index}/_doc
```

Let's create an `ACWI` ETF document in the `cf_etc` index for autogenerating the `_id`, as shown in the following screenshot:

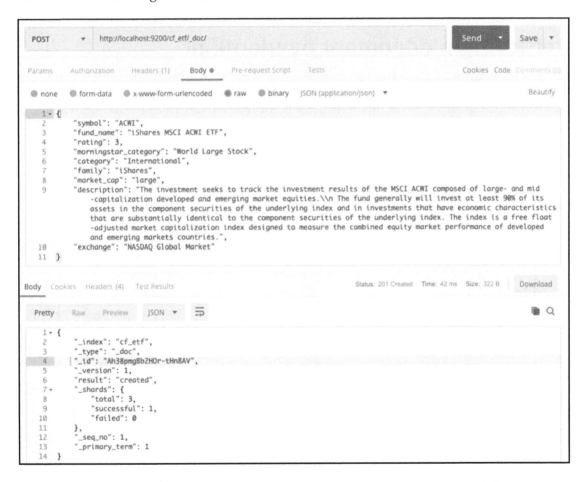

In the response body, the autogenerated `_id` is `Ah38pmgBb2HOr-tHn8AV` and the sequence number is changed to 1 from 0.

In the case of indexing with `_id`, if the `_id` does exist in the index, the original document will be replaced by the contents of the request body and treated as an update. To avoid such replacement, you can use the create API. You can use either of the following request URLs with the same request body to create a document in the `cf_etf` index with identifier 1:

```
PUT /cf_etf/_doc/1?op_type=create
PUT /cf_etf/_doc/1/_create
```

Retrieving a document by identifier

You can retrieve the whole document back by using the same index and identifier. If the mapping metadata `_source` field is not disabled, you can retrieve partial document. If it is disabled, the original JSON document will not be stored. We describe how to retrieve the document in both ways as follows:

- **Retrieve the whole document**: Let us retrieve an `ACWF` ETF document by setting `_id` as 1 and using the `cf_etf` index. In the response body, all fields in the original document are provided in the `_source` field:

- **Retrieve the partial document**: We can use the same URL as shown in the preceding screenshot with the _source request parameter and a comma-separated list of the required field. For instance, we only want the symbol, rating, and category fields back. In the response body, only the required fields in the original document are provided in the _source field:

- **Check if a document exists**: Use HEAD /{index}/_doc/{_id} to check if the document exists.

Updating a document

Elasticsearch allows you to perform a patch operation or a full reindex of a document based on a script. We will describe the operations as follows:

- **Patch**: The content changes and new fields added will be merged into the existing document. If there is no change in the content after the operation, the `result` field will be `noop` in the response body. If the document does not exist, then the response is NOT_FOUND (404) with `document_missing_exception`. Let's assume the market capitalization of the ACWF ETF has changed from `large` to `mid`. You can see in the following screenshot that the document version number, `_version`, has changed from 1 to 2:

- **A full reindex of a document based on a script**: Given a script in the request body of the document update API, Elasticsearch first gets the document from the index, then runs the script, and indexes back the results in the final stage. All operations will result in the replacement of the entire document. Let's write a script to remove the `market_cap` field from the `ACWF` ETF document, as shown in the following screenshot:

A successful update will return **200 OK**. Otherwise, it fails with an exception.

When you use a script to perform a document update operation, you can use the `upsert` parameter in the request body to handle situations when the document has been deleted. If the document exists, the update operation will be successful. Otherwise, the contents associated with the `upsert` parameter will be used to create a new document. There is a Boolean parameter, `scripted_upsert`, that allows you to always run the script when it is set to `true`. In this case, you should also use the `upsert` parameter with the empty content to create a new document for update when the document is missing.

Similar to the `upsert` parameter in the script update, there is a Boolean parameter, `doc_as_upsert`, for the patch operation. When set to `true`, it allows you to create a new document with the `doc` content when the document is missing.

- **Versioning support**: Elasticsearch has internal versioning control and also supports external version systems. However, the update API does not support external versioning.

Removing a document by identifier

You can remove a specific document by using the document identifier. Let's remove the ACWF ETF document by setting _id to 1 and using the cf_etf index. A successful removal will return **200 OK**:

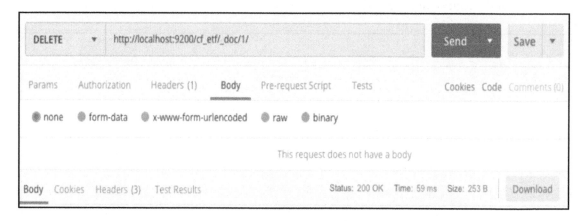

The primary shard may not be available to perform the operation while the delete request comes in. By default, the delete operation will wait up to 1 minute on the primary shard, then fail, and respond to the error. You may attach the timeout request parameter with a time period. The default wait time is 1 minutes. Use Delete /{index}/_doc/{_id}?timeout=2m to wait for a longer time (for example, 2 minutes).

Multi-document management APIs

To avoid network traffic overhead, Elasticsearch provides a set of document APIs for combining multiple requests in batch processing. You can issue a multi-document API to get multiple documents, perform multiple index/get/update/delete operations, update/delete multiple documents based on the results of the query, or reindex the document. You'll get better performance when working with a large number of documents. We'll describe them in the following subsections.

Retrieving multiple documents

The Multi get API, _mget, can retrieve multiple documents through a _docs array of index and identifier pairs given by users. Similar to the simple get API, you can also specify the required field names in the optional _source field in each pair. Before we start to run the example, let us index the removed ACWF ETF document again so that we have two documents in the cf_etf index. Recall that we have indexed two documents to the cf_view index in the last chapter. Let's issue an _mget request to retrieve one document from each index:

If all required documents are under the same index and all the document contents are retrieved, you can use the `ids` field only to simplify the request body. Let me remind you that the document identifier in the example may be different from yours:

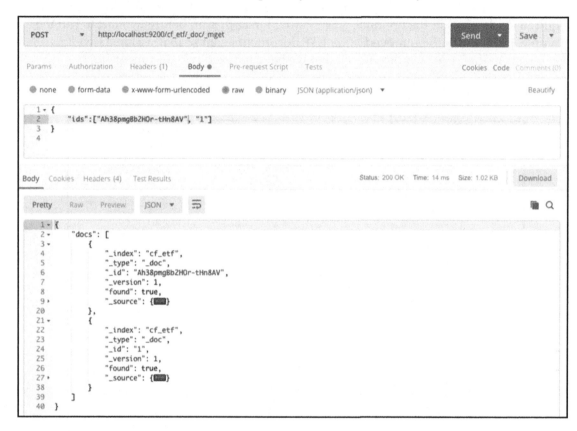

Bulk API

The bulk API allows you to operate multiple document requests, including creation, indexing, patching, replacement, and deletion, in batch mode to reduce network traffic. You can put a series of API actions and the corresponding request body pairs in the request body of the bulk API. The syntax in the request body is as follows:

```
{action_type: {metadata}}\newline
request_body}\newline
...
```

Let's practice using the bulk API with the same operations from the previous examples. The batch job involves the following steps:

1. Remove the ACWF ETF document with the _id of 1 from the cf_etf index
2. Create the ACWF ETF document that was removed in *step 1* with the same contents included
3. Update the document with the script that will remove the market_cap field from the ACWF ETF document

Remember that each line must have a line break. Otherwise, it will fail with BAD REQUEST (400) with illegal_argument_exception. If you specify the index, such as /{index}/_bulk, in the endpoint. It will be used whenever the _index term does not exist in the metadata of action_type:

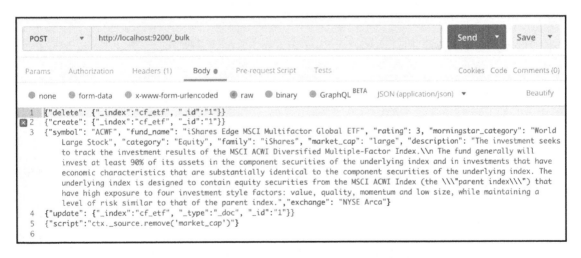

Update by query API

Similar to a single document update operation using a script, you can use the _update_by_query API to perform the same tasks for all documents that match the given condition in the script. Recall that the process in a single document update operation involves retrieving documents, running scripts, and indexing results. The first step in the _update_by_query API is to take a snapshot of the index, then run the script on the match, and index the resulting document. If any document has changed between the time the snapshot was taken and the time the index request was processed, it will fail due to a version conflict.

Getting the first failure will result in the suspension of the entire operation. However, those updates that have been executed will not be rolled back. By default, all successful updates and the aborted failure are returned in the response. There is a parameter that allows you to continue the update operation and ignore the error without interruption. The URL parameter is conflicts = proceed, or you can specify "conflicts": "proceed" in the request body. Let's update the rating field of the documents in the cf_etf index to 4 if the rating is 3. In the response body, you can see that the updated field is equal to 2 and version_of_conflicts is equal to 0. The default scripting language is Painless:

> Interested audiences can refer to the following reference for more information: https://www.elastic.co/guide/en/elasticsearch/painless/master/painless-api-reference.html.

Another useful use of `update_by_query` is to refresh the static mapping changes of the new added properties without changing the `_source`. We'll cover this feature in `Chapter 4`, *Mapping APIs*.

Delete by query API

You can perform a deletion on all documents that match a given search query. Although we have not yet introduced search APIs, let's remove the documents with the `rating` set to 4 from the `cf_etf` index by a simple query in a batch. You can also use the `conflicts = proceed` parameter to ignore any error without interrupting of the operation. In the response body, we can see that 2 documents are removed and no conflict occurs:

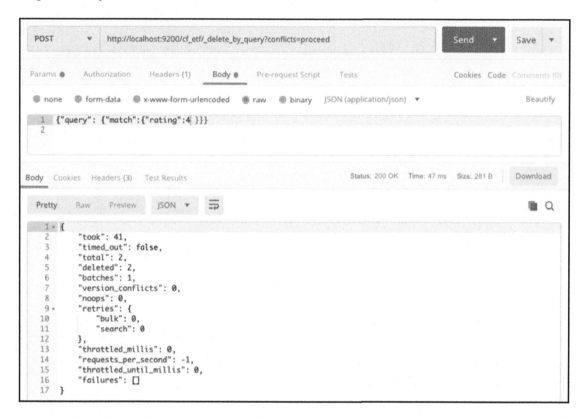

Reindex API

Your index design may not be perfect and you may need to make changes to existing fields or the analyzers. At that time, you'll have to reindex. On the other hand, due to the removal of mapping types in version 7.0, you have to perform a reindex operation if you have used multiple types in one index. Let's start with the simple Reindex API and then practice reindexing for the migration from a multiple mapping types index.

Copying documents

Before you rebuild the index, you must have the new index set up ready. The Reindex API does not copy the settings from the source index. Therefore, this API seems to simply copy the documents from the source to the target. It is only supported when the mapping metadata _source is enabled during the indexing operation on the source index, otherwise there are no sources to copy. There are several ways to copy a document from a source index, which we describe as follows:

- **Copying documents from one index**: Since the cf_etf index has no document now, let's copy documents from the cf_view index. In the response body, "created": 2 means two documents are created in the cf_etf index. If the documents do exist in the destination prior to the reindexing operation, then the existing document will get overwritten if the document identifier is the same as the one coming from the source. A version_type field can be put into the destination, dest, to control the versioning by using an internal system or external user. You may use "version_type":"external" in dest to use external control. If two documents have the same document identifier, the older version will be replaced by the newer version:

- **Copying documents from more than one index**: If you have more than one source, just put the indices into an array, for example, `"source":{"index":[cf_view1, cf_view2,..]}`.

- **Copying only missing documents**: If the destination already has documents and you only want to copy the missing documents from the source, you can specify the `op_type` option in the destination, for example, `"dest":{"index":"cf_etf","op_type":"create"}` to avoid overwriting a document.

- **Copying only the documents that match a query**: Similar to the delete by query API, you can perform a reindexing operation on all documents that match a given search query. For example, if you're only reindexing a document with a `rating` equal to 4 in the `cf_view` index, use `"source":{"index":"cf_view", "query":{"match":{"rating":4}}}`.

- **Copying from the remote Elasticsearch server**: The source can be a remote Elasticsearch server. In the request body, add the `remote` parameter with the `host`, `username`, and `password` settings into the `source`, for example, `"source":{"remote": {"host":"http://remotehost:9200", "username":"myusername", "password":"mypassword"}}`.

Migration from a multiple mapping types index

Mapping type will be deprecated in version 7.0.0 and will be removed in 8.0. Instead, only the default _doc mapping type is used. If you have an index with multiple mapping types for logical grouping documents, the reindex operation must be performed in order for each document to have no mapping type. Recall that Elasticsearch 7.0 does not launch on nodes with an index created prior to 6.0. Therefore, you must first upgrade the old version to 6.x first.

You may perform the reindex operation to remove multiple mapping types in 6.x. Then, you can upgrade to 7.0. Assume that there is one `cf_etf` index with three mapping types including `nyse`, `nasdaq`, and `cboe`. To remove the mapping types, you may create a new index for each mapping type. Let's use the same name of the mapping type to create the corresponding index. After the indices are created, we can perform the reindex operation. The command to reindex documents from the `nyse` mapping type from the `cf_etf` index to the `nyse` index is as follows:

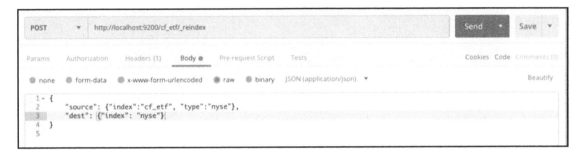

After all documents of the three mapping types are reindexed, we can remove the `cf_etf` index and create a new `cf_etf` alias for those three indices. The `cf_etf` alias can replace the old `cf_etf` index for operations.

Summary

Excellent! We have enjoyed learning about document APIs including how to store, retrieve, and manage documents in document-oriented Elasticsearch. We have delved into the document life cycle, and then we practiced the single document and multi-document APIs. Finally, we also completed the index rebuilding example for migrating indices from old versions to version 7.0.

In `Chapter 4`, *Mapping APIs*, we will drill down to the mapping APIs. A mapping in Elasticsearch is a description of how documents and their fields are stored and indexed. Although dynamic mapping is provided during indexing if you do not provide the mapping explicitly, in most cases you will still need to have your overall mapping designed properly for your search engine database. We will learn how and when to specify a custom mapping.

4

Mapping APIs

In the last chapter, we learned about the document life cycle of Elasticsearch and executed single and multiple document APIs. We introduced a commission-free ETF from TD Ameritrade and used this information to practice document APIs. We also reindexed the documents from the multiple mapping types index for migration.

In this chapter, we are going to learn about mapping APIs. In Elasticsearch, mapping is a data model that describes the structure of a document. It allows you to specify fields, field types, relationships between documents, data conversion rules, and so on. Schema-less only means that documents can be indexed without specifying the schema in advance, because the schema is dynamically derived from the first document index structure based on the built-in mapping rules in Elasticsearch. If you have a good search database design plan, you should use explicit static mapping because dynamic mapping may not be perfect for your design. We will start with dynamic mapping first with a sample document and go through the different settings and variety. By the end of this chapter, you will have covered the following topics:

- Dynamic mapping
- Meta fields in mapping
- Field datatypes
- Mapping parameters
- Refreshing mapping changes for static mapping
- Typeless APIs working with old custom index types

Dynamic mapping

The official definition of dynamic mapping is to detect the data types of new fields of the documents immediately during indexing, instead of first creating an index, defining the fields, and establishing its datatype mapping. Therefore, document indexing operations can be executed the fly without predefining the field mapping. Newly added fields can be picked up during indexing at any time. We'll first check with the mapping rules and then practice with a sample document to see the indexing result.

Mapping rules

The Elasticsearch document is in **JavaScript Object Notation (JSON)** format. In JSON, the valid datatypes are string, number, JSON object, array, Boolean, and null. The JSON data value and the mapping rules will determine the final datatype of the document field. The following table describes the mapping rules:

JSON datatype	Value	Setting in mapping	Mapped datatype
string	string		text
	date	date_detection=true	date
	integer	numeric_detection=true	long
	floating point	numeric_detection=true	float
number	integer		long
	floating point		float
JSON object			object
array	supported data type		Datatype of the first element
boolean	true/false		Boolean
null	null		Not mapped

By default, the date_detection setting is enabled and the numeric_detection setting is disabled. Let me explain with the help of an example with the two indices, default_mappings_index and custom_mappings_index. For our convenience, we use the default settings with the mapping date type in yyyy/MM/dd format.

The mappings creation is shown as the following steps:

1. Create a `default_mappings_index` index using the simple date format as shown in the following screenshot:

2. The sample document contains `12` fields to examine the variations in different JSON values and different settings. Let's first index the sample document into `default_mappings_index`, index as shown in the following screenshot:

3. The other index is designed to turn off the detection of the `date string` value and turn on the detection of the numeric string. `custom_mappings_index` is created index with the `date_detection` setting and the `numeric_detection` setting on, as shown in the following screenshot:

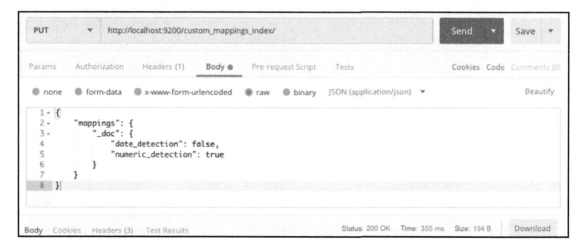

4. Index the same sample document into `custom_mappings_index`:

5. Now, get the mapping from the two indices and then compile them into a table for comparison. To get the mappings of `default_mappings_index`, use the following API, as shown in the following screenshot:

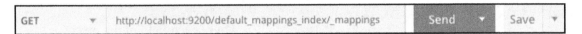

6. To get the mappings of `custom_mappings_index`, use the following API, as shown in the following screenshot:

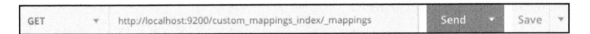

The following table shows the results from comparing `default_mappings_index` and `custom_mappings_index`:

Field	Field mapping in default_mappings_index	Field mapping in custom_mappings_index
simple_string_value	text_type_with_keyword	Same
string_w_date_value	{"type": "date","format": "yyyy/MM/dd"}	text_type_with_keyword
string_w_floating_point_value	text_type_with_keyword	{"type": "float"}
string_w_integer_value	text_type_with_keyword	{"type": "long"}
integer_value	{"type": "long"}	Same
floating_point_value	{"type": "float"}	Same
json_object	corresponding_object_type	Same
array_of_integer	{"type": "long"}	Same
array_of_float	{"type": "float"}	Same
array_of_simple_string	text_type_with_keyword	Same
array_of_integer_string	text_type_with_keyword	{"type": "long"}
array_of_float_string	text_type_with_keyword	{"type": "float"}
boolean_value	{"type": "boolean"}	Same
null_value	Not indexed	Not indexed

From the preceding table, `text_type_with_keyword` is `{"type": "text","fields":` `{"keyword":{"type":"keyword","ignore_above": 256}}}` and `corresponding_object_type` is `{"properties": {"level_1": {"properties":` `{"level2_1": {"type": "text","fields": {"keyword": {"type":` `keyword","ignore_above": 256}}},"level_2_2": {"type":` `"long"},"level_2_3": {"type": "float"}}}}}` where each field of the object follows the same mapping rules.

We can also see that the numeric detection setting has an effect on the array of numeric strings. Finally, we can establish that any field with a null value will not be indexed, and the same is true for empty arrays.

Dynamic templates

When you create an index, Elasticsearch lets you create templates for your mapping rules to augment the newly added fields with the supported mapping types. A mapping rule contains two parts: the matcher and the corresponding mapping datatype. The matcher can be performed on one of the following:

- The data type of the field: Using `match_mapping_type` for the datatype
- The name of the field: Using `match` pattern and/or `unmatch` pattern for the field name
- The full dotted path of the field: Using `path_match` and `path_unmatch` for the dotted path

Basically, the syntax of the dynamic templates is as follows:

```
"mappings":{
    "dynamic_templates" :[
        {
            "template_name_1": {
                ...mapping rules...,
                "mapping": {...}
            }
        },
        {
            "template_name_2":{...},
        },...
    ]
}
```

Let's reuse the same index name, `default_mappings_index`, to create an example to show the dynamic template. The steps to be observed are as follows:

1. Remove `default_mappings_index`, and recreate the same index with a dynamic template for the mapping
2. Index the same sample document and examine the mapping types again
3. Create three dynamic templates:
   - `integers_template` maps integer values to the `integer` type instead of the `long` type
   - `field_name_template` matches any fields to the name ending with `_simple_string`, and maps to the `keyword` type instead of the `text` type
   - `path_match_template` matches any fields with the dot path `json_object.*.level_2_3`, and maps to the `double` type instead of the `float` type:

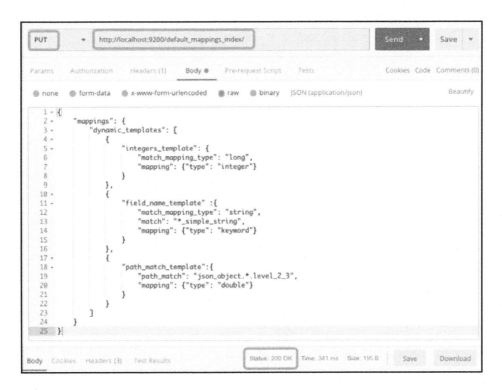

4. Once the sample document is indexed, the mapping
   of `default_mappings_index` will be as shown in the following screenshot:

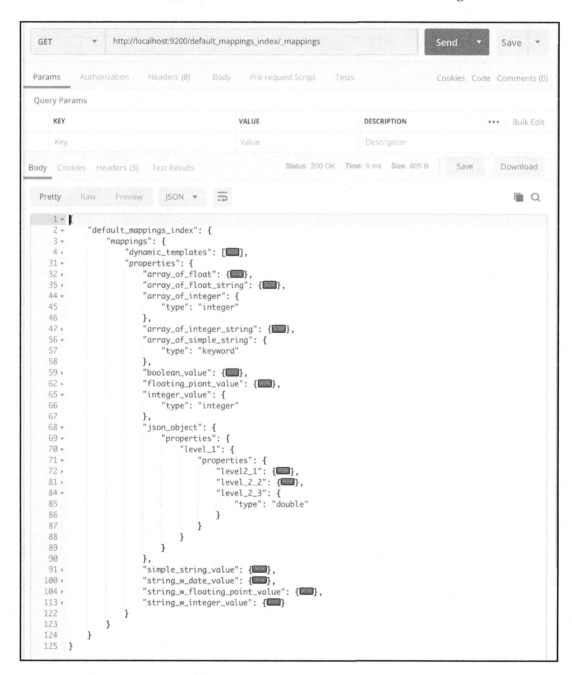

We can see that `array_of_integer` is mapped in the `integer` type, `array_of_simple_string` in the `keyword` type, and `json_object.level_1.level_2_3` in the `double` type, since those fields match the criteria in the dynamic template.

It's also worth mentioning that we can use the placeholders `{name}` and `{dynamic_type}` in the template. `{name}` and `{dynamic_type}` represent the field name and the datatype detected, respectively. In the next section, we'll look at the meta field, which defines the metadata for a document, similar to the data structure for a database table.

Meta fields in mapping

Some meta fields can be defined in the mapping to customize the indexing operation. We'll list some of the important ones and describe their usage:

- `_meta`: This is for user-defined metadata. Developers can use it to store the application-specific metadata.
- `_routing`: You can configure the routing value in the mapping to require all subsequent related operations to have the routing value specified.
- `_source`: By default, `_source` is enabled and the source document is stored. If the `_source` is disabled by a user, then the source document is not retained. The benefit to this is that it saves some storage space. The drawback is that there are no more supports for the document to reindex, update, and highlight when executing a search. Think carefully before deciding.

_meta and _routing can be updated, but _source cannot be updated. Let us use the following toy example to create an index with the mapping of the meta fields settings. We set the release equal to 1.0 and the version equal to 1 in the _meta field, the _routing field to be required, and the _source to be false:

Field datatypes

In addition to the mapped types we learned in the previous mapping rules sections, there are still many other datatypes to map for the fields in the document. Field datatypes are defined in the static mapping. In the *Dynamic mapping* section, we have shown the data structure from the response of the GET mapping request of default_mappings_index. The syntax to set the datatype of a field in static mapping is as follows:

```
"properties": {
    "field_1": {"type": "field_type_1"},
    "field_2": {"type": "field_type_2",
"mapping_parameter2a":"parameter2a_value",..}
}
```

Let us examine the description and the example usage for each mapping datatype in the following table:

Mapping datatype	Description	Example
Text	Full text value analyzed by terms.	`"field_1": {"type":"text"}`
Keyword	A string where its value can be used for filtering, sorting, or aggregation.	`"field_1": {"type": "keyword"}`
Numeric	A 6-bit signed integer between [-2^{63}, 2^{63}-1].	`"field_1": {"type":"long"}`
	A 32-bit signed integer between [-2^{31}, 2^{31}-1].	`"field_1": {"type":"integer"}`
	A 16-bit signed integer between [-32168, 32767].	`"field_1": {"type":"short"}`
	An 8-bit signed integer between [-128, 127].	`"field_1": {"type":"byte"}`
	A 64-bit IEEE-754 floating point number.	`"field_1": {"type":"double"}`
	A 32-bit IEEE-754 floating point number.	`"field_1": {"type":"float"}`
	A 16-bit IEEE-754 floating point number.	`"field_1": {"type":"half_float"}`
	A float point number using long and a scale factor.	`"field_1": {"type":"scaled_float"}`
Date	Either a date format string or a number. A long number is the elapsed milliseconds from the epoch. An integer is the elapsed seconds from the epoch. The default date format is `strict_date_optional_time||epoch_millis`.	`"field_1": {"type":"date"}`
	A long number represents a formatted date in nanosecond resolution.	`"field_1": {"type":"date_nanos"}`
Boolean	A `true` or `false` value.	`"field_1": {"type":"boolean"}`
Array	An array of values in the same datatype. The mapping type is the element's datatype; for example, [1, 2, 3, 4, 5].	`"field_1":{"type":"integer"}`
IP	IPv4 or IPv6 address.	`"field_1":{"type":"ip"}`
Alias	Another name of a field.	`"field_1": {"type": "alias", "path":"full.dotted.path.of.the.field"}`
Binary	A binary value as a Base64-encoded string. By default, it is not stored and is not searchable.	`"field_1":{"type":"binary"}`

Range	A range of values in numeric type including `integer_range`, `float_range`, `long_range`, and `double_range`.	`"field_1":{"type":"long_range"}`
	A range of values in date type.	`"field_1":{"type":"date_range", "format":{2019-02-15}`
	A range of values in IP type.	`"field_1":{"type":"ip_range"}`
Geo-point	A single location point in geo-point format.	`"field_1":{"type":"geo-point"}`
Geo-shape	A shape in GeoJSON format, such as point, circle, box, and line.	`"field_1":{"type":"geo-shape"}`
Object	A JSON format value.	`"field_1":{"properties": { "field_1_1":{"type":"type 1_1"}, "field_1_2": {"type": "type 1_2"}}}`
Nested	An array of objects. Each object is on purpose for the search.	`"field_1":{"type":"nested"}`
Token count	A value to count the number of tokens in the text.	`"field_1":{"type":"text", "fields":{"field_1_1": {"type":"token_count","analyzer":"analyzer_1"}}}`
Percolator	A JSON format value to be parsed into a native query.	`"field_1":{"type":"percolator"}`
Join	A mapping field to create a simple parent/child relation.	`"field_1": {"type": "join", "relations": {"parent_field": "child_field"}}`
	A mapping field to create multiple levels of parent/child relation.	`"field_1": {"type": "join", "relations": {"parent_field": ["child_field_1", "child_field_2], "child_field_x":"child_of_child_field_x"}}`
*Rank feature	A mapping field to provide ranking ability for the numeric field.	`"field_1":{"type":"rank_feature"}`
*Rank features	A mapping field to provide ranking ability for the numeric feature vector.	`"field_1":{"type":"rank_features"}`
*Dense vector	A mapping field to provide a dense vector of float values.	`"field_1":{"type":"dense_vector"}`
*Sparse vector	A mapping field to provide a sparse vector of float values represented in `{"dimension_1": value_1, "dimension_2":value_2, ...}`. The dimension range is between `[0,65536]`.	`"field_1":{"type":"sparse_vector"}`

The mapping parameter will be discussed in the next section.

Remark: The * symbol denotes that it is a new feature in Elasticsearch 7.0.

Static mapping for the sample document

Recall that the ETF sample document has seven fixed fields and two optional fields. The following is our static mapping for the sample document:

Field name	JSON datatype	Mapping datatype
symbol	string	keyword
fund_name	string	text
rating	integer	byte
morningstar_category	string	keyword
category	string	keyword
family	string	keyword
market_cap	string	keyword
description	text	text **with** keyword
exchange	string	keyword

Let's delete the `cf_etf` index first and recreate the same index with static mapping, as shown in the following screenshot:

The user can see that we have not included the `exchange` field in the mappings on purpose. We'll add it back to the mappings as an example in the later *Refresh mapping changes for static mapping* section. Let's reindex the two sample documents AWCF and AWCI, as we did in the *Views on a subset of documents* section of `Chapter 2`, *Index APIs*, to prepare the working environment.

Mapping parameters

The mapping parameters define the ways to store the document fields, the methodologies and options to index, the information of the fields to expose, the additional procedure to perform, and how the mapped data is analyzed during index and search. We will endeavor to explain all the supported mapping parameters in the following tables:

Mapping parameter	Description	Example
How it stores		
`store`	Whether to store the `field` value. The default value is `false`.	`"field_1":{"type":"type_1", "store":true}`
`doc_values`	It stores the same values as _source, but in a column-oriented manner. It is designed for sorting and aggregations. The default value is `true`.	`"field_1":{"type":"text", "doc_values":false}`
`term_vector`	Whether to store the information of the terms generated by the analyzer. The options are `no`, `yes`, `with_positions`, `with_offsets`, and `with_positions_offset`. The default value is `no`.	`"field_1":{"type":"text", "termvector":"yes"}`
`norm`	Whether to store the various normalization factors for scoring in query. The default value is `true`.	`"field_1":{"type":"text", "norm":false}`
How it indexes		
`index`	Whether to index the field value. The default value is `true`.	`"field_1":{"type":"type_1", "index":false}`
`index_option`	Options in indexing to provide features in search and highlighting. The options are `docs`, `freqs`, `positions`, and `offsets`.	`"field_1":{"type":"text", "index_options":"offsets"}`
`index_phrases`	Whether to provide faster phrase searches in text. The default is `false`.	`"field_1":{"type":"text", "index_phrases":true}`
`index_prefixes`	Enables faster prefix searches on text. The default action is disabled.	`"field_1":{"type":"text", "index_prefixes":{"min_chars":1, "max_chars":5}}`
`dynamic`	Whether new fields will be indexed dynamically. Options are `true`, `false`, and `strict`. The default value is `true`. The `false` option will ignore the new field. The `strict` option will throw an exception.	`"field_1":{"type":"type_1", "dynamic":false}`
`enabled`	Whether to index the field. The default value is `true`.	`"field_1":{"enabled":false}`

`fielddata`	Allows you to enable `fielddata`, which is an in-memory data structure for querying data from the text. The default value is `false`.	`"field_1":{"type":"text", "fielddata":true}`
`fields`	This provides an alternative to index the same field for a different datatype.	`"field_1":{"type":"text", "fields":{"raw":{"type":"keyword}}}`
`format`	Date format pattern for date string field values. You can customize the format or use one of the built-in formats. The default date format is `strict_date_optional_time||epoch_millis`. Interested eraders can refer to the reference: `https://www.elastic.co/guide/en/ elasticsearch/reference/7.x/mapping-date-format.html`.	`"field_1":{"type":"date", "format":"yyyy-MM-dd"}`
`ignore_above`	Allows you to set the maximum string length. Strings that are longer than the setting will be skipped, not indexed or stored.	`"field_1": {"type": "keyword_or_text_type", "igore_above": 20}`
`ignore_malformed`	Allows you to ignore invalid fields and continue indexing. The default value is `false`, and an exception is thrown.	`"field_1":{"type":"type_1", "ignore_malformed":true}`
`null_value`	Allows you to index fields with a null value.	`"field_1":{"type":"text", "null_value":"NULL"}`
`properties`	It provides a way to create sub-fields for an object data type or a nested data type.	`"field_1":{"properties": {"field_1_1":{"type":"type 1_1"},"field_1_2": {"type": "type 1_2"}}}`
`similarity`	Allows you to change the default scoring algorithm BM25 to classic, Boolean, or others.	`"field_1": {"type": "type_1","similarity": "class"}`
How it analyzes		
`analyzer`	Uses a custom analyzer or non-default analyzer.	`"field_1":{"type":"text", "analyzer":"analyzer_1"}`
`normalizer`	This is used for keyword fields. It processes in the same way as an analyzer. However, it only generates one token.	`"field_1":{"type":"keyword", "normalizer":"normalizer_1"}`
`boost`	This provides a way to weight the field value more in the relevance score used in a query. The default boost value is 1.0.	`"field_1":{"type":"type_1", "boost":1.5}`
`position_increment_gap`	This provides a fake gap for terms to separate them to prevent the phrase queries from matching across them. The default gap is 100.	`"field_1":{"type":"text", "position_increment_gap":50}`
`search_analyzer`	Uses a different analyzer at search time.	`"field_1":{"type":"text", "analyzer":"analyzer_1", "search_analyzer":"analyzer_2"}`
How it processes		
`coerce`	Allows you to convert a numeric string to a number, or round a floating number to an integer value. The default value is `false`.	`"field_1":{"type":"integer", "coerce":true}`
`copy_to`	Allows you to copy data from multiple fields into a single field so that it can be queried from that field instead.	`"field_1":{"type":"text", "copy_to":"destinated_field"}`

Refreshing mapping changes for static mapping

In Chapter 3, *Document APIs*, we introduced the **Update by Query** API for documents and also for static mappings. If static mapping is used, any fields not specified in the mappings will not be indexed and searchable; however, they are stored in _source. If we need to search for a non-mapping field later, we only need to update the static mappings to make the indexed documents take effect of the changes. No document reindexing step is required. Assume that the original mappings for our sample documents do not have the exchange field, that the document has been indexed, and that we now want it to be searchable:

1. First, we need to update the mapping, as shown in the following screenshot:

2. The next step is to issue an Update by Query request to take the static mapping changes into effect, as shown in the following screenshot:

In the response body, it shows that `total` 2 documents take effect of updates.

3. Finally, we issue a simple search request to find documents with the `exchange` field equal to `NYSE Arca`. In the response body of the following screenshot, one document is found:

In this case, this proves that the proposed indexing strategy of the static mapping approach is able to pick up the mapping changes without reindexing the documents.

The next section is the final section. We'll discuss the version compatibility issue, which deals with typeless APIs in version 7.0.

Typeless APIs working with old custom index types

Prior to version 7.0, indexes could contain a custom type. In version 6.x, only a single index type is allowed for an index. In version 6.7, a dummy index type, _doc, is used if no index type is specified. However, APIs in 7.0 are typeless but the type name _doc is still valid. A new `include_type_name` URL parameter to support the old custom type index is introduced in version 6.7.

The default value is `true` since the type name is still required in version 6.7. In version 7.0, the default value is `false`. To work with the old custom index type, you can attach the `include_type_name=false` URL parameter. You can skip the custom type in the URL since the typeless **GET** API is used. An example of retrieving index mappings without specifying the index type in the URL is shown in the following screenshot:

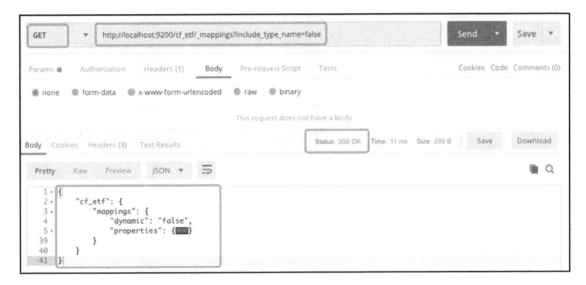

In the response body, no index type is given.

Summary

Time flies! We have completed the chapter. Now, we understand mappings and know how to index documents. We have performed mapping APIs and created our own mapping design to index the sample documents. We also dealt with the remaining task from Chapter 3, *Document APIs*, to refresh the mapping changes of static mapping in order to avoid document reindexing.

In the next chapter, we'll delve into the analyzer. With a custom analyzer, you can define how the document fields behave before storing or during search time later. You have great control over how document fields are used in your queries to make your search more accurate and efficient. We'll first learn the tokenizers, and then the filters. Then, after reviewing the built-in analyzers, we'll write our own analyzer.

5
Anatomy of an Analyzer

In `Chapter 4`, *Mapping APIs,* we learned about the mapping API; we also mentioned that the analyzer is one of the mapping parameters. In `Chapter 1`, *Overview of Elasticsearch 7*, we introduced analyzers and gave an example of a standard analyzer. The building blocks of an analyzer are character filters, tokenizers, and token filters. They efficiently and accurately search for targets and relevant scores, and you must understand the true meaning of the data and how a well-suited analyzer must be used. In this chapter, we will drill down to the anatomy of the analyzer and demonstrate the use of different analyzers in depth. During an index operation, the contents of a document are processed by an analyzer and the generated tokens are used to build the inverted index. During a search operation, the query content is processed by a search analyzer to generate tokens for matching. This chapter covers the following topics:

- An analyzer's components
- Character filters
- Tokenizers
- Token filters
- Custom analyzers
- Normalizers
- Built-in analyzers

An analyzer's components

The purpose of an analyzer is to generate terms from a document and to create inverted indexes (such as lists of unique words and the document IDs they appear in, or a list of word frequencies). An analyzer must have only one tokenizer and, optionally, as many character filters and token filters as the user wants. Whether it is a built-in analyzer or a custom analyzer, analyzers are just an aggregation of the processes of these three building blocks, as illustrated in the following diagram:

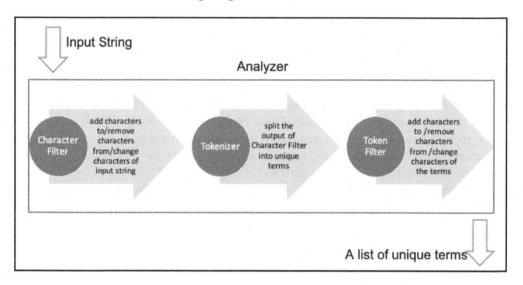

Recall from Chapter 1, *Overview of Elasticsearch 7*, (you can refer to the *Analyzer* section) that a standard analyzer is composed of a standard tokenizer and a lowercase token filter. A standard tokenizer provides grammar-based tokenization, while a lowercase token filter normalizes tokens to lowercase. Let's suppose that the input string is an HTML text string, as follows:

```
"<body>You'll love Elasticsearch 7.0.</body>".
```

After splitting the input text using the standard tokenizer, the output will be as follows:

```
[body, You'll, love, Elasticsearch, 7.0, body]
```

After converting the tokens from uppercase to lowercase using the lowercase token filter, the final output tokens will be as follows:

```
[body, you'll, love, elasticsearch, 7.0, body]
```

Let's use the Postman app to use the `_analyze` API for the two stages of the standard analyzer. The following screenshot shows an example of using the standard tokenizer:

In the response body, a list of tokens is given as an array. `start_offset` and `end_offset` represent the start and end indices in the input string, where the index starts from `0`. `position` indicates the order of the token in the token list, while `type` is the data type.

The following screenshot shows an example of using the standard tokenizer and then the lowercase token filter. In the response body, two tokens, `You'll` and `Elasticsearch`, have been converted to lowercase, that is, `you'll` and `elasticsearch`:

The same result can be obtained by using the standard analyzer instead, as shown in the following screenshot:

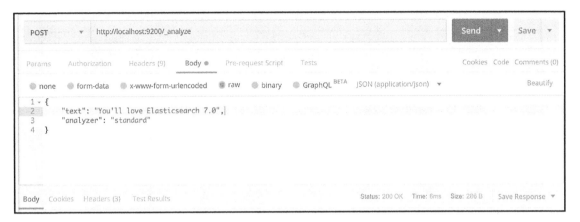

Character filters

The main function of a character filter is to convert the original input text into a stream of characters and then preprocess it before passing it as an input to the tokenizer. Three built-in character filters are supported: html_strip, mapping, and pattern_replace. We'll practice each one using the same input text string as in the previous section.

The html_strip filter

This character filter removes the HTML tags (for more information about HTML tags and entities, you can refer to https://www.w3schools.com/html/default.asp). The HTML entities are replaced by the corresponding decoded UTF-8 characters. The contents stay the same by default, but the whole HTML comment will be removed. Let's suppose that we use the same HTML input text string as the previous example; after applying the html_strip character filter, the output of the character filter will be as follows:

```
"You'll love Elasticsearch 7.0."
```

Let's apply the `html_strip` character filter, the `standard` tokenizer and the `lowercase` token filter to the input text. In the following screenshot, the `body` token does not exist in the response body because they have been stripped:

The mapping filter

You can specify a mapping using a list of key-value pairs. When the input string has such a key, the original value will be substituted by the corresponding value. The key that matches the longest string from the original value wins. There are two ways to specify the mapping:

- Using the `mappings` parameter to specify a list of key-value pairs in the text

- Using the `mappings_path` parameter to give an absolute or relative path to the configuration directory in which key-value pairs are written in each line

Let's look at an example of how to use a `mapping` character filter to replace the `You'll` input text with `You will`. Suppose that we use the same HTML input text string as we have done previously; after applying both `html_strip` and `mapping` character filters, the output of the filters will be as follows:

```
"You will love Elasticsearch 7.0."
```

Let's apply both character filters, the `standard` tokenizer and the `lowercase` token filter to the input text. In the response body of the following screenshot, you can see that the `you'll` token has been split into two tokens, `you` and `will`:

The pattern_replace filter

You can specify a regular expression (for more information, you can refer to `https://docs.oracle.com/javase/8/docs/api/java/util/regex/Pattern.html`) to match a sequence of characters. When the input string has such a sequence, the original value will be substituted by the replacement string. To define a `pattern_replace` character filter, you need to specify three parameters:

- The Java regular expression (pattern)
- The replacement string (replacement)
- The Java regular expression flag (flags)

Let's take a look at an example of how to replace the input text, `7.0`, with `v7`. We will apply all three character filters: `html_strip`, `mapping`, and `pattern_replace`. We write a regular expression matching pattern, `(\\d+).(\\d+)` to match the string `7.0`. Then we replace it with the `replacement` parameter, where we use the value `v$1`. The symbol `$1` denotes the first portion of the matching pattern, which is `(\\.d+)`. In our example, the value of the matching string is `7`. Suppose that we use the same HTML input text string as the previous examples; after applying all three character filters, the output of the filters will be as follows:

```
"You will love Elasticsearch v7"
```

Let's apply all three character filters, the `standard` tokenizer and the `lowercase` token filter to the input text. In the following screenshot, you can see that the token has been changed from `7.0` to `v7`:

```
POST   ▼   http://localhost:9200/_analyze                          Send  ▼    Save  ▼
```

Params   Authorization   Headers (9)   Body ●   Pre-request Script   Tests   Cookies Code Comments (0)

● none ● form-data ● x-www-form-urlencoded ● raw ● binary ● GraphQL ᴮᴱᵀᴬ JSON (application/json) ▼   Beautify

```
1 ▼ {
2       "text": "<body>You'll love Elasticsearch 7.0</body>",
3       "char_filter": ["html_strip", {"type": "mapping", "mappings": ["You'll=>You will"]},
4                      {"type":"pattern_replace", "pattern":"(\\d+).(\\d+)", "replacement":"v$1"}],
5       "tokenizer": "standard",
6       "filter": ["lowercase"]
7 }
```

Body Cookies Headers (5) Test Results   Status: 200 OK Time: 21 ms Size: 355 B   Save   Download

Pretty   Raw   Preview   JSON ▼   ⇥   ▣ Q

```
 1 ▼ {
 2 ▼     "tokens": [
 3 ▼         {
 4               "token": "you",
 5               "start_offset": 6,
 6               "end_offset": 9,
 7               "type": "<ALPHANUM>",
 8               "position": 0
 9           },
10 ▼         {
11               "token": "will",
12               "start_offset": 10,
13               "end_offset": 12,
14               "type": "<ALPHANUM>",
15               "position": 1
16           },
17 ▼         {
18               "token": "love",
19               "start_offset": 13,
20               "end_offset": 17,
21               "type": "<ALPHANUM>",
22               "position": 2
23           },
24 ▼         {
25               "token": "elasticsearch",
26               "start_offset": 18,
27               "end_offset": 31,
28               "type": "<ALPHANUM>",
29               "position": 3
30           },
31 ▼         {
32               "token": "v7",
33               "start_offset": 32,
34               "end_offset": 35,
35               "type": "<ALPHANUM>",
36               "position": 4
37           }
38       ]
39 }
```

Tokenizers

The tokenizer in the analyzer receives the output character stream from the character filters and splits this into a token stream, which is the input to the token filter. Three types of tokenizer are supported in Elasticsearch, and they are described as follows:

- **Word-oriented tokenizer**: This splits the character stream into individual tokens.
- **Partial word tokenizer**: This splits the character stream into a sequence of characters within a given length.
- **Structured text tokenizer**: This splits the character stream into known structured tokens such as keywords, email addresses, and zip codes.

We'll give an example for each built-in tokenizer and compile the results into the following tables. Let's first take a look at the **Word-oriented** tokenizer:

Word-oriented tokenizer		
Tokenizer		
standard	Input text	`"POST https://api.iextrading.com/1.0/stock/acwf/company /usr/local"`
	Description	This is grammar-based tokenization; it supports the `max_token_length` parameter to divide the input text into segments.
	Output tokens	`[POST, https, "api.iextrading.com", "1.0", "stock", "acwf", "company", "usr", "local"]`
letter	Input text	`"POST https://api.iextrading.com/1.0/stock/acwf/company /usr/local"`
	Description	This uses non-letters as separators to split the character stream into terms.
	Output tokens	`["POST", "https", "api", "iextrading", "com", "stock", "acwf", "company", "usr", "local"]`
lowercase	Input text	`"POST https://api.iextrading.com/1.0/stock/acwf/company /usr/local"`
	Description	Similar to the `letter` tokenizer, it uses non-letters as separators to tokenize the input text. In addition, it also converts the lettersfrom uppercase to lowercase.
	Output tokens	`["post", "https", "api", "iextrading", "com", "stock", "acwf", "company", "usr", "local"]`
whitespace	Input text	`"POST https://api.iextrading.com/1.0/stock/acwf/company /usr/local"`
	Description	This uses whitespace characters as separators to split the character stream into terms.
	Output tokens	`["POST", "https://api.iextrading.com/1.0/stock/acwf/company", "/usr/local"]`

	Input text	`"POST` `https://api.iextrading.com/1.0/stock/acwf/company /usr/local"`
`uax_url_email`	Description	This splits character streams into URL format terms and email address format terms.
	Output tokens	`["POST", "https://api.iextrading.com/1.0/stock/acwf/company",` `"usr", "local"]`
`classic`	Input text	`"POST https://api.iextrading.com/1.0/stock/acwf/company` `192.168.0.1 100-123"`
	Description	This is grammar-based tokenization. Additionally, it uses punctuation as a separator but retains some special formatting, such as dots between the non-whitespace characters, hyphens between the numbers, email addresses, and internet hostnames.
	Output tokens	`["POST", "https", "api.iextrading.com", "1.0/stock", "acwf",` `"company", "192.168.0.1", "100-123"]`
`thai`	Input text	`"คุณจะรัก Elasticsearch 7.0"`
	Description	This is similar to the standard tokenizer, but uses Thai text.
	Output tokens	`["คุณ, "จะ", "รัก", "Elasticsearch", "7.0"]`

Let's take a look at the **Partial word** tokenizer, as described in the following table:

Partial Word Tokenizer		
Tokenizer		
ngram	Input text	`"Elasticsearch 7.0"`
	Description	This slides along the input character stream to provide items in the specified length of the specified characters. It uses `min_gram` (this defaults to 1) and `max_gram` (this defaults to 2) to specify the length and `token_chars` to specify the letters, digits, whitespace, punctuation, and symbol.

	Custom tokenizer	`{"type":"ngram", "min_gram":2,`
		`"max_gram":2, "token_chars":`
		`["punctuation", "digit"]}`

	Output tokens	`["7.", ".0"]`

edge_ngram	Input	"Elasticsearch 7.0"	
	Description	This is similar to the ngram tokenizer. The difference is that each item is anchored to the starting point of the candidate words.	
	Custom tokenizer	{"type":"edge_ngram", "min_gram":2, "max_gram":2, "token_chars": ["punctuation", "digit"]}	
	Output tokens	["7."]	

Let's take a look at the **Structured text** tokenizer, as described in the following table:

Structured text tokenizer			
Tokenizer			
keyword		Input text	"Elasticsearch 7.0"
		Description	This outputs the same text as the input character steam as a term.
		Output tokens	["Elasticsearch 7.0"]
pattern		Input text	"Elasticsearch 7.0"
		Description	This uses a regular expression to perform pattern matching to process the input character stream to obtain terms. The default pattern is \W+. Use pattern to specify the regular expression; use flags to specify the flag of the Java regular expression; and use group to specify the group matched.
		Output tokens	["Elasticsearch", "7", "0"]

`char_group`	Input text	`"Elasticsearch 7.0"`
	Description	You can define a set of separators to split the input character stream into terms. Use `tokenize_on_chars` to specify a list of separators.
	Custom tokenizer	`{"type":"char_group", "tokenize_on_chars": ["whitespace", "punctuation"]}`
	Output tokens	`["Elasticsearch", "7", "0"]`
`simple_pattern`	Input text	`"Elasticsearch 7.0"`
	Description	This is similar to the `pattern` tokenizer, but with Lucene regular expressions. The tokenization is usually faster (for more information, you can refer to `https:// lucene.apache.org/core/7_0_1/core/ org/apache/lucene/util/automaton/ RegExp.html`). The following example matches words only made from letters.
	Custom tokenizer	`{"type":"simple_pattern", "pattern": "[a-zA-Z]*"}`
	Output tokens	`["Elasticsearch"]`
`simple_pattern_split`	Input text	`"Elasticsearch 7.0"`
	Description	You can define the pattern as a separator to split the input character stream into terms. Use `pattern` to specify the pattern of the separator.
	Custom tokenizer	`{"type":"simple_pattern_split", "pattern": "[a-zA-Z.]*"}`
	Output tokens	`["7", "0"]`

path_hierarchy	Input text	`"/usr/local"`
	Description	This uses the path separator to split the input character stream into terms. The following parameters can be set: `delimiter` (the separator), `replacement` (the character to replace the delimiter), `buffer_size` (the maximum length in one batch), `reverse` (this reverses the generated terms), and `skip` (the number of generated terms to skip).
	Custom tokenizer	`{"type":"path_hierarchy", "replacement":"_"}`
	Output tokens	`["_user", "_usr_local"]`

Token filters

The main function of a token filter is to add, modify, or delete the characters of the output tokens from the tokenizer. There are approximately 50 built-in token filters. We'll cover some popular token filters in the following table. You can find out more and learn about the remaining token filters at https://www.elastic.co/guide/en/elasticsearch/reference/7.x/analysis-tokenfilters.html. Each example token filter in the following table uses a standard tokenizer and a specified token filter. Note that no character filter is applied:

Token filter		
asciifolding	Input text	`"Ÿőű'ľľ ľővė Èľàśťícśèàŕćĥ 7.0"`
	Description	This transforms the terms when letters, numbers, and unicode symbols are not in the first 127 ASCII characters to ASCII. The `preserve_original` parameter (this defaults to `false`) will retain the original terms if it is `true`.
	Custom token filter	`[{"type":"asciifolding", "preserve_original":true}]`
	Output tokens	`["You'll", "Ÿőű'ľľ", "love", "ľővė", "Elasticsearch", "Èľàśťícśèàŕćĥ", "7.0"]`

ngram	Input text	`"You'll love Elasticsearch 7.0"`
	Description	This slides along the output term from the tokenizer to provide items in the specified length of the specified characters. Use `min_gram` (this defaults to 1) and `max_gram` (this defaults to 2) to specify the length.
	Custom token filter	`[{"type":"ngram", "min_gram":10, "max_gram":10}]`
	Output tokens	`["Elasticsea", "lasticsear", "asticsearc", "sticsearch"]`
edge_ngram	Input text	`"You'll love Elasticsearch 7.0"`
	Description	This is similar to the `ngram` token filter. The difference is that each item is anchored to the starting point of the candidate terms.
	Custom token Filter	`[{"type":"edge_ngram", "min_gram":10, "max_gram":10}]`
	Output tokens	`["Elasticsea"]`
lowercase (uppercase)	Input text	`"You'll love Elasticsearch 7.0"`
	Description	This converts all the letters of the terms to lowercase (from uppercase).
	Custom token filter	`["lowercase"] (["uppercase"])`
	Output tokens	`["you'll", "love", "elasticsearch", "7.0"]`
Fingerprint	Input text	`"You'll love Elasticsearch 7.0"`
	Description	Sort, deduplicate, and concatenate the terms from the tokenizer into one term. The `separator` parameter (this defaults to the space character) can be set to another character. The `max_output_size` parameter (this defaults to `255`) will restrict the emitting of the final concatenated term.
	Custom token filter	`["fingerprint"]`
	Output tokens	`["7.0 Elasticsearch You'll love"]`

keep	Input text	`"You'll love Elasticsearch 7.0"`
	Description	Only those terms defined in the list of specified words are kept. Three options are provided: the `keep_words` parameter allows you to specify a list of words in the filter; the `keep_words_path` parameter allows you to specify a list of words in the file path; and the `keep_words_case` parameter (this defaults to `false`) converts the terms to lowercase.
	Custom token filter	`[{"type": "keep", "keep_words":["Elasticsearch", "7.0"]}]`
	Output tokens	`["Elasticsearch", "7.0"]`
keep_types	Input text	`"You'll love Elasticsearch 7.0"`
	Description	Only those terms defined in the list of specified token types are kept. One option is provided: the `mode` parameter (this defaults to `include`) allows you to include or exclude specified types of terms.
	Custom token filter	`[{"type": "keep_types", "types":["<NUM>"]}]`
	Output tokens	`["7.0"]`
stemmer	Input text	`"love loves loved loving"`
	Description	This allows you to specify `stemmer` in different languages and apply it to the terms.
	Custom token filter	`[{"type": "stemmer", "name":"english"}]`
	Output tokens	`["love", "love", "love", "love"]`
stop	Input text	`"A an The and Elasticsearch"`
	Description	This allows you to specify stop words to delete from the terms. Stop words in different languages are provided, such as `_english_`, and `_spanish_`. Use `stopwords` to specify a list of words to remove. The default value is `_english_`. Use `stopwords_path` to specify a file path relative to the config location that contains a list of words to remove. Use `ignore_case` to lowercase all the terms first. Use `remove_trailing` to ignore the last term.
	Custom token filter	`[{"type": "stop", "stopwords":["_english_"], "ignore_case":true}]`
	Output tokens	`["Elasticsearch"]`

unique	Input text	`"love loves loved loving"`
	Description	This allows you to produce unique terms. The custom token filters include `stemmer` and the unique tokenizer.
	Custom token filter	`[{"type": "stemmer", "name":"english"}, "unique"]`
	Output tokens	`["love"]`
conditional	Input text	`"You'll love Elasticsearch 7.0"`
	Description	This allows you to specify a predicate script and a list of token filters. Apply the token filters to the term if the terms match. Use the `script` parameter to specify the predicate. Use the `filter` parameter to specify the list of token filters. In the following example, the predicate matches the alphanumeric token type and applies the `reverse` token filter to reverse the term.
	Custom token filter	`[{"type": "condition", "script":{"source":"token.getType()=='<ALPHANUM>'"}, "filter":["reverse"]}]`
	Output tokens	`[""ll'uoY", "evol", "hcraescitsalE", "7.0"]`
predicate_token _filter	Input text	`"You'll love Elasticsearch 7.0"`
	Description	This allows you to specify a predicate script. Remove the term if the term does not match. Use the `script` parameter to specify the predicate. You can refer to the Elasticsearch Java documentation for more information (`https://static.javadoc.io/org.elasticsearch/elasticsearch/7.0.0-beta1/org/elasticsearch/action/admin/indices/analyze/AnalyzeResponse.AnalyzeToken.html`).
	Custom token filter	`[{"type": "predicate_token_filter", "script":{"source":"token.getType()=='<NUM>'"}}]`
	Output tokens	`["7.0"]`

`word_delimiter` is a more complex token filter, so we will introduce it separately. Essentially, it uses all non-alphanumeric characters as separators to split the term from the output of the tokenizer. In addition to this, it has many parameters to shape the filter. Let's explore this in more detail in the following table; each example uses a standard tokenizer and the `word_delimiter` token filter. Note that no character filter is applied:

Parameter			
generate_word_parts	Input text	`"ElasticSearch 7.0"`	
	Description	This generates subwords from a term when the case changes.	
	Custom token filter	`[{"type":"word_delimiter", "generate_word_parts":` `true|false}]`	
	Value	`true` (by default)	`false`
	Output tokens	`["Elastic", "Search", "7", "0"]`	`["7", "0"]`
generate_number _parts	Input text	`"ElasticSearch 7.0"`	
	Description	This generates a subnumber.	
	Custom token filter	`[{"type":"word_delimiter", "generate_number_parts":` `true|false}]`	
	Value	`true` (by default)	`false`
	Output tokens	`["Elastic", "Search", "7", "0"]`	`["Elastic", "Search"]`
catenate_words	Input text	`"Elastic_Search 7.0"`	
	Description	This concatenates the split word terms, which come from the same origin term, together.	
	Custom token filter	`[{"type":"word_delimiter", "catenate_words": true|false}]`	
	Value	`true`	`false` (by default)
	Output tokens	`["Elastic", "ElasticSearch", "Search", "7", "0"]`	`["Elastic", "Search", "7", "0"]`
catenate_numbers	Input text	`"Elastic_Search 7.0"`	
	Description	This concatenates the split numeric terms that come from the same origin term.	
	Custom token filter	`[{"type":"word_delimiter", "catenate_numbers": true|false}]`	
	Value	`true`	`false` (by default)
	Output tokens	`["Elastic", "Search", "7", "70", "0"]`	`["Elastic", "Search", "7", "0"]`
catenate_all	Input text	`"Elastic_Search 7.0"`	
	Description	This concatenates the split word terms or numeric terms that come from the same origin term.	
	Custom token filter	`[{"type":"word_delimiter", "catenate_all": true|false}]`	
	Value	`true`	`false` (by default)
	Output tokens	`["Elastic", "ElasticSearch", "Search", "7", "70", "0"]`	`["Elastic", "Search", "7", "0"]`

	Input text	"ElasticSearch 7.0"	
	Description	The case changes are ignored when it is false.	
split_on_case_change	Custom token filter	[{"type":"word_delimiter", "split_on_case_change": true|false}]	
	Value	true (by default)	false
	Output tokens	["Elastic", "Search", "7", "0"]	["ElasticSearch", "7", "0"]
	Input text	"Elastic_Search 7.0"	
	Description	The original terms from the tokenizer are preserved.	
preserve_original	Custom token filter	[{"type":"word_delimiter", "preserve_original": true|false}]	
	Value	true	false (by default)
	Output tokens	["Elastic_Search","Elastic", "Search", "7.0", "7", "0"]	["Elastic", "Search", "7", "0"]
	Input text	"SN12X"	
	Description	The numeric changes are ignored when it is false.	
split_on_numerics	Custom token filter	[{"type":"word_delimiter", "split_on_numerics":true|false}]	
	Value	true (by default)	false
	Output tokens	["SN", "12", "x"]	["SN12x"]
	Input text	"Elasticsearch's analyzer"	
	Description	This removes the apostrophe from the possessive adjective.	
stem_english _possessive	Custom token filter	[{"type":"word_delimiter", "stem_english_possessive":true|false}]	
	Value	true (by default)	false
	Output tokens	["ElasticSearch", "analyzer"]	["ElasticSearch", "s", "analyzer"]

Another two parameters, protected_words and type_table, also have special usage; you can find out more about them at https://www.elastic.co/guide/en/elasticsearch/reference/7.x/analysis-word-delimiter-tokenfilter.html.

Built-in analyzers

In this section, we are going to introduce built-in analyzers. Each built-in analyzer contains a tokenizer and zero or more token filters. The corresponding parameter of the token filter that is used can be applied to the analyzer just like in the previous section. No more character filters or token filters are added in the testing. We'll cover all the supported analyzers and compile the testing results in the following table. The input text for all testing will be In Elasticsearch 7.0:

Analyzer	Composed of		Output tokens
	Tokenizer	Token filter	
standard	standard	lowercase + stop (disable in default)	["in", "elasticsearch", "7.0"]
simple	lowercase		["in", "elasticsearch"]
whitespace	whitespace		["In", "Elasticsearch", "7.0"]
stop	lowercase	stop	["elasticsearch"]
keyword	keyword		["In Elasticsearch 7.0"]
pattern	pattern	lowercase + stop	["in", "elasticsearch", "7", "0"]
fingerprint	standard	lowercase + asciifolding + stop (disable in default) + fingerprint	["7.0 elasticsearch in"]
language	english	stop	["elasticsearch", "7.0"]

The language analyzer is a special case; there are many specific languages that are supported, such as `english` and `spanish`. For more information, you can refer to `https://www.elastic.co/guide/en/elasticsearch/reference/7.x/analysis-lang-analyzer.html`.

Custom analyzers

Elasticsearch gives you a way to customize your analyzer. The first step is to define the analyzer and then use it in the mappings. You must define the analyzer in the index settings. You can then define your analyzer either in an index or in an index template for multiple indices that match the index pattern. Recall that an analyzer must only have one tokenizer and, optionally, many character filters and token filters. Let's create a custom analyzer to extract the tokens that we will use in the next chapter, which contain the following components:

- `tokenizer`: Use the `char_group` tokenizer to have separators such as whitespace, digit, punctuation except for hyphens, end-of-line, symbols, and more.
- `token filter`: Use the `pattern_replace`, `lowercase`, `stemmer`, `stop`, `length`, and `unique` filters.

Since the description text will be indexed differently, we need to delete the `cf_etf` index first, and then recreate it with the mapping and the custom analyzer. We only apply the custom `description_analyzer` analyzer for the `description` field. For the others, we still use the default `standard` analyzer. Since the `description_analyzer` analyzer involves the `stop` filter and we use the relative file path `stopwords` as the `stopwords_path`, we must download and copy the `stopwords` file from our GitHub site (`https://github.com/PacktPublishing/Mastering-Elasticsearch-7.0/tree/master/Chapter5`) to the installed Elasticsearch `config` directory.

After that, we can run the command to test our custom analyzer, as shown in the following screenshot:

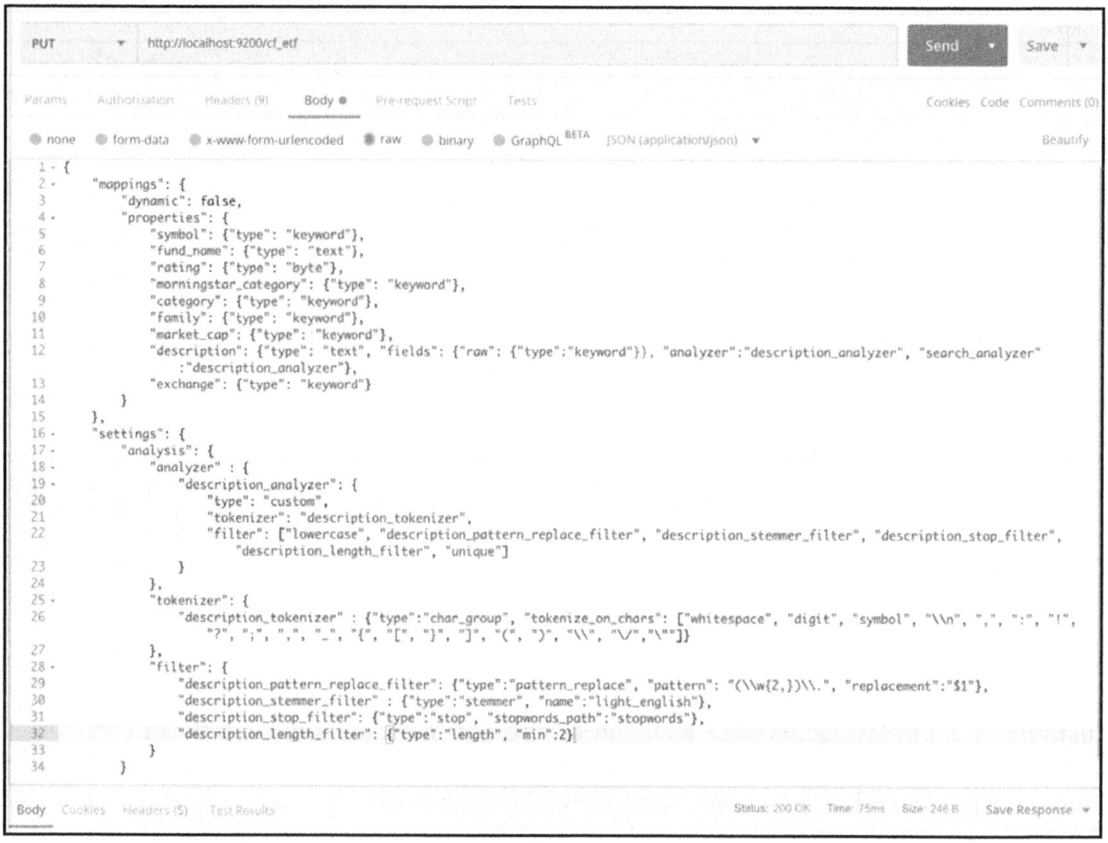

After we successfully create the description analyzer, we can test the analyzer with the sample description text. The following screenshot shows the testing with the description from one of the ETF documents as the input text. The tokens listed in the response body are `["investment", "seek", "track", "price", "yield", "performance", "fee", "expenses", "bloomberg", "barclay", "u.s.", "aggregate", "enhance", "index", "design", "broad", "capture", "grade", "fixed", "income", "security", "market", "enhance", "risk", "parameter", "constraint", "fund", "non-diversified"]`. It seems that the output tokens are meaningful for the search:

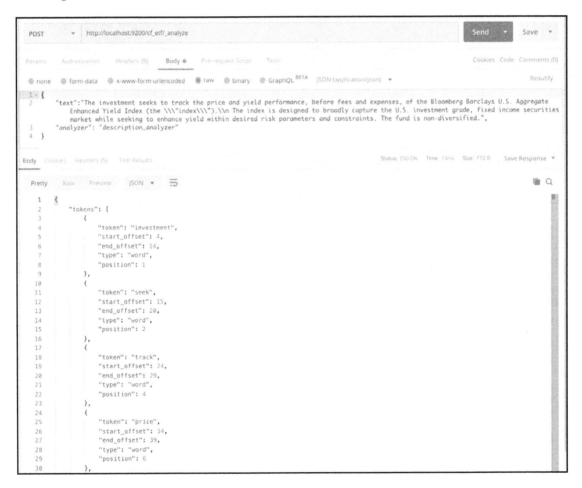

Normalizers

The normalizer behaves like an analyzer except that it guarantees to generate a single token. There is no built-in normalizer. To customize the normalizer, you only allow character-based character filters and token filters. The way to define a normalizer is similar defining to an analyzer, except that it uses the `normalizer` keyword instead of `analyzer`. Let's delete the `cf_etf_toy` index and recreate it with `lowercase_normalizer`, which contains a `lowercase` token filter:

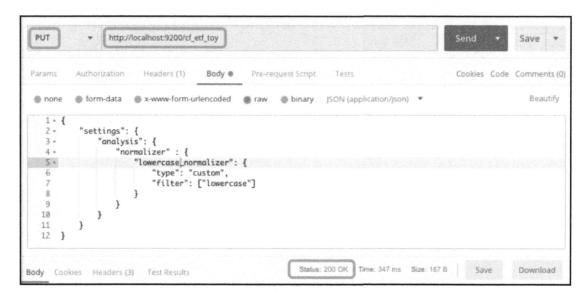

Then, we apply `lowercase_normalizer` to a sample text, as shown in the following screenshot:

In the response body, you can see that only one token is generated.

Summary

Terrific! We have understood the anatomy of the analyzer and have completed the analysis process. We have practiced different character filters, tokenizers, and token filters. We learned how to create a custom analyzer and use it in the _analyze API. Normalizers were also briefly introduced and practiced.

In the next chapter, we will focus on the search API. The basic functionality of the search API allows you to perform a search query and get back a search hit that matches the query. Elasticsearch supports the suggest API to help you improve the user experience. The explain APIs is also included; it computes the score explanation for a query and a specific document. This can provide useful feedback for scoring when you are looking for relevant issues. We will also discuss query **Domain-Specific language (DSL)** and high lighting feature in depth.

6
Search APIs

So far, what we have learned from the preceding four chapters is preparing us for searching. We prepared the index settings, the mappings, the analyzers, and then we indexed the documents. One of the ultimate goals is to execute the query and get high-quality results from the index. The Search API allows you to perform a search query and return the search hits that match the query. There are two basic ways to run a search: one is to send the search request with URL parameters, and the other is to use a request body. This chapter also provides additional information about searching related APIs, such as tuning, validating, and troubleshooting. By the end of this chapter, you will have covered the following topics:

- The URI search
- The Request body search
- The Query **domain-specific language** (**DSL**)
- The Multi-search API
- The Explain API
- The Validate API
- The Count API
- The Field capabilities API
- The Profile API
- Suggester

Indexing sample documents

You will recall that we have introduced 314 **exchange-traded funds (ETFs)** provided by TD Ameritrade. We are going to index those documents in this chapter. In our GitHub repository (`https://github.com/PacktPublishing/Mastering-Elasticsearch-7.0/tree/master/Chapter6`), you can download two files, `cf_etf_list_bulk.json` and `cf_etf_list_bulk_index.sh`. You need to make the `bash` file runnable and then you can run it to index those documents. The commands to issue are specified here. Before you issue the following command, make sure your `cf_etf` index is recreated with the static mappings and the custom analyzer. If not, delete the index and recreate it:

```
$chmod +x cf_etf_list_bulk_index.sh
$./cf_etf_list_bulk_index.sh
```

After the command runs successfully, we can use the `Postman` API to issue the count API to verify the number of indexed documents. The total number of indexed documents is `314`, as shown in the following screenshot:

Search APIs

For simple searches, you can use the simple query string as a URL parameter to execute the Search API. For complex queries, you can write JSON query strings using DSL in the request body. All Search APIs can be applied to multiple indices. Let's show three search examples, with one index, two indices, and all indices. The following screenshot shows how to search all documents with the `cf_etf` index. `314` documents are identified:

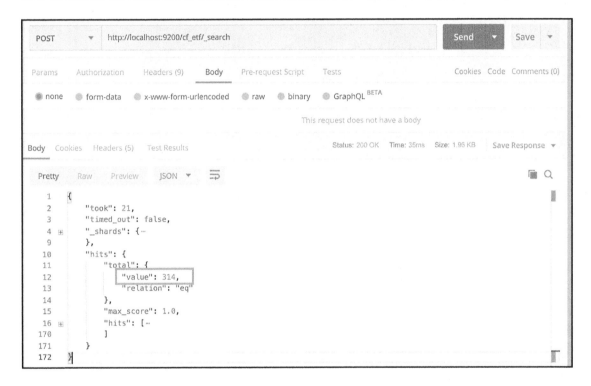

The following screenshot shows how to search all documents with two indices, the `cf_etf` index, and `cf_view` index. 316 documents are identified:

The following screenshot shows how to search all documents with all indices. 318 documents are identified:

We will first introduce the URI search and then the request body search in a separate subsection.

URI search

The URI search uses a simple query string with URL parameters to execute the Search API. We will demonstrate a number of common parameters:

- `from`: The starting item (default to 0) to return in the `hits` field.
- `size`: The number of items (default to 10) to return in the `hits` field.
- `sort`: Sort the field (default to ascending) by specifying `sort=field:asc` or `sort=field:desc`, or by the scores (`sort=_score:asc`).
- `_source`: Return the `_source` field by default. If it is set to false, no `_source` field is returned.

The following screenshot shows an example of using the `from`, `size`, `sort`, and `_source` parameters. The search result of the request will only have two items returned. The items returned start from index 2 after sorting the `symbol` field in ascending order. No _source field is returned. We use the `size=2` parameter to control the number of items returned to 2. We use the `_source=false` parameter to disable the return of the _source field. We use the `from=2` parameter to control the starting item index to 2. We use the `sort=symbol:asc` parameter to sort the `symbol` field in ascending order. You can see that the first symbol of the ETFs returned in the response body is `ACWV`, not `ACWF`:

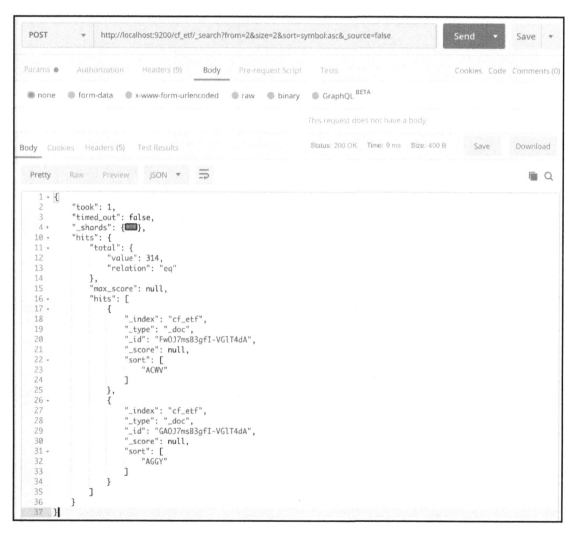

Let's continue with our explanation of the common parameters with q and
`default_operator`:

- q: Follow the DSL syntax to make a string query.
- `default_operator`: When more than one condition is in the query, you can
  specify a Boolean operator, `and|or` (default = `or`), to group them.

  The following screenshot shows an example of using the q and
  `default_operator=AND` parameters. The query is to restrict the returned
  documents where the field, `fund_name`, must contain all three words—iShares,
  Edge, and Global. Only two documents match the search criteria:

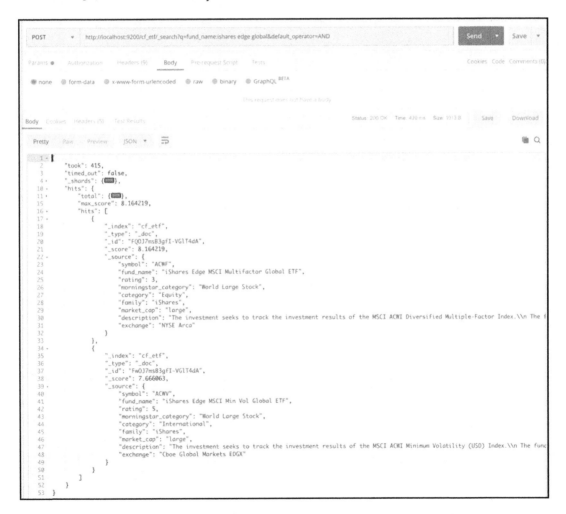

Let's continue with our explanation of the common parameters with `explain`:

- `explain`: This provides a detailed description to explain the computation of relevance scoring.

  The following screenshot shows an example of using the `explain` parameter to search the document with the `_id=oU2jLGkB_W0hQaVaoEie` identifier from the previous screenshot. In the response body, we know that the `8.183948` score is from two parts, `1.7741624` and `6.4097853`:

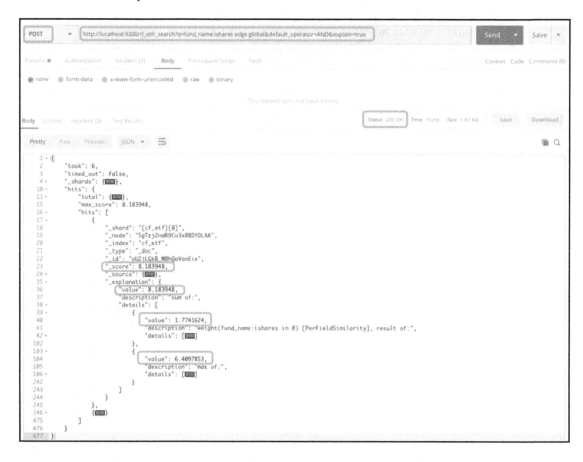

Now, let's continue with our explanation of the common parameters with `analyzer`:

- `analyzer`: This is the search analyzer to be used to analyze the input query string.

  The following screenshot shows an example of using the `keyword` analyzer instead of the default `standard` analyzer. You can see that no result is found if the `keyword` analyzer is used for the input query string:

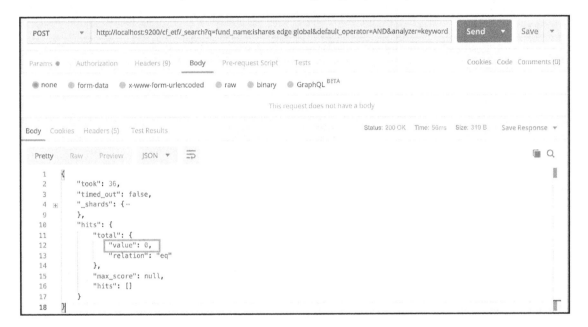

As regards the other parameters indicated in the following table, we will leave it to the interested parties to practice:

URL parameter	Description
stored_fields	This parameter retrieves those fields marked store in the mappings. Specify with a list of comma-separated fields or _none_ to disable it.
analyze_wildcard	This parameter determines whether to analyze wildcard or prefix queries. The default value is false.
allow_partial_search_results	This parameter determines whether to return partial results in the event of failure. The default value is true.
batched_reduce_size	This parameter reduces the number of temporary results collected in the coordinating node to reduce memory usage.
df	This parameter specifies the default field to search.
lenient	This parameter ignores the datatype mismatch error. The default value is false.
search_type	The query_then_fetch approach has a good relevancy scoring method, while the dfs_query_then_fetch approach is better in terms of accuracy. The default value is query_then_fetch.
timeout	This parameter specifies the time permitted to complete the search operation. The default value is no timeout.
terminate_after	This parameter specifies the number of documents that are permitted to be collected in a shard. The default value is no limit.
track_scores	This parameter allows scoring to be tracked when sorting is enabled. The default value is false.
track_total_hits	This parameter stipulates the total number of hits allowed for tracking. You can disable it with a false value. The default value is 10000.

Request body search

If the search conditions are complex, you need to follow the DSL syntax to write a JSON query string in the request body. Both HTTP GET and HTTP POST are allowed to perform search requests with the query in the request body. If you have to use HTTP GET, you can pass the body content a URL parameter named source. Let's use the same example from the *URI search* section to provide a query where the fund_name field contains all three words—ishares, edge, and global. The following screenshot shows the same search results as the example in the *URI search* section:

Most of the parameters introduced in the *URI search* section can be used in the request body search. Use the `query` parameter instead of `q`, and the `default_field` parameter instead of `df`. In addition, the `search_type` and `allow_partial_search_results` parameters must be passed as the query string parameters. The remainder of the parameters should be passed in the request body. Let's use the same example from the *URI search* section by using the request body search.

The following screenshot shows the same retrieved documents:

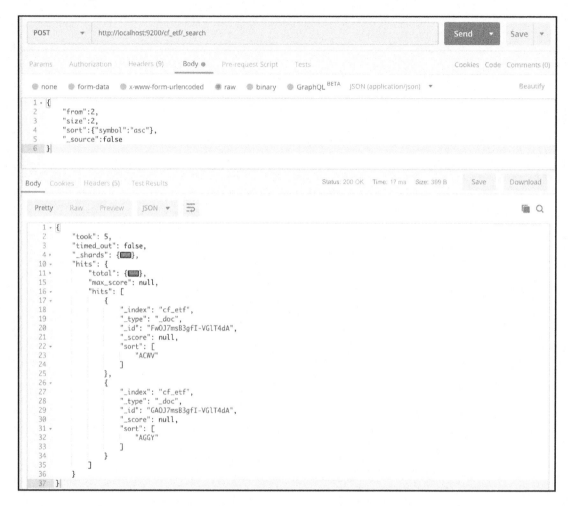

We'll choose a few parameters to practice and, as regards the rest, we will compile them into a table just for illustration purposes.

The sort parameter

You can sort by a field, multiple fields, an array, an object, or a nested object. You can sort the fields with a primitive data type or in _geo_distance.

Let's look at an example involving multiple fields. We want to obtain `ishares edge msci series commission free ETFs`. The result needs to be sorted with the `rating` field first, followed by the `symbol` field. In the following screenshot, there are six ETFs that satisfy the search criteria. You can see that the `rating` field is sorted first in descending order, followed by the `symbol` field in ascending order:

The scroll parameter

In addition to paging using the parameters, `from` and `size`, Elasticsearch also supports the `scroll` parameter, and works like a forward-only cursor. It keeps the search context active, just like a snapshot corresponding to a given timestamp.

Basically, if you need to process the returned results further and continue after the process, you need to keep such a snapshot. An identifier, `_scroll_id`, is provided in the result of the initial request so that you can use the identifier to get the next batch of results. If there are no more results, an empty array is returned in hits. You can use the `size` parameter to control the number of hits returned in the batch.

Let's look at an example where scrolling is executed three times to consume all documents. We will set the size to `313` and specify 10 minutes for the live time period.

The following screenshot is the first scroll to obtain 313 returned entries and `_scroll_id` is returned in the response body:

The following screenshot is the second scroll that uses the `_scroll_id` parameter returned from the first request to get the next batch. In the URL, `/_search/scroll` is the endpoint, and the index name, `cf_etf` should not be specified. Bear in mind that your `_scroll_id` parameter may be different. In the response body, there is only one hit entry:

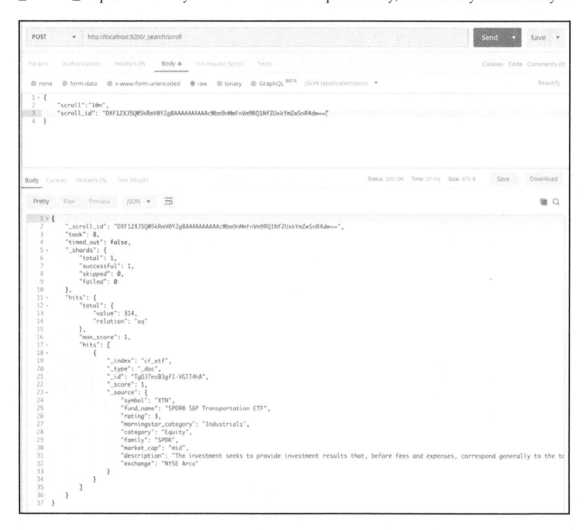

The following screenshot is the third scroll that uses the `_scroll_id` parameter returned from the second request. An empty array is returned in the `hits` field of the response body:

If you complete the process, you need to clean up the context since it still consumes the computing resource before the timeout. As shown in the following screenshot, you can use the `scroll_id` parameter to specify one or more contexts in the DELETE API:

The search_after parameter

The `search_after` parameter provides you with a cursor similar to `scroll`, but it does not keep a snapshot, hence, it is cheaper. Since the response is stateless, you cannot assume that subsequent jumps are in the same context. The use of `search_after` is based on sort and order. You need to specify the same number of values in the `search_after` parameter as in the `sort` parameter, and those values must be ordered in the same way as in the `sort` clause. When the `search_after` parameter is used, the `from` parameter should not be used.

Let's look at an example that requests a jump to an entry after `rating=5` and `symbol=EES`. The search results are first sorted with the `rating` field, followed by the `symbol` field. As shown in the following screenshot, the first hit is EMLP, and the second hit is EUSC. Both have a rating of 5:

In the prior version, the number of scroll contexts has no limit. In this version, it will be 500 open contexts per node by default. To make a change, use the cluster setting, `search.max_open_scroll_context` to set the desired number.

The rescore parameter

The `rescore` parameter gives you a way to have other scoring strategies in addition to the default scoring scheme in the query. Basically, the rescore request is examined on the basis of the number of top hits based on the `window_size` parameter (default to `10`) to recalculate the results and provide another score. Sorting is not supported, except for reverse sorting the `_score` field.

The methods to calculate the final score from the original score and rescore are shown as follows:

- Using the `query_weight` and `rescore_query_weight` parameters, both default values are 1. You can specify any numeric value to combine linearly to get the final score. The following screenshot is an example showing the original search request without rescoring. The query is to find the `description` field with the words `emerging`, `non-diversified`, `high-yield`, `global`, or `dividend`. The first hit is the `EDIV` symbol with `_score=4.9638467`:

We want to rescore the resulting documents with a higher weight if the description field contains a global word. We set the weight for the original request to 0.1, and the rescore request to 0.9. The first hit is the DEW symbol with score=2.7334738, as shown in the following screenshot:

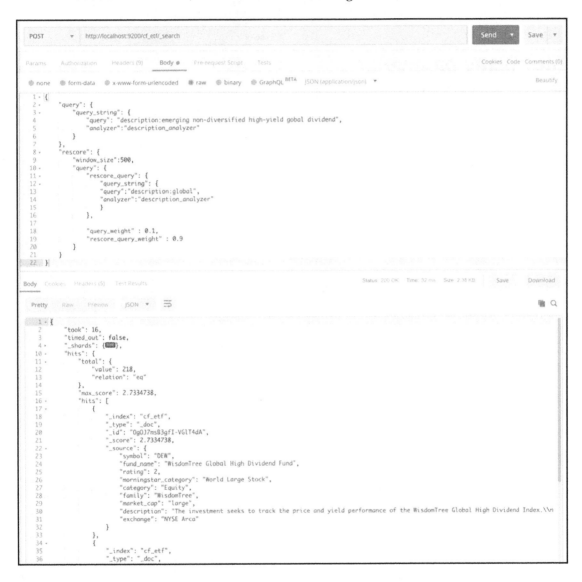

- Using the `score_mode` parameter with a choice of options, use one of `total`, `multiply`, `avg`, `max`, and `min` to combine the two scores. For practice, you can replace the `query_weight` and `rescore_query_weight` settings with `score_mode:avg` from the rescore request. The first hit will be the DGRE symbol with `_score=2.7893128` in the response body.

The _name parameter

The _name parameter gives you a way to name your queries so that you can use the name of the query as an identifier in the hit. In the following example, the _name parameter seems to only make sense for the `bool` query that allows the partial matching of queries, such as a `should` clause.

Let's look at an example of finding the `description` field containing the keyword `Asia`, `USA`, or `Europe`. However, we want to report matching keywords in the hit. Okay! We can issue a `bool` query with a `should` clause, where each query is named for a region. In the following screenshot, you can see the `matched_queries` field in the response body to report the queries to which the hit corresponds:

The collapse parameter

The `collapse` parameter gives you a way to group search results according to different field values. It seems that the search results have collapsed. Then, only the first document for each field value is collected and returned in the response body.

Let's look at an example of finding the `rating` field value greater than, or equal to, 4, and collapse it with the `rating` field. In the following screenshot, you can see that the total matches are `103` in the response body, but only two results are returned. One document is `rating=4`, and the other is `rating=5`:

The highlighting parameter

Elasticsearch allows you to emphasize the match terms in your query by means of the highlighting feature to improve the user experience. If the `store` parameter is not specified for the relevant fields in the mappings, then the highlighting fields are extracted from the `_source` parameter. All matching words will be rendered in a small portion of the original text in the `highlight` object field of the response body. Three highlighters are supported—`unified`, `plain`, and **Fast Vector Highlighter** (`fvh`). There are several parameters that can be passed in the search request to control the highlighting process, as shown in the following table. These settings can be declared in the global scope or in the local scope (field level). The local scope will override the global scope declaration:

Parameter	Description
For how to split the text field to find a matching word or phrase	
`fields`	This parameter specifies the `fields` to correspond to the word/phrase to be highlighted. Wildcards are supported for each text field and keyword field. If you use the JSON object type for `fields`, and then specify each field as its children, then the highlighting result is unordered. If you use the array type for `fields`, and then specify each field as its elements, the highlighting result is ordered.
`boundary_scanner`	It is only for `fvh` and `unified` highlighters. This parameter specifies the strategy to split the text field. There are three strategies—`chars`, `sentence`, and `word`. The `chars` strategy, only supported in the `fvh` type, involves the use of a set of characters, defined by `boundary_chars`, as the separators. The `sentence` strategy is designed to effect the split at the sentence boundary. The default strategy for the unified boundary scanner is `sentence`. When the `unified` highlighter is used and the sentence is longer than the `fragment_size` parameter, splitting will occur at the word boundary that just exceeds the size. The `word` strategy is designed to effect the split at the word boundary. For the `sentence` or `word` strategy, you can use another parameter, `boundary_scanner_locale`, to select the locale, such as en-Us, zh-cn, or en-in.
`boundary_chars`	This parameter defines the border character for the highlighted word/phrase. The default characters are .,!? \t \n. It is only supported in the `fvh` type.
`boundary_max_scan`	This setting controls the distance of the `boundary_chars` scanning. The default value is 20 characters.
`boundary_scanner_locale`	This parameter allows you to set the locale for the separator to find the boundary.
`type`	This is the highlighter type to use. The supported types are the unified highlighter (`unified`), Plain highlighter (`plain`), and Lucene (`fvh`). The default highlighter is `unified`.
`highlight_query`	If you use the rescore query, you need to use the `highlight_query` parameter to match the rescore query.
For how to fragment the field appropriately	
`number_of_fragments`	This parameter specifies the number of fragments to be returned. The default value is 5. If it is set to 0, the entire field is shown.
`fragment_size`	This parameter clips the original text portion containing the matching word/phrase to the given `fragment_size` to be rendered. The default value is 100 characters. This value is ignored when `number_of_fragments` is set to 0.

`fragment_offset`	This parameter allows you to specify the starting offset in the text field. It is only supported in the `fvh` type.
`fragmenter`	This parameter splits the text field into fragments of the same size. This setting is only supported in the `plain` highlighting type. There are two options, `simple` and `span`. Only the `span` option will attempt to preserve the integrity of the highlighting word/phrase.
`matched_fields`	This parameter allows you to combine the matching results from multiple fields into one result as a single field. This setting is only supported in the `fvh` highlighting type on those fields that have been specified with the `term_vector` mapping parameter and the `with_positions_offsets` option.
`phrase_limit`	This setting is only supported in the `fvh` highlighting type. It limits the number of matching phrases to avoid the overuse of resources. If the `match_fields` parameter is used, then it limits the number of matching phrases per matched field. The default is `256`.
For how to present the highlighting style	
`encoder`	This parameter supports a way to encode HTML tags around the matching word/phrase and add the highlighting tags. The defaults is `default`, this means there is no encoding. You can set it to `html` for the encoding.
`no_match_size`	If there is a hit to the query in the response, but there is no word/phrase matching the criteria highlighted, then no highlighted content will be returned. You can set this parameter to return the original text field length in `no_match_size` characters, starting from the beginning. Default to 0 characters returned when there is no match for highlight.
`order`	By default, the highlighting texts will be shown in the order in which they are specified in the `fields` parameter. When the unified highlighter is used, you can set the `order` parameter to `score` to sort in the relevancy scoring.
`pre_tags/post_tags`	This parameter defines the HTML tags surrounding the highlighting word/phrase. By default, the highlighted word or phrase is tagged as `<em>...</em>`.
`require_field_match`	You may specify several `field:word/phrase` matching pairs in the query. The default behavior (`require_field_match:true`) is to highlight the corresponding word or phrase in the matched pairs. When this parameter is set to `false`, it will also highlight the word or phrase from other matching pairs in the matched pairs.
`tags_schema`	This parameter specifies the schema of the tags to use. There is a built-in schema option, `styled`, which defines `pre_tags` and `post_tags` as `<em class="hltx">` and `</em class="hltx">`, where x is from 1 to 10.

Let's look at an example of using the default type, `unified`, and both boundary scanner options, `word` and `sentence`. When using a `word` type boundary scanner, you can see that the highlighted text is a single word in the following screenshot. On the other hand, an incomplete sentence is given from the `sentence` type boundary scanner, since the length of the sentence is longer than the default `segment_size` of 100 characters:

Other search parameters

Some of the request body search parameters are easy to understand and access.
Descriptions of these parameters are combined in the following table:

Parameter		
docvalue_fields	Description	This parameter allows you to get the `doc_value` fields in the response for each hit. Please refer to the Mapping parameters section in `Chapter 4`, *Mapping APIs*, for the `doc_values`.
	Example	`"docvalue_fields": ["field_1", {"field":"field_2", "format":"format_2"},...]`
script_fields	Description	This parameter allows you to specify a test script to evaluate a field and show the field in each hit of the response body.
	Example	`"script_fields": {"test": {"script": "doc['symbol']"}}`
stored_fields	Description	This is the same description as in the URI search section. Specify a list of comma-separated fields in an array, or _none_ to disable it. An empty array specified with this parameter in the request body will have the return _id and _type field of each hit in the response body.
	Example	`"stored_field":["field1", "field2",...]`
		`"stored_field":[]`
		`"stored_field":"_none"`
_source	Description	This is the same description as in the URI search section. Wildcard patterns can be used in the field names.
	Example	`"_source": false`
		`"_source":"field1"`
		`"_source":["field1", "field2",...]`
		`"_source":{"includes":["field1", "field2",...], "excludes":["field3", "field4",...]}`
search_type	Description	This is the same description as in the URI search section.
	Example	`http://localhost:9200/cf_etf/_search?q=fund_name:ishares &search_type=dfs_query_then_fetch`
explain	Description	This is the same description as in the URI search section.
	Example	`"explain":true`
min_score	Description	Only those documents with a score greater than or equal to `min_score` are returned.
	Example	`"min_score":0.7`
version	Description	This parameter is designed to return the document _version field.
	Example	`"version":true`
seq_no_primary _term	Description	This parameter is designed to return the _seq_no and _primary_term fields of the document.
	Example	`"seq_no_primary_term":true`

preference	Description	This is a URL parameter that is designed to set the selected shard copies preference to execute the search request. There are many different settings to choose from. Interested users can refer to the reference material.
	Example	`http://localhost:9200/cf_etf/_search?preference=_only_local`
request_cache	Description	This is a URL parameter that is designed to turn on caching on a per-request basis. If it is set, the index-level setting is overridden.
	Example	`http://localhost:9200/cf_etf/_search?request_cache=true`
ccs_minimize _roundtrips	Description	This parameter minimizes the network round-trips for the cross-cluster search request. The default setting is true. If it is set to false, this feature is disabled.
	Example	`"ccs_minimize_roundtrips":false`

Since the `search` parameter `inner_hits` is related to the nested object or parent-join feature, we will introduce it in the next chapter. Furthermore, `post_filter` is related to aggregation, and we will describe it in Chapter 8, *Aggregations Framework*. In the next section, we will discuss how to address the `search` result by using query language in the search request body.

Query DSL

Query DSL is a JSON-based search language for querying specific and analytical datasets. Basically, a query can be classified in two contexts—a query context and a filter context. In the filter context, the search results are based on the question relating to the match or lack of match to the query clause, where the no scoring value, `_score`, is provided in the results. In the context of the query, the search results are based on measuring the appropriateness of the match on the query clause. We will introduce a number of common query subtypes in the following subsection.

Full text queries

This type of query will use analyzers (or given search analyzers) to tokenize the query string first. Then, it uses the tokens to match the full text search fields of the document. It will provide scoring for each search result in the response body. There are several methods of working with the full text queries and they can be divided into three sub-types based on the meaning of the key word used. We are going to introduce them in the following subsections.

The match keyword

There are four kinds of queries under the match keyword:

- match: The query string is tokenized into tokens to match the search text fields and then a Boolean operator, and|or (default = or), logically groups all matches to compute the final result. Let's look at an example of using the default operator, or , to find the ETFs with the fund_name field that contains either one, ishares or global word. The following screenshot shows that there are 75 hits in total:

Another example is to use the `operator` parameter with the `and` option to find the ETFs with the `fund_name` field that contains both words. The following screenshot shows that there are 4 hits in total:

Elasticsearch provides a fuzzy matching feature for matching queries by using the `fuzziness` parameter with the value in the Levenshtein edit distance based on the length of the tokens.

Let's look at an example where we have `fuzziness=2` (this permits two edits to the token). In the following screenshot, you can see 5 hits, which is one hit more than the result without `fuzziness`. The extra ETF result, `fund_name=iShares J.P. Morgan EM Local Currency Bond ETF`, is provided from the fuzzy matching because the word `global` can be changed to `local` with two edits:

Another parameter is `zero_terms_query`. When the analyzer is unable to generate a token, no hits are returned. You can use the **all** option to return all documents instead of **none**. Another useful parameter is `cutoff_frequency`. This provides a feature to identify the importance of a token based on occurrence. Without applying a special tokenizer or token filter, most high-frequency tokens generated are the stop words.

Consequently, high-frequency words are less important, and vice versa. Low-frequency tokens are used to match the search criteria, where high-frequency tokens will increase the weight of the scoring. When you specify a fraction number to `cutoff_frequency`, this means the ratio of occurrences of the token vis-à-vis the total number of documents in the index. When you specify a number ≥ 1, this indicates an absolute occurrence. Let's look at an example to explain the `cutoff_frequency` with the absolute value.

We set the `cutoff_frequency` to `10`, which defines the occurrence of the tokens of higher importance as being less than `10`. The query is to match the `fund_name` field with the word `usa`, `global`, or `emerging`.

In the response, there are six documents with `fund_name` fields associated with the word `usa`. None of the results are associated with the words global and emerging, since both words occur with a high frequency and are treated as being less important.

The following screenshot shows what happens when the earlier steps are implemented:

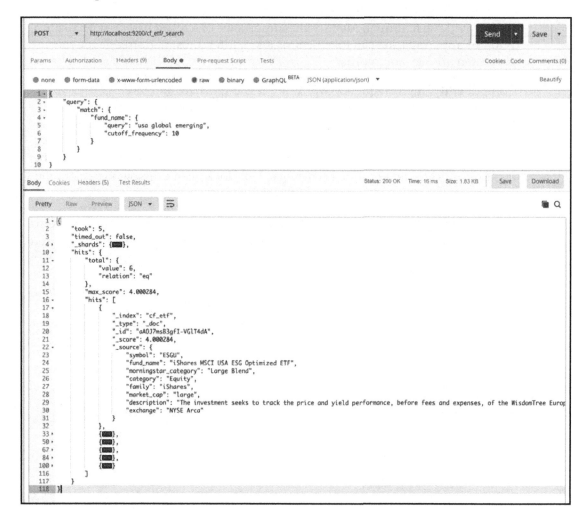

- `match_phrase`: The query string is analyzed into tokens and then generates a phrase to match the search text fields. Let's look at an example of using `match_phrase` to retrieve all `iShares msci` ETFs. In the following screenshot, 18 ETFs have a name with that phrase. The `match_phrase` query supports a `slop` parameter to allow you to specify the tolerance of the gap between the matched terms in the query string. The gap refers to the allowed number of words that can be ignored in the text:

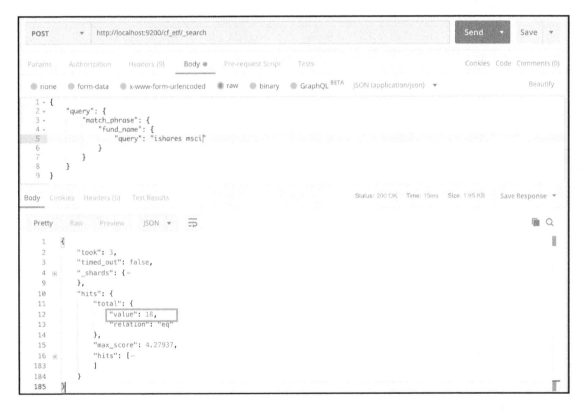

- `match_phrase_prefix`: This is similar to the `match_phrase` query, except that it is a prefix match for the phrase.

- `multi_match`: This provides a way to match the query string to multiple fields. You can use a wildcard in the field names. Since there are multiple fields, you can specify an option to define the match type among the fields as described in the following table:

The match type option	Description
`best_fields`	This ranks the results by the best score of each match.
`most_fields`	This ranks the results by the total score of each match.
`cross_fields`	This ranks the results by the best score according to the term-by-term basis blended term query to blend the score.
`phrase`	This is similar to the `best_fields` option, but uses the `match_phrase` query instead.
`phrase_prefix`	This is similar to the `best_fields` option, but uses the `match_phrase_prefix` query instead.

The query string keyword

There are two sub-types of query string keywords, `query_string` and `simple_query_string`. They use different parsers to process the query string. The syntax of the parser is quite different. If the query string is not suitable for the grammar, the parser of `query_string` will throw an exception, while the parser of `simple_query_string` will discard the invalid part and continue the process. Both parsers will split the query string with the operators and then, for each group, it splits the field and its value:

- `query_string` query: The syntax of the query string is described in the following table. If no field is specified in the query string, the setting, `index.query.default_field`, is used:

The reserved characters are +, −, =, &&, | |, >, <, !, (,), {, }, [,], ^, ", ~, *, ?, :, and \. If you use them as literals, you need to use backlash characters \ to escape it:		
Item	Description	Example
:	This is the separator between the field and the value.	`"field_1: value_1"`
()	This groups the elements to a clause.	`"field_1: (value_1 || value_2)"`

&&, ||, !	These are for Boolean operators.	`"field_1:(value_1`
		`||value_2) &&value_3 &&`
		`!value_4)"`

+, −	The plus symbol followed by a term means that the term must be matched. The minus symbol followed by a term means that the term must not be matched.	`"field_1:(+value_1 && −` `value_2)"`
>, <, =	These are mathematical symbols.	`"field_1:>=4"`
*, ?	• *: This matches zero or more characters. • ?: This matches a single character.	`"field_1:value_1*"`
"	This matches an exact phrase.	`"field_1:\"value_1\""`
~	This represents fuzzy matching.	`"field_1:(value_1~` `&& value_2~)"`
/	This is for a regular expression.	`"field_1://regular` `expression//"`
^	This is for boosting (increasing weight).	`"field_1:(value_1 value` `_2^2)"`
[,], {, }	These are for range queries. { and } mean exclusion, while [and] mean inclusion.	`"field_1:[1 TO 3}"`

Let's look at an example of the `query_string` query to find a rating range from 1 to 3, but not including 3, as demonstrated in the following table:

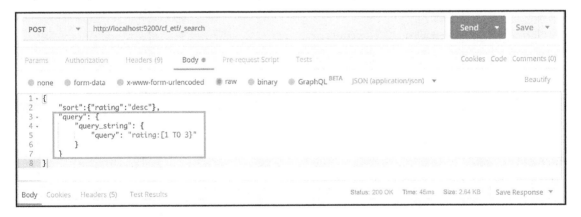

If all the criteria are applied to a single field or multiple fields, then we may rewrite the query using the `fields` parameter. In the case of multiple fields, it uses the Boolean, OR, to group the matching according to each field. The search request is shown in the following screenshot:

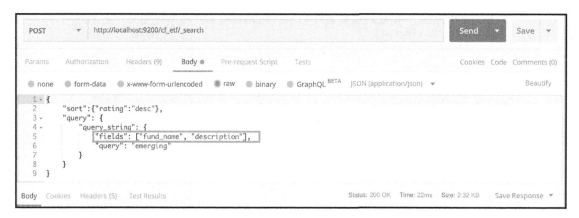

- `simple_query_string` query: The syntax of the query string is described in the following table. If there is no field specified in the query string, then the `index.query.default_field` setting is used:

The reserved characters are +, −, |, ", ~, N, *, and (). If you use them as literals, you need to use backlash characters, \, to escape them.		
Item	**Description**	**Example**
+	The Boolean AND operator.	`"value_1 + value_2"`
|	The Boolean OR operator.	`"value_1 | value_2 + value_3"`
−	This must not match the following token.	`"-value_1"`
"	This matches an exact phrase.	`"\"value_1\""`
W~, P~	If this comes after a word, W, it means `fuzziness`. If this comes after a phrase, P, it means `slop`.	`"value_1~"`
W*	This is for a prefix match if it comes after a word, W.	`"value_1*"`
()	This is for precedence.	`"(value_1 || value_2) + value_3"`

If you want to only enable some of the reserved characters, you can use the `flags` field with the options to enable those items. The options are listed in the following table:

Flag	For reserved character	Description
ALL		This is the default for all reserved characters.
NONE		Disable all reserved characters.
AND	+	Enable it.
OR	|	Enable it.
NOT	−	Enable it.
PREFIX	W*	Enable it.
PHRASE	"	Enable it.
PRECEDENCE	( )	Enable it.
FUZZY	W~	Enable ~ with the `fuzziness` feature.
SLOP/NEAR	P~	Enable ~ with the `slop` feature.
ESCAPE		Enable the backslash character \ as an escape character.
WHITESPACE		Enable the whitespace character as separators.

> Both the `query_string` and `simple_query_string` queries support quite a lot of parameters. Any users who are interested can refer to `https://www.elastic.co/guide/en/elasticsearch/reference/7.x/query-dsl-query-string-query.html`.

The intervals keyword

The `intervals` query is similar to the `span` query, which provides fine-grain control, to some extent, over the order and the gap between the words of the query text. Let's look at an example to understand the meaning. The following screenshot shows an `intervals` query that fully satisfies two criteria. The first criterion is that the ETFs `fund_name` field must have the text `MSCI Markets`, with a gap of at most one word between.

The second criterion is that the ETFs `fund_name` field must have the text `ETF`, and it must appear after `MSCI Markets`. The total number of hits is 4 ETFs:

If we change the value of `max_gaps` to 0, then no hits will be returned since there is no ETFs `fund_name` field containing the exact phrase, `MSCI Markets`. On the other hand, if we switch the order of the two queries, no hits will be returned since the text, `ETF`, is always at the end position in the `fund_name` field.

Term-level queries

These types of queries will use the exact term (not analyze) specified in the query to match the inverted index. Usually, it uses fields of a number, date, and keyword data type, rather than full text. We will describe different sub-types of the term-level query in the following table:

Sub-type	Description	Example
term	Use the exact term to match.	`"term": {"field_1": "value_1"}`
terms	Use any terms in the list to match.	`"terms":{"field_1": ["value_1", "value_2"]`
terms_set	Use any terms in the list to match, but the number of matches must reach the requisite number specified. This requires the `required_matches` parameter when you index the document and specify its value in the search query.	`"terms_set":{"field_1": {"terms":[ "field_1", "field_2", "field_3"], "minimum_should_match_field":"required_matches"`
range	Use the term to match any value within a scope. These four parameters—`gte` (greater than or equal to), `gt` (greater than), `lte` (less than or equal to), and `lt` (less than)—can specify the scope in a number or date data type.	`"range":{"field_1":{"parameter_1":"value_1", "parameter_2":"value2"}}`
exists	Use the term to check the existence and match. If the `null_value` parameter is specified as `_null_` for the field in the mappings, then the `null` value can be used to match the field for nonexistence.	`"exists":{"field_1":"value_1"|null}`
prefix	Use the term as a prefix to match.	`"prefix":{"field_1":"prefix characters"}`
wildcard	Use a wildcard term the characters `*` and `?` characters to match.	`"wildcard":{"field_1":"c*d?"}`
regexp	Use the term that is contained in the regular expression to match.	`"regexp":{"field_1": "regular expression"}`
fuzzy	Use the term to fuzzy match.	`"fuzzy":{"field_1":"value_1"}`
ids	Use the terms as a list of document identifiers to match.	`"ids":{"values":["id_1", "id_2", "id_3"]}`

Compound queries

Compound queries are used to combine multiple clauses to build a complex query. There are several sub-type queries, and each of these are described briefly in the following table.

Sub-type		
bool	Description	This query combines query clauses using Boolean equivalent operators such as `must`, `must_not`, and `should` to provide more relevant or specific results.
	Example	`"bool": {"must": {"match_phrase_prefix": {"fund_name": "ishares edge" }}, "must_not": {"match": {"fund_name":"global"}}}`

boosting	Description	When searching for multiple fields with term query, we may want to increase the weight of the score of some fields. You can specify a `positive` query and a `negative` query. A `negative_boost` parameter will be specified with a fractional number to reduce the weight of the negative query by multiplying the `_score` query.
	Example	`"boosting": {"positive": {"match_phrase_prefix": {"fund_name": "ishares edge" }}, "negative": {"term":{"category":"Equity"}},"negative_boost":0.1}`
dis_max	Description	This query has a `queries` field to collect a list of queries to match. Matching any one of the queries is a hit. However, the score of the hit is assigned to the maximum of all of the hits.
	Example	`"dis_max": {"queries": [{"match_phrase": {"fund_name": "ishares edge" }}, {"match": {"morningstar_category": "World Large Stock"}}]}`
function_score	Description	This query provides a way to recalculate the `_score` query by means of user-defined functions for the hits.
	Example	Refer to the following diagram.

Let's look at an example to show the `function_score` query. The example will retrieve all ETFs' `fund_name` fields with `ishares edge`. The score will be rescored under two rules. The score will be multiplied by 2, 1.5, or 0.5 if the morning star category is `Stock`, `Growth`, or `Blend`, respectively. You will observe that ETFs with the `stock` category are in the top hits since it has the larger weight:

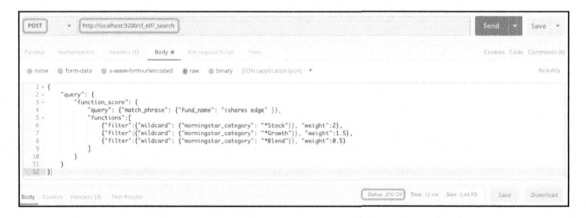

The script query

The query clause is written in a given user-defined script. Usually, it is used in the filter context where the `filter` parameter is placed in a `bool` query after `must` or `should` clauses. Let's look at an example of using a `bool` query to embed a filter with a `script` query. This example will retrieve the ETFs with the `fund_name` field starting with `ishares edge` and `rating≥4`, as shown in the following screenshot. There are 4 ETFs in total:

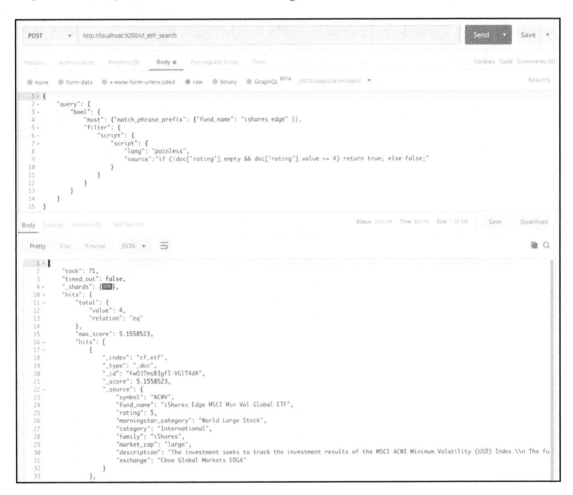

The `interval` query also supports embedding the `script` query. In the next section, we will discuss how to address the multiple search query.

The multi-search API

Similar to the `Bulk` API, Elasticsearch provides you with a way to gather multiple search (`_msearch`) requests together to send out in a batch. You need to put the header and the corresponding request body as a pair in the multi-search request body. You can specify the appropriate index names and parameters in the header, including `search_type`, `preference`, and `routing`. The header content type must be set to the newline delimited JSON format (application/x-ndjson).

Now, let's look at an example to issue an `_msearch` request that contains two sub-requests to find those EFTs in the `cf_etf` and `cf_view` indices that do not have the `rating` field. In the following screenshot, you can see that the response body has a `responses` field with the array type that contains two results corresponding to the two sub-requests:

Other search-related APIs

Elasticsearch supports a few search-related APIs to provide information to troubleshoot search issues. It can help you in preparing the complex search query to obtain more precise search results.

The _explain API

Similar to the explain parameter in the request body search, this _explain API tells you
how to calculate the score of matching for a particular document. It provides you with
useful feedback when looking for related issues and finding the reason why a given
document can be found. The following screenshot provides an explanation as to why
the GgOJ7msB3gfI-VGlT4dA document identifier satisfies the query:

The _validate API

This `_validate` API provides you with a way to provide an evaluation of your query without execution. When you try to work with time-consuming, heavy queries, you will need it to shorten your testing time. Additional parameters, such as `df`, `analyzer`, `default_operator`, `lenient`, and `analyze_wildcard`, are provided for better validation processing. Their uses are the same as what we described in the *URI search* section. Let's look at an example to validate a query that matches the `rating` field with text, while its data type is numeric. We can add a URL parameter, `?explain=true`, to get a detailed explanation as to why it fails.

In the following screenshot, you can read the explanations field to see the cause of the failure. In this case, it shows `java.lang.NumberFormatException: For input string: \"five\"`:

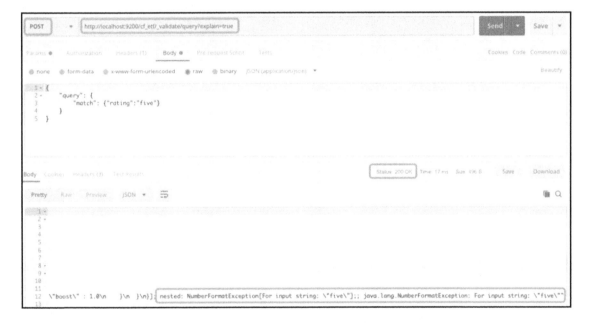

The _count API

This `_count` API gives you a count of the search results without giving the details. You can use it in a URI search or request body search query. Additional parameters, such as `df`, `analyzer`, `default_operator`, `lenient`, `analyze_wildcard`, and `terminate_after`, can be used in the query. Their usages are the same as what we described in the *URI search* section. Let's look at an example of counting the ETFs `fund_name` field containing the word `asia`. You can see that there are 5 ETFs with the `fund_name` field containing the word `asia`:

The field capabilities API

If you don't know much about the indexed fields, you can use this `_field_caps` API to familiarize yourself with the features of using the fields. Five topics are reported, including `searchable`, `aggregatable`, `indices`, `non_searchable_indices`, and `non_aggregatable_indices`. The topics names are self-explanatory, except the fact that the term `indices` refers to the name of the indices that own the field. Now, let's take a look at the `fund name` and `category` fields of the ETF documents. In the following screenshot, you can see that the `fund_name` field is `searchable`, but not `aggregateable`, because it is in the `text` datatype.

On the other hand, the `category` field is `searchable` and `aggregatable` because it is in the keyword data type:

Profiler

Through profiling, you can get very specific details pertaining to the steps in the query process. In order to obtain all these details, many low-level methods are utilized to provide a breakdown of the time spent analyzing each step. You may improve your query after you fully understand the anatomy of your query in depth. Let's look at a simple example and give a brief explanation. We want to search those ETFs containing the word `ishares` in the `fund_name` field, and the word `global` in the `description` field. In the following screenshot, you can see that the original compound `bool` query is decomposed into two `Term` child queries. One query is designed to search the `fund_name` field containing the word `ishares`, while the other query is designed to search the `description` field containing the word `global`.

The time spent is reported in the `time_in_nanos` field:

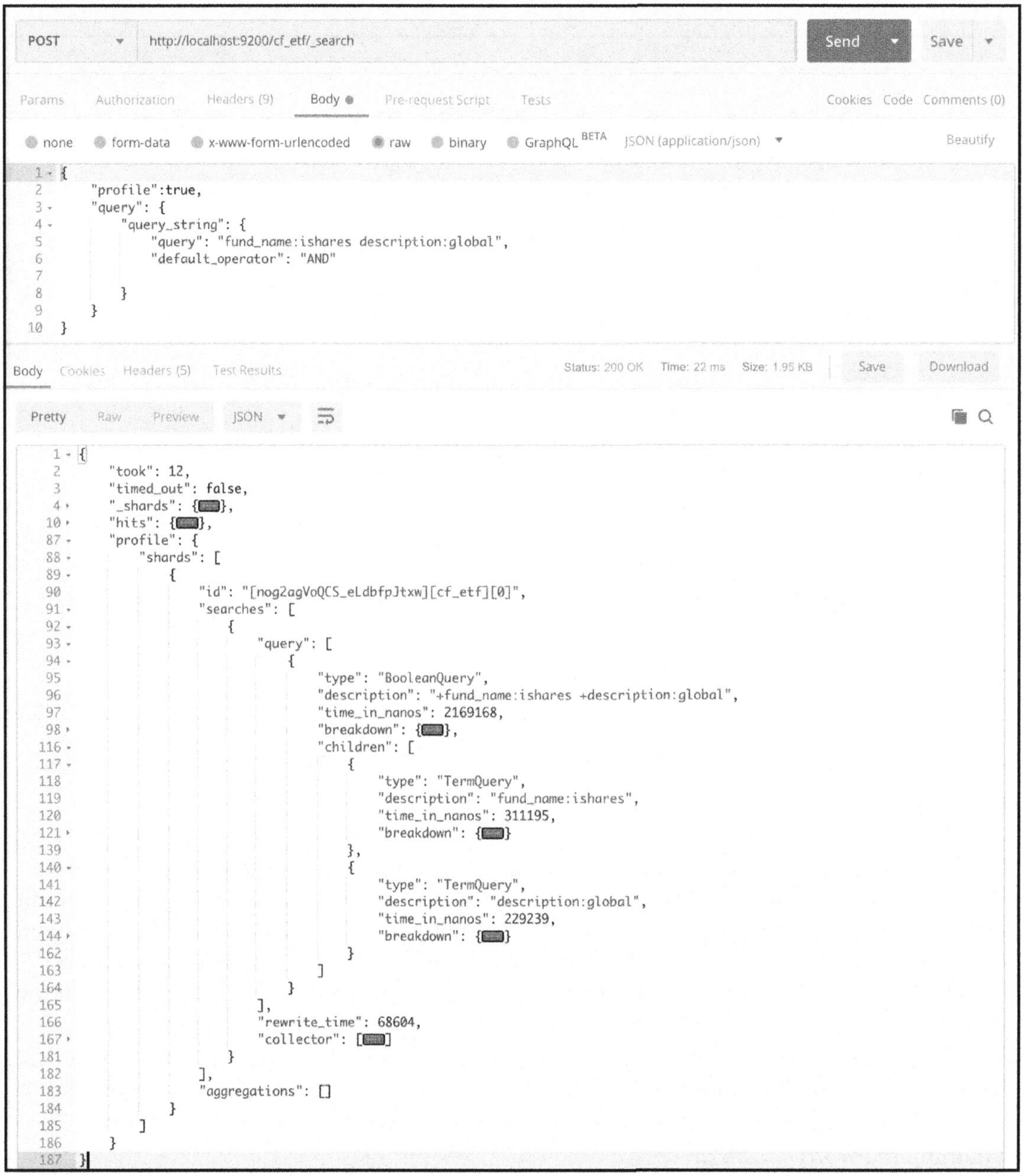

Now, let's expand the breakdown field of the `fund_name:ishares` child query to take a look. The total time spent on the `fund_name:ishares` term query is 311195 nanoseconds. If you total the numbers from the breakdown analysis, it is exactly the same. For each term in the breakdown, any users who are interested can `https://www.elastic.co/guide/en/elasticsearch/reference/7.0/search-profile-queries.html`:

```
"children": [
    {
        "type": "TermQuery",
        "description": "fund_name:ishares",
        "time_in_nanos": 311195,
        "breakdown": {
            "match_count": 0,
            "shallow_advance_count": 3,
            "next_doc": 0,
            "match": 0,
            "next_doc_count": 0,
            "score_count": 4,
            "compute_max_score_count": 4,
            "compute_max_score": 13939,
            "advance": 12445,
            "advance_count": 15,
            "score": 7760,
            "build_scorer_count": 3,
            "create_weight": 171126,
            "shallow_advance": 4894,
            "create_weight_count": 1,
            "build_scorer": 101001
        }
    },
```

Suggesters

The suggester is widely used in search solutions that improve a user's experience. This search feature is based on suggesting similar terms using the text provided by the suggester. There are four types of suggesters—term, phrase, completion, and context. Let's briefly look at each one in turn:

- **Term suggester**: This returns a list of possible suggestions with corrected terms. The following screenshot is an example of obtaining the suggestions from two suggesters. One suggester recommends searching for the term `asian` from the `fund_name` field, while the other recommends searching for the term `stock` from the `description` field.

You can see that use of the word `asia`, instead of `asian`, in the query is recommended:

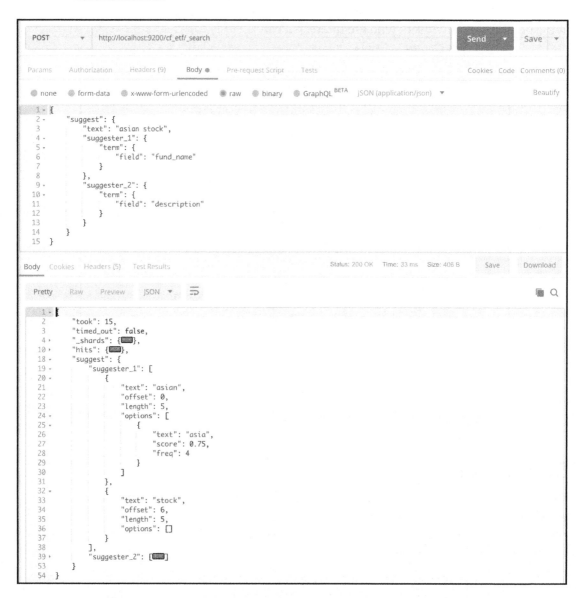

- **Phrase suggester**: This returns a list of possible corrected phrases for suggestions. This suggester is developed from the term suggester. It provides a flexible token selection methodology based on frequency and concurrency. The following screenshot is an example of obtaining the suggestions corresponding to a misspelled phrase, `divide weigh index`. You can see that several phrases are suggested. The suggested phrase `dividend weight index`, has the highest ranking:

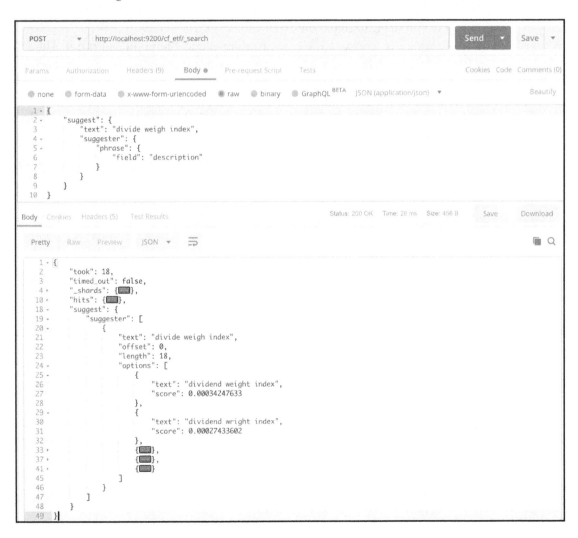

- **Completion suggester**: This provides a way of giving a suggestion to complete the typing for the user. To use the completion suggester, you must first specify the field with the `completion` type in the mappings. However, building and providing this functionality is costly. Let's look at an example where we change the `fund_name` field from the text type to the completion type. You can download three files, `cf_etf_suggester_bulk.json`, `cf_etf_suggester_mappings.json`, and `cf_etf_suggester_bulk_index.sh` from the aforementioned GitHub site in this chapter. You need to make the `bash` file, `cf_etf_suggester_bulk_index.sh`, runnable, and then you can run it. The `bash` file first deletes the `cf_etf_suggester` index if it exists. Then, it creates the `cf_etf_suggester` index with the mappings and settings. Finally, it indexes the 314 ETFs. In the following screenshot, the mapping of the `cf_etf_suggester` index is shown. You can see that the `fund_name` field is of the `completion` type:

Now we are ready to use the `completion` suggester. Let's try to get a suggestion for finding ETFs with the `fund_name` field containing the `ishares edge` prefix from the suggester. In the following screenshot, a list of ETFs with names starting with `iShares Edge` is provided by way of a suggestion. While the search text is typed by the user, search-as-you-type functionality can be provided to complete the typing from the choices provided by the suggester:

- **Context suggester**: You can associate a suggester with different contexts, for example, in short-term investment or in mid-term investment. First of all, you need to specify a list of contexts in the mappings and index the documents with the contexts so that you can search with those contexts. We will not delve into the details. Any interested users can refer to the `https://www.elastic.co/guide/en/elasticsearch/reference/7.0/suggester-context.html`.

Summary

What a lengthy chapter! Our excuse is the slogan of Elasticsearch—*You know, for Search*. Elasticsearch supports many features, and the search functionality is one of the most important topics. We have experienced different types of searches, from term-based to full-text; from exact search to fuzzy search; from a single field search to a multi-search, and then to a compound search. In short, we have explored every avenue from a simple query to a complex query. We also learned a lot about the query DSL and search-related APIs.

In the next chapter, we will focus on data modeling techniques, and some of the most common problems in data modeling and their solutions involving a variety of techniques, including the use of nested objects and parent-child relationships to process related documents. Let's see how we will resolve the data modeling issue when Elasticsearch only has minimal support for the relationship between documents.

2
Section 2: Data Modeling, Aggregations Framework, Pipeline, and Data Analytics

In this section, you will look into data modeling, the aggregations framework, and preprocessing documents in pipelines. You will also learn how to use Elasticsearch for exploratory data analysis.

This section is comprised the following chapters:

- Chapter 7, *Modeling Your Data in the Real World*
- Chapter 8, *Aggregation Frameworks*
- Chapter 9, *Preprocessing Documents in Ingest Pipelines*
- Chapter 10, *Using Elasticsearch for Exploratory Data Analysis*

Modeling Your Data in the Real World

7

In the previous chapter, we have discussed different aspects of search APIs. We started from using a simple URI search and request body search. We investigated the Query DSL to learn how to write high-quality queries. We practiced troubleshooting techniques with the Profile API, the Validate API, the Explain API, and completion suggested and completed a detailed example of search-as-you-type feature. Since we know how to search now, we need to step back and think about the design of data modeling. In this chapter, we will discuss data modeling when using Elasticsearch.

Elasticsearch is a distributed, document-oriented NoSQL database for storing, retrieving, and managing document-oriented or semi-structured data. Basically, a document is stored with minimal support for relationships between documents. This chapter focuses on some of most common issues users encounter when working with different techniques. This chapter will help you to understand some conventions and get insights for the real-world examples of denormalizing complex objects and designing and creating data structures by using nested objects to handle relationships.

Before we jump into modeling data, we will first expand our ETF system to involve the historical price information for the current documents. After that, we can perform practical data modeling. By the end of this chapter, we will have covered the following topics:

- The Investor Exchange Cloud
- Modeling data and the approaches
- Practical considerations

The Investor Exchange Cloud

IEX (**Investor Exchange**) Cloud (`https://iexcloud.io/`) is a new platform from IEX Group that is separated from the original Exchange site (`https://iextrading.com/developer/docs/`). This platform provides free access to developers and engineers to the Exchange. It can be used to build high-quality application and services. There is a lot of information in different aspects, and we will try to push our system forward one step at a time. To run the sample programs, go to the IEX Cloud login site (`https://www.iexcloud.io/cloud-login#/register`) to register a free account. Besides the different URL we will use, it also requires a token generated by the system to send out with the request. The publishable token is the one to be used in the request. A registered user can find a token a `https://iexcloud.io/console/tokens` as shown in the following screenshot:

Users should go to (`https://iexcloud.io/docs/api/` to get more information from the IEX Cloud before we start next section.

If you have **exchange-traded fund (ETFs)** stock, you can get the distribution in the form of dividends. IEX provides an API to retrieve dividends information based on the symbol (ticker). The returned data format is described in the following table:

Key	Datatype	Description
exDate	string	On the date, you must have owned the ETF in order to receive the next scheduled dividend.
paymentDate	string	On the date, the dividend checks will be mailed out.
recordDate	string	On or before the date, ETF ownership should be registered in order to receive dividends.
declaredDate	string	On the date, the next dividend payment date will be announced.
amount	number	This is the payment amount.

flag	string	This is additional information about the dividend.
currency	string	This is the currency of the dividend.
description	string	This is the description of the dividend event.
frequency	string	This indicates the frequency of the dividend.
date	string	This indicates the date of the query performed. It will be removed from the records.

To get the dividend information, we take an example to retrieve such information for the `ACWF` ETF within five years, as shown in the following screenshot:

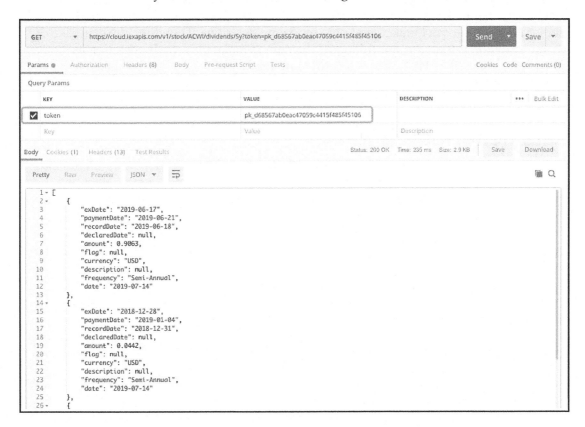

We discover that the results are in an array of each dividend announcement. For some reasons, the `flag`, `description`, and `declaredDate` fields are null. The data of the `amount` field is a `float` datatype and the data of `declaredDate`, `exDate`, `paymentDate` and `recordDate` are in `Date` string format. We will start discussing different approaches to data modeling using IEX data in the next section.

Modeling data and the approaches

The common way of data modeling for relational database is to reduce data redundancy and improve data integrity by using a normalization process. However, Elasticsearch is not ;a relational database and, as such, data modeling does not apply to it. Like most NoSQL databases, Elasticsearch treats the real world as a flat world, which means each document is independent. Basically, a single document should include all of the information used to determine whether it matches a search request. To bridge the gap between two worlds, several common techniques of data modeling are used in Elasticsearch. We'll discuss data denormalization, inner objects, nested objects, and join datatypes in the following sub-sections. No matter what kinds of technique you use, if you don't know the query that the user is running, you can't make good data modeling decisions. Therefore, the general recommendation is that you should model the data to make the search operation as lightweight as possible. We'll introduce different approaches to model this data and perform search requests on it.

Data denormalization

To denormalize data is to establish relationships by keeping one or more redundant fields in each document to maintain a flat structure. Since each document contains all of the information needed to determine whether the query is met, additional joins of the documents among the indices can be avoided. The advantage of data denormalization is speed. Let's try to practice data denormalization to expand our system. In our GitHub repository (`https://github.com/PacktPublishing/Mastering-Elasticsearch-7.0/tree/master/Chapter07`), you can download two files, `cf_etf_dividend_denormalize_bulk.json` and `cf_etf_dividend_denormalize_bulk_index.sh`. You need to make the bash file runnable and then you can run it to index these documents.

We will use the default settings and dynamic mapping to create an index named `cf_etf_dividend_denormalize`. There is a sample ETF, `ACWF`, in the `cf_etf_dividend_denormalize_bulk.json` file. We have separated each dividend record manually as a document using the IEX data. There are `10` dividend records with the `ACWF` ETF. We have also associated the corresponding `symbol` field and value with each ETF. Let's take a look at the dynamic mapping of the `cf_etf_dividend_denormalize` index generated by Elasticsearch after indexing, as shown in the following screenshot:

GET ▼ http://localhost:9200/cf_etf_dividend_denormalize/_mappings Send ▼ Save ▼

Params Authorization Headers (8) **Body** Pre-request Script Tests Cookies Code Comments (0)

● none ○ form-data ○ x-www-form-urlencoded ○ raw ○ binary ○ GraphQL BETA

This request does not have a body

Body Cookies Headers (5) Test Results Status: 200 OK Time: 10 ms Size: 363 B Save Download

Pretty Raw Preview JSON ▼

```
1  {
2      "cf_etf_dividend_denormalize": {
3          "mappings": {
4              "properties": {
5                  "amount": {
6                      "type": "float"
7                  },
8                  "currency": {
9                      "type": "text",
10                     "fields": {
11                         "keyword": {
12                             "type": "keyword",
13                             "ignore_above": 256
14                         }
15                     }
16                 },
17                 "exDate": {
18                     "type": "date"
19                 },
20                 "frequency": {
21                     "type": "text",
22                     "fields": {
23                         "keyword": {
24                             "type": "keyword",
25                             "ignore_above": 256
26                         }
27                     }
28                 },
29                 "paymentDate": {
30                     "type": "date"
31                 },
32                 "recordDate": {
33                     "type": "date"
34                 },
35                 "symbol": {
36                     "type": "text",
37                     "fields": {
38                         "keyword": {
39                             "type": "keyword",
40                             "ignore_above": 256
41                         }
42                     }
43                 }
44             }
45         }
46     }
47  }
```

The dynamic mapping automatically assigns data types based on the field values. Now, we will look at an example to retrieve documents from the index made by denormalization data modeling. declaredDate, flag, and description do not appear in the dynamic mapping since they all have a null value. This test is to find the documents with a compound bool query. Three must criteria are that the symbol must be ACWF, the exDate field on or before 2016-02-01, and the amount field greater or equal to 0.1. We use a range query with the field name specified as .exDate and amount for a search in the cf_etf_dividend_denormalize index. As shown in the following screenshot, two hits are retrieved:

It is simple to use denormalized data to solve the relationship. However, if you need to perform a query involving more than one index such as `cf_etf` and `cf_etf_hist_price`, you have no way to do it just simply using the denormalize approach. An alternative is to use a ;nested object datatype to index the document. We'll discuss this approach in a later sub-section.

Using an array of objects datatype

As we have discussed in the previous sub-section, additional work is required to manually separate dividend records into a document to perform indexing. Another way is to embed all dividend records from the ETF into a parent document using an array of objects. In this approach, you need not index a lot of documents for a single ETF. However, when a new dividend is announced to an ETF, you need to update the corresponding document. Since the frequency of distributing dividend for ETFs is not that high, it seems that this approach may be the most suitable approach.

Let's practice using an array of objects to expand our system. From the aforementioned GitHub site (`https://github.com/PacktPublishing/Mastering-Elasticsearch-7.0/tree/master/Chapter07`), you can download two other files, `cf_etf_dividend_bulk.json` and `cf_etf_dividend_io_bulk_index.sh`. There are 4 sample ETFs, *ACWF*, ACWI, ACWV and AGGY, in the `cf_etf_dividend_bulk.json` file. We will use default settings and dynamic mapping to create the index, named `cf_etf_io_dividend`. After running the bash file, the documents in the `cf_etf_dividend_bulk.json` file are indexed into the `cf_etf_io_dividend` index.

Let's take a look at the dynamic mapping of the `cf_etf_dividend_io` index, as shown in the following screenshot:

We add a field, named `announcement`, to denote the array of dividend and associate the corresponding `symbol` field and value for each ETF. As we know, there is no array type support in Elasticsearch. Instead, any field can contain zero or more values. Hence, we can see that the `announcement` field is an object.

Now, we will look at an example to retrieve documents from the index made by an array of object datatype modeling. This test is to find the ACWF ETF in the `cf_etf_dividend_io` index with the same criteria used in the previous sub-section. The only difference in the query is that you must use the long format field names. The long format field name is specified with a prefix `announcement`, which means the `exDate` and `amount` fields are inside the `announcement` object. As shown in the following screenshot, one hit is retrieved and it is the ACWF ETF:

You can see that `announcement` is an array type containing all dividend records of the ETF.

Let's use another example to remind you of the behavior of using an array of objects. You cannot query each object independently of the other objects in the array. For example, there is no record of the `ACWF` ETF meeting the criteria with `exDate` on or before `2015-12-01` and the `amount` greater or equal to `0.2`. The returned result shouldn't be a hit. However, you still get one hit in the result, as shown in the following screenshot:

Why? It is because arrays of objects are flattened into multi-value format of the object's fields and the search is performed on the match of each field, as follows:

```
"announcement":[
    "exDate":[...],
    "amount":[...].
    "paymentDate":[...],
    ...
]
```

The incorrect match is caused by the flattening; therefore, you cannot search for each individual object from the array of objects. If you want it on purpose for a search, you need to use the `nested` datatype, as described in the next sub-section.

Nested object mapping datatypes

The dividend records of an ETF has a one-to-one relationship to the origin `cf_etf` index. It will be easy to embed the whole dividend records to the `cf_etf` index. Using a `nested` object datatype will make each object indexed as a separate hidden document internally. Let's add the `announcement` object field in the mappings of the `cf_etf` index and then change the `announcement` field from an object type to a `nested` object type, as follows:

```
{
    "mappings": {
        "dynamic": false,
        "properties": {
            "symbol": {"type": "keyword"},
            "fund_name": {"type": "text"},
            ...
            "announcement":{
                "type":"nested",
                    "properties": {
                        ...
```

In the GitHub repository of this chapter (`https://github.com/PacktPublishing/ Mastering-Elasticsearch-7.0/tree/master/Chapter07`), there are another three files, `cf_etf_dividend_nested_mappings.json`, `cf_etf_dividend_nested_bulk.js on`, and `cf_etf_dividend_nested_bulk_index.sh`, for you to download to practice the `nested` object type. You can run the bash shell file to create the `cf_etf_dividend_nested` index and perform indexing for the 10 selected ETFs in `cf_etf_dividend_nested_bulk.json`. Let's issue the same search request to find the `ACWF` ETF with `exDate` on or before `2015-12-01` and the `amount` field greater or equal to `0.2` again. As shown in the following screenshot, the search result is correct now:

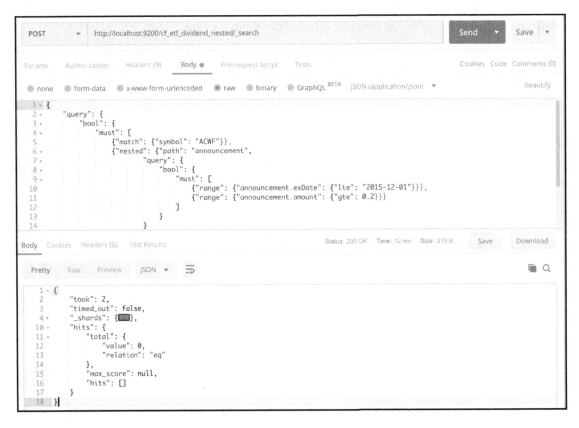

No hit is returned in the result. As you can see, you must use the nested query on the fields of the `nested` object type.

If you change the `amount` field criteria in the query to greater or equal to `0.1`, then you will get a hit with one document returned, as shown in the following screenshot:

```
none   form-data   x-www-form-urlencoded   raw   binary   GraphQL BETA   JSON (application/json)  ▼                                    Beautify
 1 ▾ {
 2 ▾   "query": {
 3 ▾     "bool": {
 4 ▾       "must": [
 5             {"match": {"symbol": "ACWF"}},
 6 ▾           {"nested": {"path": "announcement",
 7 ▾             "query": {
 8 ▾               "bool": {
 9 ▾                 "must": [
10                     {"range": {"announcement.exDate": {"lte": "2015-12-01"}}},
11                     {"range": {"announcement.amount": {"gte": 0.1}}}
12                   ]
13               }
```

```
Body   Cookies   Headers (3)   Test Results                              Status: 200 OK   Time: 23ms   Size: 1.03 KB   Save Response ▼

 Pretty   Raw   Preview   JSON ▾

  1  {
  2      "took": 11,
  3      "timed_out": false,
  4      "_shards": {-
  9      },
 10      "hits": {
 11          "total": {
 12              "value": 1,
 13              "relation": "eq"
 14          },
 15          "max_score": 3.9924302,
 16          "hits": [
 17              {
 18                  "_index": "cf_etf_dividend_nested",
 19                  "_type": "_doc",
 20                  "_id": "W1SKt2wBfLrb-Hyw96hM",
 21                  "_score": 3.9924302,
 22                  "_source": {
 23                      "symbol": "ACWF",
 24                      "fund_name": "iShares Edge MSCI Multifactor Global ETF",
 25                      "rating": 3,
 26                      "morningstar_category": "World Large Stock",
 27                      "category": "Equity",
 28                      "family": "iShares",
 29                      "market_cap": "large",
 30                      "description": "The investment seeks to track the investment results of the MSCI ACWI Diversified Multiple-Factor Index.
 31                      "exchange": "NYSE Arca",
 32                      "announcement": [
 33                          {-
 43                          },
 44                          {-
 54                          },
 55                          {-
 65                          },
 66                          {-
 76                          },
 77                          {-
 87                          },
 88                          {-
 98                          },
 99                          {-
109                          }
110                      ]
```

However, you do not know which nested object causes the match since all nested objects are returned because you can see the whole `announcement` array in the response body.

If you want to check which nested object causes the actual match, you can use the `inner_hits` parameter to embed those documents in the response body. You can also use options such as form, size, and sort to control the number of documents returned. Let's use the same preceding example and add an extra `inner_hits` parameter. In the following screenshot, you can see the response body got the `inner_hits` field, which only shows the actual match document with the `exDate` field at `2015-06-25` and `amount` is `0.111075`:

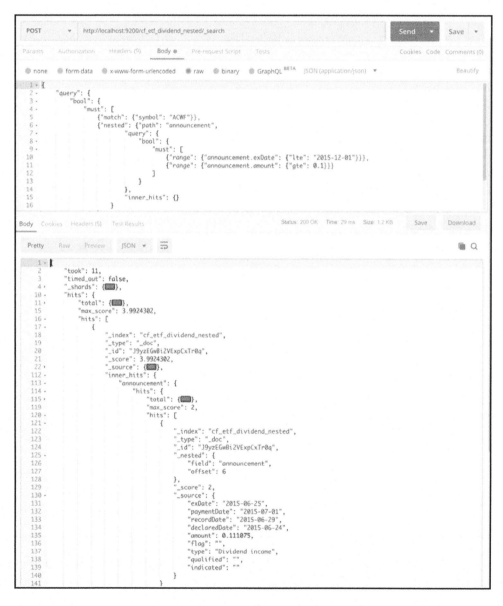

Join datatypes

If you recall in the *Field datatype* section of `Chapter 4`, *Mapping APIs*, Elasticsearch supports a special datatype called `join` to create a simple or multiple-level parent/child relationship in documents of the same index. You can define a set of possible relationships in the document with a parent field and a child field. We can establish a one-to-one relationship with the announcement, which is an array of dividend records, or a one-to-many relationship with each individual dividend record. According to the recommendations, you should only use the `join` datatype when your data contains a one-to-many relationship and the number of entities in many side significantly exceeds the other. Since there is a kind of ETF called a dividend-paying ETF, which gets dividends paid at a higher frequency, we will use the `join` datatype to expand our system.

To make it easier for understand, we look at an example of using `ACWF` as the sample ETF, in which it has got seven dividend records. From the aforementioned GitHub repository, there are four files, `cf_etf_dividend_join_mappings.json`, `cf_etf_acwf_join.json`, `cf_etf_dividend_join_bulk.json`, and `cf_etf_dividend_join_bulk_index.sh` for you to download to practice the `join` datatype. You can run the bash shell file to create the `cf_etf_dividend_join` index with the mappings in which a `cf_etf_dividend` relation is defined between the `cf_etf` and `dividend` entities, as shown in the following screenshot:

For simplicity, we use only one ETF, `ACWF`, for the parent document. After the `cf_etf_dividend_join` index is created, the bash shell file will index the parent document (`cf_etf_acwf_join.json`), as shown in the following screenshot:

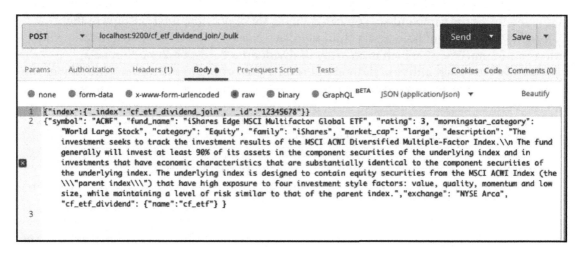

Since we use bash script to perform the indexing operation, we use a known document identifier, `12345678`, for indexing so that the known document identifier can be used to indicate the parent document when indexing the child document. It is not necessary to do so when you work on programming.

After the parent document is indexed, we index the child documents
(cf_etf_dividend_join_bulk.json). There are 10 dividend records with
the ACWF ETF; therefore, there are seven indexing operations in the _bulk operation. The
following screenshot shows the _bulk operation for indexing these seven dividend records
with the routing value:

Since it is required that the parent and the child documents must be indexed on the same
shard, the routing value is required. Recall that the default routing value is the document
identifier, which is 12345678 in this case.

Parent ID query

The goal of this type of query is to find a child document associated with the specified parent ID and the join child type. In the following screenshot, you can see that there are seven hits for the parent document with the `12345678` identifier and the join child of the `dividend` type:

has_child query

The goal of this type of query is to find the parent documents associated with a child type and meet the criteria of the children. It can be read as *which parents have children that meet the criteria?* Let's see an example to find parent documents that have the `dividend` child relation and its child document has a `currency` field equal to `USD`. As shown in the following screenshot, our sample `ACWF` ETF meets these criteria:

has_parent query

The goal of this type of query is to find the child documents that are associated with a parent type and meet the criteria of the parent. It can be read as *which children have a parent that meets the criteria*? Let's take an example to find child documents that have the `cf_etf` parent relation and the parent's `symbol` is `ACWF`. As shown in the following screenshot, all `10` records meet these criteria:

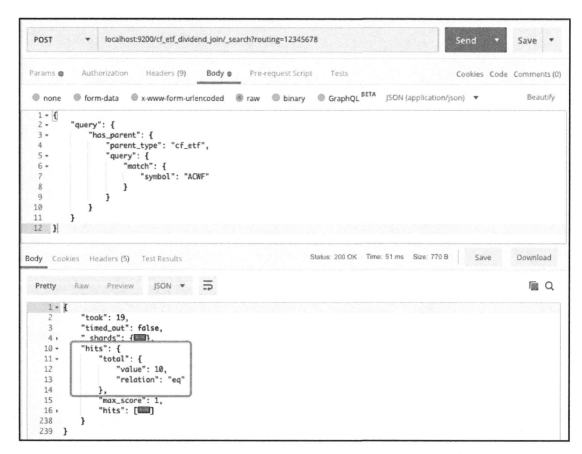

So far, we have introduced different approaches for data modeling and we will give a brief practical overview in the next section.

Practical considerations

For `join` datatypes, the parent allows re-indexing/adding/deleting specific children. However, using `has_child` or `has_parent` queries can have a significant impact on performance. If you need better performance, always use nested datatypes. Nonetheless, as long as you have to update, you need to re-index all children to their parent. The `nested` datatype approach is also easier to manage than the `join` datatype approach. You must be very careful while using the `join` datatype method because you can index children without a parent. Also, if you want to remove a parent, it is not an automatic cascading task to delete all of its children. You need to clean it up by yourself. On the other hand, if you want to update parent or child document, the `join` datatypes approach will be more convenient because you can update the values in the parent field or the child field. For `nested` datatypes, you can't just change one nested value in a nested field. You must re-index all of the nested values in the nested field.

Summary

In this chapter, we used different techniques from Elasticsearch to gain insight about data modeling using real-world examples from IEX. We used the same examples to practice with different techniques. From the general recommendation, using data denormalization can provide easier management and maintenance and compose queries for search.

In the next chapter, we will introduce the aggregation framework. Aggregation can be thought of as a technique to build analytics on a set of documents. The framework consists of many building blocks that can be combined to build a complex summary of the data selected by the search query. There are many different types of aggregations, and we will cover the common methods, such as metric aggregation, bucket aggregation, pipeline aggregation, and matrix aggregation.

8
Aggregation Frameworks

The two key features of Elasticsearch are search and data analytics. In the previous two chapters, we learned about the search API and how to design search data modeling. We also used real-world examples from the **Investor Exchange (IEX)** Cloud ETF system to practice using the search feature. In this chapter, we will discuss data analytics using the aggregation framework. Aggregation can be thought of as a unit of work for building analytic information on a set of documents. The framework consists of many building blocks that can be composed to build a complex summary of the data selected by a search query. The framework is straightforward, simple, extensible, quick to access, and awesome. It can be very helpful for our business.

By the end of this chapter, we will have covered the following topics and used IEX historical ETF data to work on supported aggregation types:

- Aggregation query syntax
- Matrix aggregations
- Metrics aggregations
- Bucket aggregations
- Pipeline aggregations
- Post filter on aggregations

ETF historical data preparation

In the previous chapter, we introduced dividend data from IEX. IEX also provides historical data such as the closing price, opening price, highest price, lowest price, and closing price change. The following screenshot will show the historical price responses from IEX. We will retrieve one month of `ACWF` ETF data:

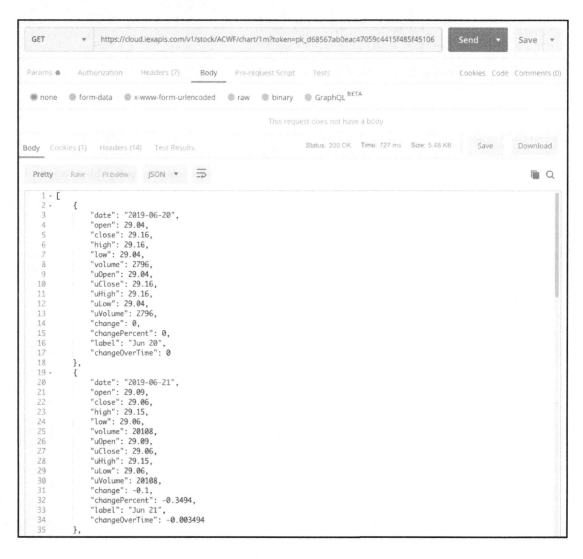

We list each returned field and give a short description for each one in the following table:

Field	Type	Description
date	date	The trading date
open	float	The adjusted opening price of the ETF on that date
high	float	The adjusted highest price of the ETF on that date
low	float	The adjusted lowest price of the ETF on that date
close	float	The adjusted closing price of the ETF on that date
volume	long	The adjusted daily trading volumes traded on that date
change	float	The closing price change between the trading day and the previous trading day
changePercent	float	The ratio of the closing price change between the trading day and the previous trading day
label	text	The given label Month Day of the trading date
changeOverTime	float	The percentage of the closing price change between the trading day and the first reported trading day
uVolume, uHigh, uLow, uOpen, uClose,	float	The unadjusted data corresponding to volume, high, low, open, and close on that date. These fields will not be used in the example.

In our GitHub repository (https://github.com/PacktPublishing/Mastering-Elasticsearch-7.0/tree/master/Chapter08), we can download three files, cf_etf_hist_price_bulk.json, cf_etf_hist_price_mappings.json, and cf_etf_hist_price_bulk_index.sh. We need to make the Bash file runnable and then we can run it to index those documents. We will use the default settings and static mapping from cf_etf_hist_price_mappings.json to create an index, named cf_etf_hist_price. All three figures of month data of 314 ETFs, starting from 2018-12-26 to 2019-03-25 and compiled for bulk index operations, are put in the cf_etf_hist_price_bulk.json file. We have separated each record manually as a document. We have also associated the corresponding symbol field and value with each ETF. We can use the _count API to count the total records, which is 19,141 in the cf_etf_hist_price index.

Let's take a look at the search all results from the `cf_etf_hist_price` index as shown in the following screenshot:

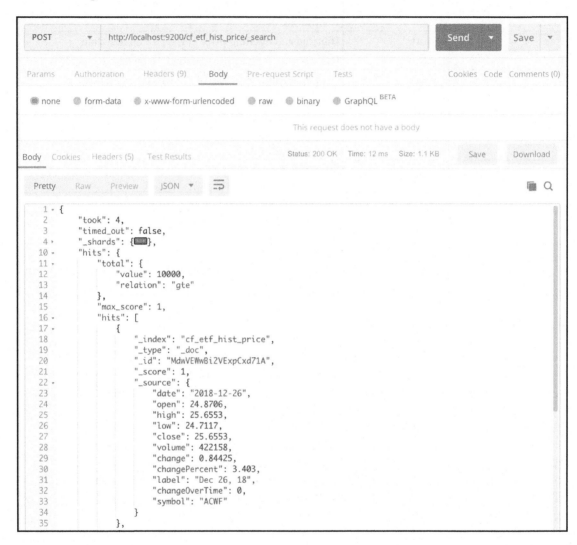

We can see that `10000` hits are reported. This is the default value of the maximum result window size setting, `index.max_result_window`, for the search results. If we want more search results, we should search with the `scroll` parameter as we described in Chapter 6, *Search APIs*. In the next section, we will introduce the basic syntax of the aggregation query.

Aggregation query syntax

The following code block in regular expression syntax demonstrates the basic structure of the aggregation query syntax:

```
"aggs":{
    "name_1": {
        "type": { body }
            [,"aggs" : {[sub aggregation]+}]?
    }
    [,"name_2":{...}]*
}
```

We can have multiple aggregations in one shot. In addition, if we have to use complex aggregation logic to solve a problem, we may use sub-aggregations. The `aggs` keyword is the short form of the `aggregations` keyword. The `name_1` word is the name of the aggregation. Elasticsearch supports more than one aggregation on the same level, such as `name_2`. The `type` word is used to define the type of the aggregation such as terms, stats, and range. The `body` word specifies the criteria of the aggregation.

One of the powerful features of aggregations is the ability to embed aggregations. The inner `aggs` keyword tells Elasticsearch to begin a new aggregation known as a sub-aggregation. The syntax of the parent aggregation and the sub-aggregation are the same. Sub-aggregation operates in the context of the individual buckets from the previous level's aggregations. The sub-aggregation allows us to continuously refine the aggregates to any number of levels. We'll learn about matrix aggregation, which provides intermediate data statistics, in the next section.

Matrix aggregations

Matrix aggregations is a family of functions, which is still being developed to provide a way to manipulate multiple fields at the same time and generate results for the fields in a matrix form. Matrix stats is the only type supported in matrix aggregations since version 5.0.

Matrix stats

This aggregation computes the numeric statistics on a set of given document fields, as shown in the following table:

Statistics measure	Description
count	The number of samples measured.
mean	The average value of the field measured from the sample.
variance	How far the values of the field measured are spread out from its mean value. The larger the variance, the more spread from its mean value.
skewness	This describes the shape of the distribution. The asymmetry measure of the distribution of the field's values.
kurtosis	This describes the shape of the distribution. It measures the tail heaviness of the distribution. As the tail becomes lighter, kurtosis decreases. As the tail becomes heavier, kurtosis increases.
covariance	A measure of the joint variability between two fields. A positive value means their values move in the same direction and vice versa.
correlation	A measure of the strength of the relationship between two fields. The valid values are between [−1, 1]. A value of −1 means the value is negatively correlated and a value of 1 means it is positively correlated. A value of 0 means there is no identifiable relationship between them.

Let's take an example to get a statistics report using the matrix_stats aggregation for the volume and changePercent fields of the ACWF ETF in the cf_etf_hist_price index. As shown in the following screenshot, we have used a request body query to only restrict the statistics on the ACWF ETF:

```
POST    ▼    http://localhost:9200/cf_etf_hist_price/_search                    Send ▼   Save ▼
```

Params   Authorization   Headers (9)   Body ●   Pre-request Script   Tests   Cookies Code Comments (0)

● none   ● form-data   ● x-www-form-urlencoded   ● raw   ● binary   ● GraphQL BETA   JSON (application/json) ▼   Beautify

```
1 ▾ {   "size": 0,
2       "query": { "match": { "symbol": "ACWF"}},
3 ▾     "aggs": {
4 ▾         "statistics": {
5 ▾             "matrix_stats": {
6                   "fields": ["volume", "changePercent"]
7               }
8           }
9       }
10  }
```

Body Cookies Headers (5) Test Results   Status: 200 OK Time: 35 ms Size: 588 B   Save   Download

Pretty   Raw   Preview   JSON ▼   ⇥   ▣ Q

```
1 ▾ {
2       "took": 23,
3       "timed_out": false,
4 ▸     "_shards": {▨},
10 ▸    "hits": {▨},
18 ▾    "aggregations": {
19 ▾        "statistics": {
20             "doc_count": 61,
21 ▾            "fields": [
22 ▾                {
23                     "name": "volume",
24                     "count": 61,
25                     "mean": 93711.57377049184,
26                     "variance": 51154224255.54864,
27                     "skewness": 4.2285941836425796,
28                     "kurtosis": 22.107908567115107,
29 ▾                   "covariance": {
30                         "volume": 51154224255.54864,
31                         "changePercent": 44266.72083865841
32                     },
33 ▾                   "correlation": {
34                         "volume": 1,
35                         "changePercent": 0.2097465625424968
36                     }
37                 },
38 ▾                {
39                     "name": "changePercent",
40                     "count": 61,
41                     "mean": 0.2386393414535482,
42                     "variance": 0.870729977029517,
43                     "skewness": 0.5615966340353099,
44                     "kurtosis": 5.479469502967177,
45 ▾                   "covariance": {
46                         "volume": 44266.72083865841,
47                         "changePercent": 0.870729977029517
48                     },
49 ▾                   "correlation": {
50                         "volume": 0.2097465625424968,
51                         "changePercent": 1
52                     }
53                 }
54             ]
55         }
56     }
```

There are 61 documents, within three months, involved in the computation. We use the `size:0` parameter to suppress the content of the hits returned. We only show the results for the `changePercent` field.

From the `covariance` and `correlation` values, we can tell that there is a positive relationship ($\approx$ 44,266) between the `volume` and `changePercent` fields and the relationship is weak ($\approx$ 0.2097).

There are four families of aggregations. We have presented two of them. The other three families are big and include a lot of different types of aggregations. In the following section, we'll introduce metrics aggregations, which contain simple data statistics.

Metrics aggregations

The metrics aggregations family provides common uses of functions to perform simple mathematical operations on values in one or more fields, and help to analyze grouped sets of documents. We will illustrate each type of aggregation in the metrics family using the fields from the `cf_etf`, `cf_etf_hist_price`, and `cf_etf_dividend` indexes in the following subsections.

avg

Compute the average of the numeric field value of the records. The following example aims to find the average change of the ACWF ETF in the `cf_etf_hist_price` index, and the value is `0.0624`:

```
"query": { "match": { "symbol": "ACWF"}},"aggs":
{"acwf_avg_close_price":{"avg": { "field": "change" }}}
```

weighted_avg

Compute the weighted average of two numeric field values according to the formula $\sum(field1*field2)/\sum(field2)$. This toy example treats the `volume` field as the weight and the `change` field as the value. The weighted average `change` field of the ACWF ETF in the `cf_etf_hist_price` index is `0.1815`:

```
"query": { "match": { "symbol": "ACWF"}},"aggs":
{"acwf_avg_change_with_vol_weight": {"weighted_avg": {"value":
{"field":"change"}, "weight": {"field": "volume"}}}}
```

cardinality

Obtain the number of unique field values. According to the reference (https://www.
elastic.co/guide/en/elasticsearch/reference/7.0/search-aggregations-metrics-
cardinality-aggregation.html), the total count is approximate. This example aims to find
the number of distinct morningstar categories in the cf_etf index. There are 80
categories:

```
"aggs": {"number_of_morningstar_category":{"cardinality": {"field":
morningstar_category"}}}
```

value_count

Obtain the number of records necessary for the field to exist. The example aims to find out
how many ETFs have been classified for market capitalization (exist
in the market_cap field) in the cf_etf index. There are 228 ETFs that have
the market_cap field:

```
"aggs": {"num_of_etfs_have_market_cap": {"value_count": {"field":
"market_cap"}}}
```

sum

Compute the summation of the numeric field value of the records. This example aims to
find the total dividends for the ACWF ETF in the cf_etf_dividend index. The total
dividend amount, sum_amount, is 1.6313:

```
"query": { "match": { "symbol": "ACWF"}},"aggs": {"sum_amount": {"sum":
{"field": "amount"}}}
```

min

Compute the minimum of the numeric field values of the records. This example aims to
find the minimum open price of the ACWF ETF in the cf_etf_hist_price index. The
minimum open price of the ACWF ETF is 24.8706:

```
"query": { "match": { "symbol": "ACWF"}},"aggs": {"minimum_open_price":
{"min": {"field": "open"}}}
```

max

Compute the maximum of the numeric field values of the records. This example aims to find the maximum open price of the ACWF ETF in the cf_etf_hist_price index. The maximum open price of the ACWF ETF is 29.51:

```
"query": { "match": { "symbol": "ACWF"}},"aggs": {"maximum_open_price":
{"max": {"field": "open"}}}
```

stats

Compute the min, max, sum, count, and avg of the numeric field values of the records in one shot. This example aims to find the stats value of the open price of the ACWF ETF in the cf_etf_hist_price index:

```
"query": { "match": { "symbol": "ACWF"}},"aggs": {"stats_open_price":
{"stats": {"field": "open"}}}
```

extended_stats

Compute the stats and sum_of_squares, variance, std_deviation, and std_deviation_bounds (±2 std_deviation from the mean) of the numeric field value of the records in one shot. This example aims to find the extend_stats value of the open price of the ACWF ETF in the cf_etf_hist_price index:

```
"query": { "match": { "symbol": "ACWF"}},"aggs":
{"extended_stats_open_price": {"extended_stats": {"field": "open"}}}
```

top_hit

This is commonly used to group documents together and then use the size to limit the groups generated from the top hits. It can be used as the buckets generator for top-level aggregation. This example aims to find the top five morningstar_category based on the number of ETFs in the cf_etf index. The top five categories are Diversified Emerging Mkts, Large Blend, Miscellaneous Region, Europe Stock, and Technology:

```
"aggs": {"category_top_hits": {"terms":
{"field":"morningstar_category","size": 5},"aggs":{"category_top_hits":
{"top_hits": {}}}}}
```

percentiles

Produce percentiles for the numeric field value of the records. The example aims to obtain the percentiles of the open price of the ACWF ETF in the cf_etf_hist_price index. The open price percentiles at *[1%,5%,25%,50%,75%,95%,99%]* are *[24.923, 25.7931, 27.3052, 28.47, 29.03, 29.4086, 29.5033]*:

```
"query": { "match": { "symbol": "ACWF"}},"aggs": {"open_price_percentiles":
{"percentiles": {"field":"open"}}}
```

percentile_ranks

Obtain the percentage of a given value in the percentiles generated from the numeric field value of the records. This example obtains a measure of the ACWF ETF at the open price of 28.5 in the cf_etf_hist_price index. The result is 51.29%:

```
"query": { "match": { "symbol":
"ACWF"}},"aggs":"open_price_percentile_rank: {
"percentile_ranks":{"field":"open","values":28.5}}
```

median_absolute_deviation

This is a measure of variance similar to the standard deviation to determine whether or not the data was distributed normally. The mathematical formula is the median absolute deviation ($|median(X) - X_i|$). This example aims to obtain such a measure of the ACWF ETF in the cf_etf_hist_price index. The result is 0.483:

```
"query": { "match": { "symbol": "ACWF"}},"aggs": {"med_change_percent":
{"median_absolute_deviation": { "field":"changePercent" }}}
```

geo_bound

Compute the bounding box from the geo_point field value of the records:

```
"aggs" : {"bounding_box" : {"geo_bounds" : {"field" : "field_1"}}}
```

geo_centroid

Compute the centroid from the `geo_point` field value of the records:

```
"aggs" : {"centroid" : {"geo_centroid" : {"field" : "field_1"}}}
```

scripted_metric

We execute the `scripted_metric` aggregation in four different stages: the init stage, the map stage, the combine stage, and the reduce stage. The corresponding script parameters are as follows:

- `init_script`: Optional parameter. A script for initialization, including an object named `state` to store the changes in the shard level.
- `map_script`: Required parameter. A script to perform at the document level if the document is included in the aggregation.
- `combine_script`: Required parameter. A script to perform in the shard level when all the documents are collected within a shard node. Finally, a value or an object is returned to the coordinating node.
- `reduce_script`: Required parameter. A script to perform in the coordinating node level when all the documents are collected from shard nodes. The named `states` object is the collection of the return results from the shard nodes.

The return value of the object from the scripts must be in one of the primitive types: the `string` type, the `map` type, or the `array` type. Let's take an example to find the maximum ratio of *changePercent/(changeOverTime*100)* for the ACWF ETF to demonstrate the `scripted_metric` aggregation. In the following screenshot, we can see that the `init_script` initializes an `ArrayList`:

map_script computes the ratio for each document. combine_script finds the maximum ratio in each shard node. reduce_script finds the maximum ratio from all shard nodes in the coordinating node. The maximum ratio is 2.7843.

Two more points should also be mentioned:

- We can write a script to generate the numeric field value and most aggregation types support it.
- The missing parameter can be used to deal with the missing value by assigning a predefined field value.

In the next section, we'll cover the largest family, bucket aggregation, which contains around 30 different types of aggregations.

Bucket aggregations

Bucket aggregation is a family that provides mechanisms for segmenting document sets into groups (buckets). Thus, each bucket is associated with a criterion, which determines whether the document in the current context *falls* into it. The following sections will illustrate each type of aggregation in the bucket family.

histogram

The purpose of the `histogram` aggregation is to group values into ranges with a fixed interval and count the documents. The starting range is 0 or a given offset. The range distance is specified by the `interval` value. The rounding formula is `bucket_key = Math.floor((value - offset) / interval) * interval + offset`. The `"extended_bounds" : {"min" : lv, "max" : uv}` parameter is used to specify the lower bound and upper bound of the buckets:

- **Example**: The purpose is to obtain the histogram of the `open` price of the `ACWF` ETF in the `cf_etf_hist_price` index, with `interval=1`, `min=24`, and `max=30`:

  ```
  "query": { "match": { "symbol": "ACWF"}},
  "aggs": { "acwf_histogram": {"histogram": {"field":
  "open","interval": 1,"extended_bounds": { "min":24, "max":30}}}}
  ```

- **Resulting buckets**: `key` is the `open` price:

  ```
  "acwf_histogram": {"buckets": [[{"key": 24,"doc_count": 1},{"key":
  25,"doc_count": 5},{"key": 26,"doc_count": 5},{"key":
  27,"doc_count": 10},{"key": 28,"doc_count": 22},{"key":
  29,"doc_count": 18},{"key": 30,"doc_count": 0}]]}
  ```

date_histogram

The purpose of the date histogram aggregation is to group date values into ranges with a fixed time unit interval and count the documents. The range distance is specified by the interval value in time units such as *millisecond, 1ms, Xms, second, 1s, Xms, minute, 1m, Xm, hour, 1h, Xh, day, 1d, Xd, week, 1w, month, 1M, quarter, 1q. year*, and *1y*, where *X* is a positive integer. We can use the `format` parameter to specify the custom date format. The starting value is respective to the time unit and we can use the `offset` parameter to adjust the starting value with ±`time_unit` to denote a positive or negative offset of the time unit:

- **Example**: The purpose is to obtain the monthly trading days of the ACWF ETF in the `cf_etf_hist_price` index:

```
"query": { "match": { "symbol": "ACWF"}},
"aggs":{"monthly_trading_days": {"date_histogram":{"field":
"date","interval": "month", format": "yyyy-MM-dd"}}}
```

- **Resulting buckets**: `key` is the timestamp and `key_as_string` is the date value according to the format:

```
"monthly_trading_days": {
"buckets": [[{"key_as_string": "2018-12-01","key":
1543622400000,"doc_count": 4}, {"key_as_string":
"2019-01-01","key": 1546300800000,"doc_count":
21},{"key_as_string": "2019-02-01","key":
1548979200000,"doc_count": 19},{"key_as_string":
"2019-03-01","key": 1551398400000,"doc_count": 17}]]}
```

auto_date_histogram

This is similar to the date histogram aggregation. The difference is using a given number of intervals (buckets) instead of the time interval:

- **Example**: The purpose is to obtain the monthly trading days of the ACWF ETF in the `cf_etf_hist_price` index. Since we already know that the data involves four months, we use `buckets=4`:

```
"query": { "match": { "symbol": "ACWF"}},
"aggs":{"monthly_trading_days": {
"auto_date_histogram":{"field": "date","buckets": "4","format":
"yyyy-MM-dd"}}}
```

- **Resulting buckets**: Same as the result in the date histogram aggregation example, but an additional parameter interval value is provided as `"interval":"1M"` denote monthly.

ranges

The purpose of the `ranges` aggregation is to group values into ranges and count the documents. Each range can be randomly defined by using the `from`/`to` keyword. Note that the `from` value is inclusive and the `to` value is exclusive:

- **Example**: The purpose is to demonstrate the number trading days of the `ACWF` ETF within different ranges specified by `from`/`to` in the `cf_etf_hist_price` index:

```
"query": { "match": { "symbol": "ACWF"}},
"aggs":{"monthly_trading_days": {
"range":{"field": "date","format": "yyyy-MM-dd",
"ranges":
[{"from":"2018-12-01"},{"to":"2019-04-01"},{"from":"2019-01-01","to
":"2019-02-01"}]}}
```

- **Resulting buckets**: The key is the specified date range in the specified format, and `from`/`to` is the epoch in milliseconds:

```
"monthly_trading_days": {"buckets": [
[{"key": "*-2019-04-01","to": 1554076800000,"to_as_string":
"2019-04-01","doc_count": 61},
{"key": "2018-12-01-*","from": 1543622400000,"from_as_string":
"2018-12-01","doc_count": 61},
{"key": "2019-01-01-2019-02-01","from":
1546300800000,"from_as_string": "2019-01-01","to":
1548979200000,"to_as_string": "2019-02-01","doc_count": 21}]]}
```

date_range

This is similar to the date range aggregation. The difference is using Date Math expression (please refer to the *API conventions* section of Chapter 1, *Overview of Elasticsearch 7*) for the from/to range. Note that the from value is inclusive and the to value is exclusive:

- **Example**: The purpose is to demonstrate the number trading days of the ACWF ETF within different date ranges specified by from/to in the cf_etf_hist_price index:

```
"query": { "match": { "symbol": "ACWF"}},
"aggs":{"monthly_trading_days": {"date_range":{"field":
"date","format": "yyyy-MM-dd",
"ranges":
[{"from":"2018-12-01"},{"to":"2019-04-01"},{"from":"2019-01-01","to
":"2019-01-01||+1M"}]}}}
```

- **Resulting buckets**: Same as the result in the ranges aggregation.

ip_range

Similar to the date_range aggregation, this is used for the IP data type field to count the documents based on the IP range:

- **Example**: The purpose is to count the documents with an IP between 192.168.0.150 and 192.168.0.255, from the ip_field IP data type field:

```
"aggs" : {"used_ips" : {"ip_range" : {"field" : "ip_field","ranges"
: [{ "to" : "192.168.0.255" },{ "from" : "192.168.0.150" }]}}}
```

filter

The purpose of the `filter` aggregation is to screen the documents that fit a specified filter and provide a total count. It generally acts as the pre-screening step to nail down the scope of documents:

- **Example**: The purpose of this is to find the average `changePercent` on the date of `2019-02-1` in the `cf_etf_hist_price` index:

  ```
  "aggs":{"avg_changePercent_at_date": {"filter":{"term":
  {"date":"2019-02-15"}},
  "aggs": {"avg_changePercent": {"avg":{"field": "changePercent"}}}}}
  ```

- **Resulting buckets**: The `avg_changePercent_at_date` value is `0.60385`. There are 314 documents involved in the aggregation:

  ```
  "avg_changePercent_at_date": {"doc_count": 314,"avg_changePercent":
  {"value": .6038535040014299}}
  ```

filters

The purpose is to provide multiple buckets based on the specified filters. Each filter provides a document count for one bucket:

- **Example**: The purpose is to count the number of times an ETF's `changePercent` is larger than or less than the `changePercent` average of `0.60385` in the `cf_etf_hist_price` index:

  ```
  "query": { "term": {"date":"2019-02-15"}},
  "aggs":{"filters_avg_changePercent": {"filters":{
  "filters": {"less_than_avg": {"range":
  {"changePercent":{"lt":0.60385}}},
  "greater_than_avg":{"range": {"changePercent":{"gte":0.60385}}}}}}}
  ```

- **Resulting buckets**: There are `159` documents with `changePercent` greater than `0.60385` and `155` documents where it is less than that value:

  ```
  "filters_avg_changePercent": {"buckets": {"greater_than_avg":
  {"doc_count": 159},
  "less_than_avg": {"doc_count": 155}}}
  ```

term

The purpose of this is to group results in buckets based on the field values. It provides a document count for each field value:

- **Example**: The purpose is to count each rating in the `cf_etf` index:

  ```
  "aggs":{"terms_on_rating": {
  "terms":{"field":"rating"}}}
  ```

- **Resulting buckets:** There are five ratings and the counts are as follows. Because the aim of the method is estimation, the document counts are approximate values, so we can see the reported `doc_count_error_upper_bound`. We may set the `show_term_doc_count_error` parameter to `true` to get the error in a worst-case scenario:

  ```
  "terms_on_rating": {"doc_count_error_upper_bound":
  0,"sum_other_doc_count": 0,
  "buckets": [{"key": 3,"doc_count": 77},{"key": 4,"doc_count":
  69},{"key": 2,"doc_count": 36},
  {"key": 5,"doc_count": 34},{"key": 1,"doc_count": 21}]
  ```

significant_terms

The purpose of this is to identify the most relevant terms that are related to a particular set of documents. The terms in the result are not simply the most popular terms in the whole document set. Instead, they have a significant change in the popularity measured between the foreground (particular set scope) and background (index scope) sets. Here's a reminder that it does not support floating fields and the document counts are approximate values:

- **Example**: The purpose is to find the significant `morningstar` category (in keyword datatype) of ETFs with `rating` as 5 in the `cf_etf` index:

  ```
  "query":{"match":{"rating":5}},
  "aggs":{"rating_vs_morningstar":{"significant_terms":{"field":"morn
  ingstar_category"}}}}}
  ```

- **Resulting buckets**: There are 34 ETFs with `rating=5`. The significant `morningstar` category for ETFs in rating 5 are `Mid-Cap Value` and `Small Blend`. The `doc_count` and `bg_count` document counts of `significant_terms` are the document counts in the foreground and background respectively:

```
"rating_vs_morningstar": {"doc_count_error_upper_bound":
0,"sum_other_doc_count": 0,
"buckets": [{"key": 5,"doc_count": 34,
"terms_on_morningstar_category": {"doc_count": 34,"bg_count":314,
"buckets": [
{"key": "Mid-Cap Value","doc_count": 3,"score":
0.522923875432526,"bg_count": 4},
{"key": "Small Blend","doc_count": 3,"score":
0.319204152249135,"bg_count": 6}]}}]}
```

significant_text

This is similar to the `significant_term` aggregation, but it is for free-text fields:

- **Example**: The purpose is to find the significant `fund_name` (in the `text` datatype) of ETFs with rating 5 in the `cf_etf` index. We use the `size` parameter to limit the return buckets to 3 and the `exclude` parameter to exclude unwanted terms:

```
"query":{"match":{"rating":5}},
"aggs":{"rating_vs_fund_name":{"significant_text":{"field":"fund_na
me", "exclude": ["us", "p", "s", "cap"], "size":3}}}
```

- **Resulting buckets**: The top three most relevant significant texts are `low`, `volatility`, and `small` for the `fund_name` field in the `cf_etf` index:

```
"rating_vs_morningstar": {"doc_count": 34,"bg_count":
314,"buckets": [
{"key": "low","doc_count": 6,"score": 1.220464656450816,"bg_count":
7},
{"key": "volatility","doc_count": 5,"score":
0.9847174163783161,"bg_count": 6},
{"key": "small","doc_count": 4,"score":
0.24452133794694353,"bg_count": 12}]}
```

sampler

Instead of an unbound number of documents to process, the `sampler` aggregation can limit its sub-aggregation results by sampling the top scores within a shard by a `shard_size` parameter (the default value is `100`).

- **Example**: The purpose is to limit the (`significant_terms`) sub-aggregation document size to `150` per shard in the `cf_etf` index:

```
"aggs": { "sampling": {"sampler": { "shard_size":150},
"aggs": {"significant_terms_category": {"significant_terms":
{"field": "category"}}}}}
```

- **Resulting buckets**: We can see that `doc_count` of the `significant_terms_category` aggregation is `150`:

```
"sampling": {"doc_count": 150,
"significant_terms_category": {"doc_count": 150,"bg_count": 314,
"buckets": [
{"key": "International","doc_count": 61,"score":
0.13425648148148153,"bg_count": 96},
{"key": "Sector","doc_count": 10,"score":
0.07288888888888888,"bg_count": 10},
{"key": "Commodity","doc_count": 9,"score":
0.05303999999999999,"bg_count": 10}]}}
```

diversified_sampler

Similar to using the `sampler` aggregation to limit the sub-aggregation results, this restricts the number of the samples to have a common value on the specified field. It reduces the bias distribution of the sample pool:

- **Example**: Here we are using `diversified_sampler` on the `family` field and setting the `max_docs_per_value=10` parameter (sampling 10 documents per bucket) with the same `significant_terms` aggregation as the `sampler` example for the `cf_etf` index:

```
"aggs": { "sampling": {
"diversified_sampler": {"field":"family", "shard_size":150,
"max_docs_per_value" : 10},
"aggs": {"significant_terms_category": {"significant_terms":
{"field": "category"}}}}}
```

According to the result of `sampler`, there are 61 documents with `International`, 10 with `Section`, and 9 with `Commodity`.

- **Resulting buckets**: We can see that the result is different from the `sampler` aggregation. If we increase `max_docs_per_value` to 61, then the result is the same as the `sampler` aggregation:

```
"sampling": {"doc_count": 72,
 "significant_terms_category": {"doc_count": 72,"bg_count":
314,"buckets": [
 {"key": "Equity","doc_count": 30,"score":
0.03386134067952249,"bg_count": 121},
 {"key": "Bond","doc_count": 19,"score":
0.020086780503447175,"bg_count": 77},
 {"key": "Commodity","doc_count": 3,"score":
0.01284722222222222,"bg_count": 10}]}}
```

nested

The purpose of this is to perform aggregation on the field of the nested object pointing by the `path` parameter, following grouping by the field of the parent document:

- **Example**: The purpose is to sum the dividend amounts for each ETF in the `cf_etf_dividend_nested` index. Recall that the `announcement` field is in the `nested` object data type. To make the return result smaller, we only list the first three ETFs in the alphabetical order of the symbol:

```
"aggs": {"per_symbol":{"terms": {"field":"symbol", "size":3},
"aggs":{"total_dividend": { "nested": {"path":"announcement"},
"aggs": {"total_amount": {"sum": {"field":
"announcement.amount"}}}}}}}
```

- **Resulting buckets**: There are 7 dividends for the ACWF ETF and the total dividend is about 1.63133:

```
"per_symbol": {"doc_count_error_upper_bound":
0,"sum_other_doc_count": 7,"buckets": [
 {"key": "ACWF","doc_count": 1,"total_dividend": {"doc_count":
7,"total_amount": {
 "value": 1.6313300058245659}}},
 {"key": "ACWI","doc_count": 1,"total_dividend": {"doc_count":
11,"total_amount": {"value": 6.54360693693161}}},
 {"key": "ACWV","doc_count": 1,"total_dividend": {"doc_count":
10,"total_amount": {"value": 8.262333989143372}}}]}
```

reverse_nested

The purpose of this is to perform aggregation on the field from the parent document after grouping by the field from the nested object:

- **Example**: The purpose is to count the total ETFs according to the category based on the grouping by the type of dividend in the `cf_etf_dividend_nested` index:

```
"aggs": {"etf_category_distribution_on_dividend_type":{"nested":
{"path":"announcement"},
    "aggs":{"by_dividend_type": { "terms":
{"field":"announcement.type"},
        "aggs": {"total_by_etf_category":{"reverse_nested":{},
            "aggs": { "category":{"terms": {"field":
"category"}}}}}}}}
```

- **Resulting buckets**: We can see that there are three dividend types: `Dividend income`, `Long term capital gain`, and `Short term capital gain`. In each dividend type, the ETFs are counted by category:

```
"etf_category_distribution_on_dividend_type": {"doc_count":
287,"by_dividend_type": {"doc_count_error_upper_bound":
0,"sum_other_doc_count": 0, "buckets": [
 {"key": "Dividend income","doc_count":
283,"total_by_etf_category": {"doc_count": 10,
"category": {"doc_count_error_upper_bound":
0,"sum_other_doc_count": 0,
"buckets": [{"key": "Bond","doc_count": 4},{"key":
"Equity","doc_count": 3},{"key": "International","doc_count":
3}]}}},
 {"key": "Long term capital gain","doc_count":
2,"total_by_etf_category": {doc_count": 2,
 "category": {"doc_count_error_upper_bound":
0,"sum_other_doc_count": 0,
"buckets": [{"key": "Bond","doc_count": 2}]}}},
 {"key": "Short term capital gain","doc_count":
2,"total_by_etf_category": {
 "doc_count": 2,"category": {"doc_count_error_upper_bound":
0,"sum_other_doc_count": 0,
 "buckets": [{"key": "Bond","doc_count": 2}]}}}]}}
```

global

The purpose of this is to perform aggregation with all documents in the index by ignoring the query:

- **Example**: The purpose is to find the average rating of the iShares family and the average rating from all ETFs in the cf_etf index:

```
"query":{"prefix": {"family":"iShares"}},
"aggs": {"ishares_avg_rating": {"avg":
{"field":"rating"}},"overall_avg_rating": {"global":{},
    "aggs":{"global_avg_rating":{"avg":{"field":"rating"}}}}}
```

- **Resulting buckets**: The average rating of the iShares family is about 3.31 and the overall average rating is about 3.25:

```
"overall_avg_rating": {"doc_count": 314,"global_avg_rating":
{"value": 3.2489451476793247}},
 "ishares_avg_rating": {"value": 3.311111111111111}
```

missing

The purpose of this is to count the documents with a missing field value:

- **Example**: The purpose is to count how many ETFs are not rated in the cf_etf index:

```
"aggs": {"not_rated_count": {"missing": {"field":"rating"}}}
```

- **Resulting buckets**: There are 77 ETFs not rated:

```
"not_rated_count": {"doc_count": 77}
```

composite

This allows us to create bucket pairs from different sources and perform paging quickly through large aggregation result sets in order:

- **Example**: The purpose is to perform aggregation to count documents for each pair of values from the `family` and `rating` fields—with ratings of 4 and 5—in the `cf_etf` index. We have limited ourselves to 5 results in the response:

```
"query": {"query_string": {"query": "rating:[4 TO 5]"}},
"aggs": { "multi_sources": {"composite": {
    "sources": [{"family": {"terms":
{"field":"family"}}},{"rating": {"terms":
{"field":"rating"}}}],"size":5}}}
```

- **Resulting buckets**: We can see that there are 5 results of the `family` and `rating` pairs. We can use the whole `after_key` expression inside the `composite` expression for the next patch retrieval:

```
"multi_sources": {"after_key": {"family": "Invesco","rating":
5},"buckets": [
{"key": {"family": "AGFiQ","rating": 4},"doc_count": 1},
{"key": {"family": "First Trust","rating": 4},"doc_count": 8},
{"key": {"family": "First Trust","rating": 5},"doc_count": 4},
{"key": {"family": "Invesco","rating": 4},"doc_count": 6},
{"key": {"family": "Invesco","rating": 5},"doc_count": 5}]}
```

adjacency_matrix

This allows users to define a set of filters and provide bucket results in an adjacency-matrix form among the filters, which means any two filters are applied together:

- **Example**: The purpose is to discover the scenario about the two filters. The first filter is to select the rating of 5 and the second filter is to select the ETFs from the `iShares` family in the `cf_etf` index:

```
"aggs": { "adjacency_filters": {"adjacency_matrix": {"filters": {
    "rating_gte_5": {"range":{"rating":{"gte":5}}},
    "family_prefix_A": {"prefix":{"family":"iShares"}}}}}}
```

- **Resulting buckets**: There are 34 ETFs rated at 5. There are 56 ETFs in the iShares family. Only 7 ETFs from the iShares family are rated at 5:

```
"adjacency_filters": {"buckets": [
{"key": "family_prefix_A","doc_count": 56},
{"key": "family_prefix_A&rating_gte_5","doc_count": 7},
{"key": "rating_gte_5","doc_count": 34}]}
```

parent

The purpose of this is to aggregate parent documents with the join data type field:

- **Example**: The purpose is to obtain a count of symbols that have dividends for the ETF in the cf_etf_dividend_join index:

```
"aggs": {"dividend":{ "parent": {"type": "dividend" },
    "aggs": {"count":{"value_count":{"field":"symbol"}}}}}
```

- **Resulting buckets**: Since we have only one symbol ACWF, the count value is 1:

```
"aggregations": { "dividend": { "doc_count": 1, "count": {
"value": 1 } } }
```

children

The purpose of this is to aggregate the child documents with the join data type field:

- **Example**: The purpose is to obtain the total amount of dividend for each symbol in the cf_etf_dividend_join index:

```
"aggs": {
"dividends_for_symbol": {
"terms": {"field": "symbol"},
"aggs": {"dividend":{ "children": {"type": "dividend" },
"aggs": {"total_dividend":{"sum":{"field":"amount"}}}}}}
}
```

- **Resulting buckets**: Since we have only one symbol ACWF, the result will show the total dividend of it:

```
"aggregations": {
    "dividends_for_symbol": {
        "doc_count_error_upper_bound": 0, "sum_other_doc_count": 0,
        "buckets": [ {
```

```
        "key": "ACWF",
        "doc_count": 1,
        "dividend": {
            "doc_count": 7,
            "total_dividend": {
                "value": 1.6313300058245659
            } } } ] } }
```

geo_distance

This is similar to the `range` aggregation, but with the `geo_point` data type field applied. The purpose is to find the documents within different `geo_distance` ranges:

- **Example**: `"aggs"` : `{"aggregation_name"` : `{"geo_distance"` : `{"field"` : `"field_1","origin"` : `"x, y","ranges"` : `[{ "to"` : `value_1 }, { "from"` : `value_2, "to"` : `value_3 },{ "from"` : `value_4 }]}}}`

geohash_grid

This aggregation works with the `geo_point` data type field. It groups documents into buckets defined by the precision (between 1 to 12; the default is 5), which is the geohash length, a well-defined dimension of grids:

- **Example**: `"aggs"` : `{"aggregation_name"` : `{"geohash_grid"` : `{"field"` : `"field_1"}}}`

geotile_grid

This aggregation works with the `geo_point` data type field. It groups documents into buckets defined by the precision (between 0 and 29; the default is 7), which is a zoom level, a well-defined dimension of grids:

- **Example**: `"aggs"` : `{"aggregation_name"` : `{"geotile_grid"` : `{"field"` : `"field_1"}}}`

In the next section, we'll cover the last family, pipeline aggregation, which is different from the first three. The second aggregation accepts the output of the previous one as the input in the consecutive aggregations.

Pipeline aggregations

As the name pipeline suggests, pipeline aggregations allow us to pass the result of an aggregation as the input to the aggregation in the next stage. To pass the result, a `bucket_path` parameter is provided to let us specify which source will be worked on in the next stage. To define the source, we need to follow this syntax:

```
<aggregation_name>[<aggregation_separator>,<aggregation_name>]*[<metric_sep
arator>,<metric>]
```

Here `aggregation_separator` is >, `metric_separator` is ., and the metric is the name of the metric produced in the previous stage. Pipeline aggregations can be classified into two families, parent and sibling. We will illustrate each aggregation of both families in the following subsections.

Sibling family

The sibling family means that two consecutive aggregations are at the same level. Supported aggregations are described in the following subsections.

avg_bucket

The purpose of this is to compute the average value of the buckets from the aggregation in the previous stage:

- **Example**: The purpose is to compute the overall average close price in addition to the monthly close price for the ACWF ETF in the `cf_etf_hist_price` index. We can see that the `overall_avg_close` aggregation is a sibling to the `monthly_avg_close` aggregation:

```
"query":{"match": {"symbol":"ACWF"}},
"aggs":{"monthly_avg_close": {"date_histogram":{"field":
"date","interval": "month","format": "yyyy-MM-dd"},
"aggs":{"avg_close_on_month":{"avg":{"field":"close"}}}},
"overall_avg_close":{"avg_bucket":{"buckets_path":"monthly_avg_clos
e>avg_close_on_month"}}}
```

- **Resulting buckets**: The `avg_close_on_month` field shows the monthly average close price:

```
"aggregations": {"monthly_avg_close": {"buckets": [
{"key_as_string": "2018-12-01","key": 1543622400000,"doc_count":
```

```
4,"avg_close_on_month": {"value": 25.791549682617188}},
 {"key_as_string": "2019-01-01","key": 1546300800000,"doc_count":
21,"avg_close_on_month": {"value": 27.266199929373606}},
 {"key_as_string": "2019-02-01","key": 1548979200000,"doc_count":
19,"avg_close_on_month": {"value": 28.888436668797542}},
 {"key_as_string": "2019-03-01","key": 1551398400000,"doc_count":
17,"avg_close_on_month": {"value": 28.97294111812816}}],
 "overall_avg_close": {"value": 27.729781849729125}}
```

max_bucket

The purpose of this is to find the maximum value of the buckets from the aggregation in the previous stage:

- **Example**: The purpose is to compute the maximum monthly close price in addition to the monthly close price for the ACWF ETF in the cf_etf_hist_price index:

```
"query":{"match": {"symbol":"ACWF"}},
"aggs":{"monthly_avg_close": {"date_histogram":{"field":
"date","interval": "month","format": "yyyy-MM-dd"},
"aggs":{"avg_close_on_month":{"avg":{"field":"close"}}}},
"overall_max_avg_close":{"max_bucket":
{"buckets_path":"monthly_avg_close>avg_close_on_month"}}}
```

- **Resulting buckets**: This is the same as the result in the avg_bucket example, except overall_avg_close is replaced by overall_max_avg_close as follows:

```
"overall_max_avg_close": {"value": 28.97294111812816,"keys":
["2019-03-01"]}
```

min_bucket

The purpose of this is to find the minimum value of the buckets from the aggregation in the previous stage:

- **Example**: The purpose is to compute the minimum monthly close price in addition to the monthly close price for the ACWF ETF in the cf_etf_hist_price index:

```
"query":{"match": {"symbol":"ACWF"}},
"aggs":{"monthly_avg_close": {"date_histogram":{"field":
"date","interval": "month","format": "yyyy-MM-dd"},
```

```
"aggs":{"avg_close_on_month":{"avg":{"field":"close"}}}},
"overall_min_avg_close":{"min_bucket":
{"buckets_path":"monthly_avg_close>avg_close_on_month"}}}
```

- **Resulting buckets**: It is the same as the result in the `avg_bucket` example, except `overall_avg_close` is replaced by `overall_min_avg_close` as follows:

```
"overall_min_avg_close": {"value": 25.791549682617188,"keys":
["2018-12-01"]}
```

sum_bucket

The purpose of this is to find the summation value of the buckets from the aggregation in the previous stage:

- **Example**: The purpose is to compute the total closing price change in addition to the monthly closing price change for the ACWF ETF in the `cf_etf_hist_price` index:

```
"query":{"match": {"symbol":"ACWF"}},
"aggs":{"monthly_change": {"date_histogram":{"field":
"date","interval": "month","format": "yyyy-MM-
dd"},"aggs":{"change_on_month":{"sum":{"field":"change"}}}},
"overall_change":{"sum_bucket": {"buckets_path":
"monthly_change>change_on_month"}}}
```

- **Resulting buckets**: The `change_on_month` field shows the monthly closing price change:

```
"monthly_change": {"buckets": [
{"key_as_string": "2018-12-01","key": 1543622400000,"doc_count":
4,"change_on_month": {"value": 1.1589900143444538}},
{"key_as_string": "2019-01-01","key": 1546300800000,"doc_count":
21,"change_on_month": {"value": 2.519999973475933}},
{"key_as_string": "2019-02-01","key": 1548979200000,"doc_count":
19,"change_on_month": {
"value": 0.5900000082328916}},{
"key_as_string": "2019-03-01","key": 1551398400000,"doc_count":
17,"change_on_month": {
"value": -0.4600000437349081}}]},
"overall_monthly_change": {"value": 3.8089899523183703}
```

stats_bucket

The purpose of this is to provide statistics metrics (`min`, `max`, `sum`, `count`, and `avg`) of the buckets from the aggregation in the previous stage:

- **Example**: The purpose is to compute the statistics of the monthly closing price change in addition to the monthly closing price change for the ACWF ETF in the `cf_etf_hist_price` index:

```
"query":{"match": {"symbol":"ACWF"}},
"aggs":{"monthly_change": {"date_histogram":{"field":
"date","interval": "month","format": "yyyy-MM-dd"},
"aggs":{"change_on_month":{"sum":{"field":"change"}}}},
"stats_monthly_change":{"stats_bucket": {"buckets_path":
"monthly_change>change_on_month"}}
```

- **Resulting buckets**: This is the same as the result in the `sum_bucket` example, except `overall_monthly_change` is replaced by `stats_monthly_change` as follows:

```
"stats_monthly_change": {"count": 4,"min":
-0.4600000437349081,"max": 2.519999973475933,"avg":
0.9522474880795926,"sum": 3.8089899523183703}
```

extended_stats_bucket

The purpose of this is to provide an extended statistics metric (the `stats` and `sum_of_squares`, `variance`, `std_deviation`, and `std_deviation_bounds`) of the buckets from the aggregation in the previous stage:

- **Example**: The purpose is to compute the extended statistics of the monthly closing price change in addition to the monthly closing price change for the ACWF ETF in the `cf_etf_hist_price` index:

```
"query":{"match": {"symbol":"ACWF"}},
"aggs":{"monthly_change": {"date_histogram":{"field":
"date","interval": "month","format": "yyyy-MM-dd"},
"aggs":{"change_on_month":{"sum":{"field":"change"}}}},
"extended_stats_monthly_change":{"extended_stats_bucket":
{"buckets_path": "monthly_change>change_on_month"}}
```

- **Resulting buckets**: This is the same as the result in the `stats_bucket` example, except `stats_monthly_change` is replaced by `extended_stats_monthly_change` as follows:

```
"extended_stats_monthly_change": {"count": 4,"min":
-0.4600000437349081,"max": 2.519999973475933,"avg":
0.9522474880795926,"sum": 3.8089899523183703,"sum_of_squares":
8.25335776961979,"variance": 1.1565641638510535,"std_deviation":
1.075436731682089,
"std_deviation_bounds": {"upper": 3.1031209514437705,"lower":
-1.1986259752845854}}
```

percentiles_bucket

The purpose is to calculate the percentiles for the buckets' aggregation values in the previous stage:

- **Example**: The purpose is to compute the percentiles of the weekly closing price change distribution in addition to the weekly closing price change for the ACWF ETF in the `cf_etf_hist_price` index:

```
"query":{"match": {"symbol":"ACWF"}},
"aggs":{"weekly_change": {"date_histogram":{"field":
"date","interval": week","format": "yyyy-MM-dd"},
"aggs":{"change_on_week":{"sum":{"field":"change"}}}},
"percentile_weekly_change":{"percentiles_bucket": {"buckets_path":
"weekly_change>change_on_week"}}}
```

- **Resulting buckets**: `percentile_weekly_change` shows the weekly closing price change distribution:

```
"weekly_change": {"buckets": [
{"key_as_string": "2018-12-24","key": 1545609600000,"doc_count":
3,"change_on_week": {"value": 0.9823900200426579}},
{...}]},
"percentile_weekly_change": {"values": {"1.0": -0.9000000283122063,
"5.0": -0.480000060349703,"25.0": -0.09000000357627869,"50.0":
0.3931000018492341,"75.0": 0.7446999922394753,"95.0":
.8315000105649233,
"99.0": 0.9823900200426579}}
```

Parent family

The parent family means that two consecutive aggregations are at different levels. Supported aggregations are described in the following subsections.

cumulative_sum

The purpose of this is to calculate the accumulative summation value of each bucket from the aggregation in the previous stage:

- **Example**: The purpose is to compute the cumulative sum of the closing price change side by side with the monthly closing price change for the ACWF ETF in the cf_etf_hist_price index. We can see that the monthly_change aggregation is the parent of the change_on_month and cumulative_change aggregations:

```
"query":{"match": {"symbol":"ACWF"}},
"aggs":{"monthly_change": {"date_histogram":{"field":
"date","interval": "month","format": "yyyy-MM-dd"},
"aggs":{"change_on_month":{"sum":{"field":"change"}},"cumulative_ch
ange":{"cumulative_sum": {"buckets_path": "change_on_month"}}}}
```

- **Resulting buckets**: The cumulative_change field shows the cumulative sum of the monthly closing price change:

```
"monthly_change": {"buckets": [
{"key_as_string": "2018-12-01","key": 1543622400000,"doc_count":
4,"change_on_month": {"value":
1.1589900143444538},"cumulative_change": {"value":
1.1589900143444538}},
{"key_as_string": "2019-01-01","key": 1546300800000,"doc_count":
21,"change_on_month": {"value":
2.519999973475933},"cumulative_change": {"value":
3.678989987820387}},
{"key_as_string": "2019-02-01","key": 1548979200000,"doc_count":
19,"change_on_month": {"value":
0.5900000082328916},"cumulative_change": {"value":
4.2689899960532784}},
{"key_as_string": "2019-03-01","key": 1551398400000,"doc_count":
17,"change_on_month": {"value":
-0.4600000437349081},"cumulative_change": {"value":
3.8089899523183703}}]}
```

derivative

The purpose of this is to calculate the derivate (first order, second order) of each bucket from the aggregation in the previous stage:

- **Example**: The purpose is to compute the derivative of the closing price change side by side with the monthly closing price change for the ACWF ETF in the `cf_etf_hist_price` index:

```
"query":{"match": {"symbol":"ACWF"}},
"aggs":{"monthly_change": {"date_histogram":{"field":
"date","interval": "month","format": "yyyy-MM-dd"},
"aggs":{"change_on_month":{"sum":{"field":"change"}},"first_order_d
erivative":{"derivative": {"buckets_path":
"change_on_month"}},"second_order_derivative": {"derivative":
{"buckets_path": "first_order_derivative"}}}}}
```

- **Resulting buckets**: The `first_order_derivative` and `second order derivative` fields show the derivate of the monthly closing price change:

```
"monthly_change": {"buckets": [
{"key_as_string": "2018-12-01","key": 1543622400000,"doc_count":
4,"change_on_month": {
"value": 1.1589900143444538}},
{"key_as_string": "2019-01-01","key": 1546300800000,"doc_count":
21,"change_on_month": {
"value": 2.519999973475933},"first_order_derivative": {"value":
1.3610099591314793}},
{"key_as_string": "2019-02-01","key": 1548979200000,"doc_count":
19,"change_on_month": {
"value": 0.5900000082328916},"first_order_derivative": {"value":
-1.9299999652430415}, "second_order_derivative": {"value":
-3.291009924374521}},
{"key_as_string": "2019-03-01","key": 1551398400000,"doc_count":
17,"change_on_month": {"value":
-0.4600000437349081},"first_order_derivative": {"value":
-1.0500000519677997}, "second_order_derivative": {"value":
0.8799999132752419}}]}
```

bucket_script

The purpose of this is to perform and process a user-defined script for each bucket from the aggregation in the previous stage. The `script` parameter lets us specify the contents of the script:

- **Example**: The purpose is to find the range value (max-min) of the closing price change side by side with the monthly closing price change. This is the min/max range for the ACWF ETF in the `cf_etf_hist_price` index:

```
"query":{"match": {"symbol":"ACWF"}},
"aggs":{"monthly_change": {"date_histogram":{"field":
"date","interval": "month","format": "yyyy-MM-dd"},
"aggs":{"change_on_month":{ "sum":{"field":"change"}},
"min_change_on_month":{"min":{"field":"change"}},
"max_change_on_month":{"max":{"field":"change"}},
"range_of_change":{"bucket_script":{"buckets_path":{"min_value":"mi
n_change_on_month",
"max_value":"max_change_on_month"},"script":"params.max_value -
params.min_value"}}}}}
```

- **Resulting buckets**: The `max_change_on_month` and `min_change_on_month` fields show the minimum and maximum of monthly close price change:

```
"monthly_change": {"buckets": [
{"key_as_string": "2018-12-01","key": 1543622400000,"doc_count":
4,"max_change_on_month": {
"value": 0.8442500233650208},"min_change_on_month": {"value":
0.04586799815297127}, "change_on_month": {"value":
1.1589900143444538},"range_of_change": {
"value": 0.7983820252120495}},
{...},
{"key_as_string": "2019-03-01","key": 1551398400000,"doc_count":
17,"max_change_on_month": {
"value": 0.41999998688697815},"min_change_on_month": {"value":
-0.6299999952316284},
"change_on_month": {"value":
-0.4600000437349081},"range_of_change": {
"value": 1.0499999821186066}}]}
```

bucket_selector

The purpose of this is to perform a filter to select the buckets from the aggregation in the previous stage:

- **Example**: The purpose is to discover the negative monthly closing price change from the buckets for the ACWF ETF in the `cf_etf_hist_price` index:

```
"query":{"match": {"symbol":"ACWF"}},
"aggs":{"negative_monthly_change": {"date_histogram":{"field":
"date","interval": "month","format": "yyyy-MM-dd"},
"aggs":{"change_on_month":{ "sum":{"field":"change"}},
"filter_positive_change_on_month":{"bucket_selector":{"buckets_path
":{"monthly_change_value":"change_on_month"},"script":"params.month
ly_change_value<0"}}}}
```

- **Resulting buckets**: The `negative_monthly_change` field shows only the negative monthly closing price change:

```
"negative_monthly_change": {"buckets": [
{"key_as_string": "2019-03-01","key": 1551398400000,"doc_count":
17,"change_on_month": {
"value": -0.4600000437349081}}]}
```

bucket_sort

The purpose of this is to perform sorting on the fields of the buckets from the aggregation in the previous stage:

- **Example**: The purpose is to sort by the total amount of dividend for each ETF from the `cf_etf_dividend_nested` index in descending order, and only return the top three entries:

```
"aggs": {"per_symbol":{"terms": {"field":"symbol"},
"aggs":{"total_dividend": { "nested": {"path":"announcement"},
"aggs": {"total_amount": {"sum": {"field":
"announcement.amount"}}}},
"sort": {"bucket_sort": {"sort":
[{"total_dividend.total_amount":{"order":"desc"}}],"from":0,"size":
3}}}}}
```

- **Resulting buckets**: The result is sorted by the `total_amount` field in descending order:

```
"per_symbol": {"doc_count_error_upper_bound":
0,"sum_other_doc_count": 0,"buckets": [
{"key": "ACWV","doc_count": 1,"total_dividend": {"doc_count":
10,"total_amount": {
"value": 8.262333989143372}}},
{"key": "AGZ","doc_count": 1,"total_dividend": {"doc_count":
62,"total_amount": {"value": 8.01299001276493}}},
{"key": "ACWI","doc_count": 1,"total_dividend": {"doc_count":
11,"total_amount": {"value": 6.54360693693161}}}]}
```

serial_diff

The purpose of this is to compute a series of value differences between a time lag of the buckets from the aggregation in the previous stage. The parameter lag is the prior n^{th} bucket used for subtraction from the current bucket:

- **Example**: The purpose is to compute a series of the differences of the weekly average changes of closing prices side by side with the weekly average changes of closing prices for the `ACWF` ETF in the `cf_etf_hist_price` index:

```
"query":{"match": {"symbol":"ACWF"}},
"aggs":{"serial_diff_weekly_avg_change":
{"date_histogram":{"field": "date","interval": "week",
"format": "yyyy-MM-dd"},
"aggs":{"weekly_avg_change":{"avg":{"field":"change"}},
"weekly_avg_serial_diff": {"serial_diff":
{"buckets_path":"weekly_avg_change","lag":1}}}}}
```

- **Resulting buckets**: The `weekly_avg_serial_diff` field shows the result for the `weekly_avg_change` field after `serial_diff` aggregation at weekly intervals:

```
"serial_diff_weekly_avg_change": {"buckets": [
{"key_as_string": "2018-12-24","key": 1545609600000,"doc_count":
3,"weekly_avg_change": {"value": 0.3274633400142193}},
{...},
{"key_as_string": "2019-03-25","key": 1553472000000,"doc_count":
1,"weekly_avg_change": {"value":
-0.05000000074505806},"weekly_avg_serial_diff": {"value":
0.046000000461936}}
```

Moving average aggregation

The purpose of this aggregation is to compute a series of average values from a subset of buckets into a specified window size from the aggregation in the previous stage. There are five different models to compute the moving average. They are `simple`, `linear`, `ewma`, `holt` and `holt_winter`. The `window` parameter is the size of the subset of buckets. Another important parameter is `settings`, which lets us specify the parameters of the selected `model`. Moving average aggregation must be processed within the `histogram` or `date_histogram` aggregations. We will show different models with the moving average using a window size of 4 for the monthly closing price change from the buckets for the `ACWF` ETF in the `cf_etf_hist_price` index. We also predict a four-week trend if the model supports prediction. All models are based on the common query and parent aggregations, as shown:

```
"query":{"match": {"symbol":"ACWF"}},
"aggs":{"monthly_change": {"date_histogram":{"field": "date","interval":
"week","format": "yyyy-MM-dd"},
"aggs": {"weekly_change":{"sum":{"field":"change"}},
```

Let's take a look at each supported model in the following subsections.

simple

The purpose of this is to calculate the moving average by simply averaging the values in each subset in window size. The rest of the aggregation for the `simple` model is as follows:

```
"weekly_moving_avg":
{"moving_avg":{"buckets_path":"weekly_change","model":"simple","window":4,
"predict":4}}}}
```

linear

The purpose of this is to calculate the moving average with the decaying method, which is a linear model. The rest of the aggregation for this linear model is as follows:

```
"weekly_moving_avg":
{"moving_avg":{"buckets_path":"weekly_change","model":"linear","window":4,"
predict":4}}}}
```

ewma

The purpose of this is to calculate the moving average with exponentially weighted method, a single exponential smoothing model where the moving average value depends on the window size, and the alpha $\in (0,1]$. `alpha` parameter defaults to 0.3. A smaller `alpha` value will produce more smoothing and more lag. The rest of the aggregation for the `ewma` model is as follows:

```
"weekly_moving_avg":
{"moving_avg":{"buckets_path":"weekly_change","model":"ewma","settings":{"a
lpha":0.3},"window":4,"predict":4}}}}
```

holt

The purpose of this is to calculate the moving average with Holt's linear method, a double exponential smoothing model where moving averages depend on window size and the alpha, beta$\in (0,1]$. `alpha` and `beta` parameters default to 0.3 and 0.1, respectively. The smaller `alpha` value will produce more smoothing and more lag. A smaller `beta` value will emphasize long-term trends. The rest of the aggregation for the `holt` model is as follows:

```
"weekly_moving_avg":
{"moving_avg":{"buckets_path":"weekly_change","model":"holt","settings":{"a
lpha":0.3, "beta":0.3},"window":4,"predict":4}}}}
```

holt_winters

The purpose of this is to calculate the moving average by the Holt-Winters method, a triple exponential smoothing model where the moving average depends on the window size and the `alpha`, `beta`, `gamma`$\in(0,1]$. `alpha`, `beta`, and `gamma` parameters default to $0.3, 0.1$, and 0.3, respectively. Holt-Winters can track seasonal aspects of data by using addition and multiplication. The corresponding setting types are `add` and `mult`. The rest of the aggregation for the `Holt-Winters` model is as follows:

```
"weekly_moving_avg":
{"moving_avg":{"buckets_path":"weekly_change","model":"holt_winters","setti
ngs":{"type" : "mult","alpha":0.8, "beta":0.3, "gamma":0.3,
"period":1},"window":4,"predict":4}}}}
```

The following chart includes all the supported moving average models corresponding to the aggregation examples in the *Moving average aggregation* section of this chapter:

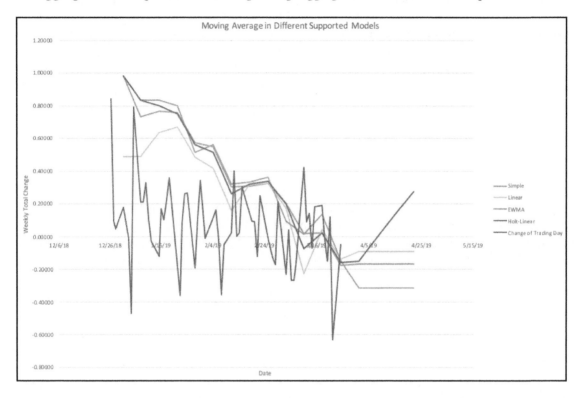

Moving function aggregation

The purpose of moving function aggregation is to execute a user-defined script with the values from the subset of buckets in a specified window size from the aggregation in the previous stage. The `script` parameter is used to specify the script to run and the `window` parameter is the size of the subset of buckets. The `moving_fn` aggregation must be processed with either the `histogram` or `date_histogram` aggregation. There are a few supported functions and we'll practice them in the following subsections. All functions are based on the common query and parent aggregation with a window size of 4 for the monthly closing price change from the buckets for the `ACWF` ETF in the `cf_etf_hist_price` index, as shown:

```
"query":{"match": {"symbol":"ACWF"}},
"aggs":{"monthly_change": {"date_histogram":{"field": "date","interval":
"week","format": "yyyy-MM-dd"},
"aggs": {"weekly_change":{"sum":{"field":"change"}},
```

max

Compute the maximum value from the subset of data in each window. The rest of the aggregation for the maximum function is as follows:

```
"max_weekly_change":
{"moving_fn":{"buckets_path":"weekly_change","script":"MovingFunctions.max(
values)","window":4}}}}}
```

min

Compute the minimum value from the subset of data in each window. The rest of the aggregation for the minimum function is as follows:

```
"min_weekly_change":
{"moving_fn":{"buckets_path":"weekly_change","script":"MovingFunctions.min(
values)","window":4}}
```

sum

Compute the summation value from the subset of data in each window. The rest of the aggregation for the summation function is as follows:

```
"total_weekly_change":
{"moving_fn":"buckets_path":"weekly_change","script":"MovingFunctions.sum(v
alues)","window":4}}
```

stdDev

Compute the standard deviation from the subset of data in each window. The rest of the aggregation for the standard deviation function is as follows:

```
"weekly_change_stdDev": {"moving_fn":{"buckets_path":"weekly_change",
"script":"MovingFunctions.stdDev(values,
MovingFunctions.unweightedAvg(values))","window":4}}
```

unweightedAvg

Compute the moving average in a simple model from the subset of data in each window. The rest of the aggregation for the unweighted average function is as follows:

```
"weekly_change_unweightedAvg":
{"moving_fn":{"buckets_path":"weekly_change",
"script":"MovingFunctions.unweightedAvg(values)","window":4}}
```

linearWeightedAvg

Compute the moving average in a linear model from the subset of data in each window. The rest of the aggregation for the linear weighted average function is as follows:

```
"weekly_change_unweightedAvg":
{"moving_fn":{"buckets_path":"weekly_change",
"script":"MovingFunctions.linearWeightedAvg(values)","window":4}}
```

ewma

Compute the moving average in a single exponential model from the subset of data in each window. The rest of the aggregation for the ewma function with the alpha parameter value set to 0.3 is as follows:

```
"weekly_change_ewma": {"moving_fn":{"buckets_path":"weekly_change",
"script":"MovingFunctions.ewma(values, 0.3)","window":4}}
```

holt

Compute the moving average by using the Holt-linear method from the subset of data in each window. The rest of the aggregation for the Holt-linear function with both the parameter values set to 0.3 is as follows:

```
"weekly_change_holt": {"moving_fn":{"buckets_path":"weekly_change",
"script":"MovingFunctions.holt(values, 0.3, 0.3)","window":4}}
```

holtWinters

Compute the moving average by using the Holt-Winters method from the subset of data in each window. The rest of the aggregation for the Holt-Winters function with the alpha (0.8), beta (0.3), gamma (0.1), and period (1) parameter values is as follows:

```
"weekly_change_holtWinters": {"moving_fn":{"buckets_path":"weekly_change",
"script":" MovingFunctions.holtWinters(values, 0.8, 0.3, 0.1, 1,
false)","window":4}}
```

Recall in Chapter 6, *Search APIs*, how we said that this chapter would discuss the post_filter request body search parameter. We will discuss it in the next section.

Post filter on aggregations

Typically, search results and aggregation results refer to the same query. If we want to display the search results and the aggregation results in different ways—such as applying filters to display narrowed-down search results—then we can run post_filter after the query. The post_filter parameter has no effect on aggregation. For example, let's use post_filter in the example of the term bucket aggregation. We only want to retrieve the rating = 5 documents in the search result, which is at the top of the result from the term aggregation on all of the rating field values.

In the following screenshot, only the rating = 4 documents are retrieved back, and the total hits is 34 instead of the total 314 documents:

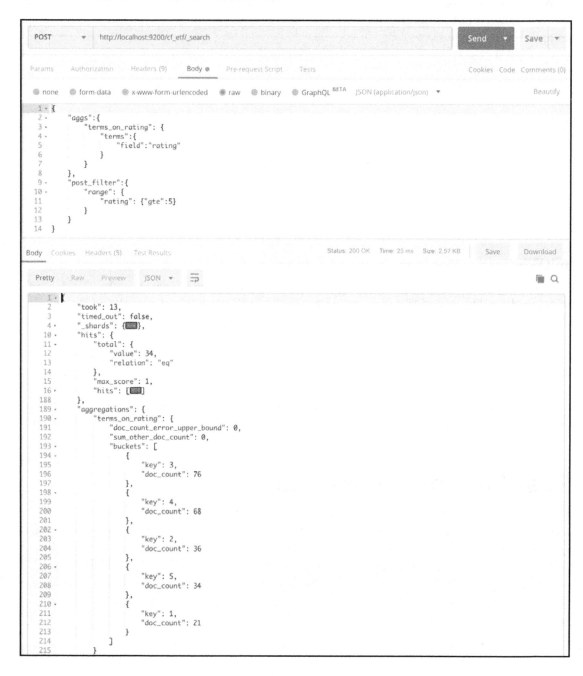

Summary

Hurrah! We have completed looking at one of the most important features in Elasticsearch. We've learned about how to perform aggregations with well-designed examples, and delved into most of the types of aggregations. We've also learned how to use IEX ETF historical data to plot a graph of different types of moving averages, including forecasted data supported by the model.

In the next chapter, we will talk about the ingest node, in which documents can be pre-processed before the actual indexing takes place. We can define a pipeline to specify a series of processors to execute in the same order as they are declared. The ingest node intercepts bulk and index requests, applies the transformation, and then passes the documents back. By default, all nodes are enabled and we can disable the functionality of the node in the configuration file.

Preprocessing Documents in Ingest Pipelines

9

In the previous chapter, we learned all four aggregation families and practiced different types of aggregations with many examples, using **investor exchange (IEX)** and **exchange-traded fund (ETF)** historical data. We have completed the study on two key features of Elasticsearch – search and aggregation. In this chapter, we'll switch to the data preparation and enrichment features. You will recall from the *Elasticsearch Architecture* section of Chapter 1, *Overview of Elasticsearch 7*, that there are four types of Elasticsearch nodes, and one of them is the ingest node. You can preprocess documents through the predefined pipeline processors before the actual indexing operation starts. All nodes are enabled as ingest by default and you can disable the capability of a node in the configuration file.

In this chapter, we will cover the following topics:

- Ingest APIs
- Accessing data in pipelines
- Processors
- Conditional execution in pipelines
- Handling failures in pipelines

Ingest APIs

Basic ingest CRUD APIs allow you to manage the entire life cycle process, from creation, update, retrieval deletion, and execution of the ingest pipeline. A pipeline is formed by a list of supported processors that are executed sequentially. Let's describe each CRUD API as follows:

- **Create/update the ingest pipeline**: To define a pipeline, you need to specify a list of processors (which will be executed in order) and a description to tell us what functions will be performed. The **PUT** request is used to create the pipeline with an identifier. If the pipeline was created previously, it will be an update request and will overwrite the original contents. Let's take an example of creating a pipeline with the range_ratio identifier by using a script processor. The range ratio is to compute the difference between the high and low price, and then set the ratio between this difference and the close price as described in the screenshot. The response is **OK (200)** if the operation succeeds and the pipeline will be available in the ingest nodes immediately:

- **Retrieve the ingest pipeline**: The **GET** API allows you to retrieve the definition of the pipeline with an identifier in the URL. The following screenshot is to retrieve the `range_ratio` pipeline using Postman. The response of a successful deletion is **OK (200)**. The **GET** response body will be similar to the previous **PUT** request to create/update the ingest pipeline:

- **Delete the ingest pipeline**: The **DELETE** API allows you to delete an ingest pipeline. You can use a wildcard asterisk expression to remove multiple pipelines as shown in the following screenshot. The response of a successful deletion is **OK (200)**, and if the identifier does not exist, it returns **Not Found (404)**:

- **Simulate the pipeline**: This valuable feature is designed to let you test your pipeline by specifying a `docs` parameter with an array of the testing documents. You can also provide an ad hoc pipeline definition in the request body to test too. Let's take an example to test the `range_ratio` ingest pipeline with an `ACWF` ETF historical price document on December 26, 2018, as shown in the following screenshot. In the response body, you can see that a new `range_ratio=0.03677992461596629` field has been reported. The `_ingest.timestamp` field is provided by the system to record the timestamp when processing occurs:

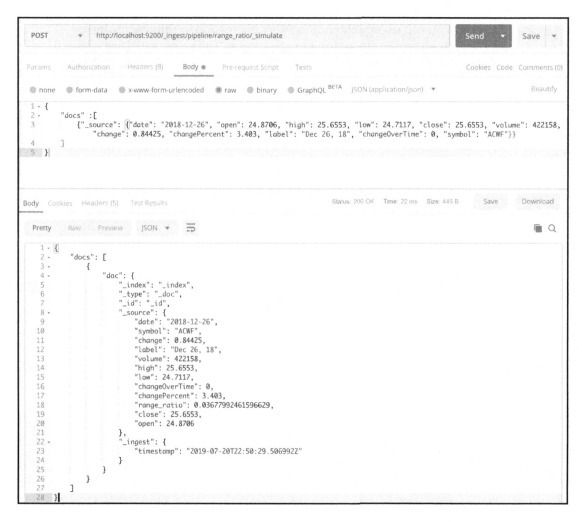

The following screenshot shows the test of an ad hoc ingest pipeline definition with the same content as the `range_ratio` pipeline. It provides the same result as the previous example:

- **Execute in the pipeline**: When you perform an index operation with a document, use the `pipeline` URL parameter with the name of the pipeline. Let's take an example; we will use the `range_ratio` pipeline while indexing the previous document to the `cf_etf_pipeline` index, with document identifier=1:

If you issue a **GET** request with document identifier=1 from the `cf_etf_pipeline` index, then you get the same document content with an extra `range_ratio=0.03677992461596629` field. In the next section, we will discuss how to access data in the pipelines.

Accessing data in pipelines

Fields in the _source field can be accessed directly in a pipeline definition simply by either using the field name or adding the _source prefix to the field name. On the other hand, if you are referring to the value of a field, then you can use the {{field_name}} template snippet to retrieve the value. Let's take an example of using a set processor to add an ingest_timestamp field to the document, which records the timestamp value when the ingest processing occurs. This value is provided by the API, as we mentioned in the result of the _simulate pipeline example. The partially relevant codes are as follows:

```
"processors": [{
    "set": {
        "field": "ingest_timestamp",
        "value": "{{_ingest.timestamp}}"
    }
}
```

Dynamic mapping fields and field values are also supported in the same way. Metadata fields such as _index, _id, and _routing can be accessed in the pipeline. For example, the following partially relevant codes show how to set the document identifier to 12345678:

```
"processors": [{
    "set": {
        "field": "_id",
        "value": "12345678"
    }
}]
```

Now that you know how to access data in the ingest processor, we can start describing each processor in the next section.

Processors

Nearly 30 processors are supported in the ingest pipeline. When the document is indexed, each processor executes as it is declared in the pipeline. A processor is defined with a name and configured with its own parameters. Before we introduce each processor, let's examine some of the common parameters as described in the following table:

Parameter Name	Description
field	The name of the field to be accessed in the processor. Most of the processors require this parameter.
target_field	The name of the destined field to be accessed in the processor. The default value depends on individual parameters. About half of the processors support this optional parameter.
ignore_missing	If the field pointed by the field parameter is missing, or the value of the field is a null value in the indexing document, it fails the execution. If this boolean parameter is set to true, then the error is ignored silently. This parameter is optional and default to false. About two-thirds of the parameters support it.
if	User-defined conditions for executing the processor. This parameter is optional and supported by all processors.
on_failure	Users define a list of processors to perform when an error occurs in the pipeline and halts execution. This parameter is optional and supported by all processors.
ignore_failure	A Boolean flag that silently ignores the failure of the processing and continues the execution of the next processor. This parameter is optional, it defaults to false, and is supported by all processors.
tag	You can specify a string for identifying the processor. This parameter is optional and supported by all processors.

Now, we can introduce each processor item by item:

- append: This processor requires parameter values and parameter fields. Suppose we have the value=X parameter and the field=Y parameter in the processor. If field=Y in the document is an array type, this processor appends X to it. If field=Y in the document is a scalar, the processor converts it to an array and then appends X to it. If the document does not have field=Y, then field=Y is created as an empty array and X is appended to it. If value=X is an array type, then the processor appends each item of X to Y:

```
"processors": [{
    "append": {
        "field": "field_name",
        "value": "value"
    }
}]
```

- bytes: This processor requires field parameters only. Suppose we have the field=X parameter. This processor converts X to a value in bytes if the string value of X is in the format of b, kb, mb, gb, tb, or pb (case insensitive) in the indexing document. The conversion value will be stored in the field specified by target_field if this optional parameter exists. Otherwise, field=X in the indexing document will be updated by the conversion value. This processor supports the ignore_missing parameter:

```
"processors": [{
    "bytes": {
        "field": "field_name_1",
        "target_field": "field_name_2",
        "ignore_missing: true|false
    }
}]
```

- convert: The convert processor requires the field and type parameters. Suppose we have parameter field X in data type Y and want to change the value of X in type Z of the indexing document. The conversion value will be stored in the field specified by target_field if this optional parameter exists. Otherwise, field X in the indexing document will be replaced by the conversion value. This processor supports the ignore_missing parameter:

```
"processors": [{
    "convert": {
        "field": "field_name_1",
        "type" : "new_data_type",
        "target_field": "field_name_2",
        "ignore_missing: true|false
    }
}]
```

- date: This processor requires the field and format parameters. Suppose we have parameter field X in a date format and we want to change it to a new date format specified in the format parameter. The parsed value will be stored in the field specified by target_field if this optional parameter exists. Otherwise, it will be stored in a new field named @timestamp. Two other supported optional parameters are timezone and locale. The timezone parameter defaults to UTC and the locale parameter is in English:

```
"processors": [{
    "date": {
        "field": "field_name_1",
        "formats": "new_date_format",
```

```
                    "target_field": "field_name_2",
                    "timezone": "PDT",
                    "locale": "en_US"
            }
    }]
```

- date_index_name: This processor requires
  the field and date_rounding parameters. Suppose we have parameter
  field X in a date format and we want to change the index name based on X after a
  round operation in the time units of y (year), M (month), w (week), d (day), h
  (hour), m (minute), or s (second). The parsed value overrides the _index meta
  field of the document. Five other supported optional parameters are timezone,
  locale, index_name_prefix, date_formats, and index_name_format.
  The timezone parameter defaults to UTC and the locale parameter is English.
  The index_name_format parameter is the date format to be used for the new
  index name. It defaults to yyyy-MM-dd. The prefix to be prepended to the result
  of the round operation to X is index_name_prefix. The expected date formats
  of X are date_formats. You can put all the expected date formats together in an
  array. The default value is yyyy-MM-dd'T'HH:mm:ss.SSSXX:

```
"processors": [{
    "date_index_name": {
        "date": "field_name",
        "date_rounding": "w",
        "date_formats": "field_name_2",
        "index_name_prefix": "weekly-"
        "index_name_format": ["yyyy-MM-dd"],
        "timezone": "PDT",
        "locale": "en_US"
    }
}]
```

- dot_expander: This processor requires a field parameter only. Suppose we have a field parameter and its value is y.z. When the y.z field exists in the indexing document with a value of k, the dot_expander processor transforms the y.z field to the nest field format, y:{z:k}. When the whole path involves more than two levels, you can use the optional parameter path to specify the parent path of a field:

```
"processors": [{
    "dot_expander": {
        "field": "field_name",
        "path": "parent_path"
    }
}]
```

- drop: This processor does not require any parameters. It is used to silently skip the indexing of documents if a user-defined condition is met:

```
"processors": [{
    "drop": {
        "if": condition_string
    }
}]
```

- fail: This processor requires the message parameter. It is used to return a user-defined failure message if a user-defined condition is met:

```
"processors": [{
    "fail": {
        "if": condition_string,
        "message": user_defined_message_string
    }
}]
```

- gsub: This processor requires
  the field, pattern, and replacement parameters. Suppose we have field=X, pattern=Y, and replacement=Z in the processor content. X in the indexing document is expected to be a string. If it is not, it raises an error. This processor will replace the occurrence of Y in X with Z. The replacement string will be stored in the field specified by target_field if this optional parameter exists. Otherwise, field=X in the indexing document will be replaced with the replacement string. This processor supports the ignore_missing parameter:

```
"processors": [{
    "gsub": {
        "field": "field_name_1,
```

```
        "target_field": "field_name_2",
        "pattern": regex_pattern,
        "replacement": replacement_string
    }
}]
```

- `join`: This processor requires the `field` and `separator` parameters. Suppose we have the `field=X` and `separator=Y` parameters. `X` is expected to be an array type in the indexing document, and `Y` is expected to be a user-defined character. This processor will concatenate each item in `X` with the `separator=Y` parameter. The concatenated string will be stored in the field specified by `target_field` if this optional parameter exists. Otherwise, `field=X` in the indexing document will be updated by the concatenated string. If `X` is not of the array type, then the processor raises an error:

```
"processors": [{
    "join": {
        "field": "field_name_1",
        "separator": separator_character,
        "target_field", "field_name_2"
    }
}]
```

- `json`: This processor requires the `field` parameter only. Suppose we have the `field=X` parameter. `X` is expected to be a JSON string. This processor will transform `X` from a JSON string to a JSON object data structure. The transformed object will be stored in the field specified by `target_field` if this optional parameter exists. Otherwise, `field=X` in the indexing document will be updated by the transformed object. Another supported optional Boolean parameter, `add_to_root`, is provided to store the transformed object at the root level of the document (if set to true). It defaults to false. If `X` is not a JSON string, then the processor raises an error:

```
"processors": [{
    "json": {
        "field": "field_name_1",
        "target_field": "field_name_2",
        "add_to_root": true|false,
    }
}]
```

- `pipeline`: This processor requires the `name` parameter only. Suppose we have the `name=X` parameter. `X` is expected to be a pipeline name. This processor will execute the predefined `X` pipeline. If `X` is not a predefined pipeline name, then the processor raises an error:

```
"processors": [{
    "pipeline": {
        "name": "pipe_name"
    }
}]
```

- `remove`: This processor requires the `field` parameter only. Suppose we have the `field=X` parameter. This processor will remove `field=X` from the indexing documents. If you want to delete multiple fields, specify `X` as an array containing the elements with the fields you want to delete. This processor supports the `ignore_missing` parameter:

```
"processors": [{
    "remove": {
        "field": ["field_name_1", "field_name_2"]
    }
}]
```

- `rename`: This processor requires the `field` and `target_field` parameters. Suppose we have the `field=X` and `target_field=Y` parameters. This processor will rename `field=X` to `field=Y` in the indexing documents. If `X` does not exist in the document or if `Y` does exist in the document, then the processor raises an error. This processor supports the `ignore_missing` parameter:

```
"processors": [{
    "rename": {
        "field": "field_name_1",
        "target_field": "field_name_2"
    }
}]
```

- `set`: This processor requires the `field` and `value` parameters. Suppose we have the `field=X` and `value=Y` parameters. This processor will set `X=Y` if `X` exists in the document. Otherwise, `field=X` is added and its value is set to `Y`. If the optional `override` parameter is set to `false` and the `field=X` parameter in the indexing document has a non-null value, the operation will be skipped:

```
"processors": [{
    "set": {
```

```
            "field":field_name_1,
            "value": "value_1",
            "override": true|false
        }
    }]
```

- `split`: This processor requires the `field` and `separator` parameters. Suppose we have the `field=X` and `separator=Y` parameters. `X` is expected to be a string in the indexing document, and `Y` is a regex expression used as a separator. This processor will break `X` into items and store them as an array according to the `separator=Y` parameter. The array of items will be stored in the field specified by `target_field` if this optional parameter exists. Otherwise, `field=X` in the indexing document will be updated by the concatenated string. This processor supports the `ignore_missing` parameter:

```
"processors": [{
    "split": {
        "field": "field_name_1",
        "separator": regex_expression,
        "target_field", "field_name_2"
    }
}]
```

- `sort`: This processor requires the `field` parameter only. Suppose we have the `field=X` parameter. `X` is expected to be an array of numbers or strings in the indexing document. This processor will sort the array numerically if the items in the array are of number types. Otherwise, it sorts the array in alphabetical order. The array of items will be stored in the field specified by `target_field` if this optional parameter exists. Otherwise, `field=X` in the indexing document will be updated by the sorted array. An optional `order` parameter is the sorting direction, which defaults to `asc` (ascending). To sort in descending order, set `order` to `desc`:

```
"processors": [{
    "sort": {
        "field": "field_name_1",
        "order": asc|desc,
        "target_field", "field_name_2"
    }
}]
```

- `trim`: This processor requires the `field` parameter only. Suppose we have the `field=X` parameter. `X` is expected to be a string in the indexing document. This processor will remove the leading and trailing whitespace character of `X`. The trimmed string will be stored in the field specified by `target_field` if this optional parameter exists. Otherwise, `field=X` in the indexing document will be updated by the trimmed string. This processor supports the `ignore_missing` parameter:

```
"processors": [{
    "trim": {
        "field": "field_name_1",
        "target_field", "field_name_2"
    }
}]
```

- `uppercase`: This processor requires the `field` parameter only. Suppose we have the `field=X` parameter. This processor capitalizes `X` in the indexing document. The capitalized string will be stored in the field specified by `target_field` if this optional parameter exists. Otherwise, `field=X` in the indexing document will be updated by the capitalized string. This processor supports the `ignore_missing` parameter:

```
"processors": [{
    "uppercase": {
        "field": "field_name_1",
        "target_field", "field_name_2"
    }
}]
```

- `url_decode`: This processor requires the `field` parameter only. Suppose we have the `field=X` parameter. This processor performs a URL decoding operation on `X` in the indexing document. The decoded string will be stored in the field specified by `target_field` if this optional parameter exists. Otherwise, `field=X` in the indexing document will be updated by the capitalized string. This processor supports the `ignore_missing` parameter:

```
"processors": [{
    "urldecode": {
        "field": "field_name_1",
        "target_field", "field_name_2"
    }
}]
```

- set_security_user: This processor requires the field parameter only. Suppose we have the field=X parameter. This processor adds field=X to the indexing document and populates the content with the currently authenticated user. If field=X exists in the indexing document, its content will be overwritten. An optional properties parameter is provided for you to select parts of content such as username, roles, email, full_name, and metadata to store:

```
"processors": [{
    "set_security_user": {
        "field": "field_name_1",
        "properties": [username, roles, email, full_name,
metadata]]
    }
}]
```

- user_agent: This processor requires the field parameter only. Suppose we have the field=X parameter. X is expected to be a user agent string used to extract detailed information from the web response. This information will be stored in the field specified by target_field if this optional parameter exists. Otherwise, it will be stored in the field named user_agent in the indexing document. An optional properties parameter is provided for you to select parts of content, such as name, major, minor, patch, build, os, os_name, os_major, os_minor, and device, to store. An optional regex_file parameter is provided to specify the custom **Yet Another Markup Language (YAML)** file under the config/ingest-user-agent directory. The YAML file has a regex expression to parse the user agent's information. Interested users can take a look at the default file shipped with the user_agent ingest (https://github.com/ua-parser/uap-core/blob/master/regexes.yaml). This processor supports the ignore_missing parameter:

```
"processors": [{
    "user_agent": {
        "field": "field_name_1",
        "properties": [name, major, minor, patch, build, os,
os_name, os_major, os_minor, device]
    }
}]
```

- `script`: This processor requires no parameters. The script content to be executed is specified in the optional `source` parameter or the `source` code stored with the `script` identifier referenced by the optional `id` parameter. An optional `params` parameter lets you specify the parameter values used in the script content. The default script language is Painless. If you use another programming language, such as Java, you can use the optional `lang` parameter to specify it:

```
"processors": [{
    "script": {
        "source": script_source
        "params": { param_1:value_1, param_2: value_2}
    }
}]
```

- `kv`: This processor requires the `field`, `field_split`, and `value_split` parameters. Suppose we have the `field=X`, `field_split=Y`, and `value_split=Z` parameters. X is expected to contain one or more key-value-like pairs strings in the indexing document. There are some S characters between each key-value-like pair string. Y is expected to be a regular expression that can match those S characters. Z is expected to be a regular expression that matches some characters in the key-value-like pair string. This processor will transform X in the indexing document into a key-value-like pair according to Y and Z. The key-value-like pairs will be stored under the field specified by `target_field` if this optional parameter exists. Otherwise, each key will be added as a field to the top level of the indexing document and assigned the corresponding value. This processor supports the `ignore_missing` parameter:

```
"processors": [{
    "kv": {
        "field": source_string
        "field_split": regex_pattern_1,
        "value_split": regex_pattern_2
    }
}]
```

Other useful optional parameters in the `kv` processor are described in the following table:

Parameter	Description
include_keys	Specifies a list of keys, that may be present in `field=X` of the indexing documents to be included. The default includes all keys in X.
exclude_keys	Specifies a list of keys that, may be present in `field=X` of the indexing documents to be excluded.
trim_key	Specifies a string of characters to trim from `field=X` of the indexing documents.
trim_value	Specifies a string of characters to trim from `field=Y` of the indexing documents.
prefix	Specifies a prefix string to add to the key of the transformed key-value pair.
strip_brackets	If set to `true`, it strips brackets such as *{}*, ◇, *[]*, ' (single quote), and " (double quote) from the value of the transformed key-value pair.

Let's take an example to illustrate the usage. Assume that the input document has only one text field, named `input_field`, and its value is as follows:

```
{"input_field":" a:b , c:d "}
```

We want to have the final document indexed as follows:

```
{"output_field": {
    "a": "b",
    "c": "d"
}}
```

According to our description, the values of X, S, Y, and Z are as follows:

```
X ⇒ "field":"input_field"
key-value-like pairs string ⇒ " a:b ", " c:d "
S ⇒ " , "
Y ⇒ "field_split" : ","
Z ⇒ "value_split" : ":"
To trim the field from " a" to "a" ⇒ "trim_key" : " "
To trim the value from "b " to "b" ⇒ "trim_value" : " "
To output as the name output_field ⇒ "target_field" : "output_field"
Add a remove processor to remove the original input_field =>
    { "remove" : { "field": ["input_field"]}}
```

The following screenshot shows the test using the _simulate API and the result of the example:

- geoip: This processor requires the field parameter only. Suppose we have the field=X parameter. X is expected to be an IP address used to extract information from the geographical lookup of the Maxmind database (interested users can refer to https://dev.maxmind.com/geoip/geoip2/geolite2). The trimmed string will be stored in the field specified by target_field if this optional parameter exists. Otherwise, the geoip field will be added to the indexing document and store the information. An optional properties parameter is provided for you to select parts of geoIP content, such as continent_name, country_iso_code, region_iso_code, region_name, city_name, and location, to store. This processor supports the ignore_missing parameter. An optional database_file parameter is provided to select one of the shipped databases, including GeoLite2-City.mmdb, GeoLite2-Country.mmdb, and GeoLite2-ASN.mmdb:

```
"processors": [{
    "geoip": {
        "field": "field_name_1",
        "target_field": "field_name_2",
        "ignore_missing": true|false
    }
}]
```

- grok: This processor requires the field and patterns parameters. Suppose we have the field=X and patterns=Y parameters. X is expected to be a text field in the indexing document, and Y is expected to be an ordered list of Logstash Grok expression (https://www.elastic.co/guide/en/logstash/current/plugins-filters-grok.html). This processor will extract from X according to pattern Y and add a key-value pair to the top level of the indexing document. Each key is a field, and each value is assigned to the corresponding field. You can customize your own patterns specified by the optional pattern_definitions parameter. Otherwise, the default patterns will be used. You can trace which patterns matched and populated into the indexing document by setting the optional trace_match Boolean parameter to true. The pattern number (starting from 0) will be reported in the response in the _grok_match_index field. This processor supports the ignore_missing parameter:

```
"processors": [{
    "grok": {
        "field": "field_name_1",
        "patterns": logstash_grok_pattern,
        "trace_match": true|false,
        "ignore_missing": true|false
```

```
          }
    }]
```

Let's illustrate the usage with an example. Assume that the input document has only one text field, named `message`, and its value is as follows:

```
{"message":"[2019-06-20T00:04:58,856][INFO
][o.e.c.m.MetaDataDeleteIndexService] [WTW.local]
[cf_etf/RiYRsKyxTGStNcHczbUxcQ] deleting index"}
```

We want to have the final document indexed as follows:

```
{
    "node": "WTW.local",
    "log-level": "INFO",
    "index_doc": "cf_etf/RiYRsKyxTGStNcHczbUxcQ",
    "action": " deleting index",
    "class": "o.e.c.m.MetaDataDeleteIndexService",
    "timestamp": "2019-06-20T00:04:58,856"
}
```

According to the message format and the Logstash `grok` expression, the `grok` patterns for `node`, `log-level`, `index_doc`, `action`, `class`, and `timestamp` are as follows:

```
timestamp ⇒ %{TIMESTAMP_ISO8601:timestamp}
log-level ⇒   %{LOGLEVEL:log-level}
class   ⇒   %{JAVACLASS:class}
node ⇒ %{DATA:node}
index_doc ⇒ %{DATA:index_doc}
action ⇒ %{GREEDYDATA:action}
space character ⇒ %{SPACE}
escape bracket ⇒ \\[, \\]
```

We also add a `remove` processor after the Grok processor to remove the original `message` field. The following screenshot shows the test using the `_simulate` API and the result of the example:

- `dissect`: Similar to the `grok` processor, the `dissect` processor also requires the `field` and `pattern` parameters. It works the same as the `grok` processor to extract from a single text field according to patterns, and adds key-value pairs to the top level of the indexing document. Each key is a field, and each value is assigned to the corresponding field in the indexing document. Unlike the `grok` processor, the `dissect` processor does not use regular expressions. Instead, it just likes a pattern to match on the text field against the user-defined pattern. The format of the pattern includes two elements: partial text segments from the original text field and keys. Each key is specified in the format of `%{key_name}`, where `key_name` is the name of the key to be added to the indexing document. The partial text segments are just used in the pattern matching stage. If the corresponding value of *key_name* cannot be found from the text field, the processor will throw an exception. If a field is referred to with more than one match, there is more than one corresponding value. All the related values are concatenated together with a separator. The default separator of the appended value is an empty string. An optional `append_separator` parameter can be used to specify the separator. This processor supports the `ignore_missing` parameter:

```
"processors": [{
    "dissect": {
        "field": "field_name_1",
        "patterns": dissect_pattern,
        "trace_match": true|false,
        "ignore_missing": true|false
    }
}]
```

Several key modifiers are supported to let you change the behavior for the `dissect` pattern. They are described in the following table:

Modifier	Example	Description
`->`	`%{key_name->}`	Ignores any right-hand side repeated characters
`+`	`%{+key_name_1}` `%{+key_name_2}`	Appends values together to the same key in order
`+ with /n`	`%{+key_name_1/2}` `%{+key_name_1/1}`	Appends values together to the same key following the order specified by the modifier
`?`	`%{?key_name}`	Skips the matched key
`* with &`	`%{*key_name}:%{&value}`	Keeps the original key name and original value
	`%{}`	Skips the matched key

Let's take the same example as the `grok` processor to illustrate how to use it. Assume that the input document has only one text field, named `message`, and its value is as follows:

```
{"message":"[2019-06-20T00:04:58,856][INFO
][o.e.c.m.MetaDataDeleteIndexService] [WTW.local]
[cf_etf/RiYRsKyxTGStNcHczbUxcQ] deleting index"}
```

According to the message format and the Logstash `grok` expression, the `grok` patterns for `node`, `log-level`, `index_doc`, `action`, `class`, and `timestamp` are as follows:

```
timestamp ⇒ %{timestamp}
log-level ⇒  %{log-level}
class  ⇒  %{class}
node ⇒ %{node}
index_doc ⇒ %{index_doc}
action ⇒ %{action}
no need to translate space character and escape the bracket.
```

The following screenshot shows the test using the `_simulate` API and the result of the example:

We have now discussed all the processors supported. In the next section, we will deal with the conditional execution of the processors in the pipeline.

Conditional execution in pipelines

As we mentioned in the *Processors* section, the optional `if` parameter is designed to let users define conditions for executing the pipeline processor. Let's demo a simple case with an example. The `rating` field of the documents in the index of *cf_etf* is a single space string when no rating is given for ETF in the original source. We can use the `remove` processor to remove the rating field in such a condition before the indexing operation, as shown in the following code block:

```
"pipeline": {
    "description":"remove the rating field if the rating is equal to a
single space string",
    "processors":[{
        "remove": {
            "field": "rating",
            "if": "ctx.rating == ' '"
        }
    }]
}
```

You will recall the dividend information in *The Investor Exchange (IEX)* section of Chapter *7, Modeling Your Data in the Real World*. We can use the nested object mapping data type to handle parent-child relationships. We can use a field in an array type named `announcement` to store the dividend records. Some ETFs may not distribute dividends, so the `announcement` object field may not exist. If we need to access the field of the `announcement` object, we have to check the existence of the `announcement`. If the parent `announcement` does not exist, `NullPonterException` will be thrown. To avoid this situation, we can also use the `ignore_missing` parameter. Another approach is to use a null safe operator (to check the null value of the parent field). If the parent field does not exist, it returns to null. Let's take another example to show three testing cases with the `_simulate` API: *(1) child exists*, *(2) child not exist*, and *(3) parent not exist* as shown in the following code block:

```
"pipeline": {
    "description":"testing parent-child relationship with ?. operator",
    "processors":[
        {"set":{
            "field": "new_id",
            "value": "{{id}}",
            "if": "ctx.parent?.child != null"
        }}
    ]
},
"docs" :[
```

```
        {"_source": {"id":1, "parent": {"child":"value"}}},
        {"_source": {"id":2, "parent": {}}},
        {"_source": {"id":3}}
    ]
```

Another recommended usage is to use conditional execution with the pipeline processor, just like a switch case statement implemented by the `if` parameter. In the `cf_etf` index, the `market_cap` field is optional and can be null for some ETFs. If we have different processing behavior for documents with null and non-null `market_cap` fields, we can provide a solution with conditional execution. The following code block shows a switch to the corresponding predefined processor according to the `market_cap` field:

```
"pipeline": {
    "description":"market_cap pre-processing",
    "processors":[
        {"pipeline":{
            "name": "for_market_cap_null_processor",
            "if": "ctx.market_cap == null"
        }},
        {"pipeline":{
            "name": "for_market_cap_processor",
            "if": "ctx.market_cap != null"
        }}
    ]
},
"docs" :[
    {"_source": {"id":1, "market_cap": null}},
    {"_source": {"id":2, "market_cap": "large"}}
]
```

We have discussed most of the conditional execution handling in ingest pipeline processing. One more item we would like to bring out is using the regular expression to write the condition for the `if` parameter. Those who are interested can refer to https://www.elastic.co/guide/en/elasticsearch/reference/current/conditionals-with-regex.html. In the next section, we'll briefly introduce error handling.

Handling failures in pipelines

As discussed in the *Ingest APIs* section of this chapter, a pipeline is formed by a list of supported processors that are executed sequentially. If an exception occurs, the whole process is halted. Let's show an exception with an example. The processor in the pipeline is to remove the `rating` field from the indexing document. However, the `rating` field is optional and it may not be present. When an error occurs, you can check out the root clause in the `error` field. When the field rating is missing in the remove processor, it shows you that the reason is **field [rating] not present as part of path [rating]**:

```
POST      ▼    http://localhost:9200/_ingest/pipeline/_simulate

Params    Headers (2)    Body ●

● none    ● form-data    ● x-www-form-urlencoded    ● raw    ● binary    ● GraphQL BETA    JSON (application/json)  ▼                            Beautify

1 ▾ {
2 ▾    "pipeline": {
3          "description":"test of hitting the exception error",
4 ▾        "processors":[{
5 ▾            "remove": {
6                  "field": "rating"
7              }
8          }]
9      },
10 ▾   "docs" :[
11         {"_source": {"id":3}}
12     ]
13  }
```

EXAMPLE RESPONSE

```
Body    Headers (5)                                                                              Status    200 OK

Pretty    Raw    Preview    JSON  ▼   ⇉                                                                      🗐  Q

1 ▾ {
2 ▾    "docs": [
3 ▾        {
4 ▾            "error": {
5 ▾                "root_cause": [
6 ▾                    {
7                          "type": "exception",
8                          "reason": "java.lang.IllegalArgumentException: java.lang.IllegalArgumentException: field [rating] not present as part of path
                                      [rating]",
9 ▾                        "header": {
10                             "processor_type": "remove"
11                         }
12                     }
13                 ],
14                 "type": "exception",
15                 "reason": "java.lang.IllegalArgumentException: java.lang.IllegalArgumentException: field [rating] not present as part of path [rating]",
16 ▾              "caused_by": {
17                     "type": "illegal_argument_exception",
18                     "reason": "java.lang.IllegalArgumentException: field [rating] not present as part of path [rating]",
19 ▾                  "caused_by": {
20                         "type": "illegal_argument_exception",
21                         "reason": "field [rating] not present as part of path [rating]"
22                     }
23                 },
24 ▾              "header": {
25                     "processor_type": "remove"
26                 }
27             }
28         }
29     ]
30  }
```

If the error can be ignored, you can set the optional `ingore_failure` parameter to `true` to silently ignore the failure and continue the execution of the next processor. Another choice is to use the `on_failure` parameter to catch the exception and perform some processing for clean-up or messaging work. Finally, the pipeline fails gracefully. In the following screenshot, we include two `set` processors inside the `on_failure` handling. The root reason for the error can be retrieved by using the `_ingest.on_failure_message` metadata. Now, the error code and error message are in the response when the simulation encounters an error:

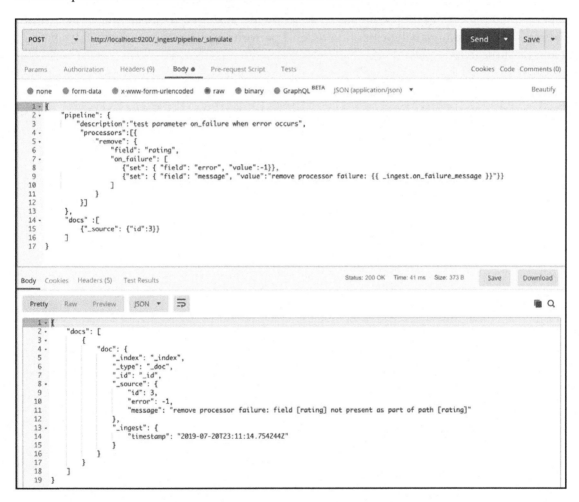

In this final section, we have completed our discussion of error handling. Before we close this chapter, let's give a brief summary in the next section.

Summary

Time flies so fast! We are in the middle of this book. In this chapter, we have performed the Ingest APIs and practiced most of the pipeline processors. We have also learned about data access to documents that pass through the pipeline processor. Finally, we have discussed how to handle exceptions when errors occur during pipeline processing.

In the next chapter, we will discuss how to use aggregation frameworks for exploratory data analysis. We'll give you a few examples, such as collecting metrics and log data generated by the system for operational data analytics, ingesting financial investment fund data before performing analytic operations, and performing simple sentiment analysis using Elasticsearch.

10
Using Elasticsearch for Exploratory Data Analysis

In the previous chapter, we learned how to preprocess documents by using ingest pipeline processors before indexing operations. We've looked at all Ingest APIs and learned how to use the processors. We were also involved in an in-depth discussion of conditional execution and error handling.

In this chapter, we'll use a powerful tool, the Aggregation Framework, to perform data analysis. According to the definition from the **Information Technology Laboratory (ITL)** at the **National Institute of Standards and Technology (NIST)** (`https://www.itl.nist.gov/div898/handbook/eda/section1/eda11.htm`), **Exploratory Data Analysis (EDA)** is an approach to carrying out data analysis by allowing the data to reveal its underlying structure and model. We'll try to use a few examples to illustrate EDA.

By the end of this chapter, we will have covered the following topics:

- Business analytics
- Operational data analytics
- Sentiment analysis

Business analytics

The general concept of business analytics is to measure past business performance by using a combination of skills, methods, and techniques to gain insight into decisions when planning for the future of the business. Elasticsearch can provide data-driven insights to help solve problems and improve efficiency. Let's take an example to investigate closing-price changes by using the Morningstar category of commission-free ETF. Recall that, in the documentation of the cf_etf_hist_price index, introduced in Chapter 8, *Aggregations Framework*, has only a symbol field. There is no way to group the documents into such a category using only the cf_etf_hist_price index unless we manually attach the Morningstar_category field during the indexing operation. Of course, this can be solved programmatically. However, we will solve it by using only Elasticsearch with the following few steps:

1. **Get all Morningstar categories**: We use a terms aggregation to get all Morningstar categories. The following screenshot shows the request of the terms aggregation:

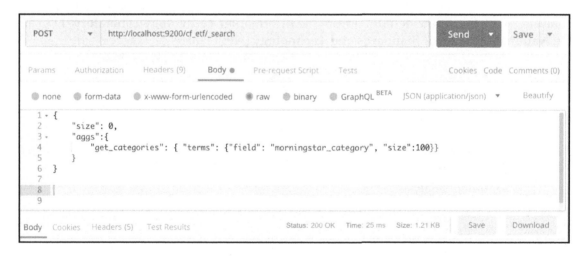

There are 80 categories in total. We will investigate the 10 largest groups in the table:

Morningstar category	Number of ETFs
Diversified Emerging Mkts	16
Large Blend	14
Miscellaneous Region	14
Europe Stock	11
Technology	11
Foreign Large Blend	9
China Region	8
High Yield Bond	8
Ultrashort Bond	8
Allocation—30% to 50% Equity	7

2. **Find all ETF symbols for each category**: For each category, we use a `terms` aggregation to get all the ETF symbols in the given category. The following screenshot shows the request of the `terms` aggregation for the `Diversified Emerging Mkts` category:

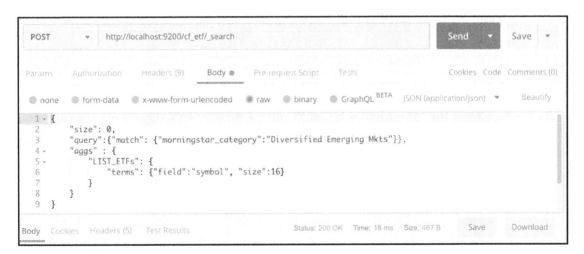

There are 16 ETFs in total under the `Diversified Emerging Mkts` category, as shown in the following table:

Funds symbol in Diversified Emerging Mkts Category	Full fund name
DEM	WisdomTree Emerging Markets High Dividend Fund
DGRE	WisdomTree Emerging Markets Quality Dividend Growth Fund
DGS	WisdomTree Emerging Markets SmallCap Dividend Fund
DVEM	WisdomTree Emerging Markets Dividend Fund
EDIV	SPDR® S&P Emerging Markets Dividend ETF
EEMX	SPDR® MSCI Emerging Markets Fossil Fuel Free ETF
EMCG	WisdomTree Emerging Markets Consumer Growth Fund
EMDV	ProShares MSCI Emerging Markets Dividend Growers ETF
ESGE	iShares ESG MSCI EM ETF
EWX	SPDR® S&P Emerging Markets Small Cap ETF
PXH	Invesco FTSE RAFI Emerging Markets ETF
QEMM	SPDR® MSCI Emerging Markets StrategicFactors ETF
RFEM	First Trust RiverFront Dynamic Emerging Markets ETF
SPEM	SPDR® Portfolio Emerging Markets ETF
UEVM	USAA MSCI Emerging Markets Value Momentum Blend Index ETF
XSOE	WisdomTree Emerging Markets ex-State-Owned Enterprises Fund

3. **Calculate the symbolic momentum value for each category**: The daily symbolic momentum of an ETF is equal to its daily transaction volume multiplied by its daily price change. The daily symbolic momentum of a category is equal to the summation of the daily momentum of each individual ETF in the given category. The following screenshot shows an example of calculating the weekly symbolic momentum of the `Diversified Emerging Mkts` category. This request includes two parts; search and aggregation:

   • The first part is to prepare the documents for aggregation. It searches all the documents belonging to the `Diversified Emerging Mkts` category from within the given time period (between `2018-12-26` and `2019-03-25`), as shown in the following screenshot:

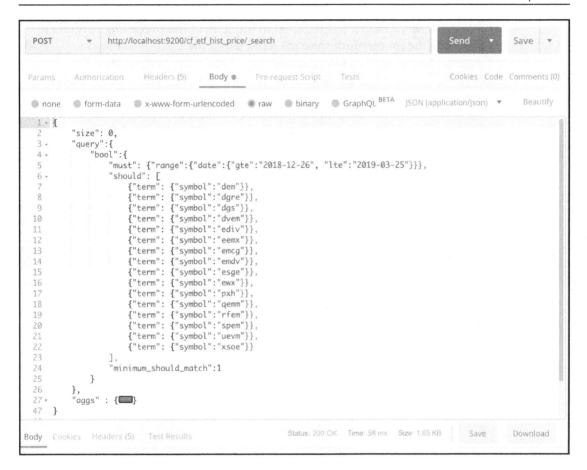

- The second part is to perform the summation of the multiplication of the volume and change for each ETF on each trading day within the same week. We want to analyze the weekly trends. The computation formula is described in the following code block:

```
morningstar_category_i ∈ (ETFi1, ETFi2, ..., ETFin)
weekly_momentum_of_category_i = (∑ETFin∑trading_day_j_of_Week volumeETFin,j *
changeETFin,j)/ (n*number_of_trading_day_in_the_week)
```

- We use *scripted* metric aggregation to implement the preceding formula to compute the momentum for each week using the `date_histogram` aggregation with a `1w` interval. There are four parts to the script. The `init_script` initializes the temporary storage. The `map_script` computes the momentum for an ETF on a given trading day. The `combine_script` computes the average momentum for two temporary results from `map_scripts`. The `reduce_script` computes the average weekly momentum for the category. Let's take a look at the *scripted* metric aggregation in the following screenshot:

- The following diagram gives a better illustration of how the scripted metric aggregation is computed. The interval of the aggregation is per week and we start from `2018-12-16`. According to the calendar, the starting day of each week will be `2018-12-24`, `2018-12-31`, `2019-01-07`, and so on:

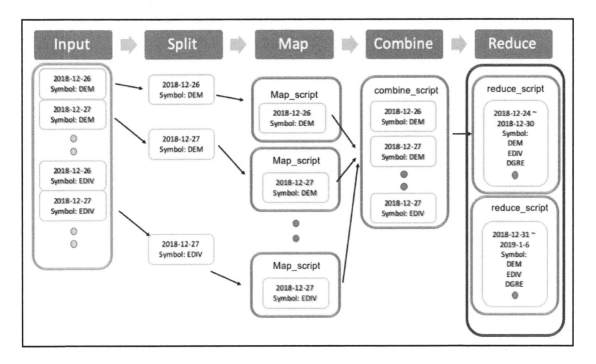

4. In the response, the `weekly_momentum` results will be marked with the first day of the week. Although our document range starts from `2018-12-26`, the first bucket is marked `2018-12-24`. The weekly average momentum, `cv`, is about `99599` for the week of `2018-12-24`, as shown in the following screenshot:

```
1 ▾ {
2        "took": 13,
3        "timed_out": false,
4 ▸      "_shards": {■},
10 ▸     "hits": {■},
18 ▾    "aggregations": {
19 ▾        "weekly_momentum": {
20 ▾            "buckets": [
21 ▾                {
22                     "key_as_string": "2018-12-24",
23                     "key": 1545609600000,
24                     "doc_count": 42,
25 ▾                   "cv": {
26                         "value": 556680.3263584425
27                     }
28                 },
29 ▾                {
30                     "key_as_string": "2018-12-31",
31                     "key": 1546214400000,
32                     "doc_count": 56,
33 ▾                   "cv": {
34                         "value": 92985.74867256165
35                     }
36                 },
37 ▾                {
38                     "key_as_string": "2019-01-07",
39                     "key": 1546819200000,
40                     "doc_count": 70,
41 ▾                   "cv": {
42                         "value": 277824.4869458773
43                     }
44                 },
```

5. After we collect the data from all 10 categories, we can plot the average weekly momentum versus the first day of the week. Let's examine the behaviors of the momentum for each Morningstar category, as shown in the following screenshot:

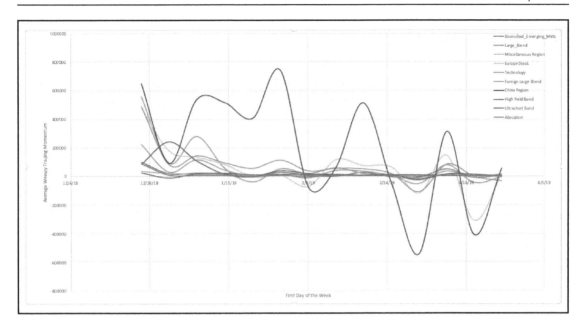

Applying business analytics concept to observe the graph, we can see that the `Diversified Emerging Mkts` category had much more momentum than other categories during the period. It also often has big fluctuations. This indicates that the momentum rebounds from the trough to the peak of the plot. When the momentum reaches its peak, it will not last for a few days. We also observe that, for the past two weeks, the `Europe Stock` category has had the same behavior as the `Diversified Emerging Mkts` category. Compared with these two categories, all other categories have had much less momentum within the past two months. From the business point of view, these two categories are much more active and may offer a way to take advantage of the price change within a short cycle. On the other hand, it also tells us that these two categories are not suitable for conservative investors.

We have produced a brief business investing analysis from the results of using EAD approach with Elasticsearch. In the next section, we will take a look at operational data analytics using the daily price change from a few ETFs.

Operational data analytics

Many professionals in the industry use the term **operational data analytics** to refer to the real-time observation of business processes. In the analytics world, operational data analytics are used to examine the latest information that businesses encounter every day, and then making the appropriate adjustments and proposing an instant solution for change. Regarding the technical stock price and volatility indicators, Bollinger Bands are a popular analysis tool to inform daily trading decisions. The band is composed of three different lines, with two standard deviations (positive and negative) away from **simple moving averages (SMA)**. Volatility is based on standard deviation. As the volatility increases, the band widens, and vice versa. The formula for Bollinger Bands is described in the following code block. Interested readers can take a look at the reference used here at https://www.investopedia.com/terms/b/bollingerbands.asp:

```
BBU = SMA(tp,window)  + n*StdDev(tp,window)
BBL = SMA(tp,window)  - n*StdDev(tp,window)
where:
BBU = Upper bound Bollinger band
BBL = Lower bound Bollinger band
SMA = Moving average using simple model
tp = typical price = (high + low + close)/3
window = number of days involved in the moving average (typically 20)
StdDev = Standard Deviation
n = a number (typically 2)
```

Recall that we introduced a simple model in the *Moving average aggregation* and *Standard deviation moving function* sections in Chapter 8, *Aggregation Framework*. We will implement the Bollinger bands using these two aggregations in this section. Let's take an example to investigate the First Trust RiverFront Dynamic Emerging Markets ETF (*symbol = rfem*) within the period of 2018-12-26 to 2019-03-25. We will see the list of instructions in following steps:

1. **Collect all the related documents with search operations**: We use the bool query with a must clause to collect documents from 2018-12-26 to 2019-03-25 with the symbol rfem. The relevant code is demonstrated in the following screenshot:

```
1 - {
2      "size": 0,
3 -    "query":{
4 -       "bool":{
5 -          "must": [
6                {"range":{"date":{"gte":"2018-12-26", "lte":"2019-03-25"}}},
7                {"term": {"symbol":"rfem"}}
8             ]
9          }
10      },
11 >    "aggs" : {▭}
55  }
```

2. **Calculate the daily typical price** (`tp`): We use the date histogram
   (`date_histogram`) bucket aggregation with the `interval=1d` parameter (which
   is equal to 1 day) and the `min_doc_count=1`parameter to perform the
   computation on the trading day. Then, we use the `scripted_metric` sub-
   aggregation to compute the typical price, `tp`, where *tp=(high + low + close)/3*. The
   relevant code is demonstrated in the following screenshot:

```
1 - {
2      "size": 0,
3 >    "query": {▭},
22 -   "aggs": {
23 -      "Bollinger_band": {
24 -         "date_histogram": {
25               "field": "date",
26               "interval": "1d",
27               "format": "yyyy-MM-dd",
28               "min_doc_count": 1
29           },
30 -         "aggs": {
31 -            "tp": {
32 -               "scripted_metric": {
33                     "init_script": "state.totals=[]",
34                     "map_script": "state.totals.add((doc.high.value+doc.low.value+doc.close.value)/3)",
35                     "combine_script": "double total=0; for (t in state.totals) {total += t} return total",
36                     "reduce_script": "return states[0]"
37                 }
38              },
39 >            "20_trading_days_moving_avg": {▭},
46 >            "20_trading_days_stdDev": {▭},
53 >            "BBU": {▭},
62 >            "BBL": {▭}
71           }
72        }
73     }
74  }
```

3. **Calculate daily SMA$_{(tp,window)}$:** We use a moving average (moving_avg) pipeline aggregation named 20_trading_days_moving_avg, with the simple model, the window parameter equal to 20 trading days, and buckets_path=tp.value to compute the daily moving average:

```
 1  {
 2      "size": 0,
 3      "query": {...},
22      "aggs": {
23          "Bollinger_band": {
24              "date_histogram": {...},
30              "aggs": {
31                  "tp": {...},
39                  "20_trading_days_moving_avg": {
40                      "moving_avg": {
41                          "model": "simple",
42                          "window": 20,
43                          "buckets_path": "tp.value"
44                      }
45                  },
46                  "20_trading_days_stdDev": {...},
53                  "BBU": {...},
62                  "BBL": {...}
71              }
72          }
73      }
74  }
```

4. **Calculate the daily StdDev$_{(tp,window)}$:** We use the moving function (moving_fn) pipeline aggregation, named 20_trading_days_stdDev, with the prebuilt stdDev() function, the window parameter equal to 20 trading days, and buckets_path=tp.value to compute the daily standard deviation:

```
 1  {
 2      "size": 0,
 3      "query": {...},
22      "aggs": {
23          "Bollinger_band": {
24              "date_histogram": {...},
30              "aggs": {
31                  "tp": {...},
39                  "20_trading_days_moving_avg": {...},
46                  "20_trading_days_stdDev": {
47                      "moving_fn": {
48                          "script": "MovingFunctions.stdDev(values, MovingFunctions.unweightedAvg(values))",
49                          "window": 20,
50                          "buckets_path": "tp.value"
51                      }
52                  },
53                  "BBU": {...},
62                  "BBL": {...}
71              }
72          }
73      }
74  }
```

5. **Calculate BBU (Bollinger Band upperbound) and BBL (Bollinger Band lowerbound)**: We use bucket script (`bucket_script`) aggregations, named BBU and BBL, with the `buckets_path` parameter, using `20_trading_days_moving_avg` and `20_trading_days_stdDev` to calculate the values:

```
22 ▾      "aggs": {
23 ▾          "Bollinger_band": {
24 ▸              "date_histogram": {▨},
30 ▾              "aggs": {
31 ▸                  "tp": {▨},
39 ▸                  "20_trading_days_moving_avg": {▨},
46 ▸                  "20_trading_days_stdDev": {▨},
53 ▾                  "BBU": {
54 ▾                      "bucket_script": {
55 ▾                          "buckets_path": {
56                               "SMA": "20_trading_days_moving_avg",
57                               "StdDev": "20_trading_days_stdDev"
58                           },
59                           "script": "params.SMA + 2 * params.StdDev"
60                       }
61                   },
62 ▾                  "BBL": {
63 ▾                      "bucket_script": {
64 ▾                          "buckets_path": {
65                               "SMA": "20_trading_days_moving_avg",
66                               "StdDev": "20_trading_days_stdDev"
67                           },
68                           "script": "params.SMA - 2 * params.StdDev"
69                       }
70                   }
71               }
72           }
```

6. **Collect the results to plot the Bollinger Band**: In the following screenshot, we show the results of each aggregation for the date of `2019-03-25`:

```
1212 ▾              {
1213                     "key_as_string": "2019-03-25",
1214                     "key": 1553472000000,
1215                     "doc_count": 1,
1216 ▾                   "tp": {
1217                         "value": 62.253334045410156
1218                     },
1219 ▾                   "20_trading_days_moving_avg": {
1220                         "value": 62.537713305155435
1221                     },
1222 ▾                   "20_trading_days_stdDev": {
1223                         "value": 0.894933210155866
1224                     },
1225 ▾                   "BBU": {
1226                         "value": 64.32757972546716
1227                     },
1228 ▾                   "BBL": {
1229                         "value": 60.7478468848437
1230                     }
1231              }
```

7. After collecting daily results, we can get a plot from `tp`,
   `20_trading_days_moving_avg`, BBU, and BBL, as shown in the following
   screenshot:

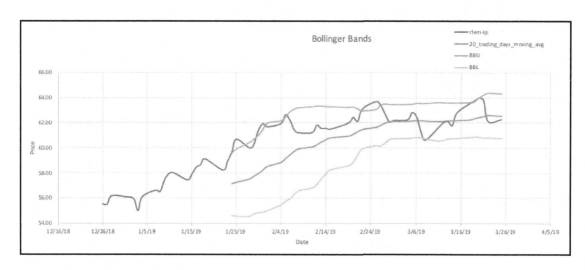

From this operational data analysis, we can conclude that the time period
of [2019-01-26, 2019-02-21] has a wider band than the time period
of [2019-02-22, 2019-03-18]. Hence, we can say it is more volatile during the first time
period. Also, it seems the band starts expanding from 2019-03-19. According to the
illustration published by IG US LLC (available at https://www.ig.com/us/glossary-
trading-terms/bollinger-bands-definition), when the market price continues to exceed
the upper limit of the Bollinger Band, it can be considered overbought, and when it moves
below the lower band, it can be considered oversold. The oversold period occurs when the
blue line is higher than the gray line. The overbought period occurs when the blue line is
lower than the yellow line. The price goes down after the overbought period at
2019-02-26. The price goes up after the oversold period at 2019-03-08. It seems that the
conclusion from our use of the Bollinger Band is that it is quite effective for daily
operational data analysis. In the next section, we will discuss how to use Elasticsearch in
sentiment analysis.

Sentiment analysis

Sentiment analysis is a research topic that analyzes opinions, attitudes, and emotions expressed in a given text. The methodology is to identify and extract subjective information by using context-mining techniques. The general purpose is to judge whether the potential emotions expressed are positive, negative, or neutral based on the source material. Many techniques, such as **natural language processing** (**NLP**), text analysis, computational linguistics, statistics, machine learning, and even biometrics, can be applied to sentiment analysis. So far, most users use Elasticsearch as the data store in sentiment analysis and the subsequent search or metric analysis. The workload for sentiment analysis is taken care of by third-party libraries. The following table introduces the two most commonly used libraries:

Name	Programming language	Description
TextBlob	Python (2 and 3)	This provides a simple API based on the **Natural Language Toolkit** (**NLTK**) and the **pattern.en** module. (More information can be found at `https://textblob.readthedocs.io/en/dev/index.html`.)
Stanford CoreNLP	Java (1.8+)	It provides a bunch of linguistic analysis tools to a piece of text. (More information can be found at `https://stanfordnlp.github.io/CoreNLP/`.)

A selection of some sentiment analysis resources available online are listed in the following table for your reference. Interested users can consult the GitHub links provided for each one:

Name	Usage	Description
`elastic-sentiment-analysis-plugin`, supported by TechnocratSid	Plugin	A plugin for sentiment analysis using Stanford CoreNLP. It is compatible with Elasticsearch 6.4.1, but will not work for 7.0. (See the repository at `https://github.com/TechnocratSid/elastic-sentiment-analysis-plugin`.)
`sentiment.py`, supported by real Python	Python programming	A project connected to the Twitter Streaming API that calculates the keyword-based sentiment of each tweet using TextBlob. The data is added to Elasticsearch after the relevant sentiment analysis process. (See the repository at `https://realpython.com/twitter-sentiment-python-docker-elasticsearch-kibana/`.)

`stocksight,` supported by shirosaidev	Python programming	A project providing stock analyzers and predictors using Elasticsearch, Twitter, news headlines, and TextBlob to implement sentiment analysis. (See the repository at `https://github.com/stdatalabs/sparkNLP-elasticsearch`.)
`twitter-sentiment-analysis,` supported by Vincent Spiewak	Scala programming	A project providing streaming tweets with Spark, language detection and sentiment analysis using StanfordNLP, dashboard with Kibana. (See the repository at `https://github.com/vspiewak/twitter-sentiment-analysis`.)
`sparkNLP-elasticsearch,` supported by stdatalabs	Scala programming	A project providing Twitter sentiment analysis using Spark and Stanford CoreNLP, with visualization from Elasticsearch and Kibana. (See the repository at `https://github.com/stdatalabs/sparkNLP-elasticsearch`.)

From our observations, the easiest way to adapt sentiment analysis with Elasticsearch is to use `elastic-sentiment-analysis-plugin`. It provides a `_sentiment` API and accepts a text field and the input text. Then, it provides the results in the response body with types and scores across five levels, which are `very_positive`, `positive`, `neutral`, `negative`, and `very_negative`. However, we need to wait for the upgrade from version 6.4.1 to 7.0. Another interesting approach we would like to highlight is proposed by Saskia Vola (for more information, see `https://www.elastic.co/blog/text-classification-made-easy-with-elasticsearch`). She suggested using the special `more_like_this` query out of the box to solve the text classification problem. If we want to develop our own method, it is worth studying this in depth.

We have given an overview of the trends to couple Elasticsearch with sentiment analysis. After the following summary, we will reach the end of this chapter.

Summary

Wonderful! We have completed a comprehensive discussion of EDA. We demonstrated how to find symbolic momentum with simple financial analysis to inform business strategies. We also provided step-by-step instructions to compute Bollinger Bands using daily operational data. Finally, we conducted a brief survey of sentiment analysis with Elasticsearch.

In this next section, we will cover the Java High Level REST Client and Java Low Level REST Client. The REST clients take care of all serialization and deserialization of the request and response objects, making the development work easy. We'll also explore the basics of Spring Data with Elasticsearch. We'll show how to use the relevant APIs for indexing, searching, and querying.

Section 3: Programming with the Elasticsearch Client

In this section, you will explore the basics of Spring Data Elasticsearch and also show how to index, search, and query in a Spring application. You will also learn how to incorporate Elasticsearch into your Python applications.

This section is comprised the following chapters:

11
Elasticsearch from Java Programming

In the last chapter, we used aggregation frameworks to explore data analysis. We drew the Bollinger Band for one of the **exchange-traded funds (ETFs)** to demonstrate operational data analysis daily. We also examined the role of Elasticsearch in sentiment analysis and showed how a number of different open source projects integrated Elasticsearch into the analysis. In this chapter, we will focus on the basics of two supported Java REST clients. We'll also explore the main features and operations for each approach. The advantage of using a REST client is that it accepts the request objects or the response objects as arguments in the APIs. The high-level REST client is responsible for the corresponding serialization and deserialization. If we choose the low-level REST client, we need to handle such operations by ourselves. Each API can be called synchronously or asynchronously. They can help us to get started on quickly integrating Elasticsearch functionality into our Java applications. In the last section of this chapter, we will discuss Spring Data Elasticsearch.

By the end of this chapter, we will have covered the following topics:

- Overview of Elasticsearch Java REST client
- The Java low-level REST client
- The Java high-level REST client
- Spring Data Elasticsearch

Overview of Elasticsearch Java REST client

You will recall that in the *Talking to Elasticsearch* section in `Chapter 1`, *Overview of Elasticsearch 7*, we discussed that Elasticsearch officially supports two protocols only. They are **HTTP** (the RESTful API) and **native**. When using the Java language, the transport client was the preferred method of the native protocol. However, transport clients such as the Java API are deprecated in Elasticsearch 7.0, and completely removed in 8.0. In short, we should use the Java high-level REST client. According to the Elasticsearch client in the Maven repository (available at `https://search.maven.org/search?q=g:org.elasticsearch.client`), we can sketch the hierarchy of the group ID and artifact ID, as shown in the following diagram:

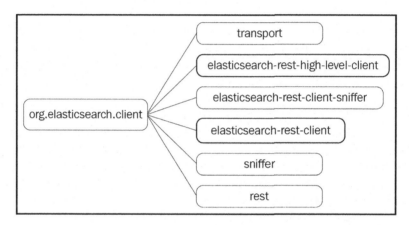

Because the length of the chapter is limited, we are only focusing on two artifacts, **elasticsearch-rest-high-level-client** and **elasticsearch-rest-client**. Be careful that the minimum required Java version is 1.8. To demonstrate the Java REST client, we will use Spring Boot 2.x to construct the Java program. We use the Spring Tools 4 IDE to create a Spring Boot starter project (for more information, see `https://spring.io/tools`). In the GitHub repository for this chapter (available at `https://github.com/PacktPublishing/Mastering-Elasticsearch-7.0/tree/master/Chapter11/java_rest_client`), we can download a Spring Boot project named `java_rest_client`. We will include a demonstration of both the Java high-level and low-level REST clients in this project. We will find the `pom.xml` file in the project base directory. What follows is a way to configure `elasticsearch-rest-client` dependencies using a Maven repository as a dependency manager. Add the following code block to the `pom.xml` file:

```
<dependencies>
    ...
    <dependency>
```

```
        <groupId>org.elasticsearch.client</groupId>
        <artifactId>elasticsearch-rest-client</artifactId>
    </dependency>
    <dependency>
        <groupId>org.elasticsearch.client</groupId>
        <artifactId>elasticsearch-rest-high-level-client</artifactId>
    </dependency>
    . . .
<dependencies>
```

The Spring Boot version that we use is 2.1.4, which, in turn, uses the default Elasticsearch client packages of version 6.4.3. We need to override this to use version 7.0.0. Add the following code block to the `pom.xml` file:

```
<properties>
    . . .
    <elasticsearch.version>7.0.0</elasticsearch.version>
</properties>
```

Spring Boot and Maven will have the corresponding transitive dependencies imported. In the next section, Java low-level REST client programming will be shown first.

The Java low-level REST client

The Java low-level REST client was released in 2016 for version 5.0.0, which is based on the Apache HTTP client. This was the first time that we could get the Java client to work in the same way as all the other language clients. Low level means that it has minimum support for Java users to build requests or to parse responses. Users have to handle the request's path, query-string construction, and the JSON response body. We are not going to elaborate on how the entire program works. Instead, we'll target only the workflow of the Java low-level REST client.

The Java low-level REST client workflow

Basically, there are three major steps involved: REST client initialization, performing a request, and handling the response. Before we look at each step, let's take a closer look at the major methods of the `org.elasticsearch.client.RestClient` class described in the following table. It involves the REST client builder, performs a request, and closes operations:

Method	Description
`public static RestClientBuilder builder(org.apache.http.HttpHost...hosts)`	Creates a new builder instance using a host or hosts to where the client will send the request.
`public void close()`	Closes the `RestClient` when it is no longer needed.
`public Response performRequest(Request request)`	Sends a request to the host specified by the client.
`public void performRequestAsync(Request request, ResponseListener responseListener)`	Sends a request to the host specified by the client asynchronously. When the request completes, the specified `ResponseListener` in the method is notified.

REST client initialization

Create a `RestClientBuilder` instance by using the static `builder()` method of the `RestClient` class with a host environment. Then, call the `build()` method of the `RestClientBuilder` instance to build the `RestClient` instance. Our example is shown in the following code block:

```
public RestClient LowLevelRestClient() {
    return RestClient.builder(new HttpHost("localhost", 9200, "http"))
        .setDefaultHeaders(new Header[] {
            new BasicHeader("accept","application/json"),
            new BasicHeader("content-type","application/json")})
        .setFailureListener(new RestClient.FailureListener() {
            public void onFailure(Node node) {
                logger.error("Low level Rest Client Failure on node " +
                    node.getName());}
        }).build();
}
```

`RestClientBuilder` provides a `setDefaultHeaders()` method to set the default request headers for each request. In addition, `RestClientBuilder` also provides a `setFailureListener()` method to set the handler to be notified when a request fails.

Performing requests using a REST client

We can send a request either synchronously or asynchronously. In synchronous mode, the calling thread is blocked until a response is received. In asynchronous mode, we provide a `ResponseListener` object with two callback methods, the `onSuccess` and `onFailure` methods, to be notified when the request completes. The declaration of the synchronous request method is shown in the following code snippet:

```
public Response performRequest(Request request) throws java.io.IOException
```

The declaration of the asynchronous request method is shown in the following code snippet:

```
public void performRequestAsync(Request request, ResponseListener responseListener)
```

Before we can send out the request, we have to construct a `Request` object. The following example is for a `POST` request with a `uRL` and a `requestBody` in a `String` type. The request is passed down to the `performRequest` method of our `RestClient` wrapper object, `11RestClient`, to perform the operation:

```
Request request = new Request("POST", uRL);
request.setJsonEntity(requestBody);
Map<String,Object> response = 11RestClient.performRequest(request);
```

The following code block describes the programming structure of the synchronous `performRequest` method. First of all, the `restClient` has been autowired to an instance created by the `LowLevelRestClient()` method. There is a try-catch block to intercept exceptions. For our own purposes, we use the `convertValue()` method from the `ObjectMapper` class to convert the response into a `Map<String, Object>` object:

```
public Map<String, Object> performRequest(Request request) {
    RestClientResponse clientResponse = new RestClientResponse();
    try {
        response = restClient.performRequest(request);
clientResponse.setStatusCode(response.getStatusLine().getStatusCode());
clientResponse.setResponseBody(EntityUtils.toString(response.getEntity()));
        clientResponse.setHeaders(response.getHeaders());
    } catch (Exception ex) {
        ...
    }
    Map<String, Object> convertValue = (Map<String, Object>) (newObjectMapper())
        .convertValue(clientResponse, Map.class);
    return convertValue;
}
```

The following code block describes the programming structure of the asynchronous `performRequestAync` method. We make the asynchronous method and the synchronous method return the same object. In our design, we can put the handling codes in the `onSuccess()` callback method in cases of success, and the error handling codes in `onFailure()` in case it should fail:

```
public Map<String, Object> performAsyncRequest(Request request) {
    RestClientResponse clientResponse = new RestClientResponse();
    restClient.performRequestAsync(request, new ResponseListener() {
        @Override
        public void onSuccess(Response response) {
            ...
        }
        @Override
        public void onFailure(Exception exception) {
        }
    });
    clientResponse.setStatusCode(200);
    Map<String, Object> convertValue =v(Map<String, Object>)
        (new ObjectMapper()).convertValue(clientResponse, Map.class);
    return convertValue;
}
```

Handing responses

Let's take a look at the returned `org.elasticsearch.client.Response` object, as described in the following table. We can use the methods provided to get the desired contents to construct our returned object:

Method	Description
public `org.apache.http.HttpEntity()`	Returns the response body in the `org.apache.http.HttpEntity` type
public `java.lang.String` `setHeader(String name)`	Returns the value of the response header corresponding to the name
public `org.apache.http.Header[]` `getHeaders()`	Returns an array of the `org.apache.http.Header` response header
public `org.apache.http.RequestLine` `getRequestLine()`	Returns the `org.apache.http.RequestLine` object that generates the response
public `org.apache.http.httpHost` `getHost()`	Returns the `org.apache.http.HttpHost` object that returns the response

`public org.apache.http.StatusLine getStatusLine()`	Returns the `org.apache.http.StatusLine` object of the response
`public java.lang.String getWarnings()`	Returns the warning string for all headers in the response
`public boolean hasWarnings()`	Returns `true` if there is a warning header returned, otherwise it returns `false`

Remember that we need to deal with exceptions. If there is any communication problem, such as a socket timeout, `IOException` will be raised. If the error originates from an HTTP response, then we need to handle `org.elasticsearch.client.ResponseException`. For detailed information about each of the low-level REST API packages, we can refer to the Java documentation at `https://artifacts.elastic.co/javadoc/org/elasticsearch/client/elasticsearch-rest-client/7.0.0/org/elasticsearch/client/package-summary.html`.

Testing with Swagger UI

We have integrated Swagger UI (refer to the reference material available at `https://swagger.io/tools/swagger-ui/`) to generate a visual testing API from the developed low-level REST client program. The step-by-step instructions are as follows:

1. Go to the `java_rest_client` directory and issue the following Maven run commands. It will clean, compile, build, and run the project:

   ```
   cd java_rest_client
   mvn clean
   mvn package
   mvn spring-boot:run
   ```

2. Then, the standard output will be similar to what is shown in the following code block:

   ```
   [INFO] Scanning for projects...
   ...

     .   ____          _            __ _ _
    /\\ / ___'_ __ _ _(_)_ __  __ _ \ \ \ \
   ( ( )\___ | '_ | '_| | '_ \/ _` | \ \ \ \
    \\/  ___)| |_)| | | | | || (_| |  ) ) ) )
     '  |____| .__|_| |_|_| |_\__, | / / / /
    =========|_|==============|___/=/_/_/_/
    :: Spring Boot ::        (v2.1.4.RELEASE)
   .....
   .....
   ```

```
2019-05-10 13:35:09.323  INFO 66332 --- [          main]
c.e.c.r.JavaRestClientApplication        : Started
JavaRestClientApplication in 3.92 seconds (JVM running for 4.408)
```

3. Now, use a web browser and
   enter `http://localhost:10010/swagger-ui.html#/low-level-rest-cli
   ent-controller` as the URL to reach the Swagger UI page for the project,
   shown in the following screenshot, and then press the **Low Level REST Client
   POST Request** bar to expand the panel:

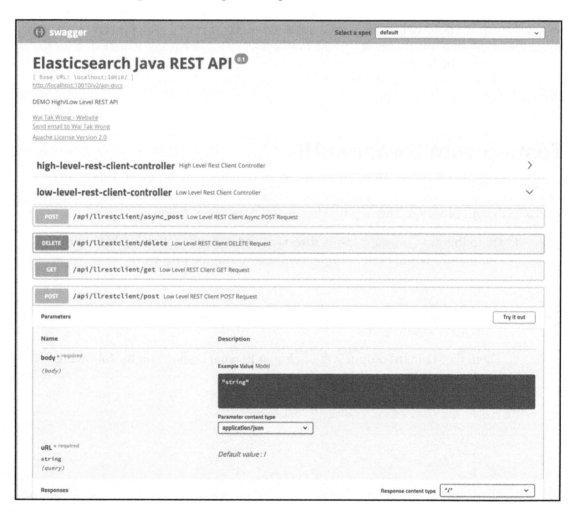

4. When the **Try it out** button is clicked, the **POST** panel will be changed to input mode. Type the request body and URL to test the REST call. For convenience, we will issue a search API with a `match_phrase` query to the `cf_etf` index. Fill the text in the **body** and **uRL** fields, as shown in the following screenshot:

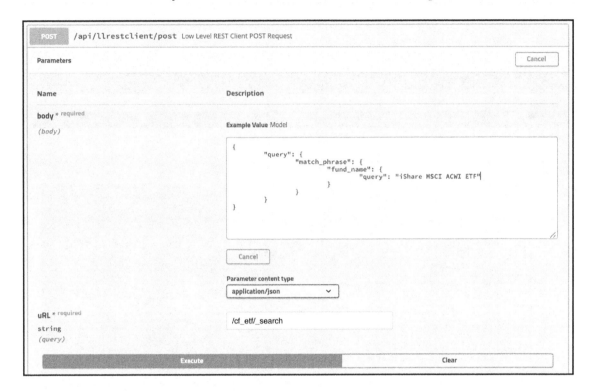

5. Hit the **Execute** button, the low-level REST client will send the request to Elasticsearch, and the response will be filled in the **Responses** panel, as shown in the following screenshot:

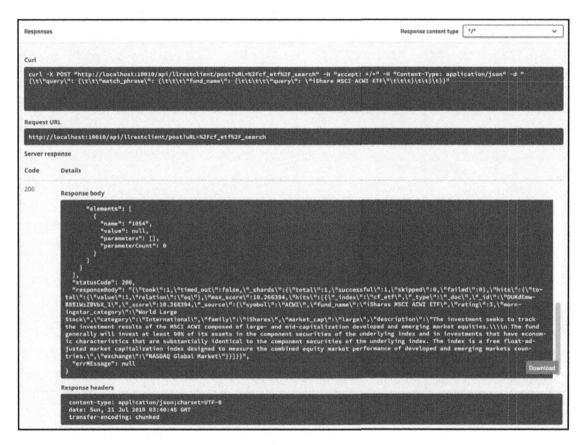

The information for the ACWI symbol is attached in the responseBody field. For the asynchronous test, use the same input and the response should be OK (200). After the asynchronous operation is done, the output will be printed in the command line when the request is completed.

New features

Two new features are related to the Java low-level REST client. Let's discuss these as follows:

- **Made warning behaviors pluggable per request**: This feature allows us to set the desired behaviors to handle the warning for each request. The `Request` class has a `setOptions` method to set the options using a `RequestOptions.Builder` class. In the `RequestOptions.Builder` class, there is a `setWarningsHandler()` method with which we can control the behavior of the handler. Two modes are provided, **permissive** and **strict**.
- **Added PreferHasAttributeNodeSelector**: This feature allows us to select a preferred node with a specified attribute. If there is no node with the specified attribute, another node will still be selected. The `RestClientBuilder` class has a `setNodeSelector()` method to take an object that implements the `NodeSelector` interface. We can use the constructor of the `PreferHasAttributeNodeSelector` class, which implements the `NodeSelector` interface, to set our desired attribute. Then, we can assign the constructed object to the `setNodeSelector()` method of the RestClientBuilder object to construct the REST client.

We have completed the demonstration of the low-level REST client. Interested users can test it out with the requests we want to try. In the following section, we will discuss the high-level REST client.

The Java high-level REST client

The Java high-level REST client is built on the top of the low-level REST client. It is responsible for the serialization and deserialization of the request and response objects. According to the official announcement from Elasticsearch (available at `https://www.elastic.co/guide/en/elasticsearch/client/java-api/7.0/transport-client.html`), the transport client will be removed in version 8.0. Using the Java high-level REST client should be the preference. Similarly to how we presented the low-level REST client, we'll target only the workflow of the Java high-level REST client.

The Java high-level REST client workflow

Similar to what we did in the previous section, there are three major steps involved. Let's take a look to see how the client is constructed first.

REST client initialization

As we've said, the high-level REST client is built on the top of the low-level REST client, so the constructor takes the `RestClientBuilder` object as an argument to build the high-level REST client object. Our example is shown in the following code block and is similar to the low-level REST client:

```
public RestHighLevelClient HighLevelRestClient() {
    return new RestHighLevelClient(
        RestClient.builder(new HttpHost("localhost", 9200, "http"))
            .setDefaultHeaders(new Header[] {
                new BasicHeader("accept","application/json"),
                new BasicHeader("content-type","application/json")})
            .setFailureListener(new RestClient.FailureListener() {
                public void onFailure(Node node) {
                logger.error("High level Rest Client Failure on node " +
node.getName());
            }
            }));
}
```

Performing requests using the REST client

The main goal of the high-level REST client is to expose each API specific methods. Hence, it tries to provide a method for each API. Some of the methods can be called directly from the REST client. Other methods can be called indirectly from the method of the REST client. In the following tables, we only cover those APIs we are interested in and that are within the scope of this book.

We first list the high-level REST client's request methods in the following table:

API	Direct call from REST client	Request and response
Document	`index()`, `indexAsync()`	`IndexResponse, IndexResponse`
	`get()`, `getAsync()`	`GetRequest, GetResponse`
	`delete()`, `deleteAsync()`	`DeleteRequest, DeleteResponse`
	`exists()`, `existsAsync()`	`GetRequest, boolean`
	`update()`, `updateAsync()`	`UpdateRequest, UpdateResponse`
	`termVectors()`, `termVectorsAsync()`	`TermVectorsRequest, TermVectorsResponse`
	`bulk()`, `bulkAsync()`	`BulkRequest, BulkResponse`
	`mget()`, `mgetAsync()`	`MultiGetRequest, MultiGetResponse`
	`mtermVectors()`, `mtermVectorsAsync()`	`MultiTermVectorsRequest, MultiTermVectorsResponse`
	`reindex()`, `reindexAsync()`	`ReindexRequest, BulkByScrollResponse`
	`deleteByQuery()`, `deleteByQueryAsync()`	`DeleteByQueryRequest, BulkByScrollResponse`
	`updateByQuery()`, `updateByQueryAsync()`	`UpdateByQueryRequest, BulkByScrollResponse`
	`reindexRethrottle()`, `reindexRethrottleAsync()`	`RethrottleRequest, ListTasksResponse`
	`updateByQueryRethrottle()`, `updateByQueryRethrottleAsync()`	`RethrottleRequest, ListTasksResponse`
	`updateByQueryRethrottle()`, `updateByQueryRethrottleAsync()`	`UpdateByQueryRequest, ListTasksResponse`
	`deleteByQueryRethrottle()`, `deleteByQueryRethrottleAsync()`	`DeleteByQueryRequest, ListTasksResponse`
Search	`search()`, `searchAsync()`, `scroll()`, `scrollAsync()`	`SearchRequest, SearchResponse`
	`clearScroll()`, `clearScrollAsync()`	`ClearScrollRequest, ClearScrollResponse`
	`msearch()`, `msearchAsync()`	`MultiSearchRequest, MultiSearchResponse`
	`searchTemplate()`, `searchTemplateAsync()`	`SearchTemplateRequest, SearchTemplateResponse`
	`msearchTemplate()`, `msearchTemplateAsync()`	`MultiSearchTemplateRequest, MultiSearchTemplateResponse`
	`fieldCaps()`, `fieldCapsAsync()`	`FieldCapabilitiesRequest, FieldCapabilitiesResponse`
	`rankEval()`, `rankEvalAsync()`	`RankEvalRequest, RankEvalResponse`
	`explain()`, `explainAsync()`	`ExplainRequest, ExplainResponse`
	`count()`, `countAsync()`	`CountRequest, CountResponse`

Script	getScript(), getScriptAsync()	GetStoredScriptRequest, GetStoredScriptResponse
	putScript(), putScriptAsync()	PutStoredScriptRequest, AcknowledgedResponse
	deleteScript(), deleteScriptAsync()	DeleteStoredScriptRequest, AcknowledgedResponse

The following tables will list our interested indirect request methods from the member object of the high-level REST client:

Under API Indices, `IndicesClient indices()` will be the member of REST client:

Call method from member	Request and response
analyze(), analyzeAsync()	AnalyzeRequest, AnalyzeResponse
create(), createAsync()	CreateIndexRequest, CreateIndexResponse
get(), getAsync()	GetIndexRequest, GetIndexResponse
exists(), existsAsync()	GetIndexRequest, boolean
delete(), deleteAsync()	DeleteIndexRequest, AcknowledgedResponse
open(), openAsync()	OpenIndexRequest, OpenIndexResponse
close(), closeAsync()	CloseIndexRequest, AcknowledgedResponse
getMapping(), getMappingAsync()	GetMappingsRequest, GetMappingsResponse
putMapping(), putMappingAsync()	PutMappingRequest, AcknowledgedResponse
getFieldMapping(), getFieldMappingAsync()	GetFieldMappingsRequest, GetFieldMappingsResponse
getSettings(), getSettingsAsync()	GetSettingsRequest, GetSettingsResponse
putSettings(), putSettingsAsync()	PutMappingRequest, AcknowledgedResponse
getTemplate(), getTemplateAsync()	GetIndexTemplatesRequest, GetIndexTemplatesResponse
deleteTemplate(), deleteTemplateAsync()	DeleteIndexTemplateRequest, AcknowledgedResponse

`existsTemplate(), existsTemplateAsync()`	`IndexTemplatesExistRequest, boolean`
`putTemplate(),putTemplateAsync()`	`PutIndexTemplateRequest, AcknowledgedResponse`
`existsAlias(),existsAliasAsync()`	`GetAliasesRequest, boolean`
`getAlias(),getAliasAsync()`	`GetAliasesRequest, GetAliasesResponse`
`updateAliases,updateAliasesAsync()`	`IndicesAliasesRequest, AcknowledgedResponse`
`refresh(),refreshAsync()`	`RefreshRequest, RefreshResponse`
`forceMerge(),forceMergeAsync()`	`ForceMergeRequest, ForceMergeResponse`
`flush(),flushAsync()`	`FlushRequest, FlushResponse`
`flushSync(),flushSyncAsync()`	`SyncedFlushRequest, SyncedFlushResponse`
`clearCache(),clearCacheAsync()`	`ClearIndicesCacheRequest, ClearIndicesCacheResponse`
`rollover(),rolloverAsync()`	`RolloverRequest, RolloverResponse`
`shrink(),shrinkAsync(),split(), splitAsync()`	`ResizeRequest, ResizeResponse`

Under API Ingest, `IngestClient ingest()` will be the member of REST client:

Call method from member	Request and response
`putPipeline(), putPipelineAsync()`	`PutPipelineRequest, AcknowledgedResponse`
`getPipeline(), getPipelineAsync()`	`GetPipelineRequest, GetPipelineResponse`
`deletePipeline(), deletePipelineAsync()`	`DeletePipelineRequest, AcknowledgedResponse`
`simulate(), simulateAsync()`	`SimulatePipelineRequest, SimulatePipelineResponse`

For other methods, interested users can refer to `https://www.elastic.co/guide/en/`
`elasticsearch/client/java-rest/current/java-rest-high.html`. Before we can send out
the request, we have to construct a `SearchRequest` object. The following code block is for
a search request to the `index` index. The `SearchRequest` object provides
a `source` method that takes a `SearchSourceBuilder` parameter, which stores the query
as a `QueryBuilder` class. We can control the paging parameter using the `from()` and
`size()` methods from the `SearchSourceBuilder` class. All API methods in the high-level
REST client support the `RequestOptions` parameter. We can use it to customize requests
without affecting the normal workflow of the execution. `SearchRequest` and
`RequestOptions` are passed down to our `RestClient` wrapper object, `hlRestClient`, to
perform the operation:

```
SearchRequest request = new SearchRequest(index);
SearchSourceBuilder sourceBuilder = new SearchSourceBuilder();
sourceBuilder.from(from);
sourceBuilder.size(size);
MatchPhraseQueryBuilder queryBuilder =
QueryBuilders.matchPhraseQuery(fieldName, fieldValue);
if (analyzer != null)
    queryBuilder.analyzer(analyzer);
request.source(sourceBuilder.query(queryBuilder));
RequestOptions options = RequestOptions.DEFAULT;
Map<String,Object> response = hlRestClient.search(request, options);
```

Each type of query must be built by the corresponding query builder class, and can then be
used in the high-level REST client. In the following table, we only cover those we are
interested in and that are within the scope of this book. For other query builders, interested
users can refer to `https://www.elastic.co/guide/en/elasticsearch/client/java-rest/`
`current/java-rest-high-query-builders.html`:

Category	Type of query	Method call in QueryBuilders
Match all queries	match_all	static MatchAllQueryBuilder matchAllQuery()
Full text queries	match	static MatchQueryBuilder matchQuery()
	match_phrase	static MatchPhraseQueryBuilder matchPhraseQuery()
	match_phrase_prefix	static MatchPhrasePrefixQueryBuilder matchPhrasePrefixQuery()
	multi_match	static MultiMatchQueryBuilder multiMatchQuery()
	query_string	static QueryStringQueryBuilder queryStringQuery()
	simple_query_string	static SimpleQueryStringBuilder simpleQueryStringQuery()

	term	`static TermQueryBuilder termQuery()`
	terms	`static TermsQueryBuilder termsQuery()`
	range	`static RangeQueryBuilder rangeQuery()`
	exists	`static ExistsQueryBuilder existsQuery()`
Term	prefix	`static PrefixQueryBuilder prefixQuery()`
queries	wildcard	`static WildcardQueryBuilder wildcardQuery()`
	regexp	`static RegexpQueryBuilder regexpQuery()`
	type	`static FuzzyQueryBuilder fuzzyQuery()`
	type	`static TypeQueryBuilder typeQuery()`
	ids	`static IdsQueryBuilder idsQuery()`
	constant_score	`static ConstantScoreQueryBuilder constantScoreQuery()`
	bool	`static BoolQueryBuilder boolQuery()`
Compound	dis_max	`static DisMaxQueryBuilder disMaxQuery()`
queries	function_score	`static FunctionScoreQueryBuilder functionScoreQuery()`
	boosting	`static BoostingQueryBuilder boostingQuery()`
Joining queries	nested	`static NestedQueryBuilder nestedQuery()`
Specialized queries	more_like_this	`static MoreLikeThisQueryBuilder moreLikeThisQuery()`
	script	`static ScriptQueryBuilder scriptQuery()`
	script_score	`static ScriptScoreQueryBuilder scriptScoreQuery()`

We can send a request either synchronously or asynchronously. In synchronous mode, the calling thread is blocked until a response is received. In asynchronous mode, we provide an `ActionListener` object with two callback methods, the `onResponse` and `onFailure` methods, to be notified when the request completes. For our convenience, we will demonstrate the `search()` and `searchAsync()` methods of the `Search` method of the high-level REST client. The following code block describes the programming structure of the synchronous search method. First of all, the `restClient` has been autowired to an instance created by the `HighLevelRestClient()` method. There is a try-catch block to intercept exceptions. For our own purposes, we use the `convertValue()` method from the `ObjectMapper` class to convert the response to a `Map<String, Object>` object:

```
public Map<String, Object> search(SearchRequest request, RequestOptions
options) {
    SearchResponse response;
    Map<String, Object> convertValue;
    try {
        response = restClient.search(request, options);
```

```
        ...
    } catch (IOException e) {
        ...
    }
    return convertValue;
}
```

The following code block describes the programming structure of the asynchronous `searchAync` method. We make the asynchronous and synchronous methods return the same object. In our design, we can put the handling codes in the `onResponse()` callback method in cases of success, and the error handling codes in `onFailure()` in case it should fail:

```
public Map<String, Object> searchAsync(SearchRequest request,
RequestOptions options) {              SearchResponse response;
    Map<String, Object> convertValue;
    restClient.searchAsync(request, options, new
ActionListener<SearchResponse>() {
        @Override
        public void onResponse(SearchResponse response) {
            ...
        }
        @Override
        public void onFailure(Exception exception) {
            ...
        }
    });
    return convertValue;
}
```

Handling responses

Each API specific method has its corresponding `response` object. Let's take the `org.elasticsearch.action.search.SearchResponse` object as an example and show the related methods that we can use to construct a `return` object in the following table:

Method	Description
public Aggregations getAggregations()	Used to get the aggregation return object
public SearchHits getHits()	The hits entries of the search
public int getTotalShards()	The total number of shards involved in the execution

`public int` `getSuccessfulShards()`	The number of shards that execute successfully
`public int` `getFailedShards()`	The number of shards that failed to execute
`public String` `getScrollId()`	The scroll ID, if the Search Scroll API is used
`public boolean` `isTimedOut()`	Does the timeout occur for the execution?
`public TimeValue` `getTook()`	How long does the execution take?
`public RestStatus` `status()`	The REST final status of the execution
`public Suggest` `getSuggest()`	The result from the suggester feature

We collect a few pieces of information, including the hits, the timed-out status, and the time taken to construct the response to send back to the caller. To preserve consistency, we use the `convertValue()` method from the `ObjectMapper` class to convert the response into a `Map<String, Object>` object:

```
public Map<String, Object> search(SearchRequest request, RequestOptions
options) {
    SearchResponse response;
    Map<String, Object> convertValue;
    try {
        response = restClient.search(request, options);
        convertValue = new HashMap<String, Object>();
        if (response.getTook() != null)
            convertValue.put("took", response.getTook().seconds());
            convertValue.put("timed_out", response.isTimedOut());
            if (response.getHits() != null)
                convertValue.put("hits", response.getHits());
    } catch (IOException e) {
        ...
    }
    return convertValue;
}
```

Testing with Swagger UI

Similar to the testing of the low-level REST client, type
the `http://localhost:10010/swagger-ui.html#/higher-level-rest-client-con troller` URL into the web browser to reach the Swagger UI page for the project, and then press the **High Level REST Client Search Request Match Phrase Query** bar to expand the panel. When we hit the **Try it out** button, the panel will be changed to input mode. We can fill in the required request parameters, including **indexName**, **fieldName**, and `fieldValue` for **match_phrase_query**. The following screenshot shows our inputs:

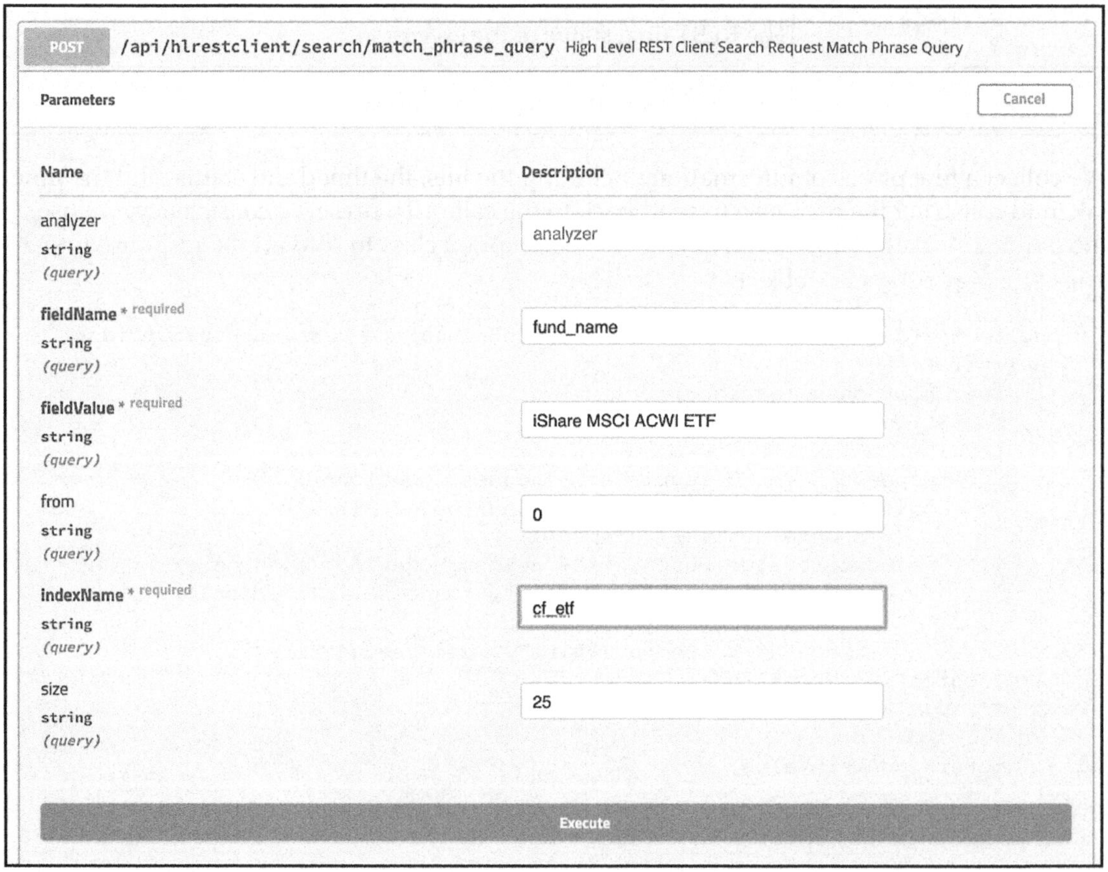

POST	/api/hlrestclient/search/match_phrase_query	High Level REST Client Search Request Match Phrase Query

Parameters   Cancel

Name	Description
analyzer string *(query)*	analyzer
fieldName * required string *(query)*	fund_name
fieldValue * required string *(query)*	iShare MSCI ACWI ETF
from string *(query)*	0
indexName * required string *(query)*	cf_etf
size string *(query)*	25

Execute

When we hit the **Execute** button, the high-level REST client will be used to send the request to Elasticsearch and the response will be filled in the **Responses** panel, as shown in the following screenshot. We can see that the `hits` field, the `took` field, and the `timed_out` field are inserted in the **Response body** as we construct the `SearchRequest` object:

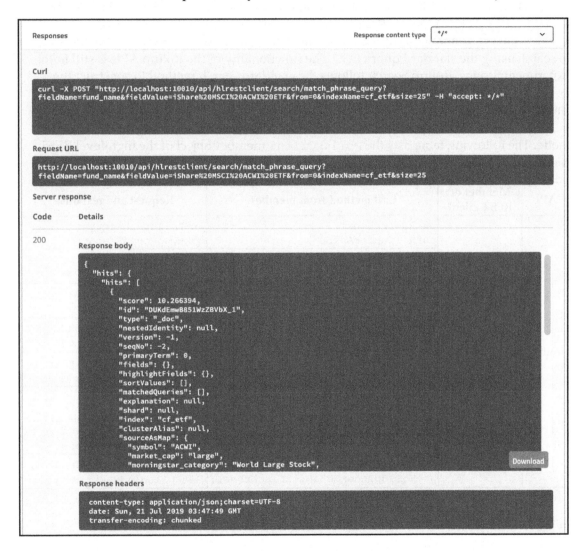

Interested users can try it out with the asynchronous search for `match_phrase_query` that we have implemented. Furthermore, we can try to implement other high-level REST API methods based on our program.

New features

The Rollup Search is a new feature in Java high-level REST client. The Rollup APIs were first introduced in X-Pack. Their objective is to store historical data with minimal storage costs so that we can use it for analysis at a later stage. There is a set of APIs at the job level to create, delete, start, stop the Rollup job, and so on. The Rollup create method, putRollupJob, generates a different document structure, but Elasticsearch still allows us to search using the standard query DSL. The functionality of the Rollup APIs is still in the experimental stage. Rollup Search follows the standard search method to construct the SearchRequest object, sends the request by the RollupClient member of the REST client, and then gets the SearchResponse object back to make everything exactly the same. RollupClient also supports the searchAsync() method for searching in asynchronous mode. The following table lists the RollupClient member object of the high-level REST client and its supported methods:

API	Member of REST client	Call method from member	Request and response
Rollup	RollupClient rollup()	putRollupJob(), putRollupJobAsync()	putRollupJobRequest, AcknowledgedResponse
		getRollupJob(), getRollupJobAsync()	GetRollupJobRequest, GetRollupJobResponse
		deleteRollupJob(), deleteRollupJobAsync()	deleteRollupJobRequest, AcknowledgedResponse
		startRollupJob(), startRollupJobAsync()	StartRollupJobRequest, StartRollupJobResponse
		stopRollupJob(), stopRollupJobAsync()	StopRollupJobRequest, StopRollupJobResponse
		search(), searchAsync()	SearchRequest, SearchResponse
		getRollupCapabilities(), getRollupCapabilitiesAsync()	GetRollupCapsRequest, GetRollupCapsResponse
		getRollupIndexCapabilities(), getRollupIndexCapabilitiesAsync()	GetRollupIndexCapsRequest, GetRollupIndexCapsResponse

In the following section, we will discuss Spring Data Elasticsearch.

Spring Data Elasticsearch

Spring Data's goal is to significantly reduce the boilerplate codes that are used to implement the data access layer. The Spring Data repository takes the domain class to manage its life cycle and provides basic functionalities such as CRUD, paging, and sorting. In order to use Spring Boot and Spring Data Elasticsearch, a new Spring Boot starter dependency is required to be added to `pom.xml`, as shown in the following code block:

```
<dependency>
    <groupId>org.springframework.boot</groupId>
    <artifactId>spring-boot-starter-data-elasticsearch</artifactId>
</dependency>
```

At the time of writing, the latest version of Spring Boot Starter Data Elasticsearch is 2.1.4, which supports Spring Data Elasticsearch 3.1.6 for Elasticsearch version 6.5.2. Interested users will need to wait for the new version to be released. Let's take an example using the contents of the `cf_etf` index as a domain class, which can be described as in the following code block. The `@Document` annotation represents a class that stores content as a document:

```
@Document(indexName="cf_etf", type="_doc")
public class Cf_etf {
    @Id
    private String symbol;
    private String fund_name;
    private int rating;
    private String morningstar_category;
    private String category;
    private String family;
    private String market_cap;
    private String description;
    private String exchange;
    ...
}
```

Next, we need to extend a repository interface, such as `ElasticsearchRepository`, which provides built-in support for CRUD, paging, sorting, and searching, among other functionalities. When Spring Data creates the corresponding repository implementation, it analyzes all the methods defined in the repository interface and attempts to automatically generate queries from the method name. It makes it easy for us to define new custom access methods. Let's create a `Cf_etf` repository corresponding to the `Cf_etf` domain class, with two additional methods:

```
public interface Cf_etfRepository extends ElasticsearchRepository<Cf_etf,
String>{
    Page<Cf_etf> findBySymbol(String symbol);
```

```
@Query("{\"query\":{\"match_phrase\":{\"fund_name\":{\"query\":\"?0\"}}}}")
    Page<Cf_etf> matchFundNamePhraseQuery(String fund_name);
}
```

There are two ways to derive queries from the method names supported by the repository interface that we can see in the preceding code block:

1. The method is derived directly from the method name (for example, findBySymbol). A list of supported keywords can be used to extend the usage of the queries. Let's give two in the following table. Interested users can refer to the documentation at https://docs.spring.io/spring-data/elasticsearch/docs/ 3.1.6.RELEASE/reference/html/ for more information:

Keyword	Method name	Query string
Is	findBySymbol	{"bool" : {"must" : {"field" : {"symbol" : "?"}}}}
And	findByCategoryAndRating	{"bool" : {"must" : [{"field" : {"category" : "?"}}, {"field" : {"rating" : "?"}}]}}

 Other keywords are Or, Not, Between, LessThanEqual, GreaterThanEqual, Before, After, Like, StartingWith, EndingWith, Containing, In, NotIn, Near, True, False, and OrderBy.

2. Manually define the query at the method using the @Query annotation—for example, the matchFundNamePhraseQuery() method in the Cf_etfRepository interface.

Before we can use Cf_etfRepository to issue a query, we must activate the repository. Using JavaConfig, annotation-based configuration is one of the easiest ways to achieve this. Let's take a look at the following code block:

```
@Configuration
@EnableAutoConfiguration(exclude={ElasticsearchDataAutoConfiguration.class})
@EnableElasticsearchRepositories(basePackages =
"com.example.client.restclient.repository")
public class SpringDataClientConfig {
    @Value("${elasticsearch.host}")
    private String host;
    @Value("${elasticsearch.transport-client-port}")
    private int port;
```

```
@Bean
public Client client() throws Exception {
    TransportClient client = new
PreBuiltTransportClient(Settings.EMPTY);
    client.addTransportAddress(new
TransportAddress(InetAddress.getByName(host), port));
    return client;
}
@Bean
public ElasticsearchOperations elasticsearchTemplate() throws
Exception {
    return new ElasticsearchTemplate(client());
}
}
```

We will notice that Spring Data Elasticsearch uses a transport client to create a communicate tunnel to talk to the server. Since Elasticsearch intends to deprecate the transport client in version 7.0, and remove it with 8.0, the Spring Data project team is working on a smoother migration by using a REST client. Interested users can check progress at the Spring Data Elasticsearch Jira issue DATES-495, available at `https://jira.spring.io/browse/DATAES-495`). We have completed the discussion with all the materials we have prepared for Java programming with Elasticsearch. We'll conclude this chapter in the following section.

Summary

Cheers! We have completed a basic study of Java programming with Elasticsearch. We should now be able to understand and access the different Elasticsearch clients in Java. We also learned how to incorporate Elasticsearch into Java applications, especially Spring Boot applications. We also outlined the basic programming concept of Spring Data Elasticsearch. We pointed out the issue that Spring Data needs to revise significantly, due to the fact that the transport client is deprecated in version 7.0 and will be removed fully in version 8.0.

In the following `Chapter 12`, *Elasticsearch from Python Programming*, we will introduce Python programming with Elasticsearch. The `elasticsearch-py` package is the official low-level client for Elasticsearch. The goal of the Python package is to provide commonality to all Elasticsearch-related codes in Python. We will also review Elasticsearch DSL, which is a high-level library built on top of the official low-level client, to provide a more convenient and versatile way to write and manipulate queries.

12
Elasticsearch from Python Programming

In the last chapter, we introduced Java programming with Elasticsearch. A sample Spring Boot project is provided to demonstrate the programming technique for both the high-level and low-level REST clients. We also used Swagger UI to create an interface to test the REST API. To make a long story short, since the transport client will not be supported anytime soon, the REST client is the method you need to go with when you program with the Java language. In this chapter, we are going to introduce the Python Elasticsearch client. You will learn about two Elasticsearch client packages, `elasticsearch-py` and `elasticsearch-dsl-py`. The `elasticsearch-py` package is the official low-level client for Elasticsearch. The goal of the Python package is to provide common ground for all Elasticsearch-related code in Python. Elasticsearch DSL is a high-level library built on top of `elasticsearch-py` to provide a more convenient and idiomatic way of writing and manipulating queries. In this chapter, we will come to understand how the client works, and how to incorporate it into a Python application. Finally, we can extend not only our skills in Elasticsearch with Java programming, but also with Python programming.

In this chapter, we will cover the following topics:

- Overview of the Elasticsearch Python client
- The Python low-level Elasticsearch client
- The Python high-level Elasticsearch library

Overview of the Elasticsearch Python client

Elasticsearch provides two types of clients for Python. The `elasticsearch-py` package provides an official low-level client. The `elasticsearch-dsl-py` package provides a high-level library that is built on top of the low-level client. The high-level library provides a more convenient way for you to manipulate queries since it is close to the Elasticsearch JSON DSL. Both clients support versions from 2.x to 7.x. Assuming that you have a working environment for Python 3.6, use the following step-by-step instructions:

1. To install the Python Elasticsearch client, you can use the `pip` command, as shown in the following code block:

   ```
   pip install elasticsearch==7.0.0
   ```

2. To install the Python Elasticsearch DSL high-level library, you can refer to the following code block:

   ```
   pip install elasticsearch-dsl==7.0.0
   ```

3. If you are working on a project, the recommended way is to set the version range in the `setup.py` file or in `requirements.txt`, as shown in the following code block:

   ```
   # Elasticsearch 7.x
   elasticsearch-dsl>=7.0.0,<8.0.0
   ```

4. After you install the Elasticsearch client and the Elasticsearch server is running, we can use a Python script to test the connection. Use the commands shown in the following code block. We are using Python version 3.6 in our working environment:

   ```
   $ python3.6
   Python 3.6.7 (v3.6.7:6ec5cf24b7, Oct 20 2018, 03:02:14)
   [GCC 4.2.1 Compatible Apple LLVM 6.0 (clang-600.0.57)] on darwin
   Type "help", "copyright", "credits" or "license" for more
   information.
   >>> from elasticsearch import Elasticsearch
   >>> es = Elasticsearch()
   >>> es.info()
   {'name': 'WTW.local', 'cluster_name': 'elasticsearch',
   'cluster_uuid': 'R9PuCbcCREK0XtPImODaVQ', 'version': {'number':
   '7.0.0-beta1', 'build_flavor': 'default', 'build_type': 'tar',
   'build_hash': '15bb494', 'build_date':
   '2019-02-13T12:30:14.432234Z', 'build_snapshot': False,
   'lucene_version': '8.0.0', 'minimum_wire_compatibility_version':
   '6.7.0', 'minimum_index_compatibility_version': '6.0.0-beta1'},
   ```

```
'tagline': 'You Know, for Search'}
>>> exit()
```

As you can see, the `es.info()` command has retrieved the information of the running Elasticsearch instance. In the following section, we will introduce the low-level client first.

The Python low-level Elasticsearch client

This low-level client is a very lightweight wrapper for Elasticsearch's REST APIs to obtain maximum flexibility. Each client is equipped with a separate connection pool to support persistent connections. By default, 10 connections are allowed to open each node. The `maxsize` parameter is used to set the maximum degree of parallelism. The Python Elasticsearch client is thread-safe. The best practice is to create a singleton to use throughout the application. However, for multiprocessing, a new client should be created after the fork is called.

Workflow for the Python low-level Elasticsearch client

To illustrate the programming, we'll target only the workflow, not the details. Basically, there are three major steps involved: client initialization, performing the request, and handling the response.

Client initialization

By using the `elasticsearch` module to import the `Elasticsearch` class, we can initialize a low-level client with a hostname or address, a port, and parameters such as maximum connections, `maxsize`. The `getInstance()` method call returns the singleton client. With the following code block, you can obtain a low-level client running on the localhost with `port=9200` and `maxsize=25`:

```python
from elasticsearch import Elasticsearch
class ESLowLevelClient:
    __es = None
    __es_lock = threading.Lock()

    @staticmethod
    def get_instance():
        if ESLowLevelClient.__es is None:
            with ESLowLevelClient.__es_lock:
```

```
        if ESLowLevelClient.__es is None:
            ESLowLevelClient.__es = Elasticsearch(['localhost'],
                                                        port=9200,
    maxsize=25)
        return ESLowLevelClient.__es

    def __init__(self):
        raise Exception("This class is a singleton!, use static method
                            getInstance()")
```

The low-level client provides a mapping from Python to REST endpoints. Similarly to the Java high-level REST client, it tries to expose each API's specific methods. Some of the methods can be called directly from the low-level client, and other methods can be called indirectly from the attributes of the low-level client. In addition, the elasticsearch.helpers module is provided to help you process bulk data. Let's take a look at the __init__() method of the Elasticsearch class in the original open source file (available at https://github.com/elastic/elasticsearch-py/blob/master/elasticsearch/client/__init__.py) in the following code block:

```
    def __init__(self, hosts=None, transport_class=Transport, **kwargs):
        self.transport = transport_class(_normalize_hosts(hosts), **kwargs)
        self.indices = IndicesClient(self)
        self.ingest = IngestClient(self)
        self.cluster = ClusterClient(self)
        self.cat = CatClient(self)
        self.nodes = NodesClient(self)
        self.remote = RemoteClient(self)
        self.snapshot = SnapshotClient(self)
        self.tasks = TasksClient(self)
        self.xpack = XPackClient(self)
```

The low-level client holds attributes such as indices to provide indirect request methods from the member object, such as IndicesClient. Using these attributes to send requests is the preferred method. In fact, these attributes are treated as proxy objects.

Performing requests

In fact, all requests are sent by the transport client in the `transport` attribute. Let's take a look at the `get()` method of `IndicesClient` (for reference, see `https://github.com/elastic/elasticsearch-py/blob/master/elasticsearch/client/indices.py`), as shown in the following code block:

```
def get(self, index, feature=None, params=None):
    if index in SKIP_IN_PATH:
        raise ValueError(
            "Empty value passed for a required argument 'index'.")
    return self.transport.perform_request(
            "GET", _make_path(index, feature), params=params)
```

We can see that the actual method call to send out the request is the `perform_request()` method of the `transport` attribute in the `Elasticsearch` object. The direct request methods are working in the same way. In the following tables, we only cover those APIs that we are interested in and that are within the scope of this book. We first list the direct request call methods from the low-level client, as shown in the following table:

API	Direct call from the low-level client
Document	`create()`, `delete()`, `deleteByQuery()`, `exists()`, `get()`, `index()`, `mget()`
Search	`field_caps()`, `msearch()`, `msearchTemplate()`, `mtermvectors()`, `reindex()`, `reindex_throttle()`, `scroll()`, `search()`, `search_template()`, `termvectors()`, `update()`, `update_by_query()`, `count()`, `explain()`, `clear_scroll()`
Script	`delete_script()`, `get_script()`, `put_script()`

The indirect request call methods from the different attributes are listed in the following table:

API	Attribute name	Member object	Call from the member object
Indices	`indices`	`IndicesClient`	`analyze()`, `clear_cache()`, `close()`, `create()`, `delete()`, `delete_alias()`, `delete_template()`, `exists()`, `exists_alias()`, `exist_template()`, `flush()`, `flush_synced()`, `forcemerge()`, `get()`, `get_alias()`, `get_field_mapping()`, `get_mapping()`, `get_settings()`, `get_template()`, `open()`, `put_alias()`, `put_mapping()`, `put_settings()`, `put_template()`, `refresh()`, `rollover()`, `shrink()`, `stats()`, `update_aliases()`, `validate_query()`
Ingest	`ingest`	`IngestClient`	`delete_pipeline()`, `get_pipeline()`, `put_pipeline()`, `simulate()`
Rollup	`xpack.rollup`	`XPackClient.RollupClient`	`delete_job()`, `get_jobs()`, `get_rollup_caps()`, `get_rollup_index_caps()`, `put_job()`, `rollup_search()`, `start_job()`

The Rollup API is located in `elasticsearch.client.xpack.RollupClient`. To access it, you need to first access the `xpack` attribute from the Elasticsearch low-level client. The `xpack` attribute is in the `XPackClient` class. Then, you can access the `rollup` attribute from the `XPackClient` and call the Rollup API methods. The following table describes the search method and parts of its method parameters (for reference, see `https://elasticsearch-py.readthedocs.io/en/master/api.html#elasticsearch`):

Parameter	Description
`index`	The index/indices to search. It can be a list of index names or a string containing a list of comma-separated index names.
`body`	Request body string using Query DSL.
`analyzer`	The analyzer to use.
`default_operator`	The default operator for a query string.
`explain`	Use explain feature to report how it scores.
`from`	Start from the entry number (the default is 0).
`size`	The number of entries to return.

sort	A string containing a comma-separated list of key-value pairs. The key is the field name and the value is the direction.
timeout	Set timeout value.

The following code block describes the programming structure of the unit test of the search method. The query uses `match_phrase_query` with the `fund_name` field equal to `iShare MSCI ACWI ETF`. The condition we check is that the return entry is equal to 1:

```
class TestLowLevelClientSearch(unittest.TestCase):
    es = ESLowLevelClient.get_instance()

    def test_match_phrase_query(self):
        body={
            "query": {
                "match_phrase": {
                    "fund_name": {
                        "query": "iShares MSCI ACWI ETF"
                    }
                }
            }
        }
        response = self.es.search(index='cf_etf', body=body)
        self.assertEqual(response['hits']['total']['value'], 1)
        print(response)
```

Handling responses

The response to the query using a low-level client is the same as the response we saw when we previously queried using Postman. Let's download the program and follow the instructions to run the test, as shown in the preceding code block. In the GitHub repository for this chapter (available at `https://github.com/PacktPublishing/Mastering-Elasticsearch-7.0/tree/master/Chapter12/cf_etf`), there is a Python project named `cf_etf`. Under the downloaded `cf_etf` directory, issue the following command to activate the virtual environment (`virtualenv`) working environment first, and then run the program. You will find that the printed response body contains the `ACWI` ETF:

```
$source venv/bin/activate
(venv)$export PYTHONPATH=.:$PYTHONPATH
(venv)$python -m unittest
com.example.test.test_low_level_client.TestLowLevelClientSearch.test_match_
phrase_query
{'took': 1, 'timed_out': False, '_shards': {'total': 1, 'successful': 1,
'skipped': 0, 'failed': 0}, 'hits': {'total': {'value': 1, 'relation':
'eq'}, 'max_score': 10.645406, 'hits': [{'_index': 'cf_etf', '_type':
```

```
'_doc', '_id': 'ok2jLGkB_W0hQaVaoEif', '_score': 10.645406, '_source':
{'symbol': 'ACWI', 'fund_name': 'iShares MSCI ACWI ETF', 'rating': 3,
'morningstar_category': 'World Large Stock', 'category': 'International',
'family': 'iShares', 'market_cap': 'large', 'description': 'The investment
seeks to track the investment results of the MSCI ACWI composed of large-
and mid-capitalization developed and emerging market equities.\\n The fund
generally will invest at least 90% of its assets in the component
securities of the underlying index and in investments that have economic
characteristics that are substantially identical to the component
securities of the underlying index. The index is a free float-adjusted
market capitalization index designed to measure the combined equity market
performance of developed and emerging markets countries.', 'exchange':
'NASDAQ Global Market'}}]}}
.
----------------------------------------------------------------
Ran 1 test in 0.009s
OK
```

Users can run the unit test for both clients, high level and low level, at the same time using the following unit test command:

```
$source venv/bin/activate
(venv) $python -m unittest discover
```

We have briefly introduced the low-level client. In the following section, we will start looking at the high-level library.

The Python high-level Elasticsearch library

The `elasticsearch-dsl-py` package provides a high-level library that is built on top of the low-level client. You can use the low-level client from what we presented in the client initialization from *The Python low-level Elasticsearch library* section. However, it is highly recommended to use the `create_connection()` method from the `elasticsearch_dsl.connections.py` module.

Illustrating the programming concept

Here, we will use three major steps to illustrate the programming concept.

Initializing a connection

Using the following code block, you can initialize a connection similar to the one that we used for the low-level client. The name of the connection is `high_level_client` and we can directly use it in the construction of different request objects:

```
from elasticsearch_dsl import connections
class ESLowLevelClientByConnection:
    __conn = None
    __conn_lock = threading.Lock()

    @staticmethod
    def get_instance():
        if ESLowLevelClientByConnection.__conn is None:
            with ESLowLevelClientByConnection.__conn_lock:
                if ESLowLevelClientByConnection.__conn is None:
                    ESLowLevelClientByConnection.__conn =
                        connections.create_connection('high_level_client',
                            hosts=['localhost'], port=9200)
        return ESLowLevelClientByConnection.__conn

    def __init__(self):
        raise Exception("This class is a singleton!, use static method
                        getInstance()")
```

Let's take a look at the `create_connection()` method of the `Connections` class in the original open source file (available at `https://github.com/elastic/elasticsearch-dsl-py/blob/master/elasticsearch_dsl/connections.py`), shown in the following code block. It contains a Elasticsearch low-level client setup. The `serializer` setting is to ensure that the request and response objects are correctly serialized into JSON every time:

```
def create_connection(self, alias='default', **kwargs):
    kwargs.setdefault('serializer', serializer)
    conn = self._conns[alias] = Elasticsearch(**kwargs)
    return conn
```

Performing requests

The high-level library provides a wrapper class around each specific API and uses the low-level client to send out the request. In the following tables, we cover those wrapper class that we are interested in and that are within the scope of this book:

API	Wrapper class	Methods supported
Indices	Index	`analyze()`, `analyzer()`, `aliases()`, `create()`, `refresh()`, `flush()`, `get()`, `open()`, `close()`, `delete()`, `exists()`, `put_mapping()`, `get_mapping()`, `get_field_mapping()`, `put_alias()`, `get_alias()`, `exists_alias()`, `delete_alias()`, `put_settings()`, `get_settings()`, `clear_cache()`, `flush_synced()`, `forcemerge()`, `shrink()`, `stats()`, `updateByQuery()`, `validate_query()`
Document	Document	`delete()`, `upgrade()`, `save()`, `search()`, `get()`, `mget()`
Search	Search	`highlight()`, `suggest()`, `count()`, `scan()`, `delete()`, `sort()`, `source()`, `execute()`
MultiSearch	MultiSearch	`add()`, `execute()`

Let's take a look at the `count()` method and the `execute()` method in the `Search` wrapper class in the original open source file (available at https://github.com/elastic/ elasticsearch-dsl-py/blob/master/elasticsearch_dsl/search.py), shown in the following code block. We can see that the `count()` method calls the `count()` method of the low-level client, and the `execute()` method calls the `search()` method of the low-level client:

```
class Search(Request):
    ...
    def count(self):
        if hasattr(self, '_response'):
            return self._response.hits.total
        es = connections.get_connection(self._using)
        d = self.to_dict(count=True)
        return es.count(index=self._index,
                     body=d, **self._params )['count']

    def execute(self, ignore_cache=False):
        if ignore_cache or not hasattr(self, '_response'):
            es = connections.get_connection(self._using)
            self._response = self._response_class(
                self, es.search(index=self._index,
                            body=self.to_dict(), **self._params))
        return self._response
```

Each wrapper class has its initialization and provides methods to perform the request. You have to study the `elasticsearch-dsl` document first, and then you'll know how it works. Let's continue the programming example with the `Search` class. After the `Search` class is initialized with a connection or a low-level client, you can call the query method to set up the query, or set the query value to the query created by the `Q()` method. To construct a query with the `Search` object, there are three ways to do it. The first one is to use the `query` method. The second one is to use the `Q()` method. The third one is to use the provided class of the query type. Once the `Search` object is constructed and initialized with the query, you can call the `execute` method to perform the search request. The following code block describes the programming structure of the unit test of the `Search` class. The query uses `match_phrase_query` with the `fund_name` field equal to `iShare MSCI ACWI ETF`. The condition we check for that the return entry is equal to 1. For each query setup method, we have a corresponding unit test:

```
import unittest
from com.example.client.config.low_level_client_by_connection import
ESLowLevelClientByConnection
from elasticsearch_dsl import Search
from elasticsearch_dsl.query import Q, MatchPhrase
```

```
class TestHighLevelClientSearch(unittest.TestCase):
    def test_match_phrase_query_via_low_level_client(self):
        # call the query method
        search = Search(index='cf_etf',
                using=ESLowLevelClientByConnection.get_instance()).query(
                    'match_phrase', 'fund_name='iShares MSCI ACWI ETF')
        response = search.execute()
        self.assertEqual(response['hits']['total']['value'], 1)
        print(response.to_dict())

    def test_match_phrase_query_via_connection(self):
        SLowLevelClientByConnection.get_instance()
        search = Search(index='cf_etf', using='high_level_client')
        # call the Q method
        search.query = Q('match_phrase', fund_name='iShares MSCI ACWI ETF')
        response = search.execute()
        self.assertEqual(response['hits']['total']['value'], 1)

    def test_match_phrase_class_via_connection(self):
        ESLowLevelClientByConnection.get_instance()
        # construct the query object using the class of the query type
        search = Search(index='cf_etf', using='high_level_client')
        search.query = MatchPhrase(fund_name='iShares MSCI ACWI ETF')
        response = search.execute()
        self.assertEqual(response['hits']['total']['value'], 1)
```

Handling responses

The response to the query using a high-level library is the same as the response of the low-level client. You can print the whole response object with the raw data by using the to_dict() method. You can use the response object as a key and use a dot to access its attribute value. Under the downloaded cf_etf directory, issue the command shown in the following code block to activate the virtual environment and run the program. You will find that the printed response body contains the ACWI ETF information:

```
$source venv/bin/activate
$python -m unittest
com.example.test.test_high_level_client.TestHighLevelClientSearch
..{'took': 1, 'timed_out': False, '_shards': {'total': 1, 'successful': 1,
'skipped': 0, 'failed': 0}, 'hits': {'total': {'value': 1, 'relation':
'eq'}, 'max_score': 10.645406, 'hits': [{'_index': 'cf_etf', '_type':
'_doc', '_id': 'ok2jLGkB_W0hQaVaoEif', '_score': 10.645406, '_source':
{'symbol': 'ACWI', 'fund_name': 'iShares MSCI ACWI ETF', 'rating': 3,
'morningstar_category': 'World Large Stock', 'category': 'International',
'family': 'iShares', 'market_cap': 'large', 'description': 'The investment
seeks to track the investment results of the MSCI ACWI composed of large-
```

and mid-capitalization developed and emerging market equities.\\n The fund
generally will invest at least 90% of its assets in the component
securities of the underlying index and in investments that have economic
characteristics that are substantially identical to the component
securities of the underlying index. The index is a free float-adjusted
market capitalization index designed to measure the combined equity market
performance of developed and emerging markets countries.', 'exchange':
'NASDAQ Global Market'}}]}}
.

```
Ran 3 tests in 0.016s
OK
```

The query class

There is a file in the original open source project (for reference, see `https://github.com/elastic/elasticsearch-dsl-py/blob/master/elasticsearch_dsl/query.py`), named `query.py`, that contains a set of classes that correspond to the query type. A list of supported query types and their provided classes are compiled in the following table. You can use the class to construct the query object:

Category	Query type	Provided class name
Match all/None query	match_all	MatchAll
	match_none	MatchNone
Full-text query	common	Common
	match	Match
	match_phrase	MatchPhrase
	match_phrase_prefix	MatchPhrasePrefix
	multi_match	MultiMatch
	query_string	QueryString
	simple_query_string	SimpleQueryString

Term-level queries	term	Term
	terms	Terms
	terms_set	TermsSet
	range	Range
	regexp	Regexp
	exists	Exists
	prefix	Prefix
	wildcard	Wildcard
	fuzzy	Fuzzy
	type	Type
	ids	Ids
Compound queries	bool	Bool
	boosting	Boosting
	constant_score	ConstantScore
	dis_max	DisMax
	function_score	FunctionScore
Joining queries	nested	Nested
	has_child	HasChild
	has_parent	HasParent
	parent_id	ParentId
Specialized queries	script	Script
	more_like_this	MoreLikeThis

The aggregations class

The aggregations framework is available in the `aggs.py` file of the `elasticsearch-dsl` package. You can use the `A()` method to define an aggregation. There are provided classes for the supported aggregation types. A list of supported aggregation types and its provided classes are compiled in the following table. You can use the class to construct the aggregation object:

Category	Aggregation type	Provided class name
Metrics	avg	Avg
	weighted_avg	WeightedAvg
	cardinality	Cardinality
	extended_stats	ExtendedStats
	max	Max
	min	Min
	percentiles	Percentiles
	percentile_ranks	PercentRanks
	scripted_metric	ScriptedMetric
	stats	Stats
	sum	Sum
	top_hots	TopHits
	value_count	ValueCount

Bucket	children	Children
	date_histogram	DateHistogram
	auto_date_histogram	AutoDateHistogram
	children	Children
	composite	Composite
	date_range	DateRange
	diversified_sampler	DiversifiedSampler
	filter	Filter
	filters	Filters
	histogram	Histogram
	ip_range	IPRange
	missing	Missing
	nested	Nested
	range	Range
	reverse_nested	ReverseNested
	sampler	Sampler
	significant_terms	SignificantTerms
	significant_text	SignificantText
	terms	Terms
Pipeline	avg_bucket	AvgBucket
	derivative	Derivative
	max_bucket	MaxBucket
	min_bucket	MinBucket
	sum_bucket	SumBucket
	stats_bucket	StatsBucket
	extended_stats_bucket	ExtendedStatsBucket
	percentiles_bucket	PercentilesBucket
	moving_avg	MovingAvg
	cumulative_sum	CumulativeSum
	bucket_script	BucketScript
	bucket_selector	BucketSelector
	bucket_sort	BucketSort
	serial_diff	SerialDiff

As an example, let's use the aggregation class to try to achieve Bollinger Bands. Recall from the Bollinger Bands in the *Operational data analytics* section of `Chapter 10`, *Using Elasticsearch for Exploratory Data Analysis*, the implementation involves the following aggregations:

- **The bucket aggregations type**: The `date_histogram` aggregation
- **The metrics aggregations type**: The `scripted_metric` aggregation
- **The pipeline aggregations type**: The `moving_avg`, `moving_fn`, and `bucket_script` aggregation

However, we cannot find the `moving_fn` aggregation supported in `elasticsearch_dsl/aggs.py` (for reference, see https://github.com/elastic/elasticsearch-dsl-py/issues/1195); therefore, we use a 0.5 constant to simulate the standard deviation for all the time periods so that the full program can run. The `DateHistogram` class, the `ScriptedMetric` class, the `MovingAvg` class, and the `BucketScript` class are equivalent to the `date_histogram` aggregation, the `script_metric` aggregation, the `moving_avg` aggregation, and the `buck_script` aggregation, respectively. The following code block is the Bollinger Band written in Python:

```
from com.example.client.config.low_level_client_by_connection import
ESLowLevelClientByConnection
from elasticsearch_dsl import Search
from elasticsearch_dsl.query import Q, Bool, Range, Term
from elasticsearch_dsl.aggs import A, DateHistogram, ScriptedMetric,
MovingAvg, BucketScript

def bollinger_band(index='cf_etf_hist_price', start_date='2018-12-26',
end_date='2019-03-25', symbol='rfem'):
    ESLowLevelClientByConnection.get_instance()
    search = Search(index=index, using='high_level_client')[0:0]
    search.query = Q(Bool(must=[Range(date={'gte': '2018-12-26',
                    'lte': '2019-03-25'}), Term(symbol='rfem')]))
    aggs = A(DateHistogram(field='date', interval='1d',
                        format='yyyy-MM-dd', min_doc_count=1))
    aggs_tp = A(ScriptedMetric(init_script='state.totals=[]',
map_script='state.totals.add((doc.high.value+doc.low.value+doc.close.value)
/3)',
        combine_script='double total=0; for (t in state.totals) {
            total += t} return total',
        reduce_script='double total=0; for (t in states) {total += t}
return total'))
    aggs_moving_avg = A(MovingAvg(model='simple', window=20,
            buckets_path='tp.value'))
    aggs_bbu = A(BucketScript(buckets_path={
```

```
                        'SMA':'20_trading_days_moving_avg'}, script='params.SMA +
    0.5'))
        aggs_bbl =
    A(BucketScript(buckets_path={'SMA':'20_trading_days_moving_avg'},
    script='params.SMA - 0.5'))
        search.aggs.bucket('Bollinger_band', aggs).pipeline('tp', aggs_tp).
                pipeline('20_trading_days_moving_avg', aggs_moving_avg).
                pipeline('BBU', aggs_bbu).pipeline('BBL', aggs_bbl)
        response = search.execute()
        print(response.to_dict())

    if __name__ == "__main__":
        bollinger_band()
```

In the preceding code block, you can see how the aggregations are linked together. Use the `aggs` attribute of the `Search` object to start with the top-level aggregation. There are three methods: `bucket()`, `metric()`, and `pipeline()`. Use the method corresponding to the aggregation category to nest the aggregations in the chain.

Under the downloaded `cf_etf` directory, issue the command shown in the following code block to activate the virtual environment and run the program that we presented in the preceding code block. You will find that the printed response body looks very similar to what we presented before in Chapter 10, *Using Elasticsearch for Exploratory Data Analysis*:

```
$ source venv/bin/activate
(venv)$ export PYTHONPATH=.:$PYTHONPATH
(venv)$ python com/example/boillinger_band/bollinger_band.py
{'took': 9, 'timed_out': False, '_shards': {'total': 1, 'successful': 1,
'skipped': 0, 'failed': 0}, 'hits': {'total': {'value': 61, 'relation':
'eq'}, 'max_score': None, 'hits': []}, 'aggregations': {'Bollinger_band':
{'buckets': [{'key_as_string': '2018-12-26', 'key': 1545782400000,
'doc_count': 1, 'tp': {'value': 55.526632944742836}}, {'key_as_string':
'2018-12-27', 'key': 1545868800000, 'doc_count': 1, 'tp': {'value':
55.51000086466471}, '20_trading_days_moving_avg': {'value':
55.526632944742836}, 'BBU': {'value': 56.026632944742836}, 'BBL': {'value':
55.026632944742836}},...
```

We have completed the presentation of all the materials we have prepared for Python programming with Elasticsearch. We'll conclude this chapter in the following section.

Summary

Incredible! We have completed Python programming with Elasticsearch, and this chapter marks the end of *Section 4* of this book. We learned about the different programming styles between the low-level client and the high-level library. We also tried to implement Bollinger Bands by using the high-level library and we discovered that the `moving_fn` aggregation type was not supported. Indeed, we can use the low-level client in case any method is missing from (or not supported in) the high-level library.

In the next chapter, we will start with Section 5, *Elastic Stack*. We will present an overview of the other components of Elastic Stack: Kibana, Logstash, and Beats. We will also learn some practical examples from an examination of some very basic usage of Kibana, Elasticsearch, Filebeat, and Logstash.

Section 4: Elastic Stack

This section will provide an overview of Elastic Stack and its components. You will be taught the very basics of creating a Kibana visualization for a dashboard application by collecting logs in Elasticsearch with Filebeat and Logstash. You will also learn how to use SQL to search and aggregate data inside Elasticsearch with the help of detailed Java programming.

This section is comprised the following chapters:

- Chapter 13, *Using Kibana, Logstash, and Beats*
- Chapter 14, *Working with Elasticsearch SQL*
- Chapter 15, *Working with Elasticsearch Analysis Plugin*

13
Using Kibana, Logstash, and Beats

In the last chapter, we introduced Python programming with Elasticsearch, and presented the low-level client and high-level library. We wrote a number of unit test programs and tried to implement Bollinger Bands with the high-level library. However, due to the fact that the `moving_fn` aggregation is not yet supported, we used a constant value for the moving standard deviation instead. If you cannot find the support function from the high-level client, you need to switch back to the low-level client. In this chapter, we will give an overview of the Elastic Stack's components, including Kibana, Logstash, and Beats. The Elastic Stack is a rich ecosystem. Knowing one piece of it is good. Two pieces are better, and three pieces are excellent. If we understand most of the components, our role could be as a fullstack engineer, and even an architect of the software project, working from end to end, from the backend to the frontend data visualization. The reason is that we not only know how to cooperate each component, but also we can build a project from the foundation.

We'll provide a brief introduction to each component and then use them all in one project.

By the end of this chapter, we will have covered the following topics:

- Overview of the Elastic Stack
- Running Elasticsearch in a Docker container
- Running Kibana in a Docker container
- Running Logstash in a Docker container
- Running Beats in a Docker container

Overview of the Elastic Stack

According to the documentation of the latest version of the Elastic Stack (available at `https://www.elastic.co/guide/en/elastic-stack/7.0/installing-elastic-stack.html`), there are six components: Elasticsearch, Kibana, Logstash, Beats, APM Server, and Elasticsearch-Hadoop. If you use more than one component, you must use the same version across the stack. Let's give a brief description of each component as follows:

- **Kibana**: In version 7.0 of the Elastic Stack, Kibana is a UI framework for working with Elasticsearch. It now supports a dark theme across the entire UI, and a responsive dashboard to take a step forward to support mobile devices.

- **Logstash**: This is an open source data collection engine that provides a real-time data processing pipeline from multiple sources and then sends the collected logs to a defined target, such as an Elasticsearch server. The data processing usually includes conversion, unification, and normalization.

- **Beats**: These are lightweight data collection agents that consume fewer system resources than Logstash. They just sit on your deployed machines and gather data. The data can be first routed to Logstash for the next level of data processing, or be sent directly to an Elasticsearch server.

- **APM**: APM is short for Application Performance Monitoring. APM is built on top of the Beats framework and provides agents for you to deploy on the machine to collect data. The agents will send data to the APM server. The APM server first transforms the data into Elasticsearch documents and then stores them in the Elasticsearch server. APM Server offers real-time user monitoring and acts as a security layer between the web browser and Elasticsearch to protect data.

- **Elasticsearch-Hadoop**: This is a self-contained open source project that lets you index Hadoop data into Elasticsearch so that you can take advantage of the real-time analytics and visualization provided by Kibana. Between Elasticsearch and Hadoop, you can easily move data in both directions.

The data flows between each component are depicted in the following diagram:

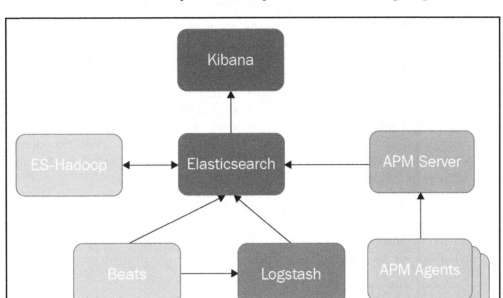

In this chapter, we will use examples involving **Kibana**, **Logstash**, and **Beats**. Due to the complication of the installation for each component, we will try to use Docker to run each component. The following section will introduce Docker and the installation of each of the Elastic Stack components.

Running the Elastic Stack with Docker

Docker is an open platform for developing, packaging, delivering, and running an application. A loosely isolated environment called a container is provided to distribute, test, and deploy your application. Without a hypervisor, the container runs directly on the host machine's kernel. A **Docker image** is a snapshot of a container in a file format, while a **Docker container** is a running instance of a Docker image. When a Docker image is started and run, it produces a container. Docker images are stored in Docker registries. The official Elastic Docker images are located at the download site at `https://www.docker.elastic.co/`. All major components are provided. The installation order for the core components is Elasticsearch → Kibana → Logstash → Beats → APM Server → Elasticsearch Hadoop. Let's complete the installation using the following step-by-step instructions:

1. **Docker installation**: We continue to the Ubuntu 16.04 operating system to host the Docker images and run the application. The following code block uses the official Ubuntu repository to install the Docker software. The version is 18.09.02 when we run the installation:

   ```
   $sudo apt-get install docker.io
   ```

   After installation, run the following command to restart the Docker service:

   ```
   $service docker restart
   ```

   Now, test Docker's functionality by running a **Hello, World!** application:

   ```
   $docker run hello-world
   Hello from Docker!
   . . .
   ```

2. **Download the Elasticsearch Docker image**: The operating system of the base image is CentOS 7. To obtain a Docker image with Elasticsearch, simply run the following Docker command:

   ```
   $docker pull docker.elastic.co/elasticsearch/elasticsearch:7.0.0
   7.0.0: Pulling from elasticsearch/elasticsearch
   ```

3. **Download the Kibana Docker image**: The operating system of the base image is CentOS 7. To obtain a Docker image with Kibana, simply run the following Docker command:

   ```
   $docker pull docker.elastic.co/kibana/kibana:7.0.0
   7.0.0: Pulling from kibana/kibana
   ```

4. **Download the Logstash Docker image**: The operating system of the base image is CentOS 7. To obtain a Docker image with Logstash, simply run the following Docker command:

```
$docker pull docker.elastic.co/logstash/logstash:7.0.0
7.0.0: Pulling from logstash/logstash
```

5. **Download the Filebeat Docker image**: The operating system of the base image is CentOS 7. To obtain a Docker image with Filebeat, simply run the following Docker command:

```
$docker pull docker.elastic.co/beats/filebeat:7.0.0
7.0.0: Pulling from beats/filebeat
```

6. **List Elastic Docker images**: Run the following Docker command to list the Elastic Stack's Docker images:

```
$docker image ls |grep elastic
```

Four Docker images will be displayed in the output, as shown in the following screenshot:

```
wai@wai:~$ docker image ls |grep elastic
docker.elastic.co/logstash/logstash               7.0.0    acb15b2d9d8f    3 months ago    765MB
docker.elastic.co/kibana/kibana                   7.0.0    7f92ab934206    3 months ago    661MB
docker.elastic.co/elasticsearch/elasticsearch     7.0.0    8f46db60ddd6    3 months ago    811MB
docker.elastic.co/beats/filebeat                  7.0.0    893591509ff0    3 months ago    288MB
```

Before we can run the Elastic Stack's Docker images, let's create a bridge network for the components to use. When a new container is created and launched by the docker run command, it automatically connects to the bridge network. Let's give a name to the bridge network – we'll use packt, as shown here:

```
$docker network create packt
```

In the following sections, we will give a brief introduction on how to run an application in a Docker container for Elasticsearch, Kibana, Logstash, and Filebeat. We will start with Elasticsearch in the next section.

Running Elasticsearch in a Docker container

On our GitHub site (`https://github.com/PacktPublishing/Mastering-Elasticsearch-7.0/tree/master/Chapter13/docker_run`), you can download a set of bash script files to run the application including `docker_create_network`, `docker_run_elasticsearch`, `docker_run_kibana`, `docker_run_logstash`, `docker_run_filebeat`, and a folder named `pipeline`, which contains the `logstash.conf` Logstash configuration file. Use the bash script file to launch an Elasticsearch server in development mode with the Elasticsearch Docker image by running the following command. However, previously you run the following command, shut down the original Elasticsearch server installed before and go to the `docker_run` folder:

```
$cd docker_run
$./docker_run_elasticsearch
```

You can check the status of the Elasticsearch Docker container to see whether it is running by using the list command, as shown:

```
$docker container ls
```

```
[wai@wai:~/book/chapter13/docker_run$ docker container ls
CONTAINER ID      IMAGE                                                COMMAND              CREATED       STATUS
                  PORTS                                     NAMES
9b45edcf5304      docker.elastic.co/elasticsearch/elasticsearch:7.0.0  "/usr/local/bin/dock…"  2 weeks ago  Up 20
seconds           0.0.0.0:9200->9200/tcp, 0.0.0.0:9300->9300/tcp  elasticsearch
```

You can see that the Elasticsearch Docker container's ID is `802d6f50ef0`. This ID is an identifier of the container for all related commands.

We can send the GET request to the Elasticsearch server with `curl` to test it. This will check whether it is healthy. Simply run the following command:

```
$curl localhost:9200 -XGET
```

The following screenshot shows the response that is received from the preceding code:

```
[wai@wai:~/book/chapter13/docker_run$ curl localhost:9200 -XGET
{
  "name" : "9b45edcf5304",
  "cluster_name" : "docker-cluster",
  "cluster_uuid" : "YzTQv81XQHuXr3nwxczBuQ",
  "version" : {
    "number" : "7.0.0",
    "build_flavor" : "default",
    "build_type" : "docker",
    "build_hash" : "b7e28a7",
    "build_date" : "2019-04-05T22:55:32.697037Z",
    "build_snapshot" : false,
    "lucene_version" : "8.0.0",
    "minimum_wire_compatibility_version" : "6.7.0",
    "minimum_index_compatibility_version" : "6.0.0-beta1"
  },
  "tagline" : "You Know, for Search"
}
```

On a production machine, the virtual memory map size must be large enough. On Linux, issue the following command to increase the limit to 262144:

```
$sysctl -w vm.max_map_count=262144
```

> It may transpire that when the Elasticsearch container is created, the error shown here occurs:
> docker: Error response from daemon: Conflict. The container name "/elasticsearch" is already in use by container "id", where "id" is a long hexadecimal string. You have to remove (or rename) that container to be able to reuse that name and you have to remove the container.
>
> If this happens, use these commands to stop the container, remove it, and re-run docker_run_elasticsearch:
> $docker container stop id
> $docker container rm id
> $./docker_run_elasticsearch

Wow! We have successfully installed and run the Elasticsearch server with a Docker container. In the next section, we will continue with Kibana.

Running Kibana in a Docker container

You can quickly launch Kibana with the Kibana Docker image. You can search, view, and analyze the Elasticsearch index in the forms of charts, tables, and maps. Run the following command to bring up Kibana:

```
$./docker_run_kibana
```

Direct your web browser to `http://localhost:5601` to communicate with Kibana. The home page of Kibana is as follows:

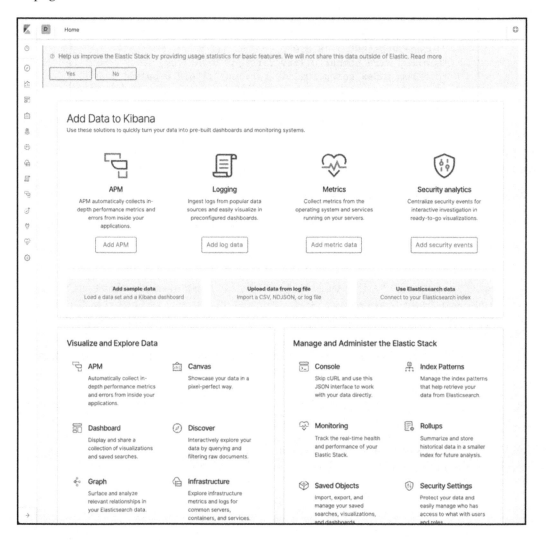

Let's try to test Kibana with the sample data provided by the official website by following these steps:

1. Press **Add sample data** hyperlink and you will see the page shown in the following screenshot:

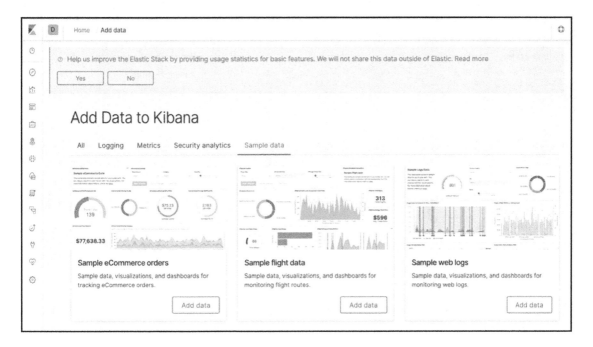

2. Now, l take the **Sample flight data**. Press the **Add data** button and you will see the page shown in the following screenshot:

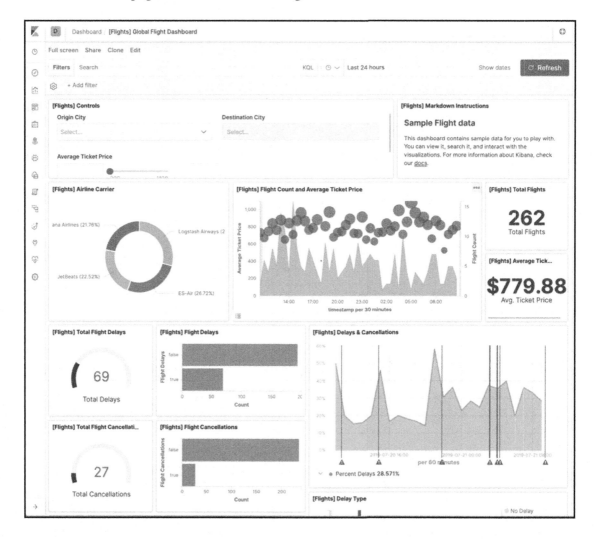

3. Amazing! What a wonderful dashboard to show the flight data. Move your mouse to the button in the left toolbar, highlighted by the a box, and press it. This will take you to the **Management** screen. Press the **Index management** hyperlink highlighted by the yellow box in the following screenshot. You will observe that the **kibana_sample_data_flight** index is created for the sample data in Elasticsearch:

4. Press the **kibana_sample_data_flight** hyperlink, and you will see a floating panel pop up, as shown in the following screenshot. The index **Settings**, **Mappings**, and **Stats** data have been collected and reported:

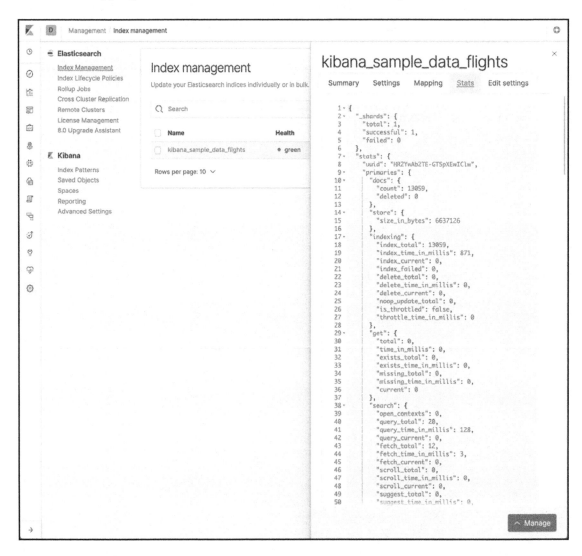

Let's populate data to the `cf_etf` and `cf_etf_hist_price` indices as we did in chapter 6, *Search APIs*, and Chapter 8, *Aggregations Framework*. After that, we can check them out in Kibana. For your convenience, we have duplicated those files and put them in the GitHub repository for this chapter at our GitHub page, available at `https://github.com/PacktPublishing/Mastering-Elasticsearch-7.0/tree/master/Chapter13/populate_data`, you can download five files: `cf_etf_list_bulk.json`, `cf_etf_list_bulk_index.sh`, `cf_etf_hist_price_bulk.json`, `cf_etf_hist_price_mappings.json`, and `cf_etf_hist_price_bulk_index.sh`. Go to the downloaded directory and run the following two commands to index data to those two indices:

```
$./cf_etf_list_bulk_index.sh
$./cf_etf_hist_price_bulk_index.sh
```

After the commands are run, you can go back to the **Index management** page in Kibana. Press the **Reload indices** button and you will see the two indices shown in the following screenshot:

How easy is it to integrate Kibana in Elasticsearch! In the next section, we are going to run and configure Logstash in a Docker container.

Running Logstash in a Docker container

Logstash receives data from multiple sources, performs data processing, and then sends the log information to the *stash*, which can mean a store. There are two types of configurations with which to configure Logstash for Docker: pipeline configuration and the settings configuration. We will use pipeline configuration for our demonstration. When the Logstash Docker container runs with pipeline configuration, it will check the path for the `logstash.conf` file. In our case, the file path is `docker_run/pipeline/logstash.conf`, as specified in the `docker_run_logstash` script file. The structure of a Logstash configuration file basically includes three parts: input, filter, and output. You specify the source of the data in the input section, and the destination in the output section. You can manipulate, measure, and create events in the filter section by using supported filter plugins. The structure of a configuration file is shown in the following code:

```
input {...}
filter {...}
output{...}
```

The following code block shows the sample configuration file we used. The input file is located in `/tmp/log/syslog`. For the syslog file type, the filter will transform each line from the input and construct a document in the Elasticsearch index. The output specifies the Elasticsearch destination with the host address, port, account name, password, and index name:

```
input {
    file {
        path => "/tmp/log/syslog"
        type => "syslog"
    }
}

filter {
  if [type] == "syslog" {
    grok {
      match => { "message" => "%{SYSLOGTIMESTAMP:syslog_timestamp} %
        {SYSLOGHOST:syslog_hostname} %{DATA:syslog_program}(?:\[%
        {POSINT:syslog_pid}\])?: %{GREEDYDATA:syslog_message}" }
        add_field => [ "received_at", "%{@timestamp}" ]
        add_field => [ "received_from", "%{host}" ]
    }
    date {
        match => [ "syslog_timestamp", "MMM d HH:mm:ss", "MMM dd HH:mm:ss"
]
    }
  }
```

Chapter 13

```
    }

output {
    elasticsearch {
        hosts => ["elasticsearch:9200"]
        index => "logstash_index"
        user => "logstash_internal"
        password => "password1"
    }
    stdout { codec => rubydebug }
}
```

To launch Logstash with the Logstash Docker image, go to the `docker_run` folder and issue the Docker command, as shown here:

```
$cd docker_run
$./docker_run_logstash
```

Let's take a look at the contents of the `docker_run_logstash` script file:

```
#!/bin/bash
docker run --name=logstash --group-add adm --net packt --rm -it -v
"`pwd`/pipeline/:/usr/share/logstash/pipeline" -v /var/log/:/tmp/log -e
xpack.monitoring.enabled=false docker.elastic.co/logstash/logstash:7.0.0
```

The command has performed a few major changes:

1. Named the docker container to `logstash`.
2. Added the Docker user's group access with the `adm` group, which is required to access the syslog file.
3. Mapped the `docker_run/pipeline` directory of the host machine to the `/usr/share/logstash/pipeline` directory of the Logstash Docker machine.
4. Mapped the `/var/log` directory of the host machine to the `/tmp/log` directory of the Logstash Docker machine. Hence, we are going to monitor and process the `/var/log/syslog` file in the Logstash Docker machine.
5. Turned off the X-Pack monitoring feature to avoid unnecessary configuration in our demonstration.

The following screenshot depicts some of messages printed after the Logstash Docker container is run:

```
wai@wai:~/book/chapter13/docker_run$ ./docker_run_logstash
2019/07/21 18:25:51 Setting 'xpack.monitoring.enabled' from environment.

Sending Logstash logs to /usr/share/logstash/logs which is now configured via log4j2.properties
[2019-07-21T18:26:06,677][INFO ][logstash.setting.writabledirectory] Creating directory {:setting=>"path.queue", :path=>"/usr
/share/logstash/data/queue"}
[2019-07-21T18:26:06,690][INFO ][logstash.setting.writabledirectory] Creating directory {:setting=>"path.dead_letter_queue",
:path=>"/usr/share/logstash/data/dead_letter_queue"}
[2019-07-21T18:26:07,007][INFO ][logstash.runner          ] Starting Logstash {"logstash.version"=>"7.0.0"}
[2019-07-21T18:26:07,028][INFO ][logstash.agent           ] No persistent UUID file found. Generating new UUID {:uuid=>"28756
a59-8696-48e4-8a40-b549a823855e", :path=>"/usr/share/logstash/data/uuid"}
[2019-07-21T18:26:12,405][INFO ][logstash.outputs.elasticsearch] Elasticsearch pool URLs updated {:changes=>{:removed=>[], :a
dded=>[http://logstash_internal:xxxxxx@elasticsearch:9200/]}}
[2019-07-21T18:26:12,581][WARN ][logstash.outputs.elasticsearch] Restored connection to ES instance {:url=>"http://logstash_i
nternal:xxxxxx@elasticsearch:9200/"}
[2019-07-21T18:26:12,615][INFO ][logstash.outputs.elasticsearch] ES Output version determined {:es_version=>7}
[2019-07-21T18:26:12,617][WARN ][logstash.outputs.elasticsearch] Detected a 6.x and above cluster: the `type` event field won
't be used to determine the document _type {:es_version=>7}
[2019-07-21T18:26:12,633][INFO ][logstash.outputs.elasticsearch] New Elasticsearch output {:class=>"LogStash::Outputs::Elasti
cSearch", :hosts=>["//elasticsearch:9200"]}
[2019-07-21T18:26:12,642][INFO ][logstash.outputs.elasticsearch] Using default mapping template
```

When the Logstash container is running, you can go back to Kibana's **Index management** page to press the **Reload indices** button. You can see that the `logstash_index`, which we specified in the `logstash.conf` file, is created as shown in the following screenshot:

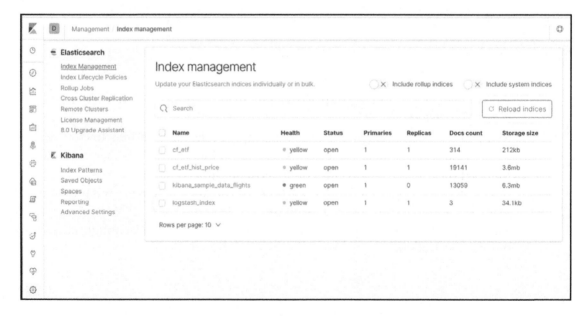

You may select `logstash_index` and look over the setting, mapping, and stats information if you would like to do so. Let's take a look at the mappings of `logstash_index`, as shown in the following screenshot. You can see that those fields specified in the filter section of `logstash.conf` have been created in the mappings:

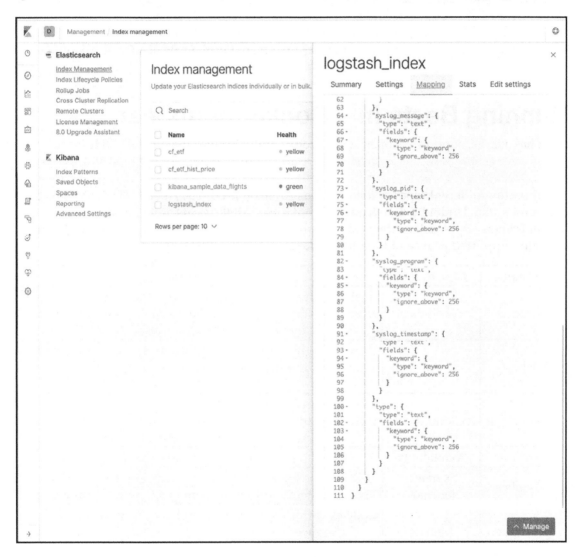

If the logstash container is kept running, it will continue to index the documents from the `/var/log/syslog` file to the `logstash_index` index. Let's stop the running Logstash container and issue the command described in the following code block to shut it down:

```
$docker container stop logstash
```

We have finished the integration of Logstash with Elasticsearch, and visualized it in Kibana! In the next section, we are going to run and configure Beats in a Docker container.

Running Beats in a Docker container

Beats has a large, supportive, open source community. Besides the official GitHub site (`https://github.com/elastic/beats`), there are about 80 other GitHub repositories (see `https://www.elastic.co/guide/en/beats/libbeat/7.0/community-beats.html`) focused on supporting different types of data, such as Amazon products, Apache HTTPD, Spring Boot, and Kafka. Undoubtedly, Beats are a hot topic. All the Beats are built on top of the libbeat framework, which contains the common packages written in the Go language. The officially supported Beats and their target data are listed in this table:

Beat name	Type of data	Description
Auditbeat	Audit data	Install it on the servers where you want to detect changes to the attributes of files or the system's events and have them sent to an output destination.
Filebeat	Log files	A lightweight version of Logstash focuses on performance to fetch information from log files and send them to an output destination.
Functionbeat	Cloud data	A lightweight data shipper for cloud data. Uses include, extracting data from Amazon Cloud software and sending it to an output destination.
Heartbeat	Availability	Used to probe the service and check availability.
Journalbeat	Systemd journals	Reads the log files from local systemd/journald-based Linux systems and sends them to an output destination.
Metricbeat	Metrics	Collects various system and service metrics such as system CPU, memory, and load, to send them to an output destination.
Packetbeat	Network packet	Collects network data from application protocols, HTTP, and low-level protocols, and sends them to an output destination.

Winlogbeat	Window event logs	Collects Windows Event Logs and sends them to an output destination.

In this section, we will continue our demonstration to integrate Filebeat to Logstash. Observe the following step-by-step instructions:

1. Before we run the `docker_run_filebeat` shell script, let's take a look at the content:

```
#!/bin/bash
docker run --name=filebeat --group-add adm --net packt -v
/var/log:/var/log -v
"`pwd`/filebeat.yml:/usr/share/filebeat/filebeat.yml"
docker.elastic.co/beats/filebeat:7.0.0
```

Similar to the `docker_run_logstash` shell script in the previous *Running Logstash in a Docker container* section, this gives a name to the Docker container, adds the `adm` group access, and maps files or directories from the host machine to the Logstash Docker machine. The Filebeat Docker container is named `filebeat`. The `docker_run/filebeat.yml` file is mapped to the `/usr/share/filebeat/filebeat.yml` file path of the Docker machine.

2. Let's now take a look at the `filebeat.yml` file, shown in this code block:

```
filebeat.inputs:
- type: log
  paths:
    - /var/log/syslog

output.logstash:
  hosts: ["logstash_filebeat:5044"]

logging.level: debug
```

This file sets the input of Filebeat to the `/var/log/syslog` log file. The file type is `log`. The output of Filebeat is sent to port `5044` of the container named `logstash_filebeat`, where the `Logstash` application is listening. The logging mode is set to debug so as to show detailed messages.

3. Run the Filebeat Docker image with the following shell script:

```
$./docker_run_filebeat
```

When Filebeat is run, it fails to connect and repeatedly tries to reconnect to the `logstash_filebeat` container at port 5044. The error message is shown as follows:

```
2019-06-29T05:32:19.954Z INFO pipeline/output.go:93 Attempting to
reconnect to backoff(async(tcp://logstash_filebeat:5044)) with 1
reconnect attempt(s)
2019-06-29T05:32:19.954Z DEBUG [logstash] logstash/async.go:111
connect
```

4. Let's run Logstash with the following shell script, which is configured to integrate with Filebeat and run at port 5044:

```
$./docker_run_logstash_for_filebeat
```

When Filebeat has successfully connected to Logstash, it keeps sending messages to Logstash when it finds unprocessed contents from the `/var/log/syslog` file. When Logstash receives the message, it will compile it and send it to the index specified in the configuration file.

5. In the screen that `docker_run_filebeat` is run, lots of messages are printed. A sample message is shown for reference. The message is extracted from the `syslog` file and sent to Logstash by Filebeat:

```
2019-06-29T07:11:38.029Z DEBUG [processors]
processing/processors.go:183 Publish event: {
    "@timestamp": "2019-06-29T07:11:38.029Z",
    "@metadata": {
        "beat": "",
        "type": "_doc",
        "version": ""
    },
    "ecs": {
        "version": "1.0.0"
    },
    "host": {
        "name": "c97e6d1a9f62"
    },
    "agent": {
        "version": "7.0.0",
        "type": "filebeat",
        "ephemeral_id": "b704a889-fe46-4804-9de2-2347518d3a17",
        "hostname": "c97e6d1a9f62",
```

```
          "id": "8d3f3e3e-ba35-4c05-ad0e-0446f3db6ade"
      },
      "message": "Jun 28 07:35:09 wai systemd-udevd[18333]: Process
'/usr/bin/nvidia-smi' failed       with exit code 12.",
      "log": {
          "offset": 0,
          "file": {
              "path": "/var/log/syslog"
          }
      },
      "input": {
          "type": "log"
      }
  }
```

6. In the screen that `docker_run_logstash_for_filebeat` is run, lots of
   messages are printed, too. A sample message is shown in the following code
   block for reference. The message is sent from Filebeat and received by Logstash.
   After processing, it is sent to Elasticsearch for document indexing:

```
{
    "agent" => {
        "version" => "7.0.0",
        "hostname" => "c97e6d1a9f62",
        "type" => "filebeat",
        "id" => "8d3f3e3e-ba35-4c05-ad0e-0446f3db6ade",
        "ephemeral_id" => "b704a889-fe46-4804-9de2-2347518d3a17"
    },
    "message" => "Jun 28 07:35:09 wai systemd-udevd[18333]: Process
'/usr/bin/nvidia-smi' failed with exit code 12.",
    "syslog_pid" => "18333",
    "syslog_timestamp" => "Jun 28 07:35:09",
    "@timestamp" => 2019-06-28T07:35:09.000Z,
    "ecs" => {
        "version" => "1.0.0"
    },
    "syslog_hostname" => "wai",
    "log" => {
        "file" => {
            "path" => "/var/log/syslog"
        },
        "offset" => 0
    },
    "received_at" => "2019-06-29T07:11:38.029Z",
    "syslog_message" => "Process '/usr/bin/nvidia-smi' failed with
exit code 12.",
    "host" => {
        "name" => "c97e6d1a9f62"
```

```
        },
        "syslog_program" => "systemd-udevd",
        "input" => {
            "type" => "log"
        },
        "@version" => "1",
        "received_from" => "{\"name\":\"c97e6d1a9f62\"}",
        "tags" => [
            [0] "beats_input_codec_plain_applied"
        ]
    }
```

7. Let's take a look at the file content of
   `docker_run_logstash_for_filebeat`, as shown in the following code block:

```
#!/bin/bash
docker run --name=logstash_filebeat --group-add adm --net packt --
rm -it -v
"`pwd`/pipeline_for_filebeat/":/usr/share/logstash/pipeline -e
xpack.monitoring.enabled=false
docker.elastic.co/logstash/logstash:7.0.0
```

   Differently to the `docker_run_logstash` shell script in the previous *Running
   Logstash in a Docker container* section, the configuration file is located at
   `docker_run/pipeline_for_filebeat/logstash.conf`.

8. Let's now take a look at the file contents of `logstash.conf`, as shown here:

```
input {
    beats {
        port => 5044
    }
}

filter {
    grok {
        match => {"message" => "%{SYSLOGTIMESTAMP:syslog_timestamp}
%{SYSLOGHOST:syslog_hostname}
%{DATA:syslog_program}(?:\[%{POSINT:syslog_pid}\])?:
%{GREEDYDATA:syslog_message}" }
        add_field => [ "received_at", "%{@timestamp}" ]
        add_field => [ "received_from", "%{host}" ]
    }
    date {
        match => [ "syslog_timestamp", "MMM d HH:mm:ss", "MMM dd
HH:mm:ss" ]
    }
}
```

```
output {
    elasticsearch {
        hosts => ["elasticsearch:9200"]
        index => "logstash_filebeat_index"
        user => "logstash_internal"
        password => "password1"
    }
    stdout { codec => rubydebug }
}
```

Logstash is listening at port `5044` and waiting for the Beats component to send messages to it. After processing according to the `grok` processor defined in the earlier code block, all documents will be sent to Elasticsearch with an index named `logstash_filebeat_index`.

9. Go back to Kibana's **Index management** page and press the **Reload indices** button. The `logstash_filebeat_index` index, shown in *step 8*, is displayed in the following screenshot. If the **Reload indices** button is clicked, the `Docs count` field of the **Index management** screen will increase. This is due to the `syslog` file growing, being read by `Filebeat`, being sent to Logstash to process, and then indexed in Elasticsearch:

We have completed the introduction, setup, and testing for Filebeat. We'll conclude this chapter with the next section.

Summary

Bravo! We have tried the major components of the Elastic Stack. You should now understand the basic concepts of the powerful Elastic Stack. We ran an example on Kibana to visualize some sample flight data from Elasticsearch. We also learned how to use Logstash to collect and parse log data from the system log file. We extended the use of Logstash as a central log-processing center by using Filebeat. We also played with the popular deployment technique of running the applications using the officially supported Elastic Stack Docker images.

In the next chapter, we will introduce Elasticsearch SQL. Yes, Elasticsearch also speaks SQL. You will learn the SQL semantics supported in Elasticsearch. You will also perform a SQL REST API with SQL statements. Also, you will work with **JDBC (Java Database Connectivity)**, the software industry standard for databases.

14
Working with Elasticsearch SQL

In the last chapter, we touched upon the major components of the Elastic Stack. We went through the entire range of data processes, starting with Filebeat, Logstash, and Elasticsearch, before finally viewing it in Kibana. Although we only gave a simple example, you can still see that once the details can be handled, the feasibility and extensibility are great. That is why the Beats are so popular and extend to different areas to collect data. In this chapter, we will introduce Elasticsearch SQL. With Elasticsearch SQL, you can access full-text search and easily extend the functionality with a familiar query syntax. You can even see your results in the tabular views. Elasticsearch provides a variety of approaches, such as the REST API interface, the command-line interface, the **JDBC (Java Database Connectivity)** driver, and the **ODBC (Open Database Connectivity)** driver, to let you use SQL to perform search and aggregation. In the final section, we'll introduce a programming example to show you how to use JDBC.

By the end of this chapter, you will have covered the following topics:

- Overview
- Getting started
- Elasticsearch SQL language
- Elasticsearch SQL REST API
- Elasticsearch SQL JDBC

Overview

The support feature for SQL was delivered with version 6.3. This was due to the popularity of SQL, while many Elasticsearch users were familiar with SQL syntax and the ability to perform SQL-like queries on indexed data had been a longstanding desire. Elasticsearch SQL is an X-Pack component, where X-Pack is an Elastic Stack extension that provides many features, including monitoring, security, and machine learning. In the default installation, Elasticsearch comes with X-Pack. You will recall from the *Mapping concepts across SQL and Elasticsearch* section of `Chapter 1`, *Overview of Elasticsearch 7*, that we constructed a table that describes the terms between SQL and Elasticsearch, comparing column and field, row and document, table and index, and database and cluster instance. You can think of Elasticsearch SQL as a translator from SQL to Elasticsearch. Nonetheless, all syntax will follow SQL standard terminology and conventions, whenever possible.

For programming with Elasticsearch SQL, nothing can be found in the reference that is related to the high-level REST client. Since SQL REST API is supported, you can use the low-level REST client to carry out the job. In addition, SQL JDBC and ODBC are supported. You can download the appropriate driver to fully integrate your application with Elasticsearch SQL (`https://www.elastic.co/downloads/jdbc-client`). In the next section, we will start with some hands-on practices involving Elasticsearch SQL on our Elasticsearch Docker container.

Getting started

Elasticsearch ships with a script, named `elasticsearch-sql-cli`, to run the SQL **CLI** (**command-line interface**) in its `bin` directory. Let's use the Elasticsearch Docker container to run the example. Assume that the container ID is `6b3d0fde663d` and issue the command, as described in the following code block, to start a `bash` shell session in the Docker container:

```
$docker exec -it elasticsearch /bin/bash
[root@6b3d0fde663d elasticsearch]#
```

You will get a prompt in response, and now you are working in the Elasticsearch Docker container. Issue the `elasticsearch-sql-cli` command to run the SQL CLI:

```
[root@6b3d0fde663d elasticsearch]# bin/elasticsearch-sql-cli
WARNING: sun.reflect.Reflection.getCallerClass is not supported. This will
impact performance.
```

When the command line starts, you will see the Elastic Stack icon and a prompt for input, as shown in the following screenshot:

```
                    asticElasticE
                 ElasticE   sticEla
           sticEl  ticEl               Elast
          lasti Elasti                  tic
       cEl          ast                 icE
      icE           as                   cEl
      icE           as                   cEl
      icEla      las                     El
    sticElasticElast                     icElas
  las            last                    ticElast
El               asti                 asti    stic
El               asticEla          Elas       icE
El           Elas  cElasticE   ticEl            cE
Ela      ticEl          ticElasti              cE
  las    astic               last             icE
   sticElas                  asti            stic
     icEl                sticElasticElast
     icE                 sticE    ticEla
     icE                 sti         cEla
     icEl                sti          Ela
      cEl                sti          cEl
       Ela              astic    ticE
        asti          ElasticElasti
        ticElasti  lasticElas
          ElasticElast

                    SQL
                    7.0.0

sql> █
```

We are now in the SQL command-line mode and can begin playing with the simple SQL **DDL (data definition language)** commands, such as **show tables**:

- The **show tables**: This lists the tables available (indices):

```
sql> show tables;
            name              |        type
------------------------------+-----------------
.kibana                       |VIEW
.kibana_1                     |BASE TABLE
.kibana_2                     |BASE TABLE
.kibana_task_manager          |BASE TABLE
.tasks                        |BASE TABLE
cf_etf                        |BASE TABLE
cf_etf_hist_price             |BASE TABLE
kibana_sample_data_flights    |BASE TABLE
logstash_filebeat_index       |BASE TABLE
logstash_index                |BASE TABLE

sql> █
```

- The **describe table**: This shows the columns, the data type in SQL, and the Elasticsearch mapping of the fields of a table (index). Let's use the `cf_etf_hist_price` index:

```
[sql> describe cf_etf_hist_price;
      column       |      type       |      mapping
-------------------+-----------------+------------------
change             |REAL             |float
changeOverTime     |REAL             |float
changePercent      |REAL             |float
close              |REAL             |float
date               |TIMESTAMP        |datetime
high               |REAL             |float
label              |VARCHAR          |text
label.keyword      |VARCHAR          |keyword
low                |REAL             |float
open               |REAL             |float
symbol             |VARCHAR          |text
symbol.keyword     |VARCHAR          |keyword
volume             |BIGINT           |long

sql>
```

- The **select statement**: This selects records from one or more tables. Let's find symbols starting with the `ACW` prefix:

```
[sql> select symbol from cf_etf where symbol LIKE 'ACW%';
      symbol
-----------------
ACWF
ACWI
ACWV

sql>
```

- The **show functions**: This lists the SQL functions supported with their function type. It supports the `like %pattern%` parameter to narrow the choices:

```
[sql> show functions like '%INU%';
      name       |      type
-----------------+----------------
MINUTE           |SCALAR
MINUTE_OF_DAY    |SCALAR
MINUTE_OF_HOUR   |SCALAR
SECOND_OF_MINUTE |SCALAR

sql> █
```

In the following section, we will drill down to the details of Elasticsearch SQL.

Elasticsearch SQL language

SQL stands for **Structured Query Language**, a programming language that is used for the following purposes:

- **Defining data** (such as create, alter, and drop commands in DDL)
- **Manipulating data** (such as insert, update, and delete in DML)
- **Resolving queries** (such as select, describe, and show in DQL)
- **Controlling data access** (such as grant and revoke in DCL)
- **Dealing with the transaction** (such as commit and rollback in TCL) for relational databases

Elasticsearch SQL does not have a **DCL** (**Data Control Language**) and **TCL** (**Transactional Control Language**) in its current version. To understand this language better, we will follow six aspects, including keywords, data types, operators, functions, and lexical structure, to study it.

Reserved keywords

Reserved keywords are part of the language syntax that the server uses to parse and analyze the statements. The following list shows the Elasticsearch SQL reserved keywords. If you use a reserved keyword as an identifier in the SQL statement, you must use double quotes to escape it:

```
ALL, AND, ANY, AS, ASC, BETWEEN, BY, CAST, CATALOG, CONVERT, CURRENT_DATE,
CURRENT_TIMESTAMP, DAY, DAYS, DESC, DESCRIBE, DISTINCT, ESCAPE, EXISTS,
EXPLAIN, EXTRACT, FALSE, FIRST, FROM, FULL, GROUP, HAVING, HOUR, HOURS, IN,
```

```
INNER, INTERVAL, IS, JOIN, LEFT, LIKE, LIMIT, MATCH, MINUTE, MINUTES,
MONTH, NATURAL, NOT, NULL, NULLS, ON, OR, ORDER, OUTER, RIGHT, RLIKE,
QUERY, SECOND, SECONDS, SELECT, SESSION, TABLE, TABLES, THEN, TO, TRUE,
TYPE, USING, WHEN, WHERE, WITH, YEAR, YEARS
```

Data type

Elasticsearch SQL almost inherits the data types from Elasticsearch. We list them as follows:

```
null, boolean, byte, short, integer, long, double, float, half_float,
scaled_float, keyword, text, binary, datetime, ip, object, nested.
```

The `datetime` data type in Elasticsearch SQL is the same as `date` in Elasticsearch. The reason for the name change is that it is not equivalent to DATE in ANSI SQL. Other data types that are only supported in Elasticsearch SQL are as follows:

```
date, interval_year, interval_month, interval_day, interval_hour,
interval_minute, interval_second, interval_year_to_month,
interval_day_to_hour, interval_day_to_minute, interval_day_to_second,
interval_hour_to_minute, interval_hour_to_second, interval_minute_to_second
```

However, these data types can only be used inside the SQL statement.

Operators

The following table lists the operators supported with their types:

Type	Operators
Arithmetic	+, - (subtraction), *, /, %, - (unary)
Comparison	=, <=>, <>, !=, <, <=, >, >=, BETWEEN, IN, IS NULL, IS NOT NULL
Logical	AND, OR, NOT
Fuzzy	LIKE, RLIKE

Functions

Elasticsearch SQL supports many built-in functions. The following table lists the functions supported with their descriptions:

These built-in functions have been categorized as per the following:

- Aggregate
- Grouping
- Date-time
- Full-text search
- Mathematic
- String
- Type conversion
- Conditional
- System

Aggregate

The following table lists the functions supported with their descriptions:

Function name	Description
AVG(field_name)	Returns the average value.
COUNT(expr)	Returns the number of records that satisfy the expression. COUNT(*) or COUNT (literal) will return all records.
COUNT(ALL field_name)	Returns the number of records with the non-null value from the field_name field.
COUNT(DISTINCT field_name)	Returns the number of records with non-null and distinct values from the field_name field.
FIRST(field_name_1 [, field_name_2])/ FIRST_VALUE(field_name_1 [,field_name_2])	Sorts the records with field_name_2 if they exist. Otherwise, sorting is affected with field_name_1. Returns the first non-null value from the field_name_1 field.

`LAST(field_name_1 [, field_name_2])/ LAST_VALUE(field_name_1 [, field_name_2])`	Sorts the records with `field_name_2` if they exist. Otherwise, sorting is affected with `field_name_1`. Returns the last non-null value from the `field_name_1` field.
`MAX(field_name)`	Returns the maximum value from the `field_name` field.
`MIN(field_name)`	Returns the minimum value from the `field_name` field.
`SUM(field_name)`	Returns the summation of the values from the `field_name` field.
`KURTOSIS(field_name)`	Returns the `field_name` per-field measurement for the shape of the distribution (refer to the `matrix_stats` aggregation).
`PERCENTILE(field_name, n)`	Returns the value at the *nth* percentage from the percentile aggregation of the `field_name` field.
`PERCENTILE_RANK(field_name, value)`	Returns the percentage rank of the value from the percentile aggregation of the `field_name` field.
`SKEWNESS(field_name)`	Returns the per-field measurement for the asymmetric distribution around the mean.
`STDDEV_POP(field_name)`	Returns the standard deviation from the population distribution of the `field_name` field.
`SUM_OF_SQUARES(field_name)`	Returns the sum of the squares of the difference in each value in the `field_name` field and its mean.
`VAR_POP(field_name)`	Returns the per-field measurement for how far removed each value in the `field_name` field is from its mean.

Grouping

The following table lists the functions supported with their descriptions:

Function name	Description
`HISTOGRAM(expr1, interval)`	Returns the histogram from `expr1` according to the `interval` value.

Date-time

The following table lists the functions supported with their descriptions:

Function name	Description
INTERVAL	This is a keyword, but it works like a function to convert the subsequent literal into a date-time interval.
CURRENT_DATE / CURRENT_DATE() / CURDATE()	Returns the current date of the server. It can be used as a keyword instead of a function.
CURRENT_TIMESTAMP / CURRENT_TIMESTAMP(precision)	Returns the current date/time of the server. The precision (defaults to 3) is the number of digits rounded off to nanoseconds. It can be used as a keyword instead of a function.
DAY_OF_MONTH(expr) / DOM(expr) / DAY(expr)	Returns the day of the month from expr.
DAY_OF_WEEK(expr) / DAYOFWEEK(expr) / DOW(expr)	Returns the day of the week from expr.
DAY_OF_YEAR(expr) / DOY(expr)	Returns the day of the year from expr.
DAY_NAME(expr) / DAYNAME(expr)	Returns the day of the week from expr.
HOUR_OF_DAY(expr) / HOUR(expr)	Returns the hour of the day from expr.
ISO_DAY_OF_WEEK(expr) / ISODAYOFWEEK(expr) / ISODOW(expr) / IDOW(expr)	Returns the day of the week according to the ISO 8601 standard.
ISO_WEEK_OF_YEAR(expr) / ISOWEEKOFYEAR(expr) / ISOWEEK(expr) / IWOY(expr) / IW(expr)	Returns the week of the year according to the ISO 8601 standard.
MINUTE_OF_DAY(expr)	Returns the minute of the day from expr.
MINUTE_OF_HOUR(expr) / MINUTE(expr)	Returns the minute of the hour from expr.
MONTH_OF_YEAR(expr) / MONTH(expr)	Returns the month of the year in a number from expr.
MONTH_NAME(expr) / MONTHNAME(expr)	Returns the month of the expr in literals.

NOW()	This is the same as CURRENT_TIME_STAMP().
SECOND_OF_MINUTE(expr)/ SECOND(expr)	Returns the second of the minute from expr.
QUARTER(expr)	Returns the quarter season from expr.
TODAY()	This is the same as CURRENT_DATE().
WEEK_OF_YEAR(expr)/ WEEK(expr)	Returns the week of the year from expr.
YEAR(expr)	Returns the year from expr.
EXTRACT(date-time-function from expr)	Applies the date-time function to expr and returns the value.

Full-text search

The following table lists the functions supported with their descriptions:

Function name	Description
MATCH(expr1, expr2 [,options])	Converts expr1 and expr2 to a match/multi-match query, where expr1 is the field name/names, and expr2 is the field value/values.
QUERY(expr [,options])	Similar to the query_string query in Elasticsearch, this converts expr to a full-text predicate with the addition of parameters from options if available.
SCORE()	Returns the scoring values (relevance) for the output records.

Mathematics

The following table lists the functions supported with their descriptions:

Function name	Description
ABS(expr)	Returns the absolute value of expr.
CBRT(expr)	Returns the cube root value of expr.
CEIL(expr)/ CEILING(expr)	Returns the smallest integer larger than, or equal to, expr.
E()	Returns Euler's number.
EXP(expr)	Returns Euler's number to the power of expr.
EXPM1(expr)	Returns Euler's number to the power of expr and then subtracts 1.
FLOOR(expr)	Returns the greatest integer less than, or equal to, expr.

LOG(expr)	Returns the natural logarithm value of expr.
LOG10(expr)	Returns the base logarithm value of expr.
PI()	Returns the PI number.
POWER(expr1, expr2)	Returns the value of expr1 to the power of expr2.
RANDOM(expr) / RAND(expr)	Returns the random number where seed=expr.
ROUND(expr1 [,expr2]))	Rounds expr1 according to expr2 and returns the value. If expr2 does not exist, then rounds expr1 according to expr2=0.
SIGN(expr) / SIGNUM(expr)	Returns 1 if expr is positive, -1 if expr is negative, and 0 if expr=0.
SQRT(expr)	Returns the square root value of expr.
TRUNCATE(expr1 [,expr2]	Truncates expr1 according to expr2 and returns the value. If expr2 does not exist, then truncats expr1 according to expr2=0.
ACOS(expr)	Returns the arccosine value of expr.
ASIN(expr)	Returns the arcsine value of expr.
ATAN(expr)	Returns the arctangent value of expr.
ATAN2(ordinate, abscisa)	Returns the 2-arguments arctangent value of expr.
COS(expr)	Returns the cosine value of expr.
COSH(expr)	Returns the hyperbolic cosine value of expr.
COT(expr)	Returns the cotangent value of expr.
DEGREES(expr)	Converts expr to degrees and returns the value.
RADIANS(expr)	Converts expr to radians and returns the value.
SIN(expr)	Returns the sine value of expr.
SINH(expr)	Returns the hyperbolic sine value of expr.
TAN(expr)	Returns the tangent value of expr.

String

The following table lists the functions supported with their descriptions:

Function name	Description
ASCII(src)	Returns the ASCII code of the leftmost character of the src string.

`BIT_LENGTH(src)`	Returns the length of the `src` string in bit units.
`CHAR(char)`	Returns the `ASCII` code of the `char` character.
`CHAR_LENGTH(src)`	Returns the length of the `src` string in character units.
`CONCAT(src1, src2)`	Returns the concatenated string of the two strings.
`INSERT(src, start, len, replacement)`	Returns the `src` string after replacing the substring beginning with the index starting at length, `len`, with the `replacement` string.
`LCASE(expr)`	Returns the string that is the lowercase conversion of the src string.
`LEFT(src, num)`	Returns the substring from the `src` string. The substring is the left `num` characters of the src string.
`LENGTH(src)`	Returns the number of characters in the `src` string.
`LOCATE(substring, src[, start])`	Returns the index of the first occurrence of substring in the `src` string. If the starting index presents, then the occurrence must be after the starting index. 0 is returned if not found.
`LTRIM(expr)`	Returns the `src` string following left-side trimming.
`OCTET_LENGTH(src)`	Returns the length in bytes of the `src` string.
`POSITION(substring, src)`	Returns the starting index of the first occurrence of substring in the `src` string.
`REPEAT(src, num)`	Returns the string from repeating concatenation of the `src` string num of times.
`REPLACE(src, pattern, replacement)`	Returns the `src` string after replacing the occurrences of the pattern with the replacement string.
`RIGHT(src, num)`	Returns the rightmost `num` of characters from the `src` string.
`RTRIM(src)`	Returns the `src` string following right-side trimming.
`SPACE(num)`	Returns a string of `num` space characters.
`SUBSTRING(src, start, len)`	Returns the substring of the `src` from the `start` index with a length, `len`, of characters (*index=0, 1, 2,..*).
`UCASE(src)`	Returns the string that is the uppercase conversion of the `src` string.

Type conversion

The following table lists the functions supported with their descriptions:

Function name	Description
CAST(expr AS dataType)	Returns the casting result. If it fails, it returns a failure.
CONVERT(expr, dataType)	Similar to the CAST() method, but works with the ODBC data types.

Conditional

The following table lists the functions supported with their descriptions:

Function name	Description
COALESCE(expr1, expr2,...)	Returns the first non-null argument. If all are null values, null is returned.
GREATEST(expr1, expr2,...)	Returns the largest argument. If all are null, null is returned.
IFNULL(expr1, expr2)	Returns expr2 if expr1 is null. Otherwise, expr1 is returned.
ISNULL(expr1, expr2)	Returns expr2 if expr1 is null. Otherwise, expr1 is returned.
LEAST(expr1, expr2, ...)	Returns the smallest argument. If all are null, null is returned.
NULLIF(expr1, expr2)	Returns null if expr1=expr2. Otherwise, expr1 is returned.
NVL(expr1, expr2)	Returns expr2 if expr1 is null. Otherwise, expr1 is returned.

System

The following table lists the functions supported with their descriptions:

Function name	Description
DATABASE()	Returns the current working database.
USER()	Returns the current user.

Elasticsearch SQL query syntax

SELECT is a very powerful statement that can be very simple, but there are also many optional parts that allow you to filter and shape the data you want to solve your complex problems. The complete syntax of the SELECT statement is complicated, but it can be described as follows, similar to what is in SQL:

```
SELECT select_expr [, ...]
[ FROM table_name [[AS] alias]]
[ WHERE search_condition_1 ]
[ GROUP BY expression [, ...] ]
[ HAVING search_condition_2]
[ ORDER BY order_expression [ ASC | DESC ] [, ...] ]
[ LIMIT [ count ] ]
```

Elasticsearch only accepts one command at a time in the current stage. Also, it does not support subqueries. Therefore, only table_name (index) is accepted in the FROM clause. To access multiple indices, you can use the asterisk (*) index pattern or SQL LIKE in the FROM clause. Although the reserved keywords include LEFT, RIGHT, INNER, OUTER, and JOIN, Elasticsearch SQL does not yet support left, right, inner, and outer join.

Now, let's describe the order of execution in the SELECT statement according to the SQL standard. This sequence determines the output from a clause in one step that is available for the input to a clause in a subsequent step:

1. FROM clause
2. WHERE clause
3. GROUP BY clause
4. HAVING clause
5. SELECT clause
6. DISTINCT/ALL clause
7. ORDER BY clause

New features

Let's discuss those new features that were mentioned in `Chapter 1`, *Overview of Elasticsearch 7*, as follows. We will use `elasticsearch-sql-cli` to play around the topics:

- `DATABASE()` and `USER()` system functions: The `DATABASE()` function returns the current working database instance, and the `user()` function returns the current user. As shown in the following screenshot, the current working database is `docker-cluster`, while there is no current user since we have not yet set up the user authentication:

```
[sql> select database();
   database()
-----------------
docker-cluster

[sql> select user();
     user()
-----------------
null

sql>
```

- `INTERVAL` keyword: This is a keyword for converting the subsequent literal into a date-time interval. Let's see how it is used. The following code block is a statement for selecting one record from the `cf_etf_hist_price` index, where the `date` field is equal to `2010-01-31`:

```
sql> select * from cf_etf_hist_price where date='2019-01-31' limit
1;
```

The following code block uses `INTERVAL` to generate a `datetime` interval of 1 day. This interval is then added to the `datetime` value generated by casting the literal value, `2019-01-31`. The calculation will produce a `2019-02-01` date-time value. Therefore, the response will be a record where its `date` field is equal to `2010-02-01`:

```
sql> select * from cf_etf_hist_price where date=CAST('2019-01-31'
AS DATETIME) + INTERVAL 1 day limit 1;
```

The calculation will produce a `2019-02-01` datetime value. Therefore, the response will be a record where its `date` field is equal to `2019-02-01`, as shown in the following screenshot:

```
sql> select * from cf_etf_hist_price where date=CAST('2019-01-31' AS DATETIME) + INTERVAL 1 day limit 1;
     change      |   changeOverTime  |   changePercent   |      close      |        date        |
     high        |     label      |     low      |      open      |    symbol    |    volume     |
----------------+-----------------+-------------------+-----------------+--------------------+
----------------+-----------------+-----------------+-----------------+-----------------+--------------+
 -0.01279999967664482|0.1099928691983223|-0.04500000178813934|28.47719955444336|2019-02-01T00:00:00.000Z|
28.539899826049805|Feb 1, 19        |28.389999389648438|28.469999313354492|ACWF          |40296

sql>
```

- HISTOGRAM grouping function: The `histogram()` function is used to generate buckets from the first parameter, the first parameter. Each bucket starts with a value and spans an interval, the second parameter. The first parameter can be a numeric expression, or a `datetime` expression. The interval will be a numeric value or a `datetime` value, respectively. Let's take an example to report the open price distribution of `symbol='RFEM'` where the interval = `0.5`. The SQL statement is written in the following code block:

```
select histogram(open, 0.5) AS open_price, count(*) AS count from
cf_etf_hist_price where symbol='RFEM' group by open_price;
```

The result of the SQL query is shown in the following screenshot:

```
sql> select histogram(open, 0.5) AS open_price, count(*) AS count from cf_etf_hist_price where
symbol='RFEM' group by open_price;
    open_price   |      count
----------------+-----------------
 55.0           |5
 56.0           |3
 56.5           |1
 57.0           |3
 57.5           |2
 58.0           |3
 58.5           |1
 59.0           |2
 59.5           |1
 60.0           |2
 60.5           |2
 61.0           |6
 61.5           |10
 62.0           |8
 62.5           |6
 63.0           |2
 63.5           |4

sql>
```

Elasticsearch SQL has numerous limitations and is still undergoing rapid development. Interested users can refer to the reference material (see `https://www.elastic.co/guide/ en/elasticsearch/reference/current/sql-limitations.html`). In the next section, we will practice some SQL statements using Elasticsearch SQL REST API.

Elasticsearch SQL REST API

The SQL REST API accepts a SQL statement in JSON format, executes it, and returns a response. The endpoint of the SQL REST API is shown in the following code block. You should use a parameter query with a SQL statement in the request body:

```
POST /_sql?format=response_format
{
    "query": "....",
     "parameter_x": parameter_x_value
}
```

Now, let's use the Kibana console to practice some examples outlined under the *Query DSL* section of `Chapter 6`, *Search APIs*:

1. To use the Kibana console from `dev_tools`, click on the button with the wrench icon on the left-hand sidebar, as shown in the following screenshot:

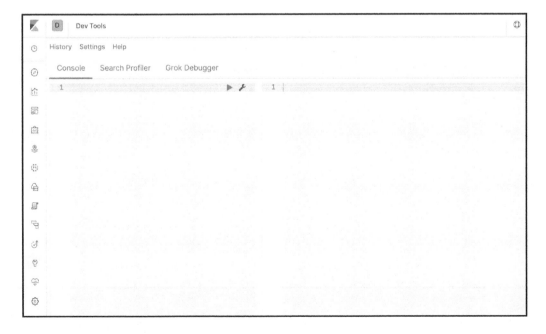

2. Then, type the SQL statement to retrieve all the records from the `cf_etf` index, as described in the following code block, in the left-hand panel and click on the green arrow button in the top-right corner of the panel:

```
POST /_sql?format=txt
{
  "query": """
  select * from cf_etf
  """
}
```

3. You will then see the response in the right-hand panel, as shown in the following screenshot:

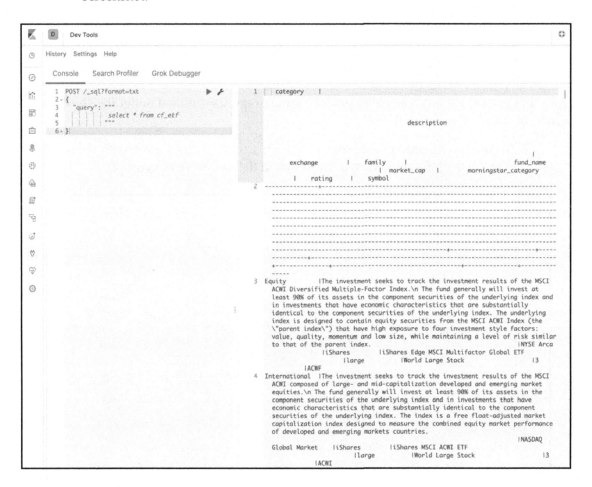

4. You can choose one of the supported data formats for the `format` parameter, such as `csv`, `json`, `tsv`, `txt`, `yaml`, `cbor`, and `smile` for the response data.

Triple quotes (`"""`) are supported in the Kibana console. It not only escapes double quotes (`"`) inside the query string, but also allows a SQL statement to be written in multiline format.

There are several supported parameters that you can set in the request body to manipulate the response and its behaviors. These are listed in the following table:

Parameter	Description
`fetch_size`	The maximum number of records to retrieve. The default setting is `1000` records.
`filter`	Supports the Query DSL filter context.
`request_timeout`	Time-out value in string format for the request. It defaults to `90 s`, where `s` means second.
`page_timeout`	Time-out value in string format to await the next request before the pagination window expires. It defaults to `45 s`, where `s` means second.
`time_zone`	Time zone used on the server. It defaults to `UTC/Greenwich`.
`field_multi_value_leniency`	If this Boolean parameter is set, it will not fail for multi-value fields. Instead, it picks one of the values (the first one for most cases) to continue the request. It defaults to a false value.
`cursor`	If the records exceed the `fetch_size` parameter, a cursor field and its value will be returned in the response body. You use it to request the records for the next page.

Now, let's show an example of how to deal with the `fetch_size` and `cursor` parameters to perform scrolling:

1. Follow the code block to specify `fetch_size=1` with the query. We also set the `page_timeout` parameter to increase to `120` seconds to let you have a sufficient time interval to play with the cursor:

```
POST /_sql?format=json
{
  "query": """
select * from cf_etf ORDER BY symbol ASC
""",
  "fetch_size":1,
  "page_timeout": "120s"
}
```

2. You will see a `cursor` field in the response body, as shown in the following screenshot:

3. Follow the previous screenshot to use the cursor field to retrieve the next page content of the same query:

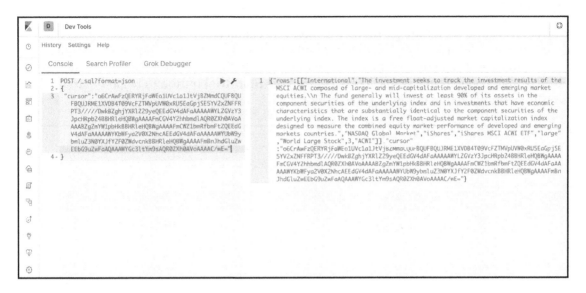

In the following section, we will study how to write a program with Elasticsearch SQL via JDBC.

Elasticsearch SQL JDBC

Elasticsearch's SQL JDBC is a type 4 driver, which means it is a pure Java driver and platform-independent. It connects directly to Elasticsearch and converts JDBC calls to Elasticsearch SQL. According to the support matrix of the official website (https://www. elastic.co/subscriptions#request-info), JDBC support is only available for the platinum license. If the Elasticsearch software is downloaded, or the open source version used, it will be a basic version. Therefore, let's follow the instructions provided in the following section to perform an upgrade.

Upgrading Elasticsearch from a basic to a trial license

To run the sample program, go to the Kibana license manager to upgrade from a basic license to a trial license, or to obtain a platinum license. To get a free trial, we must activate a 30-day trial license to use the platinum features. Go to the **Management** screen and click **License Management** in Kibana. Then, click on the **Start trial** button to begin the trial license, as shown in the following screenshot:

A license description panel appears, as shown in the following screenshot. Click on the **Start my trial** button to continue:

Finally, a notice will tell us that the Elastic Stack trial license is active and will expire after 30 days, as shown in the following screenshot:

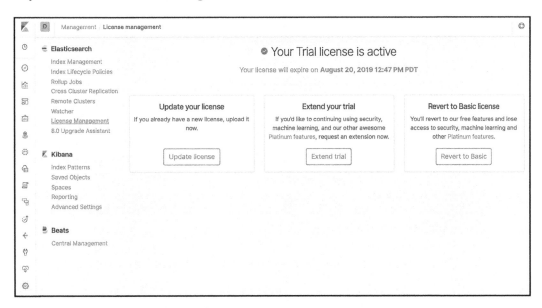

Now, let's begin our journey regarding the features of SQL JDBC.

Workflow of Elasticsearch SQL JDBC

We have to extend the SpringBoot project to support SQL JDBC from `Chapter 11`, *Elasticsearch from Java Programming*. The project is located on the GitHub site (`https://github.com/PacktPublishing/Mastering-Elasticsearch-7.0/tree/master/Chapter14/java_rest_client`) under `Chapter 14`, *Working with Elasticsearch SQL*. We are not going to detail how the whole program works. Instead, we'll target just the workflow of the Elasticsearch SQL JDBC programming in SpringBoot.

Basically, there are four major steps based on our previous SpringBoot project framework. These are configuring the Maven dependency, configuring the SQL JDBC connection, performing the JDBC `executeQuery` request, and handling the `ResultSet` response. The following is a step-by-step guide to integrating Elasticsearch SQL JDBC:

1. **Configuring the Maven dependency**: In the `pom.xml` file, add the Elastic repository and the SQL JDBC dependency:

   ```
   <repositories>
       ...
       <repository>
           <id>elastic.co</id>
               <url>https://artifacts.elastic.co/maven</url>
       </repository>
   </repositories>

   <dependencies>
       ....
       <dependency>
           <groupId>org.elasticsearch.plugin</groupId>
           <artifactId>x-pack-sql-jdbc</artifactId>
           <version>7.0.0</version>
       </dependency>
   </dependencies>
   ```

2. **Configuring the SQL JDBC client connection**: Similar to what we did in the *Java REST client initialization* section of `Chapter 12`, *Elasticsearch from Python Programming*, in the `com.example.client.restclient.configuration.SqlJdbcClientConfig.java` file, we construct a `org.elasticsearch.xpack.sql.jdbc.EsDataSource` data source to create a JDBC connection. Our example is shown in the following code block:

   ```
   package com.example.client.restclient.configuration;

   import org.elasticsearch.xpack.sql.jdbc.EsDataSource;
   ```

```
import org.springframework.beans.factory.annotation.Value;
import org.springframework.context.annotation.Bean;
import org.springframework.context.annotation.Configuration;
...

@Configuration
public class SqlJdbcClientConfig {
    ...
    @Value("${elasticsearch.host}")
    private String host;
    @Value("${elasticsearch.rest-client-port}")
    private int port;
    @Bean
    public Connection SqlJdbcClient() throws SQLException {
        EsDataSource dataSource = new EsDataSource();
        String url = "jdbc:es://" + host + ":" + port;
        dataSource.setUrl(url);
        Properties properties = new Properties();
        dataSource.setProperties(properties);
        return dataSource.getConnection();
    }
    ...
}
```

3. **Sending out the JDBC request**: In the
`com.example.client.restclient.service.impl.SqlJdbcClientService Impl.java` file, we autowire in the `Connection` object from step 2. Then, we use the `Connection` object to create a JDBC SQL statement and call the `executeQuery()` method from the JDBC SQL statement to send out the request. The sample file is shown in the following code block:

```
package com.example.client.restclient.service.impl;
import java.sql.Statement;
import java.sql.Connection;
import java.sql.ResultSet;
import java.sql.ResultSetMetaData;
import java.sql.SQLException;

@Service
public class SqlJdbcClientServiceImpl implements
SqlJdbcClientService {

    @Autowired
    Connection connection;
    @Override
    public Map<String, Object> executeQuery(String sqlStatement) {
        List<Map<String, Object>> hitList = new
```

```
ArrayList<Map<String, Object>>();
        Map<String, Object> result = new HashMap<String, Object>();
        Statement statement;
        int colCount=0, total=0;

    try {
        statement = connection.createStatement();
        ResultSet resultSet =
statement.executeQuery(sqlStatement);
        ResultSetMetaData rsmd = resultSet.getMetaData();
        colCount = rsmd.getColumnCount();
        while (resultSet.next()) {
            total++;
            Map<String, Object> map = new HashMap<String,
Object>();
            for (int i=1; i<=colCount; i++) {
                String columnName = rsmd.getColumnName(i);
                map.put(columnName,
resultSet.getObject(columnName));
            }
            hitList.add(map);
        }
    } catch (SQLException e) {
        ...
    }
    result.put("total", total);
    result.put("hits", hitList.toArray(new
HashMap[hitList.size()]));
    return result;
    }
}
```

4. **Handling the result of the response**: As shown in the preceding code block, the response from the executeQuery() method is the JDBC ResultSet object. We first call the getMetaData() method from the ResultSet object to get the ResultSetMetaData object. For each record, we retrieve the column names from the ResultSetMetaData object and then get each column value by calling the getObject() method from the ResultSet object with the column name.

Testing with Swagger UI

Now, let's use Swagger UI to test the SQL JDBC program. The step-by-step instructions are as follows:

1. Go to the `java_rest_client` directory and issue the Maven run command, as described in the following code block:

   ```
   cd java_rest_client
   mvn spring-boot:run
   ```

2. Use a web browser and type the URL, `http://localhost:10010/swagger-ui.html#/sql-jdbc-client-controller`, to reach the Swagger UI page for the project, as shown in the following screenshot, and then click on **sql-jdbc -client-controller** to expand the panel:

3. Click the **GET** button to expand the panel to see the usage:

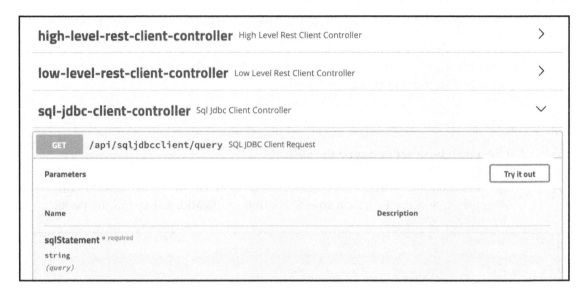

4. Click the **Try it out** button and the panel will be changed to input mode. Type the SQL statement and click the **Execute** button to perform the request. For example, let's use the following SQL statement to retrieve one record from the list ranking from the **symbol** field in ascending order. Type the SQL statement in the **sqlStatement** parameter input and then click the Execute button to run:

```
select * from cf_etf ORDER BY symbol ASC limit 1
```

The response will be shown directly in the **Responses** body sub-panel, as follows:

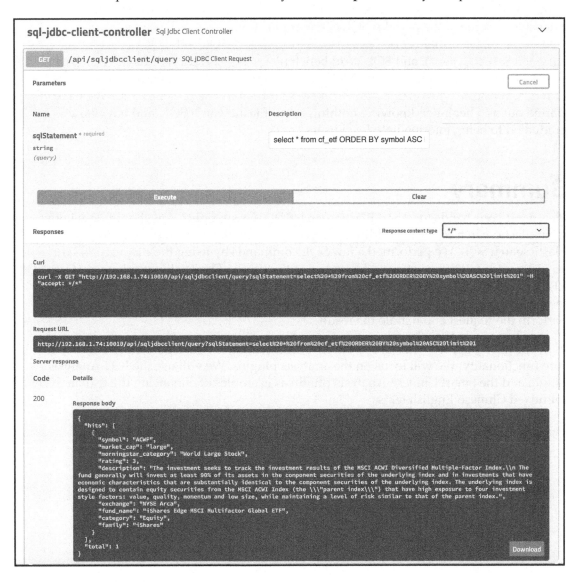

Interested users can try to run different SQL commands with different indexes. Owing to JDBC and ODBC support, third-party applications can use Elasticsearch SQL functionality extensively. Some of the popular SQL client applications, such as DBeaver (`https://dbeaver.io/`), DbVisualizer (`https://www.dbvis.com/`), SQuirreL SQL (`http://squirrel-sql.sourceforge.net/`), and SQL Workbench (`https://www.sql-workbench.eu/`), can access Elasticsearch via JDBC. For ODBC interested users, please refer to `https://www.elastic.co/guide/en/elasticsearch/reference/current/sql-odbc.html`. We have started out as a beginner, knowing nothing about Elasticsearch SQL, and have now graduated to being intermediate-level users.

Summary

Please put your hands together! Elasticsearch SQL is easy, right? You should now know what Elasticsearch SQL is. In addition, you are now familiar with the semantics of Elasticsearch SQL. We performed a few SQL commands by using the `elasticsearch-sql-cli` script. We demonstrated how to use the Kibana DevTools console to perform SQL REST API with different SQL statements and, finally, we provided some programming instructions to set up the Elasticsearch SQL JDBC driver and used the JDBC connection to perform the request and handle the result.

In the next chapter, we will learn about Elasticsearch plugin management to enhance its core functionality. We will focus on the analysis plugins. We will use the ICU Analysis plugin and the Smart Chinese Analysis plugin as examples of enhancing the text analyzer for mixed Chinese-English texts.

15
Working with Elasticsearch Analysis Plugins

In the previous chapter, we learned about Elasticsearch SQL. We started with a basic understanding of the Elasticsearch SQL language from its conceptual definition to practical examples. We have written a SQL statement in command-line mode. We have played with the SQL REST API in the Kibana Dev Tools console. We also gave a direction for programming with Elasticsearch SQL through **JDBC (Java Database Connectivity)**.

In this chapter, we will introduce the Elasticsearch plugin, which is an approach to enhance Elasticsearch's capabilities in a customized way. Elasticsearch comes with many core built-in plugins. Additionally, there are many available custom plugins that have been contributed by different communities too. In this chapter, however, we will focus only on the **Analysis Plugins**.

In this chapter, we will cover the following topics:

- What Elasticsearch plugins are
- Working with the **International Components for Unicode (ICU)** Analysis plugin
- Working with the Smart Chinese Analysis plugin
- Working with the IK Analysis plugin

What are Elasticsearch plugins?

Plugins are used to extend the basic capabilities of Elasticsearch in a customized way; for example, by adding custom mapping types, custom analyzers, native scripts, custom discovery mechanisms, and more. A plugin must contain a property file, named `plugin-descriptor.properties`, and it may optionally contain JAR files, scripts, and configuration files. The source of plugins can be classified into two types. The first one is the built-in core plugin that is part of the Elasticsearch package and is maintained by the Elastic team. The second one is developed by individuals or different communities. For example, the ICU Analysis plugin and the Smart Chinese Analysis plugin (for more information about these plugins, refer to `https://github.com/elastic/elasticsearch/tree/master/plugins`) are the core plugins shipped with the product, while the IK Analysis plugin (for more information about this plugin, refer to `https://github.com/medcl/elasticsearch-analysis-ik`) was developed by a person, named Medcl.

There are many different types of plugins that can be used to enhance Elasticsearch's functionalities in different areas. We have compiled them in the following table along with a brief description of each type:

Plugin type	Description
API extension	This plugin adds new APIs for searching or mapping features.
Alerting	This plugin adds new monitoring features for indices and for sending out alerts.
Analysis	This plugin adds new tokenizers, token filters, character filters, or analyzers to analyze texts in different languages.
Discovery	This plugin adds new mechanisms to discover nodes in the cluster.
Ingest	This plugin adds new features to the ingest node.
Management	This plugin adds new UI features to interact with the Elasticsearch server.
Mapper	This plugin adds new field data types for the mappings.
Security	This plugin addresses the security needs of an enterprise.
Repository	This plugin adds new repositories for snapshot backups and restore features.
Store	This plugin adds new storage instead of the default Lucene store.

Let's now take a look at plugin management in the following subsection.

Plugin management

The plugin script can be used to list, install, and remove installed plugins from the server. The `elasticsearch-plugin` plugin script file is located in the `bin` directory of the downloaded folder. Let's do some practice with the `elasticsearch-plugin` command by using the Elasticsearch Docker container:

- `help`: First, show all of the supported commands, as detailed in the following screenshot:

```
[root@803cf4e9c1cf elasticsearch]# bin/elasticsearch-plugin --help
A tool for managing installed elasticsearch plugins

Commands
--------
list - Lists installed elasticsearch plugins
install - Install a plugin
remove - removes a plugin from Elasticsearch
```

- `list`: Use the list of commands to list the installed plugins (we had `analysis-phonetic` plugin installed before), as shown in the following screenshot:

```
[root@803cf4e9c1cf elasticsearch]# bin/elasticsearch-plugin list
analysis-phonetic
[root@803cf4e9c1cf elasticsearch]#
```

- `install`: We can use the plugin name, the download URL, or the downloaded file to install the plugin. Let's simply install the `analysis-icu` plugin using the plugin name, as shown in the following screenshot:

```
[root@803cf4e9c1cf elasticsearch]# bin/elasticsearch-plugin install analysis-icu

-> Downloading analysis-icu from elastic
[=================================================] 100%??
WARNING: An illegal reflective access operation has occurred
WARNING: Illegal reflective access by org.bouncycastle.jcajce.provider.drbg.DRBG (file:/usr/share/elasticsearch/
lib/tools/plugin-cli/bcprov-jdk15on-1.61.jar) to constructor sun.security.provider.Sun()
WARNING: Please consider reporting this to the maintainers of org.bouncycastle.jcajce.provider.drbg.DRBG
WARNING: Use --illegal-access=warn to enable warnings of further illegal reflective access operations
WARNING: All illegal access operations will be denied in a future release
-> Installed analysis-icu
[root@803cf4e9c1cf elasticsearch]#
```

- `remove`: Next, remove the installed plugin with the plugin name from the Elasticsearch server, as shown in the following screenshot:

```
[root@803cf4e9c1cf elasticsearch]# bin/elasticsearch-plugin remove analysis-icu
-> removing [analysis-icu]...
[root@803cf4e9c1cf elasticsearch]#
```

- `update`: Note that there is no update command provided. We can remove the old version and reinstall a new one.

After we install the plugin, We must restart the Elasticsearch server. For our working environment, we need to restart the Elasticsearch Docker container. To do this, quit the Docker container, `elasticsearch`, issue the Docker `restart` command, and enter the Docker container in command-line mode:

```
$ docker restart elasticsearch
```

We will discuss the ICU Analysis plugin in the next section.

Working with the ICU Analysis plugin

The ICU Analysis plugin is a set of libraries that integrates the Lucene ICU module into Elasticsearch. Essentially, the purpose of the ICU is to add the support of Unicode and globalization to provide better text segmentation analysis of Asian languages. From Elasticsearch's point of view, this plugin provides new components in text analysis, as shown in the following table:

Components		Description
Character filter	ICU Normalizer Character Filter	The `icu_normalizer` character filter converts text into unique, equivalent character sequences. It supports three optional parameters: `name`, `mode`, and `unicode_set_filter`. The `name` parameters can be `nfc`, `nfkc`, and `nfkc_cf` (the default). The `mode` parameter can be `decompose`.
Tokenizer	ICU Tokenizer	The `icu_tokenizer` tokenizer splits a piece of text into words on word boundaries. It adds support for Asian languages such as Thai, Lao, Chinese, Japanese, and Korean.

Token filter	ICU Normalizer Token Filter	The `icu_normalizer` token filter supports two optional parameters: `name` and `unicode_set_filter`. The `name` parameters can be `nfc`, `nfkc`, and `nfkc_cf`. The `unicode_set_filter` parameter can be set to the regular expression values defined in the `Unicodeset` class (we can refer to `https://ssl.icu-project.org/apiref/icu4j/com/ibm/icu/text/UnicodeSet.html`).
	ICU Folding Token Filter	The `icu_folding` token filter performs the Unicode normalization. It supports an optional parameter, `unicode_set_filter`, to fold characters, which means converting the characters into their ASCII equivalent.
	ICU Collation Token Filter	The `icu_collation` token filter was deprecated in Lucene 5.0. Instead, use the `icu_collation_keyword` keyword for the sorting type to sort the field in the order of the specific language.
	ICU Transform Token Filter	The `icu_transform` token filter provides conversion, normalization, and script transliterations.
Analyzer	ICU Analyzer	The `icu_analyzer` analyzer contains the `icu_normalizer` character filter, the `icu_tokenizer` tokenizer, and the `icu_normalizer` token filter.

Examples

Let's use the following text in Chinese and its English translation to compare the analyzed result from the default analyzer (that is, the standard) and the `icu_analyzer` analyzer:

Language	Text
Chinese	股市投资稳赚不赔必修课：如何做好仓位管理和情绪管理
English	The stock market investment stable earning and never lose compulsory course: how to do a good positioning management and emotional management

We are going to use the Kibana Dev Tools console to perform the analysis. First, issue the command and click on the green arrow icon in the top-right side of the panel. We will see the tokens generated in the panel on the right-hand side, as shown in the following screenshot:

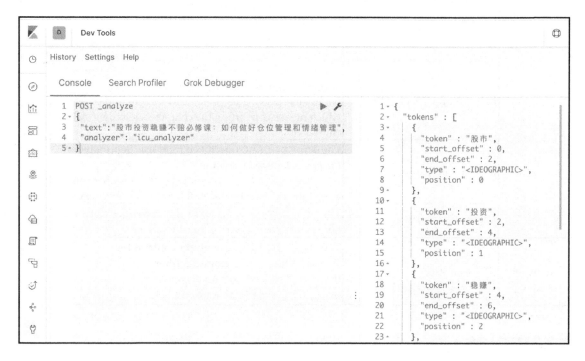

We then use the same text and perform the test again with the default analyzer and collect the tokens. In the following table, we compare the tokens from both analyzers:

Analyzer		
icu_analyzer	tokens in Chinese	股市,投资,稳赚,不,赔,必修,课,如何,做好,仓,位,管理,和,情绪,管理
	tokens in English	stock market, investment, stable earning, not, lose, compulsory, course, how, to do a good, storage, positioning, management, and, emotional, management
default	tokens in Chinese	股,市,投,资,稳,赚,不,赔,必,修,课,如,何,做,好,仓,位,管,理,和,情,绪,管,理
	tokens in English	stock, market, invest, capital, stable, earning, not, lose, must, take, course, as, how, do, good, storage, positioning, manage, supervise, and, passion, emotion, manage, supervise

In most cases, the token that is generated by the `icu_analyzer` analyzer is a two-character word, while the token that is generated by the standard analyzer is a single-character word. The total number of tokens generated from the input text by the default analyzer is 24, while it is 15 from `icu_analyzer`. Clearly, the `icu_analyzer` analyzer gains a much better understanding of the word boundaries in the text analysis.

The ICU analyzer can have multiple customized variant types by changing the method and mode parameters of the character filter and token. The following table describes the mix of different types of ICU analyzers:

Analyzer name	Character filter	Tokenizer
nfkc_cf_normalized	icu_normalizer with name=nfkc_cf and mode=compose (all in default value)	icu_tokenizer
nfc_normalized	icu_normalizer with name=nfc and mode=compose	icu_tokenizer
nfkc_normalized	icu_normalizer with name=nfkc and mode=compose	icu_tokenizer
nfd_normalized	icu_normalizer with name=nfc and mode=decompose	icu_tokenizer
nfkd_normalized	icu_normalizer with name=nfkc and mode=decompose	icu_tokenizer

Let's try the `nfkd_normalized` analyzer. Follow the definition and test it in the Kibana Dev Tools console. The response is shown in the following screenshot. However, we cannot find any difference in the results as a result of using the `nfkd_normalized` analyzer and the `icu_analyzer` analyzer:

To use the newly defined analyzer, we have to define it in the `Index Settings`, as we have done in the *Custom analyzers* section of `Chapter 5`, *Anatomy of an Analyzer*. In the next section, we will take a look at the Smart Chinese Analysis plugin.

Working with the Smart Chinese Analysis plugin

The Smart Chinese Analysis plugin integrates Lucene's Smart Chinese analysis module into Elasticsearch for analyzing Chinese or mixed Chinese-English text. The supported analyzer uses probability knowledge based on a hidden Markov model on a large training corpus to find the optimal word segmentation for Simplified Chinese text. The strategy it uses is to first break the input text into sentences and then perform segmentation in a sentence to obtain words. This plugin provides an analyzer, which is called the `smartcn` analyzer, and a tokenizer called `smartcn_tokenizer`. Note that both cannot be configured with any parameter.

To install the `smartcn` Analysis plugin in the Elasticsearch Docker container, use the commands shown in the following screenshot. We then restart the container to make the plugin effective:

```
[wai@wai:~/book/chapter13/docker_run$ docker exec -it elasticsearch /bin/bash
[[root@803cf4e9c1cf elasticsearch]# bin/elasticsearch-plugin install analysis-smartcn
-> Downloading analysis-smartcn from elastic
[=================================================] 100%??
WARNING: An illegal reflective access operation has occurred
WARNING: Illegal reflective access by org.bouncycastle.jcajce.provider.drbg.DRBG (file:/usr/share/elasticsearch/
lib/tools/plugin-cli/bcprov-jdk15on-1.61.jar) to constructor sun.security.provider.Sun()
WARNING: Please consider reporting this to the maintainers of org.bouncycastle.jcajce.provider.drbg.DRBG
WARNING: Use --illegal-access=warn to enable warnings of further illegal reflective access operations
WARNING: All illegal access operations will be denied in a future release
-> Installed analysis-smartcn
[root@803cf4e9c1cf elasticsearch]# █
```

Examples

We will use the same input text and perform our analysis using the Kibana Dev Tools console. First, issue the command and click on the green arrow button in the top-right side of the panel. We collect the tokens generated in the panel on the right-hand side, as shown in the following screenshot. Then, we compile all the tokens generated into a table and list the English translation for each token:

Analyzer		
smartcn	tokens in Chinese	股市,投资,稳,赚,不,赔,必修课,如何,做,好,仓,位,管理,和,情绪,管理
	tokens in English	stock market, investment, stable, earning, not, lose, compulsory course, how, to do, a good, storage, positioning, management, and, emotional, management

The total number of tokens generated from the input text by the `smartcn` analyzer is 16. We can see that a three-character word is generated by `smartcn`. It seems to be better at text segmentation than the `icu_analyzer` analyzer. However, note that we have also observed a pair of two-character words that can be obtained from `icu-analyzer`, which `smartcn` cannot provide. In the next section, we will introduce the IK Analysis plugin to see whether we can obtain a better result.

Working with the IK Analysis plugin

The IK Analysis plugin belongs to the community contributed plugin category. It is an open source project (`https://github.com/medcl/elasticsearch-analysis-ik`) that provides a lightweight Chinese word segmentation toolkit based on the Java language. It integrates the Lucene IK Analyzer into Elasticsearch and supports a customized dictionary. It works with English and Chinese and is also compatible with Korean and Japanese characters. It supports hot swapping to update dictionary contents without the need to restart the Elasticsearch server. This plugin provides two types of analysis: fine-grained and coarse-grained. Fine-grained analysis includes the `ik_max_word` analyzer and the `ik_max_word` tokenizer. They will generate more tokens and they are suitable for the `term` query. Coarse-grained analysis includes the `ik_smart` analyzer and the `ik_smart` tokenizer. They will generate fewer, but more precise, tokens so that they are targeted to the phrase query.

Since the IK Analysis plugin is not maintained by the Elastic team, we need to get it from the author's GitHub site (`https://github.com/medcl/elasticsearch-analysis-ik/releases/download/v7.0.0/elasticsearch-analysis-ik-7.0.0.zip`). We can download it first or run the installation with the URL. To install the IK Analysis plugin in the Elasticsearch Docker container, use the following commands:

```
$bin/elasticsearch-plugin install
https://github.com/medcl/elasticsearch-analysis-ik/releases/download/v7.0.0
/elasticsearch-analysis-ik-7.0.0.zip
```

Next, take a look at the commands in the following screenshot:

```
[root@803cf4e9c1cf elasticsearch]# bin/elasticsearch-plugin install https://github.com/medcl/elasticsearch-analy
sis-ik/releases/download/v7.0.0/elasticsearch-analysis-ik-7.0.0.zip
-> Downloading https://github.com/medcl/elasticsearch-analysis-ik/releases/download/v7.0.0/elasticsearch-analysi
s-ik-7.0.0.zip
[=============================================] 100%??
@@@@@@@@@@@@@@@@@@@@@@@@@@@@@@@@@@@@@@@@@@@@@@@@@@@@@@@@
@     WARNING: plugin requires additional permissions     @
@@@@@@@@@@@@@@@@@@@@@@@@@@@@@@@@@@@@@@@@@@@@@@@@@@@@@@@@
* java.net.SocketPermission * connect,resolve
See http://docs.oracle.com/javase/8/docs/technotes/guides/security/permissions.html
for descriptions of what these permissions allow and the associated risks.

Continue with installation? [y/N]y
-> Installed analysis-ik
[root@803cf4e9c1cf elasticsearch]#
```

After installation, we restart the container to make the plugin effective and enter the Elasticsearch Docker container to perform the testing.

Examples

We will use the same input text and perform analysis using the Kibana Dev Tools console. First, issue the command and click on the green arrow button in the top-right side of the panel. If we use the `ik_smart` analyzer, we will get the response that is shown in the following screenshot:

In the preceding response, we can see that there is a four-character word token. The meaning of the token is *stable earning and never lose*, which is a correct Chinese phrase. The total number of tokens generated is 12, which is less than the icu-analysis analyzer and the smartcn analyzer. If we use the ik_max_word analyzer, we will get the response that is shown in the following screenshot:

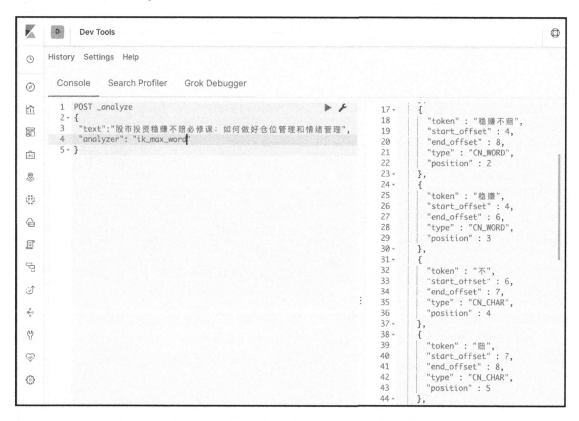

In the preceding response, we can see that the four-character word token appears, and it also derives another three sub-tokens that are covered by the bounding box. As we know, the purpose of the `ik_max_word` analyzer is to generate more tokens for the term query search. However, it seems to me that one more token should be generated, which is *never lose*. The total number of tokens generated is 18, which is about 1.5 times more than the number of tokens generated by `ik_smart`. Let's now take a look at the tokens generated by the two analyzers alongside their English translation:

Analyzer		
ik_smart	tokens in Chinese	股市,投资,稳赚不赔,必修课,如何,做好,仓,位,管理,和,情绪,管理
	tokens in English	stock market, investment, stable earning and never lose, compulsory course, how, to do good, storage, positioning, management, and, emotional, management
ik_max_word	tokens in Chinese	股市,投资,稳赚不赔,稳赚,不,赔,必修课,必修,修课,如何做,如何,做好,仓,位,管理,和,情绪,管理
	tokens in English	stock market, investment, stable earning and never lose, not, lose, compulsory course, compulsory, take course, how to do, how, to do good, storage, positioning, management, and, emotional, management

One thing that I am disappointed by is that none of the analyzers mentioned can generate the two-character token for *positioning* or the four-character token for *positioning management and emotional management*. The reason may be that the phrases are professional terms so they do not exist in the dictionary of the IK Analysis plugin system. One way to make this analyzer more powerful is to add a new vocabulary to the self-defined dictionary of the IK Analysis plugin.

Configuring a custom dictionary in the IK Analysis plugin

In this subsection, we will demonstrate how to make the IK analyzer more powerful by adding a custom dictionary. In the Elasticsearch Docker container, a `IKAnalyzer.cfg.xml` configuration file is located at `/usr/share/elasticsearch/config/analysis-ik`, as shown in the following screenshot:

```
[root@803cf4e9c1cf elasticsearch]# ls -l /usr/share/elasticsearch/config/analysis-ik/
total 8260
-rw-rw---- 1 elasticsearch root     625 Jul 22 16:13 IKAnalyzer.cfg.xml
-rw-rw---- 1 elasticsearch root 5225922 Jul 22 16:13 extra_main.dic
-rw-rw---- 1 elasticsearch root   63188 Jul 22 16:13 extra_single_word.dic
-rw-rw---- 1 elasticsearch root   63188 Jul 22 16:13 extra_single_word_full.dic
-rw-rw---- 1 elasticsearch root   10855 Jul 22 16:13 extra_single_word_low_freq.dic
-rw-rw---- 1 elasticsearch root     156 Jul 22 16:13 extra_stopword.dic
-rw-rw---- 1 elasticsearch root 3058510 Jul 22 16:13 main.dic
-rw-rw---- 1 elasticsearch root     123 Jul 22 16:13 preposition.dic
-rw-rw---- 1 elasticsearch root    1824 Jul 22 16:13 quantifier.dic
-rw-rw---- 1 elasticsearch root     164 Jul 22 16:13 stopword.dic
-rw-rw---- 1 elasticsearch root     192 Jul 22 16:13 suffix.dic
-rw-rw---- 1 elasticsearch root     752 Jul 22 16:13 surname.dic
[root@803cf4e9c1cf elasticsearch]#
```

Use `vi` editor to edit the file `IKAnalyzer.cfg.xml`. Once the file is opened, it may show non-printable codes. Use the `vi` command in the following code block to update the encoding:

```
:set encoding=utf-8
```

The file content will be shown correctly as the following code block:

```
<feff><?xml version="1.0" encoding="UTF-8"?>
<!DOCTYPE properties SYSTEM "http://java.sun.com/dtd/properties.dtd">
<properties>
        <comment>IK Analyzer 扩展配置</comment>
        <!--用户可以在这里配置自己的扩展字典 -->
        <entry key="ext_dict"></entry>
         <!--用户可以在这里配置自己的扩展停止词字典-->
        <entry key="ext_stopwords"></entry>
        <!--用户可以在这里配置远程扩展字典 -->
        <!-- <entry key="remote_ext_dict">words location</entry> -->
        <!--用户可以在这里配置远程扩展停止词字典-->
        <!-- <entry key="remote_ext_stopwords">words_location</entry> -->
</properties>
```

To support hot swapping dictionary contents for updates, we must use the remote approach by using the `remove_ext_dict` tag pair as shown in the previous code block. Since it is not our main concern, we will only demonstrate adding the dictionary with the local file. We will put our dictionary file, named `mydictionary.dic`, in the `/usr/share/elasticsearch/config/analysis-ik/custom` directory. To do this, perform the following steps:

1. Make the custom directory under `/usr/share/elasticsearch/config/analysis-ik/`. Issue the following command in the Docker Elasticsearch container:

```
# cd /usr/share/elasticsearch/config/analysis-ik/
# mkdir custom
```

2. Before we can edit it, we need to set the working environment with the correct `Locale` for any editor. Issue the following commands:

```
# export LANG="en_US.utf8"
# export LC_ALL="en_US.utf8"
# export LC_CTYPE="en_US.utf8"
```

3. Go to the `custom` directory and use an editor such as `vi` to add a file, named `mydictionary.dic`. The content of the file has three lines, as follows:

```
[root@803cf4e9c1cf analysis-ik]# cat mydictionary.dic
仓位
仓位管理
情绪管理
[root@803cf4e9c1cf analysis-ik]#
```

4. Edit the `IKAnalyzer.cfg.xml` configuration file and update the content of the lines to add the custom dictionary file path, as described in the following code block:

```
<feff><?xml version="1.0" encoding="UTF-8"?>
<!DOCTYPE properties SYSTEM "http://java.sun.com/dtd/properties.dtd">
<properties>
        <comment>IK Analyzer 扩展配置</comment>
        <!--用户可以在这里配置自己的扩展字典 -->
        <entry key="ext_dict">mydictionary.dic</entry>
         <!--用户可以在这里配置自己的扩展停止词字典-->
        <entry key="ext_stopwords"></entry>
        <!--用户可以在这里配置远程扩展字典 -->
        <!-- <entry key="remote_ext_dict">words_location</entry> -->
        <!--用户可以在这里配置远程扩展停止词字典-->
        <!-- <entry key="remote_ext_stopwords">words_location</entry> -->
</properties>
```

5. Close the configuration file, quit the Elasticsearch container, and then restart the container.

6. Rerun the testing with the `ik_smart` analyzer and the same input text. We will get the response that is shown in the following screenshot. We will discover that we can now get the two favorite four-character tokens. The new add `custom dictionary works` as follows:

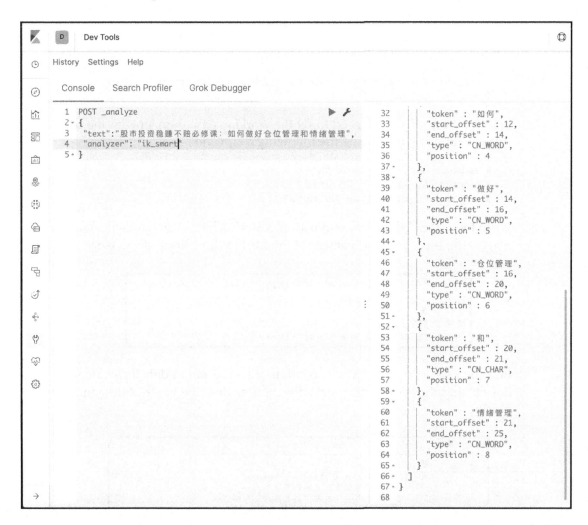

Summary

Voila! We have completed this chapter. We should now understand what Elasticsearch plugin management is and how it enhances the core functionality of Elasticsearch.

In this chapter, we introduced Analysis Plugins and deep dived into their details. We practiced the ICU Analysis plugin, the Smart Chinese Analysis plugin, and the IK Analysis plugin to perform analysis for Chinese texts. It seems that the IK Analysis plugin is better than the other two plugins due to its ability to segment word boundaries. We also added a new custom dictionary to improve word segmentation in order to make it work better.

In the next chapter, we will study the machine learning support that is available in Elasticsearch and use a Python scikit-learn package to work with Elasticsearch. We will follow two examples; the first one will create a single metric job to track the custom indicator to detect anomalies in sample data, while the second one will involve *k*-means clustering from the Python scikit-learn library for integration with Elasticsearch.

Section 5: Advanced Features

In this section, you will be looking into some hot topics, such as machine learning and Apache Spark support with Elasticsearch. You will also be shown how to solve a text classification problem by using Elasticsearch and scikit-learn. You will also learn how to read data from an Elasticsearch index, perform some computations using Spark, and then write the results to another Elasticsearch index. And, at the end of the section, you will need to put most of what you learned in the previous chapters together to build the final project, that is, building Analytics RESTful Services.

This section is comprised the following chapters:

- Chapter 16, *Machine Learning with Elasticsearch*
- Chapter 17, *Spark and Elasticsearch for Real-time Analytics*
- Chapter 18, *Building Analytics RESTful Services*

16
Machine Learning with Elasticsearch

In the last chapter, we learned about the Elasticsearch analysis plugins. We tried three different plugins; two from the official Elastic Team and one from the community. It seems to me that the two core Analysis plugins, ICU Analysis and Smart Chinese analysis, do not meet with the expectations. At least in the simple testing, both plugins do not produce good resulting tokens. In contrast to the two officially supported Analysis plugins, the Lucene IK Analysis plugin from the community works better. In this chapter, we will learn about the advanced features supported by Elasticsearch. We will start with the machine learning feature.

In the context of Elasticsearch, machine learning can be thought of as a natural extension of search and analysis. Recall that we looked at Bollinger Bands in `Chapter 10`, *Using Elasticsearch for Exploratory Data Analysis*, and that it is an analysis of time series data. The machine learning feature supported by Elasticsearch can automatically analyze the time series data by running a metric job that contains one or more detectors that define the fields that will be analyzed. It can help us identify the anomalies in single-variable time series data and show us what the normal situation may look like.

On the other hand, scikit-learn provides a set of Python modules for machine learning, data mining, and data analysis. Classification is a type of supervised machine learning problem. We'll provide an example of solving the classification problem by using Elasticsearch and scikit-learn.

By the end of this chapter, we will have covered the following topics:

- Machine learning with Elastic Stack
- Machine learning using Elasticsearch and scikit-learn

Machine learning with Elastic Stack

Earlier, one of the main issues related to machine learning while using Elasticsearch is that of solving anomaly detection. It can be traced back to the hot topics discussed in 2014 and earlier (see `https://www.businesswire.com/news/home/20140826005072/en/Prelert-Extends-Anomaly-Detection-Elasticsearch` and `https://speakerdeck.com/elasticsearch/real-time-analytics-and-anomalies-detection-using-elasticsearch-hadoop-and-storm`). Basically, anomaly detection is a statistical problem that can be solved in a simple way, by marking the irregularities from the common statistical properties of the input data distribution. However, we can solve the problem with machine learning-based approaches, such as cluster-based anomaly detection and support vector machine-based anomaly detection. The machine learning feature provided by Elastic Stack can involve the data visualizer from Kibana, job management, scheduler, and metrics aggregation for the statistical tasks from Elasticsearch. We can even use Beats to collect data; for example, using Metricbeat to collect system-level resource usage statistics.

Before we can go forward with using the machine learning feature in Elasticsearch, be sure the Platinum license is installed. If the Elasticsearch software is downloaded or the open source version is used, it will be the basic version. We must activate a 30-day trial license to use the Platinum features as shown in the *Upgrading Elasticsearch from a basic to a trial license* section in `Chapter 14`, *Working with Elasticsearch SQL*. Now, let's start the journey of using the Elastic Stack machine learning feature. We will take a look at the machine learning APIs first.

Machine learning APIs

The machine learning feature involves 10 resources, and most of the APIs revolve around these resources. We have compiled the relevant APIs into the following table:

Resource	API URL	Description
Calendars	GET _ml/calendars/[<calendar_id>|_all]	Get a calendar resource with the given <calendar_id> identifier, or all calendar resources.
	PUT _ml/calendars/<calendar_id>	Create a calendar resource with the given <calendar_id> identifier for associating scheduled event resources later.
	DELETE _ml/calendars/<calendar_id>	Remove the calendar resource with the given <calendar_id> identifier and its associated scheduled events.

Calendars, events	`GET_ml/calendars/[<calendar_id>|` `_all]/events`	Get all the scheduled events from the calendar resource. An event contains attributes such as `description`, `start_time`, `end_time`, `calendar_id`, and `event_id`.
	`POST_ml/calendars/<calendar_id>/events`	Add event resources to a calendar with the given `<calendar_id>` identifier. Each event resource is specified in the `events` array in the request body.
	`DELETE _ml/calendars/<calendar_id>` `/events/<event_id>`	Remove an event with the given `<event_id>` identifier from the calendar resource, using the `<calendar_id>` identifier.
Jobs	`GET _ml/anomaly_detectors/[<job_id>` `|<job_id>,<job_id>|_all]`	Get the job resource with the given `<job_id>` identifier, multiple job resources with multiple `<job_id>` identifiers separated by commas, or all job resources.
	`DELETE _ml/anomaly_detectors/<job_id>`	Delete the job resource with the given `<job_id>` identifier.
	`POST_ml/anomaly_detectors/` `{job_id}/_open`	To open a job means to start receiving new data from where it left off last time and continue the analysis.
	`POST _ml/anomaly_detectors/[<job_id>|` `<job_id>,<job_id>|_all]/_close`	This API can close one, multiple, or all job resources. To close a job means to stop receiving data and analysis operations. However, we can still read the job resource.
	`POST _ml/anomaly_detectors/` `<job_id>/_update`	Update the properties of the job resource with the `<job_id>` identifier.
	`POST_ml/anomaly_detectors/` `<job_id>/_data`	Send data to a job resource with the `<job_id>` identifier. The data must be in JSON format in the request body. The job must be opened first.
	`POST_ml/anomaly_detectors/` `<job_id>/_flush`	Flush the data to the job resource while data is being sent for analysis. After the `flush` operation, the job is still opened.
	`GET _ml/anomaly_detectors/[<job_id>|` `<job_id>,<job_id> |_all]/_stats`	Get statistics from one, multiple, or all job resources.
Jobs, forecast	`POST_ml/anomaly_detectors/` `<job_id>/_forecast`	Predict the future result of the job with the given `<job_id>` identifier.
	`DELETE _ml/anomaly_detectors/<job_id>` `/[_forecast|[/<forecast_id>|_all]`	Delete the forecast resource with the given `<forecast_id>` identifier and the job resource with the given `<job_id>` identifier, or all forecasts.
Calendars, jobs	`PUT_ml/calendars/<calendar_id>` `/jobs/<job_id>`	Add a job resource with the given `<job_id>` identifier to a calendar resource with the `<calendar_id>` identifier.
	`DELETE_ml/calendars/<calendar_id>/` `jobs/<job_id>`	Delete a job resource with the given `<job_id>` identifier.
Jobs, results, buckets	`GET _ml/anomaly_detectors/<job_id>` `/results/buckets` `/[<timestamp>]`	Get the bucket aggregation result with the `<timestamp>` identifier, or get all buckets from the job resource with the `<job_id>` identifier.

Jobs, results, overall buckets	`GET _ml/anomaly_detectors/[<job_id>|`
	`<job_id>,<job_id>|`
	`_all]/results/overall_buckets`
		Provide a summary of bucket aggregation results over multiple jobs where the longest bucket span is used.

Jobs, results, records	`GET _ml/anomaly_detectors/<job_id>` `/results/records`	Get the anomaly records from the results of the job resource with the given `<job_id>` identifier.
Jobs, results, influencers	`GET _ml/anomaly_detectors/<job_id>` `/results/influencers`	Get the influencer information from the job resources with the `<job_id>` identifier.
Datafeeds	`GET _ml/datafeeds/[<_feed_id>|` `<feed_id>,>feed_id>|_all]`	Get a datafeed resource with identifiers from one, multiple, or all datafeed resources.
	`PUT _ml/datafeeds/<feed_id>`	Create a datafeed resource for the job resources to use later. The datafeed can be an aggregate or a query.
	`DELETE _ml/datafeeds/<feed_id>`	Delete the datafeed with the given `<feed_id>` identifier.
	`POST _ml/datafeeds/<feed_id>/_update`	Update the properties of the datafeed with the given `<feed_id>` identifier.
	`GET _ml/datafeeds/[<_feed_id>|` `<feed_id>,>feed_id>|_all]/stats`	Get statistics from one, multiple, or all datafeed resources.
	`POST _ml/datafeeds/<feed_id>/_start`	Start the datafeed and be ready to retrieve data from Elasticsearch.

	`POST _ml/datafeeds/[<_feed_id>|`
	`<feed_id>,>feed_id>|_all]`
	`/_stop`
		Stop receiving data for the datafeeds resources in Elasticsearch.

	`GET` `_ml/datafeeds/<datafeed_id>/_preview`	Preview a datafeed.
Filters	`GET _ml/filters/[<filter_id>]`	Get the filter resource with the given `<snapshot_id>` identifier or all snapshot resources.
	`PUT _ml/filters/<filter_id>`	A filter defines a list of strings, which is referenced by the detector attribute of the `job` resources.
	`POST _ml/filters/<filter_id>/_update`	Update the properties of the filter resource.
	`DELETE _ml/filters/<filter_id>`	Delete the filter resource with the given `<filter_id>` identifier.

Jobs, model snapshots	`GET _ml/anomaly_detectors/<job_id>/`
	`model_snapshots`
	`/[<snapshot_id>]`
		Get the `snapshot` model resource with the `<snapshot_id>` identifier or all snapshot resources.

	`POST_ml/anomaly_detectors/<job_id>`
	`/model_snapshots`
	`/<snapshot_id>/_update`
		Update the properties of the `snapshot` model resource with the given `<snapshot_id>` identifier, and the job resource with the given `<job_id>` identifier.

	`DELETE _ml/anomaly_detectors/<job_id>/`
	`model_snapshots`
	`/<snapshot_id>`
		Delete the snapshot model resource with the given `<snapshot_id>` identifier.

	`POST _ml/anomaly_detectors/<job_id>/`
	`model_snapshots`
	`/<snapshot_id>/_revert`
		Reset the state of the snapshot model with the given `<snapshot_id>` identifier, of the job resource with the given `<job_id>` identifier, to the previous record.

The following table is for the miscellaneous APIs, regardless of any specific resources:

API URL	Description
`DELETE_ml/_deleted_expired_data`	Deletes all resources, data, and results if they are expired.
`POST _ml/find_file_structure`	Finds the file structure of a file. The data of the file must be suitable for Ingest APIs.
`POST _ml/set_upgrade_mode`	If the enabled parameter is set to true, it enables the `upgrade_mode` setting to prepare the indices used by machine learning for an upgrade.

Machine learning jobs

Kibana 7.0 supports four types of machine learning jobs, described as follows:

- **Single-metric jobs**: Data analysis is performed on only one index field.
- **Multi-metric jobs**: Data analysis can be performed on multiple index fields; however, each field is analyzed separately.
- **Advanced jobs**: Data analysis can be performed on multiple index fields. Advanced jobs provide full configuration settings for detectors and influencers.
- **Population jobs**: Data analysis of the distribution behavior for less common data, such as detecting outliers in a population.

Let's look at an example of a single-metric job using Kibana.

Sample data

The data in the `cf_etf_hist_price` index is time series data; however, it is not continuous. The data is only for trading days. Before we can practice our machine learning task, we must provide another set of data that will fill in the non-trading days using the corresponding price data from the previous trading day. In our GitHub repository (`https://github.com/PacktPublishing/Mastering-Elasticsearch-7.0/tree/master/Chapter16`), three files can be downloaded: `cf_rfem_hist_price_bulk_index.sh`, `cf_rfem_hist_price_bulk.json`, and `cf_rfem_hist_price_mappings.json`. It contains the `RFEM ETF` data symbol with trading days and non-trading days. Go to the download directory and run the following command to index data to the new `cf_rfem_hist_price` index:

```
$ ./cf_rfem_hist_price_bulk_index.sh
```

After the command is run, we can go back to the `Index Management` page in Kibana. Click on the **Reload indices** button and we'll find that the new index, **cf_rfem_hist_price**, is shown (see the following screenshot). There are 90 documents, which include data from 61 trading days and 29 non-trading days:

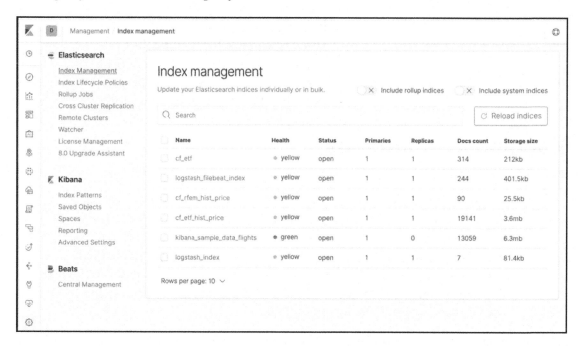

For our convenience, to demonstrate machine learning jobs, let's use the Kibana user interface and show the single-metric job.

Running a single-metric job

Basically, a single-metric job uses only one field from the indexed documents as a detector for the analysis. The step-by-step instructions to run a single-metric job for the `volume` field are described as follows.

Creating index patterns

For creating index patterns, we need to do the following:

1. Go the **Index Management** screen and click on the **Index Patterns** selection of Kibana.

2. Click on the **Create index pattern** button. The **Create index pattern** panel is shown in the following screenshot:

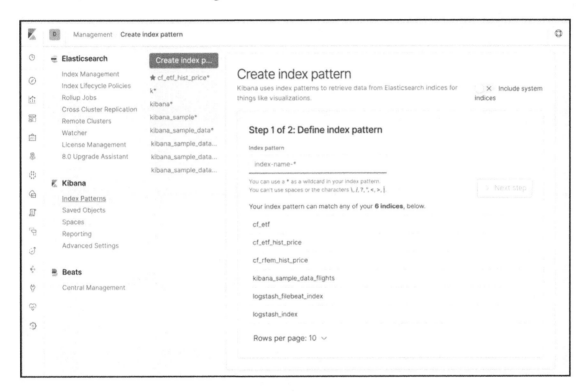

3. Fill in the **Index pattern** field with `cf_rfem_hist_price` and click on the **Next step** button, as shown in the following screenshot:

4. The next step is to fill in the **Time Filter field name** section. Select the **date** option from the dropdown and then click on the **Create index pattern** button, as shown in the following screenshot:

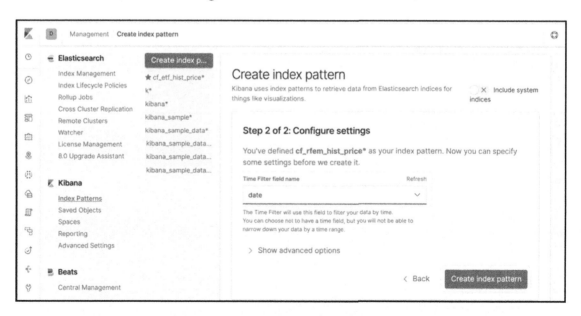

The `cf_rfem_hist_price` index pattern is created and can be used in the machine learning job.

Creating a new machine learning job

To create a single-metric machine learning job, we need to do the following:

1. Click on the machine learning button on the left-hand toolbar, highlighted in the following screenshot, and the right-hand pane will show the machine learning panel.
2. From the top menu, select **Job Management**. Click on the **Create new job** button, as shown in the following screenshot:

3. The panel will let us choose the source data, which comes from a new search, a selected index, or a saved search. Click on the **cf_rfem_hist_price** index, as shown in the following screenshot:

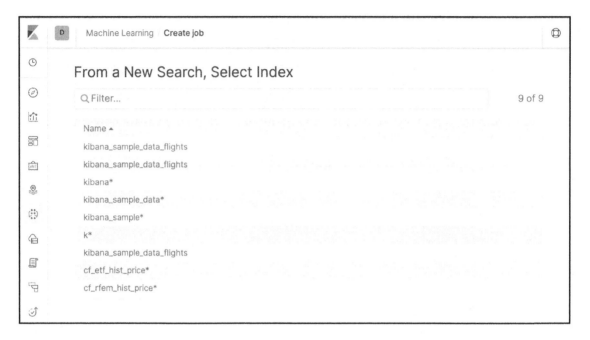

4. There are several job types to use to define the machine learning job. Let's choose a single-metric job, as shown in the following screenshot:

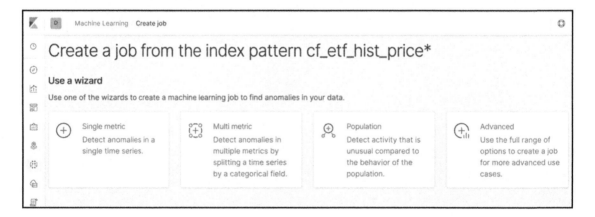

5. A single-metric job must use aggregation. Since our data is a daily record and the bucket span (interval) is one day, the aggregation is the same whether we choose **Sum**, **Mean**, or **Median** aggregation.

6. We will choose the **Sum** aggregation and the **volume** field to check the anomaly. Follow the steps shown in the screenshot to fill the data with the `job` identifier.

7. Click on the **Use full cf_rfem_hist_price data** button. We want to see the chart for the data of the **volume** field. Finally, click on the arrow button and we can see that the **Validate Job** and **Create Job** buttons are enabled:

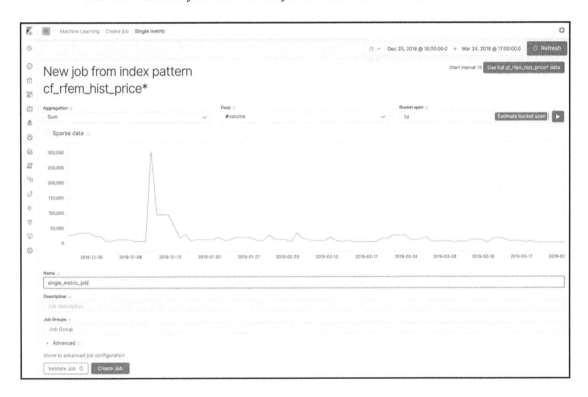

8. Click on **Validate Job** before we create it. This shows the validation messages. If there are any errors, it shows us the error messages in red. The following screenshot shows that everything is valid.

9. Click on the **Close** button and then click on the **Create Job** button to create the machine learning job:

10. Congratulations! We have successfully created a single-metric machine learning job. We will see a band, as shown in the following screenshot, which is an anomaly warning determined by Elasticsearch:

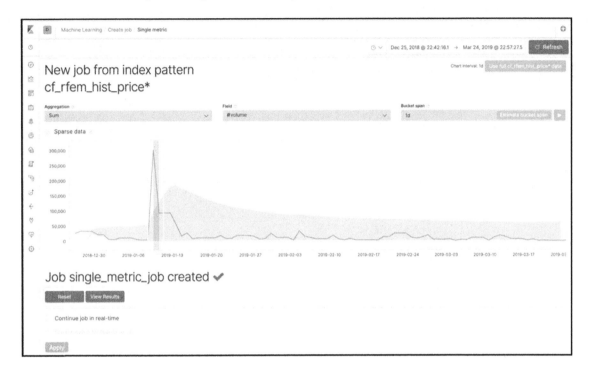

Examining the result

Let's take a look at the detailed information of the result as follows:

1. Click on the **View Results** button to check the details of the anomaly, as shown in the following screenshot:

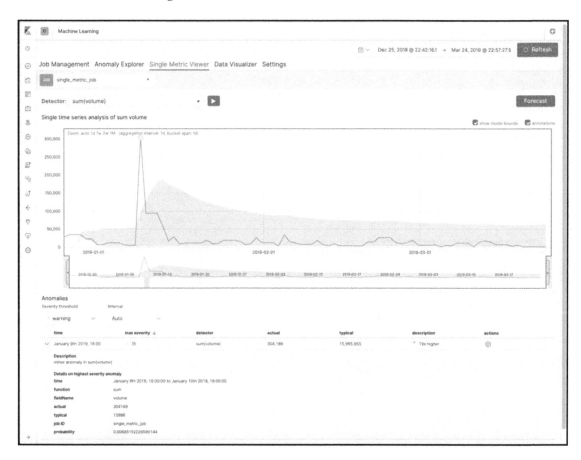

2. Try the forecast function by clicking on the **Forecast** button in the top right-hand corner. Let's forecast 7 days and click on the **Run** button from the pop-up panel, as shown in the following screenshot:

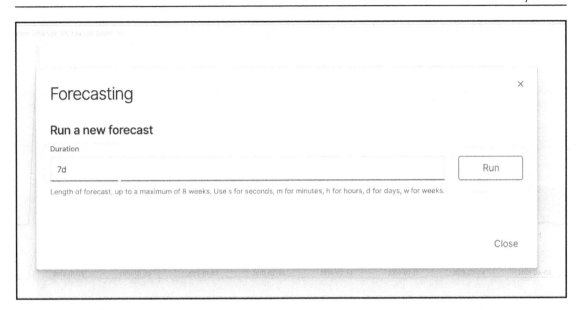

We use a bounding box to cover the prediction part, as shown in the following screenshot:

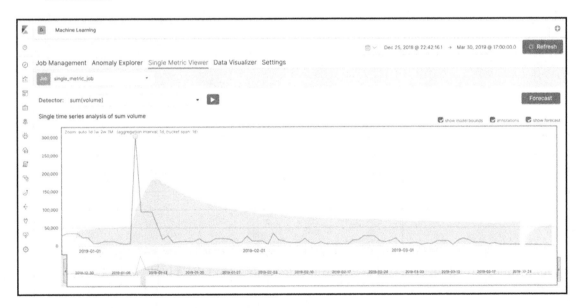

3. Finally, let's take a look to see the content of the `single_metric_job` machine learning job that we defined using the Kibana DevTools console. The detector to analyze is the addressed `volume` field:

```
D  Dev Tools                                                                    ⊕

History  Settings  Help

Console    Search Profiler    Grok Debugger

  1  GET _ml/anomaly_detectors/single_metric_job    ▶ ⚙     1 ▾ {
  2                                                          2      "count" : 1,
                                                             3 ▾    "jobs" : [
                                                             4 ▾      {
                                                             5          "job_id" : "single_metric_job",
                                                             6          "job_type" : "anomaly_detector",
                                                             7          "job_version" : "7.0.0",
                                                             8          "description" : "",
                                                             9          "create_time" : 1563861489275,
                                                            10          "finished_time" : 1563861969709,
                                                            11 ▾        "analysis_config" : {
                                                            12            "bucket_span" : "1d",
                                                            13            "summary_count_field_name" : "doc_count",
                                                            14 ▾          "detectors" : [
                                                            15 ▾            {
                                                            16                "detector_description" : "sum(volume)",
                                                            17                "function" : "sum",
                                                            18                "field_name" : "volume",
                                                            19                "detector_index" : 0
                                                            20 ▾            }
                                                            21 ▾          ],
                                                            22            "influencers" : [ ]
                                                            23 ▾        },
                                                            24 ▾        "analysis_limits" : {
                                                            25            "model_memory_limit" : "10mb",
                                                            26            "categorization_examples_limit" : 4
                                                            27 ▾        },
                                                            28 ▾        "data_description" : {
                                                            29            "time_field" : "date",
                                                            30            "time_format" : "epoch_ms"
                                                            31 ▾        },
                                                            32 ▾        "model_plot_config" : {
                                                            33            "enabled" : true
                                                            34 ▾        },
                                                            35          "model_snapshot_retention_days" : 1,
                                                            36 ▾        "custom_settings" : {
                                                            37            "created_by" : "single-metric-wizard"
                                                            38 ▾        },
                                                            39          "model_snapshot_id" : "1563861489",
                                                            40          "results_index_name" : "shared"
                                                            41 ▾        }
                                                            42 ▾    ]
                                                            43 ▾ }
                                                            44
```

After completing the Elasticsearch machine learning job, it seems that it only supports anomaly detection in the current stage. Interested users can take a look at the fundamental algorithm (see `http://www.ijmlc.org/papers/398-LC018.pdf`) developed by the Elastic's engineers Thomas J. Veasey and Stephen J. Dodson for more details. In the next section, we will go through a brief introduction of using Elasticsearch and scikit-learn in machine learning.

Machine learning using Elasticsearch and scikit-learn

Scikit-learn is a Python machine learning library built on the top of NumPy, SciPy, and Matplotlib. It provides simple tools for data mining and data analysis. According to the description on its website (see `https://scikit-learn.org/stable/`), we can use it in six major areas:

- **Classification**: A supervised learning approach for learning given data and using it to generate a model for a classifier. Then, we use the model to predict new data in order to identify the category with the classifier.
- **Regression**: Using a statistical methodology to predict continuous values using a given set of data.
- **Clustering**: Grouping data into different categories.
- **Dimensionality reduction**: Reducing the dimension of the data.
- **Model selection**: Tuning the hyperparameters of the model.
- **Preprocessing**: Feature extraction and normalization.

In the last section, *Machine learning with the Elastic Stack*, we practiced anomaly detection with the machine learning feature of Elasticsearch. Now, we will try to solve the same problem using a simple k-means clustering library function provided by scikit-learn. The purpose of k-means clustering is to divide the number of *n* data into *k* clusters, where each item of data belongs to a cluster with the nearest mean. We will use the data from the `cf_rfem_hist_price` index for analysis. For the `single_metric_job` machine learning job in the *Create new machine learning job* section, we only looked at the `volume` field. In this section, we will look at three fields: `volume`, `changeOverTime`, and `changePercent`. A small Python project, solving the classification problem using Elasticsearch and scikit-learn, can be downloaded from our GitHub repository, available at `https://github.com/PacktPublishing/Mastering-Elasticsearch-7.0/tree/master/Chapter16/cf_rfem_hist_price`). After downloading it, take a look at the `cf_rfem_hist_price` directory. We are extending and rewriting the same Python project from `Chapter 12`, *Elasticsearch from Python Programming*. The `etl.py` file—shown in the following code block—uses the low-level client to perform the search request. The query and the date histogram aggregation is reused to search the same set of data. Then, we only collect the data for the three fields and put it in a three-dimensional array, which is the returned content of the `etl()` function:

```
from com.example.client.config.low_level_client_by_connection import
ESLowLevelClientByConnection
from elasticsearch_dsl import Search
```

```
from elasticsearch_dsl.query import Q, Bool, Range, Term
from elasticsearch_dsl.aggs import A, DateHistogram

def etl(index='cf_rfem_hist_price', start_date='2018-12-26',
end_date='2019-03-25', symbol='rfem'):
    ESLowLevelClientByConnection.get_instance()
    search = Search(index=index, using='high_level_client')[0:100]
    search.query = Q(Bool(must=[Range(date={'gte': '2018-12-26', 'lte':
'2019-03-25'}),                             Term(symbol='rfem')]))
    aggs = A(DateHistogram(field='date', interval='1d', format='yyyy-MM-
dd', min_doc_count=1))          response = search.execute()
    hits = response['hits']
    hits=hits['hits']
    XX=[]
    for hit in hits:
        X=[]
        X.append(hit['_source']['changeOverTime'])
        X.append(hit['_source']['changePercent'])
        X.append(hit['_source']['volume'])
        XX.append(X)
    return(XX)

if __name__ == "__main__":
    XX=etl()
    for X in XX:
        print(X)
```

The `kmeans.py` file—shown in the following code block—uses the `KMeans` class for clustering. We instantiate a `KMean` object with the `n_clusters=2` parameter to see whether we can divide the data into a normal group and an anomaly group. We read the data from the `etl()` function and then put it into the `fit()` function of the `KMeans` class. It generates a label for each data point: `0` for the first group and `1` for the second group. Then, we use the `matplotlib.pyplot()` function to plot the data with the label assigned. Let's take a look at the `kmeans.py` file, as shown in the following code block:

```
from etl import etl
import matplotlib.pyplot as plt
from sklearn.cluster import KMeans
from mpl_toolkits.mplot3d import Axes3D

points = etl()
Kmean = KMeans(n_clusters=2)
Kmean.fit(points)
labels = Kmean.labels_
fig = plt.figure()
ax = fig.add_subplot(111, projection='3d')
for item,label in zip(points, labels):
```

```
    if label == 0:
        ax.scatter(item[0], item[1], item[2], c='r', marker='o')
    else:
        ax.scatter(item[0], item[1], item[2], c='b', marker='s')

ax.set_xlabel('changeOverTime')
ax.set_ylabel('changePercent')
ax.set_zlabel('volume')
plt.show()
```

To run the program, follow the step-by-step instructions in this code block:

```
$ cd cf_rfem_hist_price/
$ source venv/bin/activate
(venv)$ export PYTHONPATH=.:$PYTHONPATH
(venv)$ python com/example/kmeans/kmeans.py
```

The program will generate a graph, as follows:

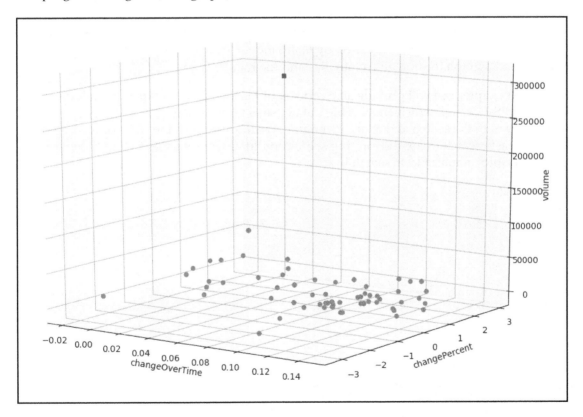

The dots represent the data labeled with 0, and the square represents the data labeled with 1. As our sample data is ideal for showing the anomaly, we don't need any further processes. If you are interested, you may want to expand your analysis to other fields such as `changePercent`. Moreover, you can write a plugin by using the code for practice. We will draw a present conclusion in the following section.

Summary

Hooray! We have completed the first part of the advanced feature of this book; that is, machine learning with Elasticsearch. We have introduced the machine learning feature of the Elastic Stack. We created a single-metric job to track the `volume` field to detect anomalies in the data of the `cf_rfem_hist_price` index. We have also introduced the Python scikit-learn library and the unsupervised learning algorithm, k-means clustering. The `KMean` class is provided in the `sklearn.cluster` package. We have extracted data from the `cf_rfem_hist_price` index and used three fields, `changeOverTime`, `changePercent`, and `volume`, to construct multidimensional input data, in order for the k-means clustering to find the anomalies. By using the `matplotlib.pyplot()` function, we have plotted a graph to show the anomalies and the regular data.

In the next chapter, we will provide an overview of Elasticsearch for Apache Hadoop, known as ES-Hadoop, which enables big data businesses to enhance their Hadoop workflows with the search and analytics engine. We'll learn about the skills of reading data from an Elasticsearch index, performing some computations using Spark, and then writing the results into another Elasticsearch index.

17
Spark and Elasticsearch for Real-Time Analytics

In the previous chapter, we looked at the machine learning feature of Elastic Stack. We used a single metric job to track one-dimensional data (with the `volume` field of the `cf_rfem_hist_price` index) to detect anomalies by using Kibana. We also introduced the scikit-learn Python package and performed the same anomaly detection, but with three-dimensional data (with two more fields: `changePercent` and `changeOverTime`) by using Python programming.

In this chapter, we will look at another advanced feature, which is known as **Elasticsearch for Apache Hadoop (ES-Hadoop)**. The ES-Hadoop feature contains two major areas. The first area is the integration of Elasticsearch with Hadoop distributed computing environments, such as Apache Spark, Apache Storm, and Hive. The second area is the integration of Elasticsearch to use the Hadoop filesystem as the backend storage so that you can index Hadoop data into the Elastic Stack to take advantage of the search engine and visualization. In this chapter, our focus is on ES-Hadoop's Apache Spark support. Apache Spark is an open source processing engine for analytics, machine learning, and overcoming a range of data challenges. We'll practice reading data from an Elasticsearch index, performing some computations using Spark, and then writing the results back to Elasticsearch.

By the end of this chapter, we will have covered the following topics:

- Overview of ES-Hadoop
- Apache Spark support
- Real-time analytics using Elasticsearch and Apache Spark

Overview of ES-Hadoop

As we mentioned, the ES-Hadoop feature contains two major areas: distributed computing and distributed storage. The main goal of ES-Hadoop is to seamlessly connect Elasticsearch and Hadoop so that they can benefit each other with distributed computing, distributed storage, searching, analytics, visualization, and more. We can import **Hadoop Distributed File System** (**HDFS**) data to Elasticsearch for search and analysis, and export the Elastisearch data to HDFS for snapshot and restore. ES-Hadoop fully supports the Spark framework, including Spark, Hive, Pig, Storm, Cascading, and sure, the standard MapReduce. Let's take a look at the data flow between Elasticsearch, ES-Hadoop, and components in the Hadoop ecosystem, as shown in the following screenshot:

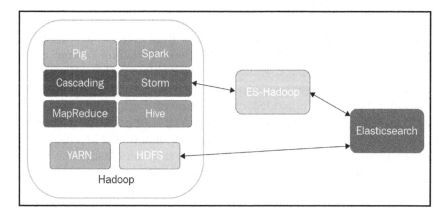

In short, we can think of ES-Hadoop as a data bridge between Elasticsearch and the Hadoop big data ecosystem, through which it provides real-time, or near-real-time, interactive analysis. We will also provide a brief description of each component in the following table:

Component	Description
HDFS	HDFS is an individual filesystem. It can manage a huge amount of data that may span hundreds of machines. When you refer to a file path, the actual data may be stored on many different machines. However, you don't need to know where the data is located.
MapReduce	MapReduce is the first-generation computing engine for HDFS. Although HDFS can manage data located on different machines, the batch data processing is too slow.
Spark	Spark is the second-generation computing engine for HDFS. Spark is much faster than MapReduce and can perform real-time data analysis when running in memory, especially in machine learning applications such as online product recommendations, network security analysis, and more.
Storm	Storm is another distributed computing engine working with Hadoop. Unlike MapReduce and Spark, it does not collect data and store it. Instead, it receives streaming data over the network, processes it in real time, and then returns the result directly.
Hive	Since MapReduce was cumbersome to write, Hadoop users wanted to have a higher-level language for programming. The Hive software project was developed to provide a SQL-like query language called **HiveQL**. It transparently converts SQL queries to MapReduce programs.
Pig	The reason why Pig was developed is similar to Hive. It is a high-level scripting language for expressing data analysis programs. It consists of a compiler that converts the scripts to MapReduce programs.
Cascading	Cascading is a software abstraction layer for Apache Hadoop. It allows you to create and execute data processing workflows on Hadoop by using JVM-based languages such as Java. In fact, it hides the underlying complexity of MapReduce jobs.
YARN	**Yet Another Resource Negotiator** (**YARN**) is a central management system that supports resource management and job scheduling/monitoring management for Hadoop 2.0 or higher. The YARN framework gave Hadoop the ability to run non-MapReduce jobs.

In the next section, we will focus on integrating Apache Spark using ES-Hadoop.

Apache Spark support

Apache Spark is one of the most popular big data tools. It is a second-generation computing engine that works with Hadoop as an alternative to MapReduce. It provides in-memory computing capabilities to achieve high-performance analytics. The major components in Spark include Spark SQL, Spark Streaming, SparkR, **Machine Learning Library (MLlib)**, and GraphX. Spark is built on the Scala programming language and also supports APIs for Java, Python, and R. The following diagram depicts the ecosystem of Spark:

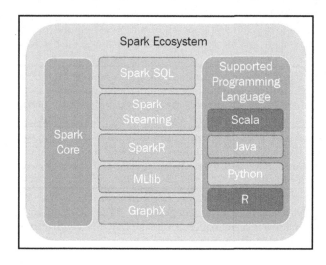

Spark provides a hybrid processing framework, which means it supports both batch processing and stream processing. Let's look at these brief descriptions of each type of processing:

- **Batch processing**: Usually, this applies to blocks of data that have been stored for a period of time and it takes a long time to complete the process. Spark handles all the data in memory and only interacts with the storage layer to load the data and retain the final result. All intermediate results are managed in memory. To implement in-memory batch processing, Spark uses a data model called **Resilient Distributed Datasets (RDDs)** to represent a collection of data and process the data in memory. The operation on an RDD produces a new RDD. Each RDD can track its family tree through its parent RDD and, eventually, it can trace back to the data on disk.

- **Stream processing**: This allows us to process data in real time as it arrives and quickly detect conditions within a short time after receiving the data. This is ideal to use with analysis tools in order to get results as soon as the data comes in. Stream processing is provided by Spark Streaming, which is based on a concept called micro-batches. This strategy is designed to treat live input data streams as a series of very small batches, which are then processed by the Spark engine to generate the final stream of results in batches. In fact, this method works quite well, but it cannot compare with the real stream processing framework. The following diagram depicts the streaming process based on micro-batches:

Although memory cost is much higher than disk space, the performance improvement will completely offset the costs when it is needed.

Real-time analytics using Elasticsearch and Apache Spark

We will use the same anomaly detection example from the previous chapter. Instead of using the simple k-means clustering library function provided by scikit-learn, we will use ES-Hadoop, Spark SQL, and Spark MLlib to solve the problem. From our GitHub download site (`https://github.com/PacktPublishing/Mastering-Elasticsearch-7.0/tree/master/Chapter17/eshadoop`), there is a project that involves using the Python 3.6 **Virtual Environment** (**virtualenv**) to create an isolated environment for the project to have its own dependencies in its site packages. The project is self-contained and allows you to run it on its working environment. The following section is a reference for you if you're interested in building a virtual environment.

Building a virtual environment to run the sample ES-Hadoop project

The following step-by-step instructions are for building the virtual environment with the required libraries to run the project:

1. Build a virtual environment folder. We assume that you have Python and virtualenv installed. We have Python 3.6 and virtualenv 15.0.1 installed. Let's name the folder eshadoop and run the command in the code block:

    ```
    $virtualenv -p python3.6 eshadoop
    ```

2. Run the following command and take a look at the eshadoop folder you've created:

    ```
    $ ls eshadoop
    bin include lib pip-selfcheck.json share
    ```

3. Run the source command to use the virtual environment built for eshadoop:

    ```
    $ source eshadoop/bin/activate
    (eshadoop) $
    ```

4. Run this command to go to the working directory:

    ```
    (eshadoop) $cd eshadoop
    ```

5. Create a text file named requirements.txt with the content described:

    ```
    #ES-Hadoop 7.0
    pyspark==2.4.3
    pandas==0.24.2
    matplotlib==3.1.0
    numpy==1.16.4
    ```

6. Run the install command to download the required third-party libraries:

    ```
    (eshadoop) $pip install -r requirements.txt
    Collecting pyspark==2.4.3 (from -r requirements.txt (line 2))
    Collecting pandas==0.24.2 (from -r requirements.txt (line 3))
    ...
    ```

7. Go to the `jar` folder of the `site-packages` folder and run the `wget` command to download the `elasticsearch-spark` JAR file:

```
(eshadoop) $cd lib/python3.6/site-packages/pyspark/jars
(eshadoop) $wget
http://central.maven.org/maven2/org/elasticsearch/elasticsearch-spa
rk-20_2.11/7.0.0/elasticsearch-spark-20_2.11-7.0.0.jar
Resolving central.maven.org (central.maven.org)... 151.101.188.209
Connecting to central.maven.org
(central.maven.org)|151.101.188.209|:80... connected.
.....
```

8. Go back to the `eshadoop` folder, make an `src` folder, and put the source file into the folder:

```
(eshadoop) $mkdir src
(eshadoop) $cd src
```

The next subsection describes how to run the sample program.

Running the sample ES-Hadoop project

We assume that you have downloaded the ES-Hadoop project, which is located in the `eshadoop` folder. The following step-by-step instructions are for running the sample ES-Hadoop project:

1. Show the downloaded folder and take a look at the contents of the `eshadoop` folder. It is almost the same as what you got after you performed the steps in the last section:

```
$ ls
bin include lib pip-selfcheck.json requirements.txt share src
```

2. Run the `source` command to use the virtual environment built for `eshadoop`:

```
$ source bin/activate
(eshadoop) $
```

3. Run this command to go to the `src` working directory:

```
(eshadoop) $cd src
```

4. Take a look at the `eshadoop/src/com/example` folder:

```
(eshadoop) $ ls com/example/*
com/example/spark:
kmean_model run.py spark-warehouse

com/example/spark_ml:
kmeans.py __pycache__
```

5. Set `PYTHONPATH` to include the current folder in the Python execution path:

```
(eshadoop) $export PYTHONPATH=.:../lib/python3.6/site-
packages:$PYTHONPATH
```

6. Use the following command to run the program as shown in the code block:

```
(eshadoop) $ python com/example/spark/run.py
19/06/09 12:47:19 WARN Utils: Your hostname, wai resolves to a
loopback address: 127.0.1.1; using 192.168.1.74 instead (on
interface enp0s31f6)
19/06/09 12:47:19 WARN Utils: Set SPARK_LOCAL_IP if you need to
bind to another address
...
```

7. It will first show a similar graph to the anomaly detection that you saw in the *Machine learning using Elasticsearch and scikit-learn* section of Chapter 16, *Machine Learning with Elasticsearch*:

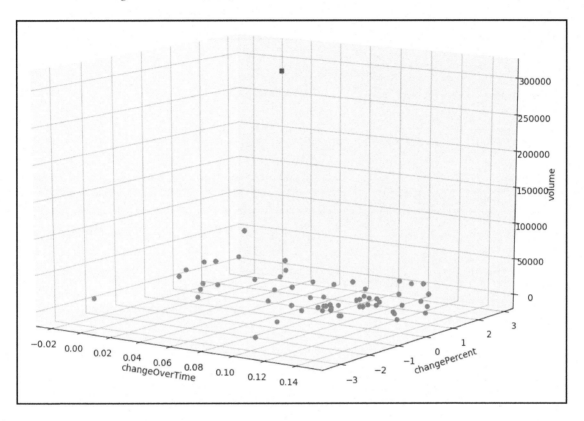

8. SparkContext provides a web UI running on port `4040` (or port `4041` if port `4040` is being used). We can use a web browser to monitor the Spark application when it is launched and running. Let's take a look at the metrics. In the following diagram, the screen text shows a list of completed **Spark Jobs**:

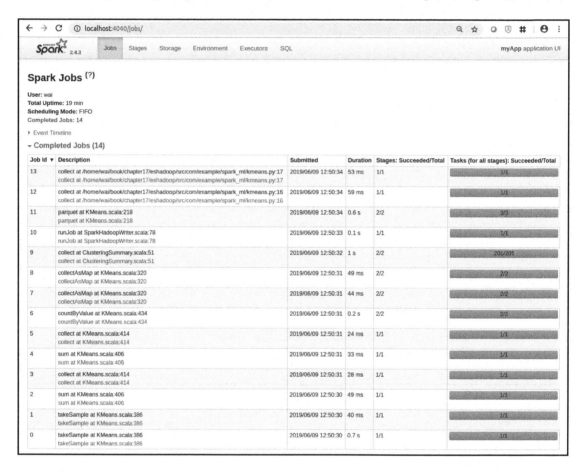

Let's take a look at **Job 13**. Click the hyperlink (**collect at ~/eshadoop/src/com/example/spark/ml/kmeans.py:17**) from the panel. It will show you the **Directed Acyclic Graph (DAG)** and the stages of **Job 13**. This DAG is created according to the program and submitted to the DAG Scheduler to spit the tasks from the graph into stages. Let's take a look at the details of **Job 13**:

We can look further into **Stage 18** of **Job 13**. Click the hyperlink (**collect at ~/eshadoop/src/com/example/spark/ml/kmeans.py:17**) from the panel. The DAG Scheduler splits the Spark RDD into the relevant stages, and when you select a stage, for example, **Stage 18** is the stage view, the RDD of **Stage 18** are analyzed in detail:

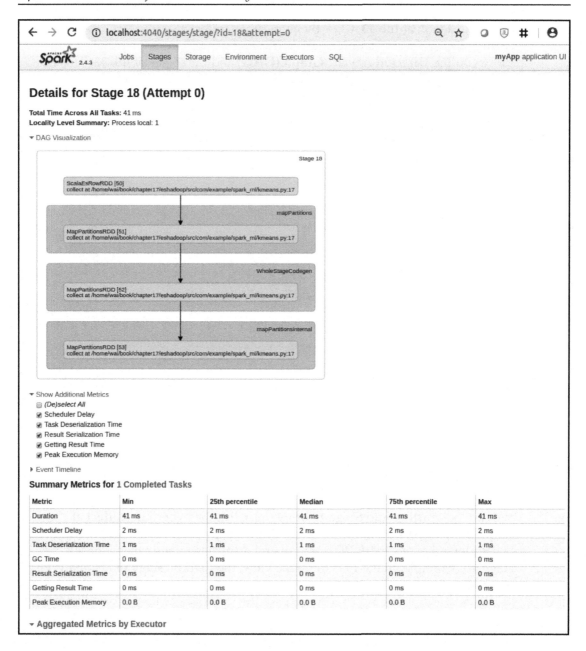

Since we are using Spark SQL to retrieve data from Elasticsearch via ES-Hadoop, let's take a look at the SQL from the menu too. As shown in the following screenshot, we have used the `createTempView` function and the command is collected in the program:

If you're interested, you can continue to take a look at other items from the menu in the panel.

9. Click the cross button in the top-left corner to close the previous figure from the anomaly detection in order to continue the program flow. The program will run to the end. It will use the centers of the two detected clusters to feed into the live anomaly detection model and predict their class labels. The labels are printed on the screen, as shown in the code block. For example, `changeOverTime=0.08200053870677948`, `changePercent=0.22583146393299103`, `volume=15841.62890625`, and `prediction=0`:

```
...
[[0.08200053870677948, 0.22583146393299103, 15841.62890625, 0],
[0.041152264922857285, 1.1649999618530273, 304189.0, 1]]
```

Running the sample ES-Hadoop project using a prepared Docker image

We have prepared a Docker image, named `eshadoop`, located on the Docker Hub website (`https://cloud.docker.com/repository/docker/wtwong316/waitakwong`). Follow the instructions and run the Python program:

1. Pull the Docker image; issue the following command to download the Docker image:

   ```
   $docker pull wtwong316/waitakwong:eshadoop
   ```

2. Verify the `eshadoop` Docker image; issue the following command to find the image identifier from the IMAGE ID column, which is `42141517aefa`:

   ```
   $ docker images
   REPOSITORY TAG IMAGE ID CREATED SIZE
   wtwong316/waitakwong eshadoop 42141517aefa 42 minutes ago 1.29GB
   ```

3. Run the `eshadoop` Docker image; issue the following command to run the `eshadoop` application. The result shows the information of the two clusters:

   ```
   docker run --rm --network packt --name eshadoop -it 42141517aefa
   /usr/app/commands.sh
   19/06/30 09:49:37 WARN NativeCodeLoader: Unable to load native-
   hadoop library for your platform... using builtin-java classes
   where applicable
   ......
   [[0.08200053870677948, 0.22583146393299103, 15841.62890625, 0],
   [0.041152264922857285, 1.1649999618530273, 304189.0, 1]]
   ```

The figure of the anomaly detection will not be shown since it runs in the Docker image. Unless the Xserver Display setting is specified, the figure will not be shown in the host. We will skip this setting since it is out of our scope. If you're interested in building the `eshadoop` Docker image by yourself, refer to the download folder from our GitHub site (`https://github.com/PacktPublishing/Mastering-Elasticsearch-7.0/tree/master/Chapter17/eshadoop_docker`).

Source code

There are two source files. The first one is located at
`eshadoop/src/com/example/spark/run.py` and the second one is located at
`eshadoop/src/com/example/spark_ml/kmeans.py`. First, let's look at the main
workflow in the `run.py` file, as described in the code block:

```
from pyspark.sql import SparkSession
import pyspark.sql.functions as f
from pyspark.sql.types import *
from pyspark.sql.functions import expr, lit
from pyspark.ml.feature import VectorAssembler
from com.example.spark_ml.kmeans import create_anomaly_detection_model,
find_anomalies
import pandas

......
if __name__ == '__main__':
    spark_session = create_spark_session()
    df_data, es_data = extract_es_data(spark_session)
    df_labels, centers = create_anomaly_detection_model(es_data)
    write_es_data(df_data, df_labels)
    df_centers_features = convert_data_to_features(spark_session, centers)
    center_labels = find_anomalies(df_centers_features)
    print(center_labels)
```

The steps of the main workflow in the `run.py` file can be described as follows:

1. Create `SparkSession`. This was introduced in Spark 2.0. Using
   `SparkSession` can eliminate the need for developers to worry about different
   contexts such as `SparkContext`, `SQLContext`, and `StreamingContext`. By
   accessing `SparkSession`, we can access `SparkContext` automatically. In the
   `create_spark_session()` function, we use the `getOrCreate()` function from
   the `SparkSession.Builder` class to create `SparkSession`:

   ```
   # Create Spark Session
   def create_spark_session():
       spark =
   SparkSession.builder.master("local").appName("anomalyDetection").ge
   tOrCreate()
       spark.sparkContext.setLogLevel("ERROR")
       return spark
   ```

2. Extract Elasticsearch data by using `SparkSession`. In the `extract_es_data()` function, we use `spark.read.format()` to open a connection to the Elasticsearch server by using `SparkSession`. Then, we read the documents into a DataFrame from the `cf_rfem_hist_price` index via ES-Hadoop. Since we are using the Spark SQL from `SparkSession`, we must register the `cf_rfem_hist_price` index as a temporary database view by using the `createTempView()` function from the DataFrame. The lifetime of the database view is tied to `SparkSession`. Then, we use the `spark_session.sql()` function to extract three fields (`changeOverTime`, `changePercent`, and `volume`) for the input of anomaly detection. We convert the data to a suitable format for the `KMeans()` Spark MLlib clustering method:

```
# Extract data from elasticsearch and select the fields for the
anomaly detection
def extract_es_data(spark):
    reader = spark.read.format("org.elasticsearch.spark.sql") \
                .option("es.read.metadata", "true") \
                .option("es.nodes.wan.only",
"true").option("es.port", "9200") \
                .option("es.net.ssl", "false").option("es.nodes",
"http://localhost")
    df = reader.load("cf_rfem_hist_price")
    df.createTempView("view1")
    df2 = spark_session.sql("Select volume, changePercent,
changeOverTime from view1")
    vec_assembler = VectorAssembler(inputCols=["changeOverTime",
"changePercent", "volume"],                   outputCol="features")
    df_features = vec_assembler.transform(df2).select('features')
    return df, df_features
```

3. Create an anomaly detection k-means model from the extracted data. In the `create_anomaly_detection_model()` function of the `com.example.spark_ml.kmeans` package, the data extracted from the `cf_rfem_hist_price` index is used to build and store the k-means model. Finally, it returns all the predicted groups (group 0 or group 1) and the centers of the classified groups.

4. To update the Elasticsearch document with the predicted group number, we use `write_es_data()` method to write the data back to the Elasticsearch index via ES-Hadoop. In the `write_es_data()` function, the `df_es` DataFrame read from Elasticsearch cannot be modified since it is immutable. Instead, we use the `select()` function to select the `document _id` column from the `_metadata` field to create a new DataFrame. To make it possible for SQL to join the operation, we add a new `row_index` column to both DataFrames: `df_id` and `df_lablels_add`. The newly created `df_update` DataFrame is written back to the Elasticsearch server using the `update` operation as we set the `"es.write.operation":"update"` option:

```
def write_es_data(df_es, df_labels_add):
    df_id = df_es.select(expr("_metadata._id as id"))
    df_id_row_index = df_id.withColumn("row_index",
f.monotonically_increasing_id())
    df_labels_row_index = df_labels_add.withColumn("row_index",
f.monotonically_increasing_id())
    df_update = df_id_row_index.join(df_labels_row_index,
on=["row_index"]).drop("row_index")
    df_update.write.format("org.elasticsearch.spark.sql") \
        .option("es.write.operation", "update") \
        .option("es.mapping.id", "id").option("es.mapping.exclude",
"id")\
        .mode("append").save('cf_rfem_hist_price')
```

In the `write_es_data()` function, we use the newly created `df_update` DataFrame, which contains two fields: ID and prediction. We set the `"es.mapping.id"="id"` option so that Elasticsearch will use the ID field as an `_id` identifier. Also, we set the `"es.mapping.exclude"="id"` option so that Elasticsearch will ignore the ID field in the `update` operation. Finally, the prediction field is appended to the documents.

5. Convert the returned data (the center of clusters) to test the k-means model. We convert the data returned from the `create_anomaly_detection_model()` function by using the `convert_data_to_features()` function to fit the data format in the `find_anomalies()` function:

```
def convert_data_to_features(spark, data):
    schema = StructType([StructField("changeOverTime",
FloatType()), \
                StructField("changePercent", FloatType()),
StructField("volume", FloatType())])
    df_temp_data = spark.createDataFrame(pandas.DataFrame(data),
schema)
```

```
    vec_assembler = VectorAssembler(inputCols=["changeOverTime",
"changePercent", "volume"], \
outputCol="features")
    df_features =
vec_assembler.transform(df_temp_data).select('features')
    return df_features
```

The Python Spark MLlib's k-means model uses a single column to store the input features. In the `extract_es_data()` function, we use the following two lines to make the DataFrame with a single column, named `features`, to embed those three fields from the Elasticsearch document:

```
vec_assembler =
VectorAssembler(inputCols=["changeOverTime",
"changePercent", "volume"], outputCol="features")
df_features =
vec_assembler.transform(df_temp_data).select('features')
```

6. Feed the data to the anomaly detection k-means model. This function will return the corresponding labels predicted by the stored k-means model for the input data.
7. Print the return labels.

We describe the functions in the `kmeans.py` file as follows:

- `create_anomaly_detection_model()`: This instantiates a Spark ML `KMeans` object to use the k-means clustering algorithm to separate data into two (`k=2`) groups. Then, it stores the model in a file by calling the `model.write().overwrite().save()` function from the model created. Then, it calls `model.transform().select()` to get the label for each input data and plot the data with the label by calling `plot_points_with_label()`:

```
from pyspark.ml.clustering import KMeans, KMeansModel
import matplotlib.pyplot as plt
from mpl_toolkits.mplot3d import Axes3D
import numpy as np
import os

cur_model = None

def create_anomaly_detection_model(df_input):
    kmeans = KMeans(k=2, seed=0).setFeaturesCol('features')
    model = kmeans.fit(df_input)
    current_path = os.getcwd()
    model.write().overwrite().save(current_path + "/kmean_model")
```

```
df_labels = model.transform(df_input).select('prediction')
plot_points_with_label(df_input, df_labels)
centers = model.clusterCenters()
return centers
```

- `find_anomalies()`: If the Spark ML k-means model does not exist, it loads the model from the stored file using the `KMeansModel.load()` function. Then, it uses the model to predict the input data and return the label with the input data:

```
def find_anomalies(points):
 global cur_model
 if cur_model is None:
 model_path = os.getcwd() + "/kmean_model"
 cur_model = KMeansModel.load(model_path)
 labels = cur_model.transform(points).select('prediction')
 points_array = np.asarray(points.collect())
 labels_array = np.asarray(labels.collect())
 results = list()
 for item, label in zip(points_array, labels_array):
 temp = list()
 temp.append(item[0][0])
 temp.append(item[0][1])
 temp.append(item[0][2])
 temp.append(label[0])
 results.append(temp)
 return results
```

- `plot_points_with_label()`: This uses the `matplotlib.pyplot()` function to plot the data (the `changeOverTime`, `changePercent`, and `volume` fields) with the label (group 0 or group 1), where data with label=0 uses red-colored bullets and data with label=1 uses blue-colored squares:

```
def plot_points_with_label(df_input, df_labels):
    labels = df_labels.collect()
    points = df_input.collect()
    points_array = np.asarray(points)
    labels_array = np.asarray(labels)
    fig = plt.figure()
    ax = fig.add_subplot(111, projection='3d')
    for item, label in zip(points_array, labels_array):
        if label == 0:
            ax.scatter(item[0][0], item[0][1], item[0][2], c='r',
marker='o')
        else:
            ax.scatter(item[0][0], item[0][1], item[0][2], c='b',
marker='s')
    ax.set_xlabel('changeOverTime')
```

```
ax.set_ylabel('changePercent')
ax.set_zlabel('volume')
plt.show()
```

Let's examine the `cf_rfem_hist_price` index to see the document with a `prediction` field value equal to 1 (the group number). Use a web browser via `http://localhost:5601` to communicate with Kibana and click the wrench icon on the left sidebar to use the DevTools console. The REST API needed to retrieve the documents with prediction=1 and their results are shown in the following screenshot. There is only one document with prediction=1:

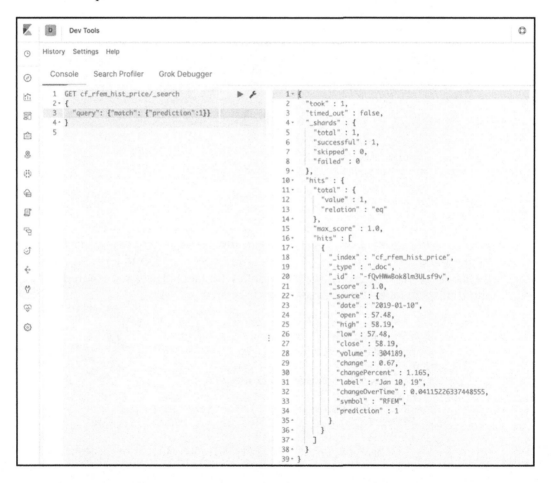

We have completed the introduction, setup, testing, and explanation for using Spark from ES-Hadoop. We'll conclude this chapter in the next section.

Summary

Unbelievable! We have completed the study of Spark and Elasticsearch for real-time analytics via ES-Hadoop. We started with the basic concepts of Apache Hadoop. We learned how to configure ES-Hadoop for Apache Spark support. We read the data from Elasticsearch, processed it, and then wrote it back to Elasticsearch. We learned about the `find_anomalies()` function, which is a real-time anomaly detection routine based on the k-means model, which was created from past data using the Spark MLlib. This can tell you whether the input data is an anomaly.

The next chapter is the final chapter of this book. We will use Spring Boot to build a RESTful API to provide search and analytics backed by Elasticsearch. We will revisit what we have learned before and glue it together to make a real-world use case project. Finally, we will visualize the results produced by the project by using Kibana.

18
Building Analytics RESTful Services

So far, we have learned about basic features such as mapping, using the document analyzer, indexing, searching, and aggregation. We have also learned about advanced features such as Elasticsearch SQL, Elasticsearch **Machine Learning (ML)** jobs, and **Elasticsearch-Hadoop (ES-Hadoop)** for Apache Spark. In addition, we have studied how to write the programs with the Java high-level REST client and Spring Boot. In this chapter, we'll put these materials together to build an end-to-end real-world final project to help the readers understand how they fit together. We'll reuse some of the codes provided earlier and glue them together. This project provides a search analytics REST service powered by Elasticsearch. The data flow will be retrieved from Elasticsearch using the REST client. The data is then used to build a k-means clustering model and accept the real-time data for anomaly detection using the Spark ML library and Spark SQL. Finally, the predicted class and the Bollinger Band-related data are written back to Elasticsearch by using ES-Hadoop. The results of the analysis display the newly stored data in Kibana. We also use Spring Scheduler to perform automatic data updates. Really fun and exciting!

By the end of this chapter, we will have covered the following topics:

- Building a RESTful web service with Spring Boot
- Integration with the Bollinger Band
- Building a Java Spark ML module for k-means anomaly detection
- Testing Analytics RESTful services
- Working on Kibana to visualize the analytics results

Building a RESTful web service with Spring Boot

In this project, we want to view the Bollinger Band on the Kibana **Visualize** page. There may be more than one way to do it. What we are going to do is pre-compute the related values of the Bollinger Band and index them when the trading price of the targeted symbol is ready. In addition to the fields from the **cf_etf_history_price** index, we are going to index fields such as the standard deviation and the moving average of 20 trading days, the upper and lower bounds of the Bollinger Band, the *typical price = (high+low+close)/3*, and the predicted anomaly class from the k-means model. We will create a Bollinger Band visualization with Kibana, as shown in the following screenshot:

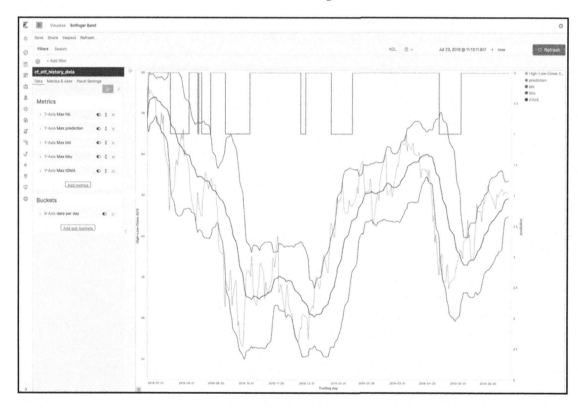

There are five lines on the chart. The uppermost line on the chart represents the predicted class that uses the k-means model for the 20-day standard deviation. The line that is just below the k-means model prediction is the upper bound of the Bollinger Band. The line at the bottom of the chart is the lower bound of the Bollinger Band. The line in the middle of the lower and the upper bounds of the Bollinger Band is the 20-day moving average. The last line, whose behavior fluctuated, is the typical price. This chart can monitor the mid-term or long-term trends of the **Extended-Traded Funds** (ETF) price.

We also create an ML job to analyze the standard deviation of 20 trading days to monitor the typical price variance; however, no matching anomalies are found. According to the 1-week forecast, the standard deviation will increase a little within the next week, as the data in the bounding box shows:

Finally, the system will automatically perform daily updates for the registered ETF symbols. Let's first take a look at the Spring Boot project program structure.

Project program structure

In the GitHub repository of this chapter (`https://github.com/PacktPublishing/Mastering-Elasticsearch-7.0/tree/master/Chapter18/sprintboot-es-analytics`), we can download a Spring Boot project named `springboot-es-analytics`.

We can use SpringToolSuite4 IDE to edit, compile, and run the data. The project program structure is shown in the following screenshot, which is extracted from the IDE:

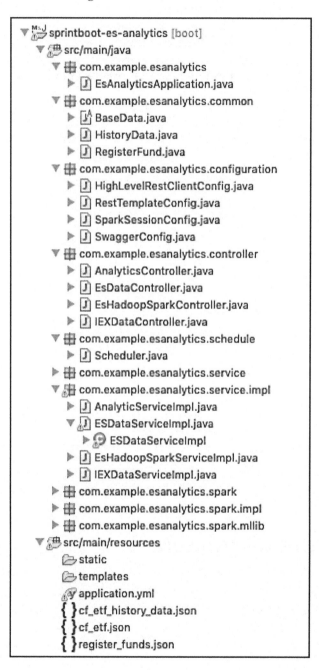

Each major package is briefly described as follows:

- The main method of the Spring Boot project is in
  `EsAnalyticsApplication.java`, under the `com.example.esanalytics`
  package.
- There are two **Plain Old Java Objects (POJOs)**, the `HistoryData` and
  `RegisterFund` classes, which contain the structure of the documents to be
  indexed. Both are from the `BaseData` class. They are under
  the `com.example.esanalytics.common` package.
- In `HighLevelRestClientConfig.java`, we configure the high-level REST
  client to communicate with Elasticsearch. In `RestTemplateConfig.java`, we
  configure the Spring Framework REST client to communicate with the IEX
  server. In `SparkSessionConfig.java`, we configure the ES-Hadoop Spark
  client to communicate with Spark. In `SwaggerConfig.java`, we configure
  Swagger for the GUI testing interface. They are under
  the `com.example.esanalytics.configuration` package.
- There are four controllers, which have corresponding service classes. In fact, the
  main workflow exposed to the user is only involved with
  the `AnalyticsController` class. Another three controller classes,
  `IEXDataController`, `EsDataController`, and `EsHadoopSparkController`,
  are written for testing purposes for their service classes. The controller classes are
  located in `com.example.esanalytics.controller`. The corresponding
  service classes and their implementations are located in
  `com.example.esanalytics.service` and
  `com.example.esanalytics.service.impl`, respectively.
- For the scheduling of the daily update data, we use Spring Scheduler with a cron
  schedule. The workflow is in `Scheduler.java`.
- Two indices are created: `cf_etf_history_data` and `register_funds`. Their
  mappings and settings are stored in the corresponding JSON
  files: `cf_etf_history_data.json` and `register_funds.json`.
- The `com.example.esanalytics.spark` package will be described in the
  Building a Java Spark ML module for k-means anomaly detection section.

The following diagram depicts the major methods of the `AnalyticsController` class:

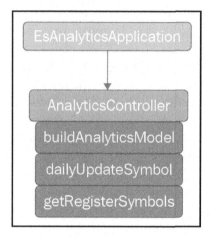

The purpose of the three major methods in the `AnalyticsController` class are as follows:

- `buildAnalyticsModel()`: Call the `buildAnalyticsModel()` method with the symbols, fields, and the time period from the `AnalyticService` Spring Bean in order to build the Bollinger Band and the k-means analytics model. All related data is indexed in Elasticsearch.
- `dailyUpdateSymbol()`: Call the `dailyUpdateSymbol()` method with the symbol from the `AnalyticsService` Spring Bean in order to perform daily data updates for the Bollinger Band and the predicted class from the built k-means analytics model, which is from the symbols the model was built with.
- `getRegisterSymbols()`: Call the `getRegisterSymbols()` method from the `AnalyticsService` Spring Bean, in order to get the registered symbols from the `register_funds` Elasticsearch index.

We will run the program and examine the APIs in practice.

Running the program and examining the APIs

We have integrated the Swagger UI to generate a visual testing API from the developed program. To run the program, we must use **Java Development Kit** (JDK) 8 since it is required by the Spark ML library. Perform the commands as follows:

1. Go to the `springboot-es-analytics` directory of the `Download` folder and issue the Maven run command, as follows:

   ```
   cd springboot-es-analytics
   mvn spring-boot:run
   ```

2. The standard output will be similar to what it is shown:

   ```
   [INFO] Scanning for projects...
   [INFO]
   [INFO] ----------------------< com.example:esanalytics >-----------
   ------------
   [INFO] Building sprintboot-es-analytics 0.0.1-SNAPSHOT
   ......

     .   ____          _            __ _ _
    /\\ / ___'_ __ _ _(_)_ __  __ _ \ \ \ \
   ( ( )\___ | '_ | '_| | '_ \/ _` | \ \ \ \
    \\/  ___)| |_)| | | | | || (_| |  ) ) ) )
     '  |____| .__|_| |_|_| |_\__, | / / / /
    =========|_|==============|___/=/_/_/_/
    :: Spring Boot ::  (v2.1.4.RELEASE)
   ......
   2019-06-24 00:27:28.035 INFO 50492 --- [ main]
   c.e.esanalytics.EsAnalyticsApplication : Started
   EsAnalyticsApplication in 5.608 seconds (JVM running for 10.021)
   ```

3. Now, use a web browser and type
   `http://localhost:10010/swagger-ui.html#/` to reach the Swagger UI
   page for the project and then expand each controller in the panel, as follows:

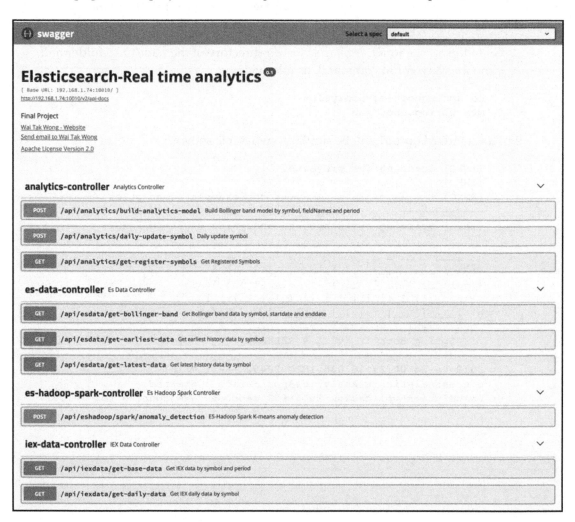

According to this screenshot, Analytics Controller has three endpoints that support the main workflow of the project:

- The `/api/analytics/build-analytics-model` URI calls the `buildAnalyticsModel()` method of the controller to build the model.
- The `/api/analytics/daily-update-symbol` URI calls the `dailyUpdateSymbol()` method of the controller to perform daily data updates.
- The `/api/analytics/get-register-symbol` URI calls the `getRegisterSymbols()` method of the controller to get the registered symbols.

If we don't use JDK 8 to run the project, then we will get `illegalArgumentException`. The error stack trace will look like this:

```
java.lang.IllegalArgumentException: null
at org.apache.xbean.asm5.ClassReader.<init>(Unknown
Source) ~[xbean-asm5-shaded-4.4.jar:4.4]
```

Main workflow anatomy

In this subsection, we will give a brief description of the main workflow for each task. There are three major tasks. We must first succeed in the task of building the analytic model, and then we can perform the daily update data. To get registered symbols, our task is to get all the symbols for daily data updates from the scheduler. The next few sections provide brief descriptions of each task.

Building the analytic model

This diagram shows us how the task of building the model works:

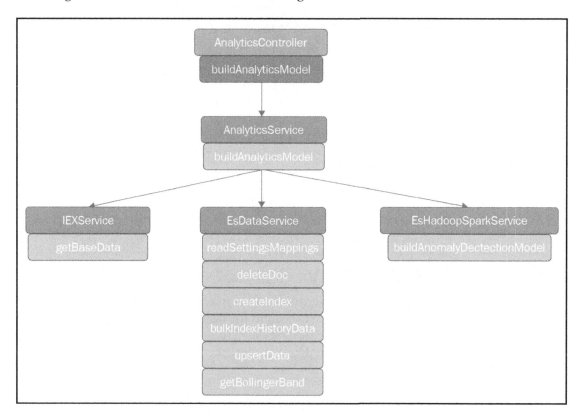

The step-by-step instructions for this are as follows:

1. Call the `getBaseData()` method from the `IEXService` Spring Bean to extract the IEX historical price data for the given funds, starting from the given time range.
2. Call the `readSettingsMappings()` method from the `EsDataService` Spring Bean to read the settings and mappings from the `cf_etf_history_data.json` and `register_funds.json` files for the `cf_etf_history_data` and `register_funds` indexes.
3. Call the `deleteDoc()` method from the `EsDataService` Spring Bean to delete the documents of the given symbol in the `cf_etf_history_data` index, if they exist.

4. Call the `createIndex()` method from the `EsDataService` Spring Bean to create the `cf_etf_history_data` and `register_funds` indexes with the mappings and settings, if they do not exist.
5. Call the `bulkIndexHistoryData()` method from the `EsDataService` Spring Bean to index the IEX data into the `cf_etf_history_data` index.
6. Call the `upsertData()` method from the `EsDataService` Spring Bean to update or insert the data into the `register_funds` index.
7. Call the `getBollingerBand()` method from the `EsDataService` Spring Bean to compute the Bollinger Band-related data.
8. Call the `buildAnomalyDetectionModel()` method from the `EsHadoopSparkService` Spring Bean to construct the required data, according to the field provided, to build the k-means clustering model and give the class label for each item of data. Finally, we update the data with the fields, including the standard deviation of 20 trading days and moving average, the upper and lower bounds of the Bollinger Band, the typical price, and the predicted class label, into Elasticsearch.

After we build the analytic model for a symbol, we need to maintain the data for each trading day. The next subsection shows the data update workflow.

Performing daily update data

This diagram shows us the task of updating the data for the registered symbols:

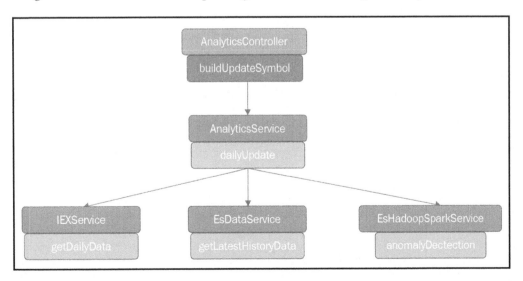

The step-by-step instructions are as follows:

1. Call the `getBaseData()` method from the `IEXService` Spring Bean to extract the up-to-date data of the given symbol.
2. Call the `getLatestHistoryData()` method from the `EsDataService` Spring Bean to get the latest data from the `cf_etf_history_data` index.
3. If the data in Elasticsearch needs to be updated, then call the `anomalyDetection()` method from the `EsHadoopSparkService` Spring Bean to predict the class label. Finally, we update the data into Elasticsearch.

We can update data for a given symbol; however, we need to maintain the data automatically for each trading day. The next subsection shows the workflow for getting the registered symbols to update.

Getting the registered symbols

If a symbol has performed the `buildAnalyticsModel` workflow successfully, then the symbol is stored in the `register_funds` index and treated as registered. To update all the registered symbols, we need to know all the registered symbols.

The `getRegisterFunds()` method from the `EsDataService` Spring Bean is used to get all the registered symbols. To perform a search request to retrieve all symbols, we construct a `SearchRequest` object, which embeds a `SearchSourceBuilder` object to create a match all query. The following code block shows the source code:

```
SearchRequest request = new SearchRequest(registerIndexName);
SearchSourceBuilder sourceBuilder = new SearchSourceBuilder();
RequestOptions options = RequestOptions.DEFAULT;
request.source(sourceBuilder.query(
    QueryBuilders.matchAllQuery()).sort("symbol", SortOrder.DESC));
......
response = restClient.search(request, options);
```

In the next section, we will discuss the final task: building the scheduler to update data automatically.

Building the scheduler

We need a scheduler to update the data for each trading day automatically. Spring Scheduler is an easy-to-use Spring component that we adopt in `Scheduler.java`. The user-defined cron schedule, `scheduler.cron`, is defined in `application.yml`. Once the task starts, it first calls `getRegisterFunds()` to get all the symbols. If the symbol has been performed by `buildAnalyticsModel`, then it is registered and it proceeds with the following workflow:

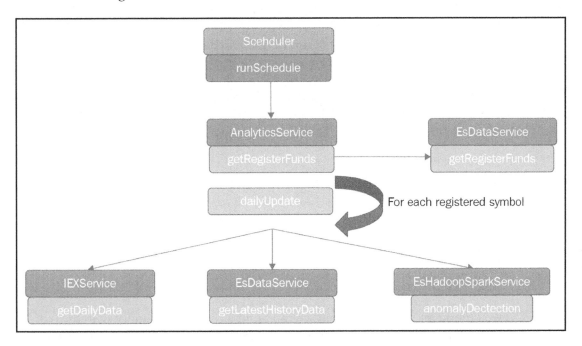

In the *Python high-level Elasticsearch library* section of `Chapter 12`, *Elasticsearch from Python Programming*, we implement the Bollinger Band. In the next section, we will use the Elasticsearch Java high-level REST client to implement it.

Integration with the Bollinger Band

In the last section, we introduced the workflow of `buildAnalyticsModel`. After we insert/update the ETF data to the `cf_etf_history_data` index, we compute the data for the Bollinger Band. Let's recall the details to compute the Bollinger Band from the *Operational data analytics* section of `Chapter 10`, *Using Elasticsearch for Exploratory Data Analysis*, to work on Java programming. The step-by-step instructions are as follows:

1. Collect all the related documents by performing a search operation: `symbol` and `period` are given by the user. `startDate` and `endDate` can be derived from the period. We have learned how to use Elasticsearch's high-level REST client to build a `SearchRequest` object in the *Java high-level REST client* section in `Chapter 11`, *Elasticsearch from Java Programming*. The following code block is extracted from the `getBollingerBand()` method in the project's `EsDataServiceImpl.java` file, and helps us learn about how to build a `SearchRequest` object:

```
SearchRequest request = new SearchRequest(dataIndexName);
SearchSourceBuilder sourceBuilder = new SearchSourceBuilder();
BoolQueryBuilder boolQueryBuilder = QueryBuilders.boolQuery();
boolQueryBuilder.must(QueryBuilders.termQuery("symbol", symbol));
boolQueryBuilder.must(QueryBuilders.rangeQuery("date").gte(startDat
e).lte(endDate));
request.source(sourceBuilder.query(boolQueryBuilder));
......
RequestOptions options = RequestOptions.DEFAULT;
response = restClient.search(request, options);
```

Two criteria must be met so that we can build a `boolQuery` query with the two `must` subqueries. The first criterion is that the symbol of the document is equal to the given symbol. Hence, we use `termQuery()` to match the symbol. The second criterion is that the date field of the document must be between the start date and end date. Hence, we use `rangeQuery()` to match the date range.

2. Calculate the daily typical price (tp). Since it is a trading day basis computation, we use a dateHistogram aggregation to produce buckets for each trading day. We give the name bollingerBand to the aggregation. We use the scriptedMetric aggregation to compute *tp*, where *tp=(high + low + close)/3*. We give the name *tp* to the aggregation. Both the dateHistogram and scriptedMetric aggregations use the AggregationBuilders class to build the aggregation. The bollingerBuilder.subAggregation() method adds the tpBuilder aggregation as its sub-aggregation. The following code block is a program flow of a typical price aggregation:

```
AggregationBuilder bollingerBuilder =
AggregationBuilders.dateHistogram("BollingerBand")
.field("date").dateHistogramInterval(DateHistogramInterval.days(1))
    .format("yyyy-MM-dd").minDocCount(1L);
AggregationBuilder tpBuilder =
AggregationBuilders.scriptedMetric("tp")
    .initScript(new Script("state.totals=[]"))
    .mapScript(new Script(
"state.totals.add((doc.high.value+doc.low.value+doc.close.value)/3)
"))
    .combineScript(
        new Script("double total=0; for (t in state.totals) {total
+= t} return total"))
    .reduceScript(new Script("return states[0]"));
......
......
bollingerBuilder.subAggregation(tpBuilder).subAggregation(tDMA).sub
Aggregation(tDStdDev)
    .subAggregation(bbu).subAggregation(bbl);
```

3. Calculate the moving average of 20 trading days: tdMA. Since the moving average aggregation is deprecated, we use a moving function aggregation instead. To create a moving function aggregation, we call the movingFunction() method of the PipelineAggregatorBuilders class. The bucket path is tp.value, where tp is the name of a typical price aggregation:

```
MovFnPipelineAggregationBuilder tDMA =
PipelineAggregatorBuilders.movingFunction("tdMA",
    new Script("MovingFunctions.unweightedAvg(values)"),
"tp.value", 20);
```

4. Calculate the standard deviation of 20 trading days: `tdStdDev`. Similar to the moving average, the standard deviation can be computed as follows:

```
MovFnPipelineAggregationBuilder tDStdDev =
PipelineAggregatorBuilders.movingFunction(
    "tdStdDev", new Script("MovingFunctions.stdDev(values,
        MovingFunctions.unweightedAvg(values))"), "tp.value", 20);
```

5. Calculate **Bollinger Band Lower Bound (BBU)** and **Bollinger Band Upper Bound (BBL)**. To compute the values of `BBU` and `BBL`, we just use the `bucketScript` pipeline aggregation to add/subtract double the standard deviation value to/from the moving average. `bucketScript` needs `bucketPath` to specify the parameter value. The following code block depicts the computation:

```
Map<String, String> bucketPath = new HashMap<String, String>();
bucketPath.put("SMA", "tdMA");
bucketPath.put("StdDev", "tdStdDev");
BucketScriptPipelineAggregationBuilder bbu =
PipelineAggregatorBuilders.bucketScript(
    "bbu", bucketPath, new Script("params.SMA + 2 *
params.StdDev"));    BucketScriptPipelineAggregationBuilder bbl =
PipelineAggregatorBuilders.bucketScript(
    "bbl", bucketPath, new Script("params.SMA - 2 *
params.StdDev"));
bollingerBuilder.subAggregation(tpBuilder).subAggregation(tDMA).sub
Aggregation(tDStdDev)
.subAggregation(bbu).subAggregation(bbl);
```

6. Add the aggregation to the source of the `SearchSourceBuilder` object and call the `search()` method of the REST client:

```
sourceBuilder.aggregation(bollingerBuilder);
......
response = restClient.search(request, options);
```

In the *Real-time analytics using Elasticsearch and Apache Spark* section of Chapter 17, *Spark and Elasticsearch for Real-Time Analytics*, we implemented k-means clustering for anomaly detection by using ES-Hadoop, Spark SQL, and Spark MLlib with the Python programming language. In the next section, we will implement it by using the same skills with the Java programming language.

Building a Java Spark ML module for k-means anomaly detection

According to the Spark MLlib guide (see `https://spark.apache.org/docs/latest/ml-guide.html`), starting from Spark 2.0, the RDD-based APIs in the `spark.mllib` package will be retired. Users should use the DataFrame-based ML API in the `spark.ml` package. In this project, we import several classes from this new library to build the anomaly detection model. The following code block shows a few lines from the `AnomalyDetection` class in the `com.example.esanalytics.spark.mllib` package:

```
import org.apache.spark.ml.clustering.KMeansModel;
import org.apache.spark.ml.feature.VectorAssembler;
import org.apache.spark.ml.clustering.KMeans;
```

The following diagram helps us to learn about the steps to build the model within the scope of ES-Hadoop, Spark SQL, and Spark MLlib:

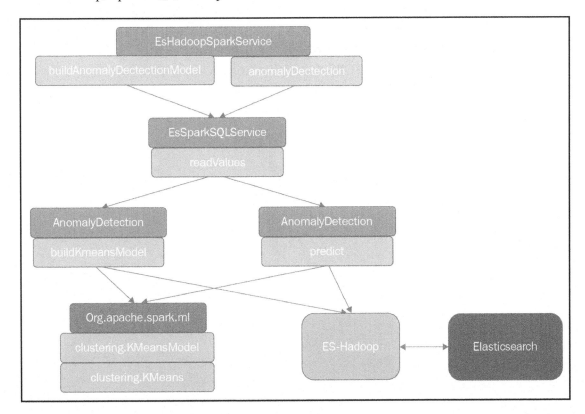

The step-by-step instructions are as follows:

1. There are two major methods, `buildAnomalyDectionModel()` and `anomalyDetection()`, from the `EsHadoopSparkService` Spring Bean in `EsHadoopSparkServiceImpl.java`, which is from the `com.example.esanalytics.service.impl` package in this project. The first method is used to build the k-means model. The second method uses the built k-means model.

2. Both methods use the `readValues()` method of the `EsSparkSQLService` Spring Bean to convert the IEX data into `org.apache.spark.sql.Dataset`, which is the data structure supported in `KMeansModel`. In the `readValues()` method, the `SparkSQL` relational data processing from `SparkSession` is used to collect the input fields selected by the users.

3. The `buildKMeansModel()` method of the `AnomalyDetection` component is called when the required workflow builds the model.

4. When the workflow predicts a class of the typical price of the trading day, the `predict()` method of the `AnomalyDetection` component is called.

5. Both methods use the `org.apache.spark.ml` library to build the model and predict the class from the built model. Then, they use `Elasticsearch-Hadoop` to update the Elasticsearch index.

Source code

Let's recall how to build the k-means model from the *Source code* section of Chapter 17, *Spark and Elasticsearch for Real-Time Analytics,* in order to work on Java programming. We briefly describe some important methods with the source codes in EsSparkSQLImpl.java, which is from the com.example.esanalytics.spark.impl package, as follows:

- readValues(): The major function of this method is to use the createDataFrame() method from SparkSession to convert the IEX data into org.apache.spark.sql.Dataset. Then, it extracts some of the values by using the sql() method (from SparkSession) into another dataset, named dataSetAD, according to user-selected field names. The selected fields are used to create the anomaly detection model. However, we need to create a database view by using createOrReplaceTempView() from the dataset first, before we can use the sql() method. This method returns both datasets. The detailed source codes are shown in the following code block:

```
public Map<String, Dataset<Row>> readValues(HistoryData[]
historyData, String[] fieldNames) {
    String statement =
        String.format("select %s from view1",
StringUtils.join(fieldNames, ","));
    Dataset<Row> dataSetAD = null;
    Dataset<Row> dataSet = null;
    try {
        dataSet =
sparkSession.createDataFrame(Arrays.asList(historyData),
HistoryData.class);
        dataSet.createOrReplaceTempView("view1");
        dataSetAD = sparkSession.sql(statement);
    } catch (Exception ex) {
        logger.error(ex.getMessage());
    }
    Map<String, Dataset<Row>> dataSetMap = new HashMap<String,
Dataset<Row>>();
    dataSetMap.put("dataSet", dataSet);
    dataSetMap.put("dataSetAD", dataSetAD);
    return dataSetMap;
}
```

- buildKmeansModel(): The major function of this method is to use the dataSetAD dataset, which is extracted from the readValues() method to build and store the k-means model. The org.apache.spark.ml.clustering.KMeans class accepts a single column element as a setter method. The VectorAssembler class transforms the user-selected fields into the single-column dataset. We provide name and features for that single column. The created k-means model is stored in a file, named kmeansModel, which will be used later in the anomalyDetection() method. Finally, it returns all the predicted groups (group 0 or group 1):

```
public Dataset<Row> buildKmeansModel(Dataset<Row> dataset, String[]
fieldNames, int numOfClass) {
    VectorAssembler assembler = new
VectorAssembler().setInputCols(fieldNames)
                .setOutputCol("features");
    Dataset<Row> features = assembler.transform(dataset);
    KMeansModel model = null;
    try {
        KMeans kmeans = new
KMeans().setFeaturesCol("features").setK(numOfClass).setSeed(1L);
        model = kmeans.fit(features);
        String kmeansModelpath = APPLICATION_ROOT_PATH +
"kmeansModel";
        model.write().overwrite().save(kmeansModelpath);
    } catch (IOException ex) {
        logger.error(ex.getMessage());
    }
    Dataset<Row> prediction = null;
    if (model != null)
        prediction =
model.transform(features).select("prediction");
    return prediction;
}
```

- `predict()`: The major function of this method is to load the k-means model from the stored file, named `kmeansModel`, and then perform the class prediction. The daily IEX data is extracted from the `readValues()` method and passed in the dataset. The `VectorAssembler` class transforms the user-selected fields into the single-column dataset. Finally, it returns the predicted group for the input data in the dataset:

```
public Dataset<Row> predict(Dataset<Row> dataSet, String[]
fieldNames) {
    KMeansModel model = null;
    Dataset<Row> prediction = null;
    VectorAssembler assembler =
newVectorAssembler().setInputCols(fieldNames)
        .setOutputCol("features");
    Dataset<Row> features = assembler.transform(dataSet);
    String kmeansModelPath = APPLICATION_ROOT_PATH + "kmeansModel";
    boolean exists = Paths.get(kmeansModelPath).toFile().exists();
    if (exists) {
        model = KMeansModel.load(kmeansModelPath);
        prediction =
model.transform(features).select("prediction");
    } else {
        logger.error("Kmeans model not found");
    }
    return prediction;
}
```

In the next section, we will discuss testing with the Swagger UI.

Testing Analytics RESTful services

We are going to present the testing of the `build-analytics-model` and `get-register-symbols` APIs from the analytic controller. The step-by-step instructions are described in the following subsection.

Testing the build-analytics-model API

This API builds the analytics model based on the user's input, such as the symbol, period, and fields to analyze. We will use `rfem` for the symbol, 1 year (`1y`) for the past period, and the 20 days standard deviation (`tDStDev`) as input. Please follow these step-by-step instructions:

1. Use a web browser and type
   `http://localhost:10010/swagger-ui.html#/analytics-controller/bu`
   `ildAnalyticsModelUsingPOST` to reach the Swagger UI page for the build-analytics-model API, and then click the *Try it out* button. We will see a panel that's similar to this screenshot:

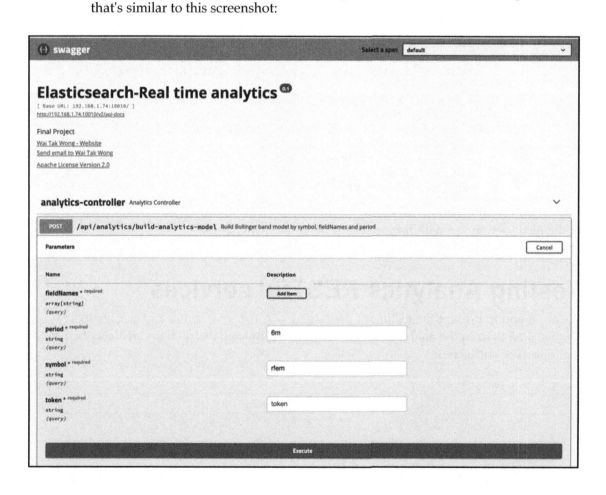

2. Click the **Add item** button to add the `tDStDev` field, type `1y` for the **period** and give the IEX Cloud token, as we described at the beginning of this chapter. It should look like this:

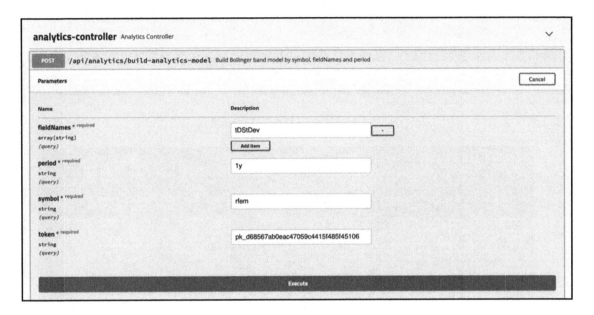

3. Click the **Execute** button, and we will get a response similar to the following screenshot. The label and some of the fields are listed in the response:

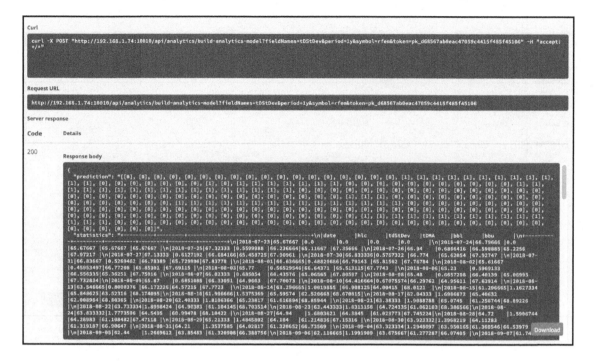

4. Once the `build-analytics-model` API has run successfully and the program is running, Spring Scheduler will kick off the `dailyUpdate()` routine every day at 5:00 a.m.

Testing the get-register-symbols API

This API gets the registered symbols that have successfully used the `build-analytics-model` API. Please follow these step-by-step instructions:

1. Use a web browser and type `http://localhost:10010/swagger-ui.html#/analytics-controller/getRegisterSymbolsUsingGET` to reach the Swagger UI page for the `get-register-symbols` API, and then click the **Try it out** button. We will see a panel that is similar to the following screenshot:

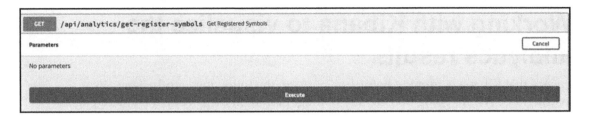

2. Since we have successfully used the `build-analytics-model` API for the `rfem` symbol, we can see the information about the `rfem` symbol in the response after we click the **Execute** button, as shown in the following screenshot:

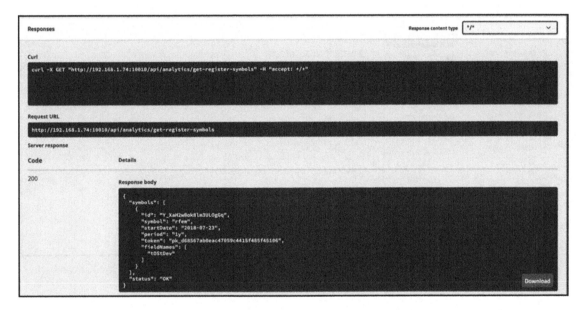

In the next section, we will discuss how to obtain the results in the Kibana **Visualize** page.

Working with Kibana to visualize the analytics results

Ensure that Kibana is running before we perform the following step-by-step instructions. We are going to draw the Bollinger Band on the Kibana **Visualize** page:

1. Similar to the *Creating index pattern* subsection of Chapter 16, *Machine Learning with Elasticsearch*, let's create a Kibana index pattern named `cf_etf_history_data`, as shown in the following screenshot:

2. Use a web browser and type
   `http://localhost:5601/app/kibana#/visualize?_g=()` to reach the
   Kibana **Visualize** page. We will see a panel that is similar to the following
   screenshot:

3. Click the **+** button cover, which is by the search box, to get into the **New Visualization** panel, as shown in the following screenshot:

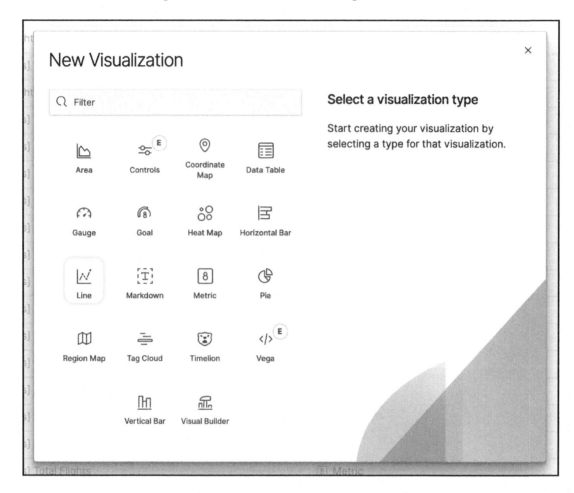

4. Click the **Line** button to create a line chart and Kibana will pop up a new panel to let us select the index pattern for the new line input. Select the **cf_etf_history_data** index, as shown in the following screenshot:

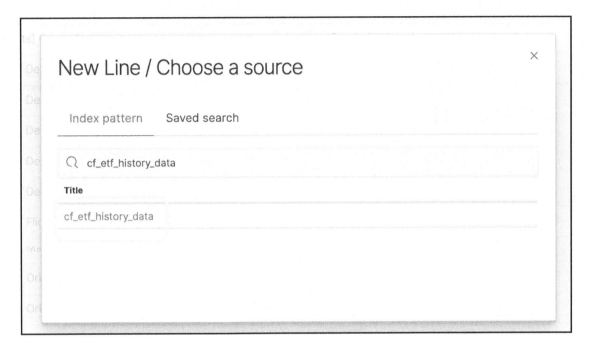

5. We can define our multiple line chart in the **Create** panel, as shown in the following screenshot. **Y-Axis**, which is covered by the bounding box, is used to add a new line. **X-Axis**, which is covered by the bounding box, specifies the line's x-axis:

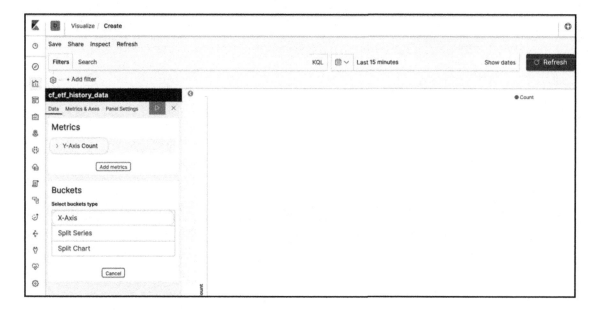

6. First, we will specify **X-Axis**. Just click it and it accepts the aggregation input. Specify **Date Histogram**, set **Field** to **date** and set **Interval** to **Daily**. Also, set the label of **X-Axis** to `Trading day`. The following screenshot shows all the inputs:

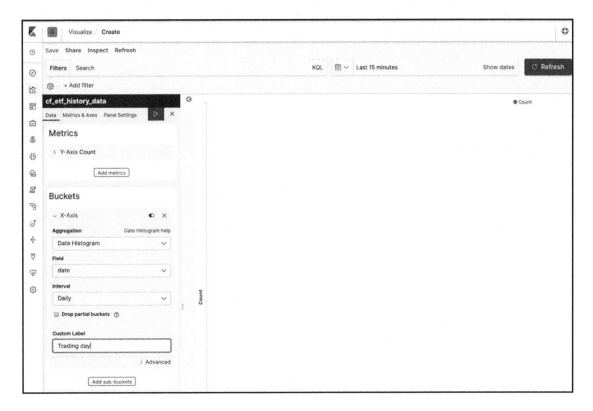

7. There are five lines in the chart. They are `tDMA` (20-day moving average), `bbu` (BBU), `bbl` (BBL), `hlc` (typical price), and prediction. We only show the step to draw the `tDMA` line. For others, just follow the same instructions as seen in the previous step to achieve them. Click **Y-Axis** to add the first line. Set **Aggregation** to **Max**, **Field** to **hlc**, and label the line as `High-Low-Closefor`.

8. Click the **Show dates** hyperlink, as shown in this screenshot, and a panel with a calendar or the time frame selector will pop up. Select the date range to examine the data. In our case, we select **Absolute** mode for the starting date and relative mode for the ending date: **July 23, 2018** to **now**. In the **Metrics & Axes** panel, we also set **Value Axis** to LeftAxis-1 and specify **Set Axis Extents**, with **Min** as 53 and **Max** as 68. After that, click the **Refresh** button denoted by the bounding box. After that, the line chart is plotted:

9. Since the scale of the line chart of the anomaly detection is different from the others, we can add another **Y-Axis** for it. Let's add the line for prediction and add a new axis on the right-hand side. The value of the predicted class label is 0~1 and we want the line on the top. Click the plus sign button of **Y-Axes** to expand the menu, and then **Set Axis Extents**. Take a look at the following screenshot to see the right places:

10. When the chart is done, click the **Save** hyperlink in the top-left corner. The **Save visualization** panel pops up, as shown in the following screenshot. Let's store it with the title `Bollinger Band`, and click the **Confirm Save** button:

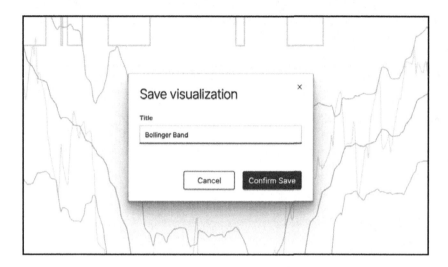

In the *Running a single metric job* section of `Chapter 16`, *Machine Learning with Elasticsearch*, we discussed the instructions to create a single metric job. Just follow the same instructions to create an ML job to analyze the standard deviation of 20 trading days (`tDStDev`). The following screenshot is an intermediate step during the job creation:

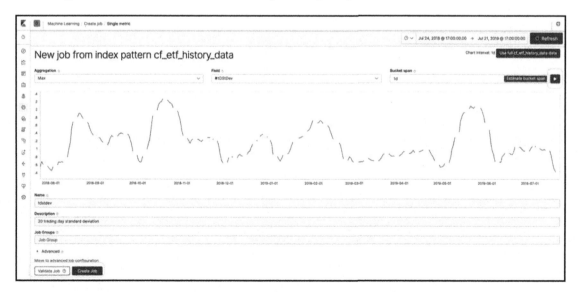

The right arrow button loads the data to show the chart. The **Create Job** button creates the ML job.

We have completed the illustration of the final project, including setup, testing, and source code explanation. We'll conclude this chapter in the next section.

Summary

Woohoo! We have completed the final chapter. We glued together the knowledge we have learned and presented the result on the Kibana **Visualize** page. We believe that it is not easy to digest all the materials from this book. However, we are very confident that this book opens the way for readers who start out as beginners and quickly become skilled users. We have covered many advanced topics, such as Elasticsearch SQL, ES-Hadoop, ML, File Beat-Logstash-Elasticsearch-Kibana integration, and the Analytics plugin. Besides this, we have used the two most popular programming languages, Java and Python, to show the implementation of integrating Elasticsearch to build analytics applications. We hope that all readers will achieve great success in their careers with Elastic Stack.

Other Books You May Enjoy

If you enjoyed this book, you may be interested in these other books by Packt:

Elasticsearch 7.0 Cookbook - Fourth Edition
Alberto Paro

ISBN: 9781789956504

- Create an efficient architecture with Elasticsearch
- Optimize search results by executing analytics aggregations
- Build complex queries by managing indices and documents
- Monitor the performance of your cluster and nodes
- Design advanced mapping to take full control of index steps

Learning Elastic Stack 7.0 - Second Edition
Pranav Shukla, Sharath Kumar M N

ISBN: 9781789954395

- Install and configure an Elasticsearch architecture
- Solve the full-text search problem with Elasticsearch
- Discover powerful analytics capabilities through aggregations using Elasticsearch
- Build a data pipeline to transfer data from a variety of sources into Elasticsearch for analysis
- Create interactive dashboards for effective storytelling with your data using Kibana
- Learn how to secure, monitor and use Elastic Stack's alerting and reporting capabilities
- Take applications to an on-premise or cloud-based production environment with Elastic Stack

Leave a review - let other readers know what you think

Please share your thoughts on this book with others by leaving a review on the site that you bought it from. If you purchased the book from Amazon, please leave us an honest review on this book's Amazon page. This is vital so that other potential readers can see and use your unbiased opinion to make purchasing decisions, we can understand what our customers think about our products, and our authors can see your feedback on the title that they have worked with Packt to create. It will only take a few minutes of your time, but is valuable to other potential customers, our authors, and Packt. Thank you!

Index

Made in the USA
Coppell, TX
30 January 2021